Governance, Management and Development

Governance, Management and Development

Making the State Work

2nd edition

Mark Turner
David Hulme
and
Willy McCourt

 macmillan education palgrave

First edition 1997
Second edition 2015

Published by
PALGRAVE

Palgrave in the UK is an imprint of Macmillan Publishers Limited,registered in England, company number 785998, of 4 Crinan Street, London, N1 9XW.

Palgrave Macmillan in the US is a division of St Martin's Press LLC, 175 Fifth Avenue, New York, NY 10010.

Palgrave is a global imprint of the above companies and is represented throughout the world.

Palgrave® and Macmillan® are registered trademarks in the United States, the United Kingdom, Europe and other countries.

ISBN 978–0–333–98463–5 hardback

ISBN 978–0–333–98462–8 paperback

This book is printed on paper suitable for recycling and made from fully managed and sustained forest sources. Logging, pulping and manufacturing processes are expected to conform to the environmental regulations of the country of origin.

A catalogue record for this book is available from the British Library.

A catalog record for this book is available from the Library of Congress.

Typeset by MPS Limited, Chennai, India.

Printed in China.

For Lulu, Georgina and Glynnis

Contents

Figures, Tables and Boxes

Figures

Tables

Boxes

Preface

The idea for this book arose over a conversation over the breakfast table in Canberra in 1990. At that time, two of us (David and Mark) had deep concerns about the role and nature of the public sector in developing countries. We had even deeper concerns about the newly dominant policy agenda which focused on minimizing the role of the public sector, rolling back the state until it almost disappeared while naively waving the new banner of 'good government' for all to cheer. The breakfast conversation started in 1990 has continued, later incorporating another academic colleague (Willy) bringing fresh insights and ideas, and now with experience of working with the world's leading financier of reform.

From David and Mark's years of working at the Administrative College of Papua New Guinea and from research and consultancy in many countries across the developing world by all three of us, we were well aware of just how difficult it is to improve the performance of government organizations. However, we were convinced that public sector activity can make a major contribution to the achievement of developmental goals and the creation of reasonably stable societies that can meet the material, social, and, perhaps, spiritual needs of the bulk of their populaces. In part this was an analytical conclusion of our readings of East and Southeast Asian development and of the history of Western Europe. It was also grounded in our personal experiences – two Liverpudlians (David and Mark) who had benefited from high quality state education, a national health service free at the point of delivery and the knowledge that a public social security net underpinned our efforts to secure livelihoods and careers. These were experiences also shared by Willy while growing up in Belfast.

While elements of ideology no doubt support our belief that the public sector has a major role to play in development, we are not ideologues. The claims of the far left ('the state must do everything') and the far right ('the market can do everything') have always appeared to be fallacious to us. Such 'either...or' analyses have been tempered in the twenty-first century by realization that more can be achieved through collective effort although strong biases still exist among some development stakeholders.

We, however, strongly believe that to secure the development outcomes we want, the public sector must work in partnership, sometimes critically, sometimes cooperatively, with both the private sector and civil society.

The first edition of this book rolled of the production line in 1997 when policy debate about governance and discussions about the future of non-governmental organizations in development were in their infancy. Privatization was *de rigueur* for the World Bank and IMF while public private partnerships were novel arrangements in developing countries. Since then, much has happened. The environments in which the organizations of developing countries operate have been true to the form described in the first edition – turbulent and uncertain. There have been many changes in policies and prescriptions although some ideas have held fast. Also, there have been profound changes in the geopolitical and economic landscape such as the rise of China and the other BRICs, increased globalization, more democratization and more wars and civil conflicts. These are all taken into account in the new edition of the book.

There were a couple of attempts to produce a second edition of the book in the early 2000s but other work and diversions prevented this from happening despite a couple of promising but false starts. It was not until Willy was recruited to be the catalyst for our final attempt that the project really gained momentum. His energy and capacity to produce finished chapters forced the issue. But what we discovered early on was that so much had changed and so much more had been written since 1997 that the second edition would not be an update. Rather it would be a rewrite – in some chapters an almost total rewrite making them unrecognizable from the 1997 edition. Details of major changes are presented in the next paragraph.

In Chapter 1, we have updated the material on development theory and development management to incorporate new and emerging modes of analysis since the mid-1990s and the resulting recommendations for reform. There is also a new section on the rise of 'good governance' and some of the critical reactions to the concept and its usage. Chapter 2 on organizational environments has incorporated much new data and many new references to keep abreast of rapidly changing environmental conditions in the developing world. There is also a new section on the natural environment involving consideration of the leading global issues of sustainability, environmental degradation and climate change. Chapter 3 on law and order is a completely new addition to the book made necessary by the unfortunate prevalence of insecurity, crime, conflict and violence in many developing countries. Policy-makers and development managers in such countries are daily faced with these conditions and must work creatively to still make development happen.

Chapter 4 on the policy process has taken a modified analytical focus as compared to the first edition of the book. The first part of the chapter now asks how policy arises, is analysed and implemented. The second half of the chapter looks at who are the actors trying to push policy along or block it. Chapters 5 and 6 have had major overhauls from the first edition where one chapter examined bureaucracy in the Third World and the other set out major reform initiatives. This transformation was necessitated by considerable activity in public sector reform since the first edition. Thus, in the second edition, while analysis of bureaucracy is necessarily retained we also have consideration of the benefits and problems of structural change over management change. New sections on executive agencies, strategic management, human resource management and bottom-up reforms are included. Also new are in-depth discussion of New Public Management (NPM) which was in its infancy in developing countries in the mid-1990s, and pay and employment reform that has been so prominent since the first edition.

Chapter 7 on planning has been updated to include the revitalization of national development planning, albeit in a different form from its heyday. Also, included are the latest experiments in project planning. Overall, the chapter reflects the sense of realism that has overtaken development planning and what we can expect it to achieve. Chapter 8 on decentralization acknowledges that since the book's first edition when decentralization was becoming popular we are now in a period when decentralization is the norm. In this second edition, more attention is paid to the political motives for decentralization while a new problem-oriented section addresses the factors that can make decentralization successful. Chapter 9 on economic development and the public sector moves beyond exclusive focus on state-owned enterprises (SOEs) and privatization. Data and trends for these items are updated but the chapter now includes detailed treatment of public private partnerships (PPPs) and the role of the state in creating enabling environments for private sector development. Finally, Chapter 10 still maintains its focus on non-governmental organizations (NGOs) but this time contextualizes NGOs in the broader field of civil society. Also included are the critiques of NGOs that have been increasingly common in recent years, and consideration of whether NGOs can return to their roots and promote participatory paths to empowerment.

There is, however, continuity in the book as we provide a historical context for both thinking about development and its management. We feel it essential to contextualize our subject matter historically so readers can appreciate the emergence of key ideas and policies and what effect they had. But we can still see their persistence in ostensibly 'new' ideas and policies as the foundations on which they were erected. Building on these foundations and taking in the newer developments in the field, the reader will find that s/he has a vast interdisciplinary range of concepts and analytical frameworks to explore. On one side is the development studies literature with its roots in economics, sociology and politics. On the other is the literature on management, psychology and business studies. We have tried to relate these literatures to the problems of development and to bridge the gap that often exists between them and hope that we have achieved some success in this endeavour.

No book of this sort could be produced without the help and assistance of other people. We name only a few here but our sincere thanks to those who have indirectly helped us in our task, those with whom we have been intellectually and practically engaged. First, mention must be made of our long-suffering publisher, Steven Kennedy, who persisted (eventually successfully) in urging us to undertake a second edition and gave great support. We believe his recent retirement is not related in any way to the stress of dealing with us. Thanks also to Stephen Wenham who took over the baton from Steven Kennedy and also to Madeleine Hamey-Thomas at Palgrave. Second, special thanks to Niki Banks at Manchester for excellent support for writing the chapter on civil society and to Jessica Hawkins, also at Manchester, for equally excellent support in writing the chapter on law and order. Third, thanks to colleagues and students at the Universities of Canberra and Manchester, and colleagues at the World Bank for the daily interactions that feed into an intellectual venture such as this. Also, we have learned from the numerous individuals we have encountered, worked alongside and sometimes shared a beer with in the developing countries where we research and consult.

Last but not least we thank our partners, Lulu, Georgina and Glynnis for tolerating our absences and absent-mindedness caused by our preoccupations with governance and management, as we struggled to find the time to write this book. In the first edition, this demand on time led to the observation in the Preface that 'We have all learnt that lawns do not need cutting'. Mark solved this by moving to a house with no lawn, David went the other way and got a bigger lawn while Willy left his lawn behind as he departed for Washington DC.

Acknowledgements

The authors and publisher would like to thank the following who have kindly given permission for the use of copyright material: John Wiley & Sons, Inc. for Figure 4.1, originally published in *Policy Analysis* by W. Jenkins, London: Martin Robinson (now John Wiley & Sons, Inc.); Elsevier Ltd. for Figure 4.4; Taylor & Francis for Figure 7.2, originally published in *Planning in Complexity: An Introduction to Collaborative Rationality for Public Policy* by J. Innes and D. Booher (2010), pg. 35; and World Bank for Table 6.5 under the Creative Commons License.

Chapter 1

Administration, Management, Governance and Development

The decades since the end of World War Two have witnessed an unprecedented drive for economic and social development by the majority of the world's nations. The leaders of these countries (often referred to as developing countries, the Third World or South) have exhorted their citizens to strive for development and have formulated policies and implemented programmes towards this end. However, the rapid achievement of development goals in the late twentieth century proved elusive for the majority of countries except a small number of 'tigers' in East Asia. More recently, however, a number of emerging powers have made significant progress – China, India and Brazil – and a group of emerging 'middle powers', sometimes called the Next 11, are achieving economic growth and improved welfare for many of their citizens. Many processes and factors have been identified as contributing to the differing levels of achievement, and prominent amongst these has been the argument that public sector organizations have often performed poorly. They have failed to provide politicians with sound advice on policy, have not delivered services effectively, have taken on inappropriate roles and have been both inefficient and corrupt. Less commonly heard but of equal significance is the argument that countries that have experienced rapid sustained development – for example, South Korea, Taiwan, Singapore, China, Chile, Brazil and Malaysia – have had effective public sector organizations.

Among contemporary development practitioners and academics there is widespread agreement on the proposition that the nature and performance of public sector organizations are critical elements in determining developmental success. It is this topic that is the focus of our present work. In this book we seek to:

- explore the complex and diverse contexts of development and public sector organizations both in terms of intellectual history

1

and practice and through environmental factors that provide opportunities for and constraints on what public sector managers and organizations can do and achieve;

• analyse the ways in which public sector organizations influence development policies and programmes and the effects this has on results achieved;

• identify and discuss the appropriateness of approaches for improving the contribution that the public sector makes to development; and

• argue the case for a vital and prominent role for public sector organizations in development.

We do not claim that public sector organizations are the only influences or necessarily the most significant ones. We do, however, argue that they are important and, in many cases, in need of innovation and reform. Unfortunately, there is ample evidence of dysfunctional bureaucracies avidly devouring scarce resources but failing to produce anticipated outcomes. It is not difficult to find policies that serve to keep ineffective and/or illegitimate governments in office rather than attending to strengthening the economy and improving welfare for the poor. There has been considerable criticism of official aid agencies that give or lend money for projects that bring limited gains to target populations. There are many instances where development achievements have proved unsustainable due to lack of budgetary foresight, excessive reliance on footloose foreign experts and preoccupation with prestige rather than with solid but unspectacular gains. Many initiatives have foundered on poor management, inappropriate planning, weak implementation and an unwillingness to involve the beneficiaries in the organization of changes that will affect their lives.

These negative views of development and its administration remain common but there are positive experiences that give cause for optimism in some contexts. The widespread progress towards achieving the Millennium Development Goals (MDGs) in all regions of the world is the clearest demonstration. The last 25 years have seen the most rapid economic growth and the biggest increases in life expectancy in human history. Still, between 1.5 billion and 3.0 billion people live in poverty and at least one third of the world's countries are classed as fragile or very badly governed (Hulme, 2015).

These contrasting positions can be best appreciated with reference to several of this book's underlying assumptions and themes. First, the organizational aspects of development cannot be reduced to a technical fix. Metaphors which liken organizations to machines can be extremely misleading as they suggest that changing a spark plug or adding a transformer are somehow equivalent to adopting a new management strategy or re-orienting staff development and training. Management systems, administrative techniques and organizational designs are not neutral value-free phenomena. Thus, administrative reform and innovation are not simply a matter of installing some piece of managerial technology which has proved effective elsewhere. There are no universal principles of management and no universal management tool kits.

The second theme concerns the importance of organizational environments, that envelope of factors and forces in which organizations operate. Although the air-conditioned, high-rise accommodation of public service agencies in some developing countries may appear to divorce them from society, organizations are not closed technical systems. They are necessarily involved in multiple relationships with other organizations and individuals. Complex webs of relationships are thus woven between these actors and have profound effects on the operation of organizations. There are also social and economic forces which impact on organizational activity. For example, declining exchange rates and falling commodity prices will mean reduced government income and will exert severe pressure on public service budgets. National culture may be a key determinant of the way in which activities are conducted and may influence operational norms and practices as much as the public service manual of procedures. And the influence is unlikely to be one way. Organizations are not simply acted upon but can also influence their environments. The whole purpose of development, and organizations that are there to promote it, is in fact to alter environments in ways that are beneficial to citizens and/or target populations.

The third theme emphasizes one aspect of the administrative environment, that is the importance of political considerations in administrative analysis and practice. Organizational action takes place in political contexts. Power and authority permeate relationships between organizational members and between these persons and those in the external environment. The range of patterns and possibilities is enormous and is reflected in a wide diversity of practice. Technical rationality will frequently be a poor guide to decisions and behaviour. The explanations of particular policy choices, planning decisions, implementation successes and failures, and unlearned lessons of evaluation will be found in political analysis. If, for example, we wish to comprehend why rural organizations for the poor have often failed we need to understand the political landscape in which those organizations attempt to operate. Society, state and business are enmeshed in political relationships. Competition over resource control and allocation is ubiquitous and for the analyst, practitioner and potential beneficiary alike the map of power and authority is an essential guide, more useful than the latest scientific planning tool.

The fourth theme flows from the environmental issues. It is that organizational improvement is not a panacea for development. Development is multi-faceted and success or failure are based on more than organizational design, administrative reform or human resource management. Such items have a strong bearing on whether developmental progress will occur but they are never the sole determinants. As Schaffer (1969: 202) observed more than four decades ago, 'The whole lesson is that development administration works only in conjunction with other factors of change'. Furthermore, public sector organizations can be utilized to oppress or to defend the privileges of certain classes and groups in society. They are not innately benign but must be directed towards the attainment of developmental goals. But what is development?

Development: a contested concept

Since the Second World War, development has been synonymous with economic, social and political changes in the countries of Africa, Asia, Latin America, the Caribbean and the South Pacific (and later some former Soviet republics). These countries have been variously labelled as underdeveloped, less-developed, developing, the Third World and the South. They are a diverse group – indeed some think they are so diverse they can no longer be called a group – but united in their commonly declared commitment to development. But there is no consensus about the meaning of development. It is a contested concept and there have been a number of battles to capture its meaning. In this section we review these ideological engagements (see Box 1.1 for a range of meanings – can you identify which meaning in the box belongs to which theoretical perspective outlined below?).

Until the end of the 1960s, the modernization perspective on development held sway. Development was seen as an evolutionary process in which countries progressed through an identified

---

Box 1.1   Competing meanings of development

'Modernization is a "total" transformation of a traditional or pre-modern society into the types of technology and associated social organization that characterize the "advanced" economically prosperous and politically stable nations of the Western World.' (Moore, 1963: 89)

'[T]hese capitalist contradictions and the historical development of the capitalist system have generated underdevelopment in the peripheral satellites whose economic surplus was expropriated, while generating economic development in the metropolitan centres which appropriate that surplus – and, further, that this process still continues.' (Frank, 1971: 27)

'We in Africa, have no more need of being "converted" to socialism than we have of being "taught" democracy. Both are rooted in our past – in the traditional society which produced us. Modern African socialism can draw from its traditional heritage, the recognition of "society" as an extension of the basic family unit.' (Nyerere, 1966: 170)

'What happened [i.e. economic development] was in very large measure the result of the individual voluntary responses of millions of people to emerging or expanding opportunities created largely by external contacts and brought to their notice in a variety of ways, primarily through the operation of the market. These developments were made possible by firm but limited government, without large expenditures of public funds and without the receipt of large external subventions.' (Bauer, 1984: 31)

'Rural development is a strategy to enable a specific group of people, poor rural women and men, to gain for themselves and their children more of what they want and need. It involves helping the poorest among those who seek a livelihood in the rural areas to demand and control more of the benefits of development.' (Chambers, 1983: 147)

'Development always entails looking at other worlds in terms of what they lack, and obstructs the wealth of indigenous alternatives.' (Sachs, 1992: 6)

'[E]nhancement of human freedom is both the main object and the primary means of development .... The people have seen, in this perspective, as being actively involved – given the opportunity – in shaping their own destiny, and not just as passive recipients of the fruits of cunning development programs.' (Sen, 1999: 53)

---

series of stages to become modern. The form of the future did not require the imagination and speculation evident in earlier evolutionary theorists such as Marx, Durkheim and Weber. The future for the developing countries was already in existence and could be seen in the form of the advanced Western societies, most especially the USA (for example, Moore, 1963). The means of getting there was also clearly delineated. The tools of scientific planning would enable the 'underdeveloped' nations to escape from this undesirable status and become fully modern in a few decades. This faith in rational planning was exported to newly independent nations and eagerly absorbed and broadcast by elites and dominant classes.

This ideology of development was at once optimistic and ethnocentric. It was optimistic in assuming that the 'problems' of underdevelopment such as poverty, inadequate social services and low levels of industrial production were amenable to straightforward solution by the application of rational management techniques. It was ethnocentric in that modernity was perceived as being purely Western and that Western technology, institutions, modes of production and values were both superior and desirable.

The approach was also heavily oriented to economic growth as the driving force. Changes in social and political institutions would simultaneously contribute to economic growth and be inevitable companions to and outcomes of such growth. Results did not match expectations. By the late 1960s, there was increased poverty, growing indebtedness, political repression, economic stagnation and a host of other ills. Development needed rethinking, and it came both in liberal reformulations and in more dramatic form through various neo-Marxist interpretations.

The liberal reformulations questioned the meaning attached to development and proposed new definitions which lessened the role of economic growth. Authentic development was seen as progress towards a set of welfare goals such as the elimination of poverty, the provision of employment, the reduction of inequality and the guarantee of human rights. The changed definition had practical implications summed up in slogans such as 'redistribution with growth', in policies such as 'the basic needs approach', and in planning packages such as 'integrated rural development'. As the biggest provider of developmental aid and as a leading think-tank on development practice, the World Bank was often viewed as the prime agency promoting such liberal reformulation. Its critics alleged it paid lip-service to the new objectives or that they were unattainable in the prevailing global context.

The neo-Marxists did not dispute the changed emphasis in the meaning of development. They disputed whether improvements in human welfare could be achieved under the prevailing political economy. Why had countries in the Third World largely failed to make the transition to fully developed capitalist economies? The neo-Marxists rejected the modernization school's explanations concerning the tenacity of tradition and institutional shortcomings and looked to historically grounded analysis of political economy.

One group, called the dependency school, argued that the global economic structure was an exploitative system which generated and maintained 'the development of underdevelopment' in nations of the periphery (for example, Frank, 1971; Wallerstein, 1979). The nations of the core had since the advent of a world economy in the late fifteenth and early sixteenth centuries enforced a system of inequitable domination on the periphery through such techniques as conquest, threat, market restriction and industrial protection. These tactics enabled strong states to perpetuate the weakness of the peripheral states. Development could only occur through radical solutions which altered relationships in the world economy. Suggested actions included development programmes which emphasized self-sufficiency, substantial even total de-linking from the world economy and socialist revolution.

Other neo-Marxists, while accepting the usefulness of the concept of the world capitalist system, were concerned about 'simple reductionism [that] can remove from history all its ambiguities, conjectures and surprises' (Cardoso, 1977: 21). They looked at the variety of experience – the rise of the newly industrializing countries such as Singapore and South Korea compared with stagnant GNIs (gross national income), political instability and immiseration in many African, Asian and Latin American nations. Could one overarching theory explain such massive differences? Diversity demanded closer attention to detail, in-depth studies on a smaller scale with less theoretical ambition. In order to achieve this, many authors employed the notions of mode of production and social class as their major analytical tools. They selected particular countries or regions and looked at the specific ways in which different modes of production (for example, pre-capitalist and capitalist) were 'articulated' to make distinctive social formations. They traced the historical development of social classes. These more fine-grained analyses found that some development was possible in peripheral societies but the benefits were restricted to dominant classes and their allies. Nobody suggested any possibility for autonomous development in the prevailing world economy. The metropolitan bourgeoisie was always lurking in the background able to determine the structural constraints within which any development would take place and to whom the benefits would flow.

While obviously different in many respects, the modernization and neo-Marxist approaches to development do share some fundamental similarities. Harrison (1988) observes that both derive from European experience and have been formulated by intellectuals, planners and politicians who have been socialized into this tradition. Both have visions of before (traditional or pre-capitalist society) and after (the modern capitalist society or the idealized socialist society) with an intermediate stage which is what exists now. Finally, neither perspective has ascribed much importance to the 'views, wants, ambitions and wishes of those about to be developed' (Harrison, 1988: 151–2).

Such views are allegedly incorporated into neo-populist types of thinking although even here one can find evidence of populist ideology being imposed from above or from outside on people who are passively mobilized or who actively oppose their own mobilization. Neo-populists are the creators of 'alternative development strategies' which Kitching (1982: 98) characterizes as focusing on 'small-scale enterprises, on the retention of a peasant agriculture and of non-agricultural petty commodity production and on a world of villages and small towns rather than industrial cities'. Equity considerations are always prominent. The neo-populists thus perceive a different meaning to development than both modernization and neo-Marxist theorists, and in the new populist forms means and ends frequently overlap and are sometimes identical.

Julius Nyerere's attempt to establish a revitalized and improved authentic African socialism in Tanzania in the 1960s and 1970s is a classic example of neo-populism in action. Unfortunately, the results were not as predicted by the theory. Economic growth was disappointing; the public sector expanded but gave poor service; and there was peasant opposition to forced 'villagization' and communal agriculture.

Other neo-populists could include E.F. Schumacher (1973) and his famous advocacy of 'small is beautiful'; Michael Lipton (1977) and his critique of the urban bias in development; or Bernard Narokobi (1983) and his rejection of Westernization and promotion of indigenous cultural values, 'the Melanesian Way', as the guide to true development for Papua New Guinea and other Pacific island peoples. There were ecodevelopers, so-called because of their belief in 'an ecologically sound development' (Glaeser and Vyasulu, 1984: 23) necessary to save the planet and its people from impending, self-induced, environmental doom.

Much of today's attack on developmental orthodoxy derives from the neo-populist tradition. But it has been boosted by voices associated with post-development and post-modernism. The assault on dominant development paradigms is forcefully articulated by NGOs, communities, students, intellectuals and others disenchanted with what they regard as the mixed record of development and particularly rising global inequality and the environmental unsustainability of contemporary economic growth. They make direct links between the negative effects of so-called development and crises affecting the world, notably arms proliferation and violence, the oppression of women, environmental degradation and disasters, climate change, the persistence of poverty and the repression of human rights. They see previous explanations of both modernization and neo-Marxist variety as deficient and identify a variety of leading villains – the state, dominant social classes, multinational corporations and banks, and the World Bank. Aided by allies in the economically prosperous countries, these villains are accused of peddling developmentalism, an ideology which 'defines the principal social objectives of all countries as consumption and accumulation' (Ekins, 1992: 205). They have created 'a domain of thought and action' that is development which is imposed on others, notably the poor and weak (Escobar, 1995: 10). Thus, 'the forms of knowledge' in which development appears are put into practice through 'systems of power' that create 'forms of subjectivity' through which people self-classify as developed and underdeveloped. For such critics development as it is currently framed does more harm than good. For post-developmentalists, true development seems to involve some combination of grassroots action instigated and directed by the marginalized preferably at the local level and which is ecologically sound. They have absorbed from post-modernism the rejection of 'grand narratives' about history and progress that characterize both modernization and neo-Marxist interpretations of the world. They are 'interested not in development alternatives but in alternatives to development' (Escobar, 1995: 215).

The post-developmentalists have emerged from the neo-populist tradition and incorporate aspects of post-modernism, and as such have become a diverse church under whose roof we find community movements, ecofeminists, the homeless, indigenous peoples, environmentalists and many others. While retaining their specific identities and goals they have partially coalesced into an anti-globalization movement – somewhat paradoxically a global phenomenon – that came to the world's attention in 1999 with the 'Battle for Seattle' where a 'kaleidoscopic crowd' attempted to disrupt the meeting of the World Trade Organization (WTO) (Greig et al., 2007: 215). Since then, civil society organizations opposed to imperialism and capitalist development have networked to form the World Social Forum that facilitates a 'world process of building alternatives to neo-liberal policies' (FSM, 2013) and have taken to the streets with the Occupy movement.

Like the neo-populists, neo-liberalism emerged as a critique of modernization and neo-Marxism. But the proponents of neo-liberalism have been much more successful: seizing control of the development agenda by imposing new meaning and practice on the concept of development, poles apart from those proposed by the neo-populists and their descendants. While the neo-classical economists who championed neo-liberalism are hardly ideological bedfellows with the neo-populists they do share a strong dislike of government intervention and of past development strategies. Collectively identified as the 'counter-revolutionaries' by Toye (1987) the neo-classicists advocated policies restricting state intervention in the economy and society. They pointed to inefficiency and ineffectiveness in planned development and celebrated the optimal resource allocation which reliance on the market allegedly provided. They successfully competed to define development theory and practice over the 1980s and 1990s and found champions in Western governments, notably USA and UK, in official multilateral and bilateral aid agencies, and in the ministries of finance and central banks of developing countries. Their policy prescriptions for development were summarized by Williamson (1990) and labelled the Washington Consensus to reflect the convergence of economic thinking among the influential institutional residents of that city (see Box 1.2). Although strongly rejected by Williamson (2004: 7) as 'a thoroughly objectionable perversion of its original meaning', the Washington Consensus was nevertheless widely interpreted as an attempt to impose privatization, liberalization and macro-economic stability measures on developing countries through a 'strong faith – stronger than warranted – in unfettered markets' and a concerted effort to weaken, if not minimize, the role of the state in development (Stiglitz, 2004: 1).

The failure of the Washington Consensus to produce the predicted outcomes has led to a rethink and toning down of neo-liberal prescriptions. This became evident in the late 1990s in the run up to the UN General Assembly's Millennium Meeting. A series of global summits identified poverty eradication as the primary goal of development (Hulme, 2015). These built up into the Millennium Declaration and in

Box 1.2   The elements of the Washington Consensus

- Fiscal discipline – strict criteria for limiting budget deficits
- Public expenditure priorities – moving them away from subsidies and administration towards previously neglected fields with high economic returns
- Tax reform – broadening the tax base and cutting marginal tax rates
- Financial liberalization – interest rates should ideally be market-determined
- Exchange rates – should be managed to induce rapid growth in non-traditional exports
- Trade liberalization
- Increasing foreign direct investment (FDI) – by reducing barriers
- Privatization – state enterprises should be privatized
- Deregulation – abolition of regulations that impede the entry of new firms or restrict competition (except in the areas of safety, environment and finance)
- Secure intellectual property rights (IPR) – without excessive costs and available to the informal sector
- Reduced role for the state

2001 to the MDGs (see Box 1.3) to halve poverty by 2015 with a major focus on publicly financed social policies. The Goals, and their implementation, were a compromise between the Washington Consensus' neo-liberalism and the UN's human development agenda. The MDGs were to be achieved by innovative public-private partnerships (such as the Global Alliance on HIV/AIDS and the Global Fund) but they also accorded a central role for the state in poverty eradication. There are other versions of this Post-Washington Consensus. For example, the World Health Organization (WHO) sees it in terms of:

- Managing liberalized trade, finance and monetary systems
- Including the creation of enforceable codes and standards, and concessions to social welfare through targeted social safety nets
- Creating vertical and horizontal policy coherence
- Including businesses and firms in a Global Compact for Development and the PRSP [Poverty Reduction Strategy Papers] process.

The Global Financial Crisis of 2008 gave the process a further boost as the crisis hit very hard in the USA, the very epicentre of neo-liberal policy transmission to the Third World. Birdsall and Fukuyama (2011) note that in the post-Global Financial Crisis

---

Box 1.3   The Millennium Development Goals (MDGs)

- Goal 1: Halve extreme poverty and hunger
- Goal 2: Achieve universal primary education
- Goal 3: Promote gender equality and empower women
- Goal 4: Reduce child mortality
- Goal 5: Improve maternal health
- Goal 6: Combat HIV/AIDS, malaria and other diseases
- Goal 7: Ensure environmental sustainability
- Goal 8: Develop a global partnership for development

Source: The UN Millennium Project.

---

world, while capitalism in its various forms is still dominant and a global capitalist system is still adhered to, there are changes in the nature of development. Firstly, the era of 'foreign finance fetish' involving the unimpeded flow of capital around the world has weakened. Second, countries are recognizing the benefits of 'a sensible social policy' and receive support for this from the World Bank and IMF (International Monetary Fund). Third, the visible hand of government, rather than the invisible hand of the market, is making a comeback in terms of intervention in industry policy. Fourthly, there is a clear imperative for 'making bureaucracy work' so that it manages and coordinates policies more effectively. Finally, the world is moving towards multi-polarity with the emergence of new and significant players like China, India and Brazil, and a set of new 'middle powers' including Mexico, Indonesia, Nigeria and Turkey.

The clearest and most concrete manifestation of a successor to the Washington Consensus are the Sustainable Development Goals (SDGs) which follow the MDGs'. They build on the MDGs human development and capabilities approach. Its intellectual foundation derives from Amartya Sen (1999) and his notion of 'development as freedom'. It was about giving people the freedoms to enable the expansion of the '"capabilities" of persons to lead the kinds of life they value' (Sen, 1999: 18). Freedom is simultaneously a 'primary means' and a 'principal end' of development. The goals of human development are interlinked and involve the freedom to develop capabilities by those most in need, ideally assisted by those who are not. The SDGs, under negotiation at the time of writing, are more ambitious than the MDGs. They highlight environmental sustainability alongside poverty eradication and include proposed goals for reducing inequality, implementing human rights and improving governance. The specification of governance goals is, however, politically contested and technically very challenging (Hulme, Savoia and Sen, 2014).

As our brief and selective survey of 'what is development?' has shown, there has been and is considerable contestation over the definition, explanation and practice of development. This struggle over meaning is intense today. It is not a discrete semantic debate conducted by academics but has a direct impact on the lives of billions of people. The struggle over meaning relates to critical policy matters such as what actions will be taken to alleviate poverty or promote economic growth, who will have access to what resources, and who will be empowered? It is perhaps clearest in contemporary negotiations over the post-2015 development goals. The intensity of the debate reflects a widespread disappointment with the results of development after seven decades of practice and can be seen as a political battle to determine the nature of future practice.

We agree with Goulet (1992: 470) that development is 'a two-edged sword which brings benefits, but also produces losses and generates value conflicts'. In the benefit column Goulet lists clear improvements in material well-being as Charles Kenny (2011) has also more recently argued in *Getting Better*. Examination of the statistics for income, health and education in the World Bank's annual *World Development Report* and the UNDP's *Human Development Report* bears out this assertion. Goulet (1992) also notes technological gains which relieve people from burdensome physical tasks, institutional specialization, increased freedom of choice, a higher degree of tolerance and greater worldwide interdependence. Such gains will be felt differentially according to who you are and where you live, and according to the values one places on the meaning of development you may not feel they are gains at all.

There have been severe losses, misguided interventions and poor results in development practice – and one does not have to be a neo-classicist or radical post-developmentalist to appreciate this. It is unfortunately easy to identify the persistence of extreme poverty (still at least 1.2 billion in 2013 according to the United Nations), deepening environmental crises, war and social dislocation, increasingly unequal relations within countries and continuing unequal relations between nations. Differential developmental success between nations (compare the records of Singapore and China with those of Malawi and Nepal) can hardly escape attention, and even within nations micro success may contrast with macro failure and vice versa. Goulet's list of losses includes some less conventional but equally important items. He focuses on the destruction of culture and community and the rise of acquisitive personal orientations. There is pervasive social alienation produced in the turmoil of development and 'the meaning systems of numerous cultural communities are evacuated' (Goulet, 1992: 471).

Development requires rethinking and renewal and should be a constant process. As critics point out, development has often degenerated into mere rhetoric in which admirable official goals, such as the satisfaction of basic needs, job provision and better social services, are supplanted by operational goals which focus on debt-servicing, crisis-management and the defence of privilege. But this does not mean that the concept of development should be discarded, rather that it should be rejuvenated. It should be subject to critique and there should be efforts to make official and operational goals

---

Box 1.4   Gross National Happiness in Bhutan

The small Himalayan kingdom of Bhutan has grabbed global attention for its innovative approach to national development through its philosophy of Gross National Happiness (GNH). First articulated by the Fourth King, GNH is a values-driven approach to development that explicitly avoids excessive concern with GNP. It is based on a longstanding legacy in the 1729 legal code where it states that 'if the government cannot create happiness for its people, there is no purpose for the government to exist'. These sentiments are echoed in the 2008 constitution that directs the government to 'promote those conditions that will enable the pursuit of GNH'. But what is GNH? It takes place when material and spiritual development of society occur side by side to complement each other. It is holistic, balanced, collective, sustainable and equitable, and pays high regard to living in harmony in nature. In practical terms it is comprised of four pillars:

• Sustainable and equitable socio-economic development
• Environmental conservation
• The preservation and promotion of culture
• Good governance

It is not simply subjective well-being but is multidimensional and can be measured on the GNH Index which, in 2010, also included health, education, culture, time-use, good governance, community vitality, ecological diversity and resilience, and living standards. The results show consistent progress but there is still a way to go before all Bhutanese can be classified as 'happy'.

coincide. There should also be a clear appreciation that any definition will be value-laden, a product of personal preferences and that there will never be universal agreement on a single meaning and policy package. However, we believe that approaches such as the case of Bhutan do hold out hope for the future and capture the multidimensional nature of development and the importance of ethics and wisdom in determining what it should be (see Box 1.4).

From development administration to development management

With the invention of development by the Western nations in the immediate post-war period and its adoption as state ideology by the governments and emerging elites of the former colonial nations, the question arose as to how the promised social transformation was to be achieved. 'The primary obstacles to development are administrative rather than economic', declared Donald Stone (1965: 53). Others agreed and the discipline and practice of development administration was created to play a major role in facilitating development.

Development administration represented the practical application of modernization theory. Its promoters saw it as 'a midwife for Western development – creating stable and orderly change' (Dwivedi and Nef, 1982: 62). It was a form of social engineering imported from the West and embodying faith in the application of rational scientific principles and the efficacy of Keynesian welfare economics. In its early days at least, it reflected the naive optimism and ethnocentricity of modernization theory, that there were straightforward technical solutions for underdevelopment and the West possessed them. It was also perceived by the US government, its allies and some of its practitioners as an integral element of the Cold War. Development administration would wage an unarmed managerial struggle against communism in the underdeveloped nations by engineering the transformation to capitalist modernity, economic growth and mass consumption.

Development administration was a US-led movement with funds and personnel for its study and practice coming largely from US sources. In Britain, some academics and administrators saw it as an attack on the colonial record or believed that it was something already familiar. But an international orthodoxy emerged that there were important differences between public administration in poor countries and in high-income countries. The distinguishing element was that in the developing countries there was 'that inconvenient combination: extensive needs, low capacities, severe obstacles', many of which are still evident today (Schaffer, 1969: 184).

While the modernization perspective did not entail a monolithic approach to development administration several generalizations can be made. First, it was based on the notion of big government 'as the beneficent instrument of an expanding economy and an increasingly just society' (Esman, 1988: 125). Development administration was synonymous with public administration which itself was synonymous with bureaucracy. Second, there was an élitist bias. An enlightened minority, such as democratic politicians, engineers, economists and planners, would be committed to transforming their societies into replicas of the modern Western nation-state. They would establish themselves in urban centres and using bureaucracy as their principal instrumentality would spread the benefits to the rural areas. Third, development administration would tackle head on the 'lack [of] administrative capability for implementing plans and programmes [through] the transfer of administrative techniques to improve the central machinery of national government' (Stone, 1965: 53). Development administration was thus perceived as the transfer and application of a bag of tools. Fourth, foreign aid was the mechanism by which the missing tools of public administration would be transferred from the West to the developing countries. Fifth, traditional culture was early recognized as an impediment to the smooth functioning of Western tools and dominant Weberian models of bureaucracy. Development administration had to overcome such cultural obstacles which were seen as the sources of bureaucratic dysfunctions.

The management theory which supported this approach was drawn from the Classical School (see Box 1.5 for a brief chronology of major approaches to management). This was the world of the 'scientific manager' (Taylor, 1911), of 'principles' of administration (Fayol, 1949) and Weber's 'ideal-type' bureaucratic form of organization (Gerth and Mills, 1948). This approach to organizing public services retained its dominance in developing countries while being usurped or at least supplemented by newer theories in the West. For example, in the 1960s and 1970s the revitalization of the Human Relations school which stressed motivation, leadership and non-hierarchical forms had little effect on the bureaucratic model in developing countries (for example, Argyris, 1957; Bennis, 1966). Even participatory development initiatives, such as the community development movement, ended up being bureaucratized in developing countries.

The attacks on modernization theory in the late 1960s and 1970s were parallelled by challenges to development administration. On the financial front, US funding for public administration projects declined rapidly and sharply after 1967 as did academic spending. The blame for poor developmental performance was in large part attributed to a failure of development administration, and development experts and institutions looked for new solutions. According to Siffin (1976: 66) there was a shift towards 'more complex and more economically oriented problem perspectives'. Also, people began to question the assumption that big government was the route to development, a theme which gathered great momentum and power in the 1980s. In the West, this was the period which saw open systems and contingency theories of management become the dominant paradigm (for example, Lawrence and Lorsch, 1967). These theories argued that there were multiple ways of organizing and that the chosen option depended on the situation. The organizational environment was elevated to an extremely important position in these theories and the principal task of managers was to fit organizational sub-systems to those of the environment. Despite these profound shifts in Western management theory, the closed systems of Classical Management theory still maintained strong practical support in developing countries and, to this day, Indian civil servants talk proudly of having a 'British' administrative system without realizing this indicates its lack of fit with India's contemporary needs.

Academics had entered a period of self-criticism, reflection and uncertainty about development administration. Schaffer (1969) pointed to a 'deadlock' in development administration and raised questions about whether bureaucracy could bring about societal transformation. Bureaucracy was, after all, dedicated to incrementalism and the *status quo* and was characteristically inefficient. A seminal symposium in *Public Administration Review* (1976) featured much criticism of previous ideas. Evolutionary models were discarded; the Western values imported with the administrative tools were exposed and judged inappropriate; and the nature of culture and its relation to administration was questioned. Siffin (1976), in reviewing development administration in the period 1955–75, wrote of a 'costly learning' experience both for recipients and disseminators. Among other things he noted that the administrative technology transfer had aimed more at 'maintenance' needs rather

Box 1.5   A brief chronology of management thought

In contemporary development management are found strands from many schools of management thought. Most approaches originated in the private sector and have been absorbed only slowly into the mainstream of development management. All are still evident to a greater or lesser degree and in various combinations.

Approach	Date	Selected features
Classical	1900	Organizations perceived as closed systems; stress on efficiency and the bureaucratic form
Behavioural/ Human Relations	1930	Emphasis on people rather than machines; close attention to factors such as group dynamics, communication, motivation, leadership and participation
Quantitative	1940	Quantitative tools to support managerial decision-making; found in management science, operational management, management information systems and business process re-engineering
Quality Movement	1955	Strongly pursued in post-war Japanese industrial development and much later elsewhere; continuous improvement by working together and client focus; seen in total quality management, benchmarking, performance measurement and ISO 9000
Open Systems/ Contingency	1965	Organizations seen as systems of interrelated parts linked to the environment; emphasis on 'fitting' organizational structure to the specific environment of the organization

$\rightarrow$

than 'developmental' needs; that mechanistic views of organizations focusing on technical expertise and 'purposive objectivity', although instrumentally important, were not the 'crucial creative levers of development'; and that public administration training and scholarship in developing countries had been emulative of the West rather than innovative.

Meanwhile the neo-Marxist assault on modernization theory identified development administration as a device to legitimate and

Approach	Date	Selected features
Power/Politics	1965	Organizational decision-making not guided by technical rationality but is determined by political processes; a dominant coalition will be the major locus of organizational power
Managerialism	1980	Adoption by the public sector of private sector management practices; application of public choice theory and neo-classical economics to public sector management; often known as new public management (NPM)
Strategic Management	1990	Determining organizational objectives and the policies and plans to achieve them involving the allocation and alignment of resources; concern with external environment and use of tools like Balanced Scorecard
Change Management	1995	Focus on designing and implementing methods of organizational change borrowing ideas and techniques from other approaches; strong concern for change leadership
Critical Management	2000	Drawing on diverse theories, critical management challenges the authority, relevance and morality of mainstream management theory and practice
Managing Innovation	2010	Innovation increasingly found to be the key to organizational success. Search for systems to encourage and manage innovation.

promote the interests of the bureaucratic bourgeoisie (that is, top bureaucrats) and other dominant classes and/or elites. It was both an ideological prop and practical tool in perpetuating inequitable relations between classes. The technology of administration could not unilaterally promote the beneficial changes delineated in the meaning of development. Radical alterations in power structure were necessary before administration could be employed to such a purpose. There was an obvious impasse for development administration in this thinking. Administration was not an independent variable. It could only be a facilitator of development under a radically different political order.

Class interests were an important explanatory variable for Hirschmann (1981) in his commentary on the disappointing results of more than two decades of development administration in Africa. Like Schaffer, he also described a 'deadlock' but Hirschmann's deadlock moved beyond the inward-looking reflections of an intellectually unsure sub-discipline. He acknowledged that there had been many innovative and imaginative ideas in development administration but that they had been frequently ignored by leading African administrators. Why? The answer, said Hirschmann, was that bureaucrats focused on defending their class interests which put them in conflict with the majority of the population. Common development administration ideas such as less-stratified organizations with strong client orientation could be seen as revolutionary threats by the bureaucratic defenders of the status quo. Hirschmann was providing a social class version of the power-politics theories of management which had been advocated from the late 1960s onwards but surprisingly little used in development administration. These theories explained managerial decision-making in terms of the power of the 'dominant coalition' within organizations (Thompson, 1967) and argued that while organizational contingencies may constrain management decisions they did not determine them. In fact, managers had some latitude to make 'strategic choices' (Child, 1972).

Dwivedi and Nef (1982) went beyond 'deadlock' and asserted that development administration was in 'crisis'. Using a dependency-style framework they argued that development administration had been a 'dismal failure' responsible for 'anti-development', bureaucratic authoritarianism and seemingly everything that was wrong with development. They pointed to the 'incompatibility between bureaucracy, as a form of institutionalized social control, and development defined as quality of life for the population' (p. 65).

The environment in which administration is practised and the origins and maintenance of its ideological support are always in evidence in Dwivedi and Nef's (1982) article. These considerations had, by necessity, been creeping into work on development administration as the 'administration as neutral technology' paradigm had become increasingly discredited and the importance of politics in administrative analysis and action had become ever more obvious. The most important difference between administration in developing countries and in the West was being increasingly identified as that envelope of factors and forces which we collectively call the organizational environment. Whether it was the social class context, the influence of the World Bank, the type of political regime, the nature of the policy-making process or simply the prevailing culture, the centrality of the environment for understanding administrative action and paralysis was becoming firmly established. There was, however, an obvious lag in development administration between the generation and dissemination of environmentally oriented management theories and their widespread acceptance and application.

A second development forcefully advocated by Dwivedi and Nef (1982) was the search for alternative forms of organizational approach to development. Instead of simply criticizing the failures, people began to look at the successes and innovations. What had the experience of indigenous experiments in China, Tanzania and Brazil taught us? What had populist approaches to offer? Why had some organizations in Thailand, India, Sri Lanka and Bangladesh produced excellent development outcomes and considerable organizational growth (Korten, 1980) while others had not? Were these experiences replicable or were there principles of organizational design that could be easily modified according to changes in organizational environment? Rondinelli (1983) was keen to identify lessons from past experience that could enhance development administration in the future. His analysis indicated that the main reason for poor past performance in the public sector was the failure to cope with the complexity and uncertainty of organizational environments in developing countries. The remedy lay in changing structures and procedures so that experimentation and learning occurred. This creative hybrid comprises a human-relations type of management theory coupled with a contingency-style acknowledgement of highly variable environmental conditions, including the political environment.

By the 1990s, the neo-classical economists had gained considerable influence in policy circles and were also pointing to inefficiency and ineffectiveness in the public sectors of developing countries. While they agreed with Rondinelli's notion of experimentation they also recommended that the state should be 'rolled back'. Big government had not been effective government and it was time the principles of the market were allowed to operate. Reducing the size of the state and restricting the operations of the state would bring considerable savings. Programmes to raise bureaucratic capacity and efficiency and to encourage private sector growth through market mechanisms would then ensure that development would take place.

This radical and highly influential approach to administration and governance in developing countries was already in full swing in countries like the UK, Australia and the USA. Its intellectual origins lay in public choice theory (for example, Ostrom and Ostrom, 1971; Baker, 1976). In practical terms it encouraged 'managerialism' or the 'New Public Management' (NPM) which drew heavily on the innovations and trends in private sector management (Pollitt, 1993; Zifcak, 1994). The old distinction between public sector and private sector management became blurred. The dissemination of this model to developing countries was undertaken by enthusiastic Western advocates and influential multilateral financial institutions such as the World Bank and IMF. It was seen as a reform model which could move easily across international boundaries at last bringing about the elusive institutional convergence predicted decades before in modernization theory (Minogue, 2001). Its adoption would promote efficiency and effectiveness in public sector management in developing countries and support the quest for economic development.

But once again, the environment in developing countries did not necessarily prove accommodating to NPM. Some countries selected particular items from the long menu of NPM-style initiatives. No country embraced NPM in its entirety. In some places there is little evidence of any NPM-inspired reforms (Turner, 2002a). The results of NPM have been described as 'perplexingly equivocal' featuring both successes and failures (Polidano, 2001: 60). Whether NPM was ever a dominant paradigm for developing countries has also been questioned (Manning, 2001). Public sector reform programmes often continued to incorporate items drawn from sources other than NPM. But a terminological change had taken place. Development 'administration' had become development 'management'. The proponents of this relabelling said that it acknowledged the dynamism of the sub-discipline and its practice in realizing the potentialities of the public sector. Some critics believed that nothing had happened and that the relabelling was simply an effort to legitimize existing and longstanding practice (Cooke, 2001).

So how do we characterize the contemporary practice of development management? It has split into two opposed camps, the reformers and the radicals (Gulrajani, 2010). The reformers comprise the majority as they include not only academics but also numerous practitioners. They acknowledge the failures and disappointments of earlier management interventions but maintain faith in the possibility of such interventions to produce desired changes. They show diversity in their approaches. For example, they may accept certain approaches drawn from the NPM menu in particular circumstances. They may strongly favour participatory approaches or award ethical concerns high priority. They are always on the search for new or modified methods for engineering social change but they demonstrate different degrees of trust in the rationality of the technology of management. All have come to accept the importance of politics in development policy and its management but vary in the importance they attach to it and the ways to deal with it. The reformers exhibit different degrees of support for the state but acknowledge its important role in promoting development whether directly through its own officials or indirectly through the private sector, civil society organizations and communities.

The radical camp depicts reformist development management as a smokescreen hiding the 'inequality, violence and power of development management over subalterns in the Global South' (Gulrajani, 2010: 144). They see development management as claiming technical neutrality while facilitating domination of the change process through leaders and managers (Mowles, 2010). Development management, they say, is inescapably managerialist, 'in the sense that the *means* of management inevitably supplant the *ends* of policy' in a context where managers' interests are most often not aligned with the interests of the poor and marginalized (McCourt and Gulrajani, 2010: 83). For Cooke (2001; 2003), the roots of contemporary practice extend way back into colonial administration but have survived and been replicated in modified form in the contemporary era. The exploitative nature of colonial administration is still pre-eminent in development management making the latter incapable of generating true development for the poor and marginalized.

While the radical analysis forcefully reminds us that management is not a neutral technology and that power is the key element in determining development trajectories, there is vagueness about what they see as the way forward. Mowles (2010) talks of 'complexity and emergence' while others seem to tread the post-developmentalist path but with little advice on what policies and practices should be introduced for empowerment and development. For example, what should Indonesia's grand bureaucracy reform programme look like?

How should local governments be organized and oriented in sub-Saharan Africa? And are the MDG achievements despite or because of development management?

There are several possibilities for future directions. Gulrajani (2010) has suggested drawing on the Romantic tradition to bridge the gap between reformers and radicals. This involves seeing that 'administrative modernisation is inherently pluralistic and political' (Gulrajani, 2010: 142). It must also embrace 'practical reason' and the valuing of experiential knowledge with practice that is 'flexible, contingent, intuitive and sensitive' (Gulrajani, 2010: 143). The practice will be necessarily disorderly and be characterized by 'improvised political steering rather than planned social engineering' (Gulrajani, 2010: 143). Finally, 'professional reflexivity' is also essential to enable practitioners to fully understand their positions in the development process and as a basis for 'emergent ethics'.

Other critical reformists have identified the way forward as refocusing attention on institutions and their vital role in managing development. Rodrik (2008) believes that the move has already started with a transition from 'getting prices right' to 'getting institutions right'. He notes that there are many options for creating 'appropriate institutions' and warns against the misguided attempts in the 1980s and 1990s to impose 'best practice' in contexts where failure was inevitable. He advocates a 'second-best mindset' that can identify, design and deliver institutions that fit the context.

Acemoglu and Robinson (2012) utilize a broad canvas in their quest to explain 'why nations fail'. Their answer is because of the application of normative theories that don't work and the consequent transfer of inappropriate institutions. What developing countries need are inclusive institutions in the political sphere that distribute political power while still maintaining some amount of centralization, and in the economic sphere that 'enforce property rights, create a level playing-field, and encourage investments in new technologies and skills' (Acemoglu and Robinson, 2012: 429). While there may be a moral agenda behind such processes, progressive institutions are commonly far from ideal. They are usually achieving the selfish goals of elites more than of the wider citizenry but, they are incrementally including more people and groups in benefit flows and influencing decisions. What must be avoided are extractive institutions that suck resources from the many for the few and where power is highly concentrated.

Another innovative and very applied proposal for improved development management is problem-driven iterative adaptation (PDIA).

Andrews (2013) argues that reforms often fail because they don't fit the diverse conditions of developing countries – a message that we stress in this book. The reformers end up putting 'square pegs in round holes' (Andrews, 2013: 2). Inappropriate best practice interventions with limited domestic support have 'poor functionality' and simply make governments look better rather than perform better. In PDIA, the process is as important as the product and involves problem identification and analysis followed by the gradual crafting of solutions through experimentation that is 'politically acceptable and practically possible' (Andrews, 2013: 3). Furthermore, successful solutions arise from the involvement of many actors and the distribution of leadership and ownership throughout networks of organizations rather than relying on individual champions. Some of Andrews' ideas can be found in the World Bank's (2012a) latest 'Approach' to public sector management reform including:

- Emphasis on diagnostic approaches in designing and implementing reform
- Emphasis on explicitly formulating and empirically testing theory about what works in public sector management reform
- Emphasis on flexible problem-solving

The Bank claims to have been moving from 'best practice' to 'best fit' and to understand what works and why with the explicit acknowledgement of solutions as being 'context-contingent'. It remains to be seen whether the Bank's declared intentions are manifested in practice (Grindle, 2013; Polidano, 2013).

The rise of good governance

While development administration was being rethought and relabelled by some and chastised by others, a more significant intellectual innovation was taking place and gaining ascendancy in the political sphere. This was the emergence of the concept of good governance (often referred to as good government in the early 1990s). It burst onto the scene in 1990, months after the end of the Cold War, and quickly established ascendancy among multilateral and bilateral donors who promoted it vigorously in developing countries. No sooner had the dust settled over the collapsed Berlin Wall than donors began to revisit Western notions of political and economic liberalization, often forgotten when propping up authoritarian regimes and dictators as bulwarks against communism. It also coincided with donor unhappiness over the results of foreign aid. The culprit was identified as unaccountable recipient governments which lacked authority, suffered from incompetence and were riddled with corruption. Development needed good governance to overcome such disabilities and to satisfy rich country aid constituencies which scrutinized aid budgets more closely as part of the new managerialism in public sector management. Good governance was the framework for reshaping the Third World state.

Although some authors regard good governance as having 'too many meanings to be useful' (Rhodes, 1997: 52–3), the competing definitions do contain 'similar ideas and similar terminologies' (Minogue, 2002: 118). These include the traditional focus of development administration – efficient and effective public sector management. But they go much further to encompass the legitimacy of government; legal frameworks and the rule of law; accountable public officials; transparency in government and freedom of information; participation of citizens in governance; and a major role for civil society (UNDP, 1995; 1998; World Bank, 1992; ADB, 1999; ODA, 1993). Good governance is not supposed to be about government controlling development: Governance is not something the state does to society, but the way society itself, and the individuals who compose it, regulate all the different aspects of their collective life. Theoretically it involves partnership between government and the many different constituencies in society, from the rich and powerful to the poor and vulnerable people. Government may be the leader but it should also be an enabler and facilitator in creating the institutional environment necessary for effective development. Policies alone are not enough. They require the framework for good governance if they are to be successful in bringing about improvements in human development, private sector growth and popular participation. In this sense, good governance becomes a synonym for 'sound development management' (ADB, 1999).

But the idea and promotion of good governance have raised a number of critical issues. Firstly, the wide scope of good governance involving multiple interactions between state, market and society means that vagueness attends the notion, and interpretations can differ markedly in practice. This is at once a strength and a weakness: a strength in that it allows good governance to be designed to suit different circumstances and a weakness in that it is so diffuse that it becomes a convenient catch-all and justification for all sorts of initiatives. Whether the decision of the UN High Level Panel on the post-2015 development agenda to recommend that good governance become a development goal after 2015 will lead to clarification, and indeed measurement, of the concept remains to be seen (UN High Level Panel, 2013). It could even be a synonym for development. Secondly, there is the allegation that good governance strategies often oversimplify the relationship between economic and political change. Minogue (2002) argues that good governance carries assumptions that political reforms must precede and will produce economic reforms yet much evidence points to the contrary or reveals complex interrelationships rarely captured in donor statements about good governance.

A third criticism is that good governance may be old modernization theory dressed up in new clothing. It is a normative concept that defines 'good' in terms of Western democratic and capitalist institutions. Good governance promotes Western-style democracy and capitalism, just like modernization theory, and does not take account of the different political and economic development trajectories found in the Third World. Furthermore, the political conditionalities which accompany foreign aid and which focus on good governance agendas are interpreted by some as a reassertion of Western domination. Whether Western-style democracy produces improved development outcomes is difficult to determine. Empirical reviews of development results under different political regimes are inconclusive with few demonstrated correlations let alone causal connections so neither critics nor defenders can claim a cast-iron case (World Bank, 1991; Moore, 1995). For example, the advocates of good governance often seem to avoid confronting the rapid developmental gains made by industrializing East Asian states under authoritarian or semi-democratic rule. China doesn't conform to the good governance ideal with its democratic deficits. But it has made huge advances in improving citizens' welfare. However, critics must surely admit that standard items on the good governance menu such as improved government accountability, reduced corruption and better services are generally what people want from development.

A fourth criticism concerns the prominent position often given to human rights in the good governance discourse. This has been challenged for promoting a Western consensus under the umbrella of universality. It is ethnocentric in 'its overriding preoccupation with political rights, to the neglect of economic and social rights' (Minogue, 2002: 128). Alternative perceptions from other societies are overridden and undervalued. Thus, Cheung (2013) takes issue with those who discard the 'Asian values' discourse too quickly and reduce it to an elite device simply intended to maintain power, privilege and inequity. He contends that 'Traditions give a nation its moral strength and cultural identity that are equally important to its "governance" as modernity and modernization achievements' (Cheung, 2013: 253). Thus, after the demise of Chairman Mao's brand of communism in the 1970s, Chinese leaders combined a market economy with the restoration of Confucian values of social harmony to create 'a sustainable political and social realm' (Cheung, 2013: 254).

When examining the results of good governance initiatives it is difficult to come to firm conclusions because of their diversity, the difficulty of measurement and the highly varied environments in which they take place. There is an assumption that everybody is in favour of them when in practice some powerholders may feel extremely threatened by proposed changes to the status quo. There can also be surprisingly little attention to the underlying causes of bad governance. Moore (2001) argues that only by understanding the roots of political underdevelopment can we find the way to encourage good governance. He acknowledges the diversity of states of the South but identifies a set of international factors which, in different combinations, have strongly influenced the political underdevelopment of current state configurations (see Box 1.6). This has led to bad governance which aid agencies have attempted to overcome by 'institutional transfer for its own sake' rather than, as Moore (2001: 410) suggests, exerting increased effort in creating 'the environmental conditions that will encourage the emergence of more productive state-society relations within poor countries'. In the next chapter we examine these environmental conditions which prevail in developing countries.

It has been realized by many that adopting and implementing all the tenets of good governance is an impossible task for poor developing countries even if they were inclined to do so. The broad definitions of good governance read like 'ideal types', far removed from Third World realities. Good governance has also been expanding – for example, from 45 aspects in the World Bank's 1997 *World Development Report* to 116 in 2002 (Grindle, 2004: 527). It is thus extremely difficult for governments in developing countries to decide on priorities from the long list presented to them. Grindle (2004) has suggested a compromise in the form of 'good enough governance' in which we think strategically about the priorities in governance reforms. In doing this it is necessary to consider such things as which actions will most benefit the poor; which actions are easier to undertake; what conditions are most conducive to obtaining the desired results; and what capacity

Box 1.6   The causes of political underdevelopment

- Unnatural birth: states created by rapid European conquest, especially in the nineteenth century in Africa with artificial borders.
- Incomplete state formation: poor states with areas never brought under bureaucratic control which are ruled by local elites often relying on coercion. The areas sometimes become havens for illegal activities.
- History of external control: many states in the South have a history of direct or indirect control.
- The declining cost of military superiority: rulers of poor countries have the opportunity to use state income to purchase military hardware that constitutes overwhelming force in relation to their civilian populations. Previous reliance on large numbers of their populations for such military superiority has been lost.
- International criminal networks: state elites in poor countries are often involved in relationships with international criminal operations concerned with activities such as smuggling narcotics, timber and precious stones or money laundering.
- Unearned state income: many poor states rely on mineral revenues or foreign aid (unearned income) and have limited incentives to negotiate with their citizens over resources or 'to institute or respect democratic processes around public revenue and expenditure'.
- Competitiveness of aid donors: in aid-dependent state the organization of foreign aid often involves competition between donors and leads to a loss of central control over expenditure and diminished state accountability.

Source: Modified from Moore, M. (2001) 'Political underdevelopment: what causes 'bad governance', *Public Management Review*, 3(2): 385–418.

does the government have to design, implement and embed reforms. Such strategic priority setting is highly political as it will involve conflicts among different actors with different interests. But coalition-building, finding common ground, compromise and trade-offs can be used to determine what is politically feasible. From such political processes, governance priorities appropriate to the circumstances can be selected and implemented by governments in the knowledge that there is strong domestic support rather than simply paying lip-service to foreign donors. As a government official once confided to one of the authors in a conversation of metaphors about an internationally financed governance project, 'you don't nurture somebody else's child like your own'.

Chapter 2

Organizational Environments: Comparisons, Contrasts and Significance

All organizations exist in and relate to environments that affect their operations. The environments in which administrators and policy-makers operate in developing countries are both distinctive and diverse. They are distinct from those environments encountered by their counterparts in the rich countries of the Organisation for Economic Co-operation and Development (OECD), but between and sometimes within developing countries there are substantial differences. This means that management models and policies which are successful in one place may be inappropriate in a different environment. Thus, the practices and prescriptions of management in rich countries may be particularly prone to failure when transplanted to radically different developing country contexts. Even South–South transfers must be treated with great care and consideration.

The organizational environment influences the nature of policy, administrative reform or any programme of planned change. Managers at all levels who have a good appreciation of the environment and reflect that in their decisions and actions have a far greater chance of success than those who choose to underestimate or ignore the significance of the environment.

In this chapter we will first explore the concept of environment and indicate some of the ways in which organizations interact with their environment. Then we will describe some of the components of the environment which have been identified as important by politicians, public servants, academics and other development professionals. Finally, we will draw some general conclusions about developing-country environments and what this means for policy-makers, administrators and development.

Making sense of the environment

To appreciate the vastness and complexity of the environment we can begin with Robert Miles's instruction to 'take the universe, subtract from it the subset that represents the organization, and the remainder is environment' (Miles, 1980: 36). There are economic forces, social institutions, demographic patterns, other organizations, international agencies and many additional elements which make up this enormous general or macro environment (Robbins et al., 2011). Collectively, they set the limits to organizational discretion (Aldrich, 2008). But it is too broad a definition of environment for practical purposes as, by incorporating everything, it fails to distinguish what is of immediate significance for the organization. To do this we can identify the 'specific' or 'task' environment as that part of the environment which is directly relevant to the organization in its specific work and in achieving its goals (Samson and Daft, 2014). For example, the constituencies which influence and interact with a Department of Health will show variation from those identified for a Department of Public Works. Delineating the boundary between the general and task environments is obviously difficult but the broad distinction is still useful. Some management texts also identify an internal environment for organizations. This is comprised of culture, operating technology, work practices, intra-organizational politics and other elements found within organizations. We will not pursue this concept here as the items which it embraces necessarily appear in other chapters of this book. In this chapter we are concerned only with the external environment.

While dividing the environment into different parts makes a useful start to our analysis, the critical questions from a management perspective focus on the degree of uncertainty and complexity in the environment. For many years, authors have suggested that if organizations are to remain effective and efficient they must take steps to 'fit' their structures and strategies to the demands of the environment (Emery and Trist, 1965). According to management writers and certainly in the popular perception, the environment is changing at an ever increasing pace generating increasing uncertainty and complexity that organizations must deal with in their unceasing change strategies. Others have been less persuaded by such determinism and have employed the distinction between the 'influenceable' and 'appreciated' environments (Smith et al., 1981). While managers will control certain decision areas in the organization (for example, deployment of staff, allocation of resources) they will not have such power outside. They may, however, be able to influence certain decisions by organizations and actors operating in the same or related areas. But there are other factors which are recognized and appreciated but which lie beyond the control of these managers. Such a view coincides with the 'resource dependence perspective' which gets away from notions of environmental determinism and identifies ways in which organizations can be proactive in influencing events and decisions in their environment especially in the extraction of resources from it (Pfeffer and Salancik, 2003).

Whether managers and policy-makers take a deterministic or proactive view of the environment they all need to engage in environmental scanning. This involves monitoring and evaluating changes in the environment so that appropriate actions can be made to organizational strategies and structures, and to national or local government policies. There is a huge range of scanning techniques, from informal but astute observation and analysis of current political trends to sophisticated data collection and computer analysis. For example, forecast-based planning examines quantitative data of past trends to predict what is going to happen while scenario planning 'takes an inductive, qualitative approach' when exploring alternative futures and the risks associated with them (Graetz et al., 2011: 55). They can adopt time-frames which vary from long-term scenarios of 20 years or more to those which focus on next year only. Whatever the methods employed and whether the organization is in the public or private sector, it appears that organizations which pay attention to their environments have a much greater chance of performing well than those which ignore environmental scanning. Furthermore, as developing-country environments are typically uncertain and growing in complexity the importance of environmental scanning as an input to public policy and management is increasing. If scant attention is paid to such data gathering and analysis, decision-making will become entirely ad hoc, and may simply degenerate into desperate steps by officials to hold on to power. Such an orientation does nothing to satisfy the developmental needs and demands of the millions of people who live in conditions of poverty and insecurity in developing countries.

There are some additional complications in dealing with the environment. The environment is not an objective reality with an existence of its own. Different people perceive it in different ways.

They may 'enact' the environment creating the very information and realities to which they then respond (Weick, 1977). Thus, organizations or policy-makers respond to what they have constructed – what is influenceable and what is appreciated. What they perceive and how they perceive it may vary. An organizational response may then be characterized as a 'strategic choice' which usually reflects the way in which the organization's power elite, its 'dominant coalition', enacts the environment (Hatch, 2013). The environment is anything but a clear empirical reality. Information can be ignored or emphasized, institutions overlooked or awarded significance. It is a zone of contestation where political process and analysis are of great importance.

Another zone of contestation is how far organizations are themselves discrete entities easily distinguished from their environments. Do they have clear boundaries? The buildings? The employees? Or should they be seen in terms of 'flux and transformation' (Morgan, 2006) where 'structure is best represented as a flow or process, not as a fixed hierarchy or static state or form' (McKenna, 1999: 221). This is the province of network analysis where we look for reciprocal relationships and where boundaries can be fuzzy. For example, a public hospital seems at first sight like a clearly bounded organization. At its operating core are the doctors but they may also work in private practice and at other hospitals. They may seek advice from doctors attached to different hospitals and they will be members of professional organizations that define standards and entry requirements. There are in-patients and out-patients receiving treatment or other services in the hospital and suppliers of materials and equipment. There are regulators in government and contractors who undertake the catering, cleaning and perhaps back-office services in finance and records management. Some of the latter may even be in a different country, conducting all transactions electronically. There will be multiple reciprocal relationships of cooperation and competition among these actors which are best depicted as a network in which the organizational boundaries are at best fuzzy. Going further down this line of thinking we can end up with the proposition that 'the very notion of organization and environment as separate is misleading' (Grey, 2009: 98). However, we shall avoid this possibility here and make the assumption that we can draw some sort of distinction between organizations and their environments as we need to identify significant forces and actors that impact on organizing for development.

Elements of the environment

In this section we will describe some of the important elements of the environment which have been consistently appreciated, influenced and enacted by policy-makers and administrators in developing countries – and by academic analysts. Although we use convenient categories to package our environmental components remember that this is an analytical device and that life is not so easily compartmentalized in practice. There is a complex causal texture between parts of the environment and in their engagement with the organization. We should therefore beware of crude generalizations about cause and effect in explaining administrative and policy behaviour. With these considerations in mind we have divided the environment into five segments: economy, culture, demography, politics and physical environment, each of which is itself subdivided.

Economic factors

Making the economy grow and sharing out the results of such growth are fundamental concerns of governments and societies engaged in development. To pursue this strategy it is necessary to know what is happening in the domestic and international economy. Administrators and policy-makers need information about such items as growth rates of the gross national income (GNI), the availability of capital, changes in the structure of production and the labour market, and projections of international debt. They are simultaneously items which the government is trying to change and elements of the environment which affect those planned changes. They will offer opportunities or place constraints on policies in the economic and other sectors. Also, they are interrelated with the other variables in the environment and will both affect them and be affected by them.

Gross national income

The most commonly cited statistics in the study of development are the closely related GNI per capita and gross domestic product (GDP) per capita. GNI (formerly GNP – gross national product) per capita is calculated by 'estimating the money value of all goods and services produced in a country in a year, plus net factor income (from labour and capital) from abroad, and dividing by the estimated mid-year population' (Hulme and Turner, 1990: 18). GDP includes only what is produced in a country and can be seen as GNI minus the net factor income from abroad. For example, worker remittances and investment income from other countries are not included in GDP. Both GNI and GDP are measures of production and are utilized to compare levels of economic development between countries. The major division is between high-income economies found in Western Europe, East Asia, North America and Australasia and the developing economies of Africa, Asia, Latin America, the former Soviet bloc and the Pacific. The division is sometimes viewed as that separating rich and poor, North and South, wealthy OECD countries and the rest, or First and Third Worlds. However, these divisions are too crude, as within the developing world there is considerable differentiation. Since most of the nations of the world and the global population are classified as developing then such diversity should be no surprise.

The World Bank divides the developing world into three categories according to GNI per capita: in the fiscal year 2015, these were low income (US$1,045 or less per capita per year), lower-middle income (US$1,046–4,125) and upper-middle income economies (US$4,126–12,746). It is questionable whether some upper-middle income economies such as Turkey, Hungary and Mexico would be recognized as 'developing'. Even excluding such cases the range is enormous – from Burundi with US$280 per capita to Venezuela with US$12,550 per capita. Contrasts in GNI and other economic data between countries can be seen in Table 2.1.

While the GNI measure does reveal a great deal about economic conditions there are limitations to its use. The adoption of GNI expressed as purchasing power parity (PPP) represents a useful advance as it removes exchange rate distortions from GNI figures to produce a measure of what the dollars would actually buy in particular countries. But even the PPP GNI per capita says nothing about income distribution, and also makes huge assumptions about informal and subsistence production which are ubiquitous in developing countries, and it is still not an accurate guide to general levels of welfare. A human development index (HDI) constructed by the United Nations Development Programme (UNDP) is a far better guide to welfare as it incorporates three basic dimensions of human development – a long and healthy life, knowledge and a decent standard of living – to give a composite measure of human welfare. Countries are grouped according to their level of development as expressed in the composite HDI measurement: human development that is very high (49 countries in 2014), high (52 countries), medium

Table 2.1   *The economic environment*

Country	GNI per Capita Atlas method (Current US$) 2013	GNI per Capita (2011 PPP$) 2013	Poverty Headcount ratio at national poverty line (% of population) Various years	Agriculture Value added (% of GDP) 2012 and 2013	Expected Years of schooling 2013	HDI Rank out of 187 and category 2013
Low Income						
Madagascar	440	1,333	75.3	29	10.3	155 (Low)
Ethiopia	470	1,303	29.6	49	8.5	174 (Low)
Bangladesh	900	2,713	31.5	17	10.0	142 (Low)
Lower Middle Income						
Ghana	1,760	3,532	28.5	22	11.5	138 (Medium)
Bolivia	2,550	5,552	45.0	13	13.2	113 (Medium)
Indonesia	3,580	8,970	11.4	14	12.7	108 (Medium)
Upper Middle Income						
China	6,560	11,477	4.6	10	12.9	91 (High)
Gabon	10,650	16,977	32.7	4	12.3	112 (Medium)
Brazil	11,690	14,275	9.0	5	15.2	79 (High)
High Income						
United Kingdom	39,110	35,002		1	16.2	14 (V. High)
Japan	46,140	36,747		1	15.3	17 (V. High)
Australia	65,520	41,524		2	19.9	2 (V. High)

Sources: World Bank data: Countries and economies. Available from: http://data.worldbank.org/country; UNDP, Human Development Reports, Data, 2014. Available from http://hdr.undp.org/en/data

(41 countries) and low (42 countries) (UNDP, 2014). In Table 2.1 it can be clearly seen that GNI ranking does not necessarily correlate with the standing of a country on the HDI.

Structure of production

Other economic indicators help to elaborate the crude GNI per capita figure. Examination of the structure of production, for example, reveals that all developing countries have a greater reliance on natural resource exploitation including agriculture, mining, forestry and fisheries than the rich nations. For most rich countries agriculture provides under 2 per cent of GDP. The developing countries stand in marked contrast, particularly the low-income economies. For example, in Sub-Saharan Africa, agriculture accounted for up to 35 per cent of GDP in 2012, and, in South Asia, 18 per cent in Bangladesh and 20 per cent in Pakistan (see Table 2.1). But the range is considerable among the developing nations with middle-income economies often possessing substantial industrial sectors and sometimes revealing production structures nearer to the high-income than to the low-income economies. The overall trend, however, is one of declining importance of agriculture in the GDPs of developing countries and increasing importance for industrial production and the service sector. But with burgeoning urban populations could the agricultural sector in some countries be set for a comeback?

Labour

The human resources profile also provides contrasts both within the developing world and with the OECD nations. The latter invariably possess more educated populations and more highly skilled labour forces. Literacy rates within the developing nations vary widely and do not necessarily correlate with the GNI per capita figure (see Table 2.2). Some economies with modest GNIs such as Sri Lanka, Vietnam and Tajikistan have superior adult literacy rates to economies with significantly higher incomes such as Morocco, Egypt and Saudi Arabia. Skills are often in short supply. In some places, highly educated persons either do not have the particular skills needed by the economy or they migrate abroad for better opportunities. For example, in 2006, there were reportedly more Malawian doctors practising in the British city of Manchester than in their home country (McDonald, 2012; disputed by Lizi et al., 2013) while in 2004 it

Table 2.2   *Gender inequality*

Country	Gender inequality index rank 2013 (n=151)	Maternal mortality rate (deaths per 100,000 live births) 2010	Women's share of seats in parliament (%) 2013	% of population with at least some secondary education 25 years + female (male) 2005–2012
Low income				
Madagascar	n/a	240	15.8	n/a
Ethiopia	121	350	25.5	7.8 (18.2)
Bangladesh	115	240	19.7	30.8 (39.3)
Lower Middle Income				
Ghana	123	350	10.9	45.2 (64.7)
Bolivia	97	190	30.1	47.6 (59.1)
Indonesia	103	220	18.6	39.9 (49.2)
Upper Middle Income				
China	37	37	23.4	58.7 (71.9)
Gabon	108	230	16.7	53.8 (34.7)
Brazil	85	56	9.6	51.9 (49.0)
High Income				
United Kingdom	35	12	22.6	99.8 (99.9)
Japan	25	5	10.8	87.0 (85.8)
Australia	19	7	29.2	94.3 (94.6)

Source: UNDP, Human Development Reports, Data, 2014. Available at http://hdr.undp.org/en/data.

was estimated that at least 1 million university degree-holders from the 50 poorest countries were living and working in rich countries, a brain drain of 15 per cent of the skilled university-educated population (Deen, 2006). Even allowing for remittances of income from abroad this appears to represent a huge loss of investment in the type of skilled human resources required for national development.

A more recent problem, especially in Sub-Saharan Africa, has been the HIV/AIDS epidemic which has wrought havoc on all sections of the population. When HIV hits rural households, agricultural production and income fall. More of the remaining income is then spent on health-related expenditures. But HIV/AIDS has also removed large numbers of skilled, experienced and irreplaceable professionals from the workforce. In the mid-2000s, 100 primary school teachers were dying of AIDS-related illnesses each month in Tanzania while in Kenya it was thought that 14,500 teachers were HIV-positive and up to 77 per cent of teacher absenteeism in countries with high prevalence rates was due to HIV/AIDS (IATT, 2008). In Zambia, HIV/AIDS was greatly responsible for making the average age of death of health professionals a mere 37.7 years (Feely et al., 2004). It was estimated that it would be necessary to increase the numbers of clinical staff by 80 per cent to offset AIDS-related mortality.

Capital

A further distinction between rich and poor countries is implicit in this very categorization. The latter generally experience scarcity in both public and private domestic capital, the resources that are needed for investment in productive enterprises. Not only are GDPs low but also are savings rates, with a few exceptions such as China and India. This is to be expected given the many persons who exist in poverty or near to it and who must attend to current consumption rather than to saving. Even middle classes may be similarly affected.

Large companies receive good service from banks in developing countries. Microfinance institutions, such as the Grameen Bank and BRAC in Bangladesh, have also made good progress providing loans to 105 million poor borrowers in developing countries in 2010 with 80 per cent of the beneficiaries women and 70 per cent living in rural areas (Microfinance Barometer, 2012). However, potential clients greatly outnumber those already served by 4 to 1. Small and medium enterprises suffer greatly from lack of access to capital. This is due to weak property rights rendering collateral a problem, poor quality of financial institutions, low capacity for assessing SME lending opportunities and risks, lack of reliable credit data, the absence or poor development of credit markets, and entrepreneur skill deficits for receiving risk capital.

While foreign direct investment (FDI) will not solve the capital problems of developing countries, governments generally believe that it can make a useful contribution to economic development. Its proponents argue that it facilitates economic growth, technology transfer, skills transmission and growth in government revenue. Others warn that it can lead to foreign control over domestic firms, undue external policy influence, foreign firms borrowing on restricted local capital markets and repatriation of profits. In 2011, $755 billion of

FDI flowed into developing and transitional economies. However, the large emergent economies of the BRIC countries (Brazil-Russia-India-China) have been the destinations for almost half of this flow since 2005, especially China. Success in attracting FDI depends largely on country-specific factors, for example rich natural resources, an educated workforce, a large domestic market, a reliable legal system, but in general it is the more economically developed nations that attract more resources as they have more to offer. The main source of FDI has been rich countries but China has also been leading a South–South campaign of FDI with US$43.9 billion invested in Latin America and the Caribbean with 92 per cent going to Caribbean tax havens (Shixue, 2012). In Africa, a similar story has been unfolding with China's stock of foreign investment increasing from US$56 million in 1991 to US$4.46 billion in 2007 and with over US$2.52 billion invested in 2012 alone (Renard, 2011; Xinhua, 2013). Chinese firms are apparently less risk averse than western companies, have less social and economic concerns and consider their investment longer-term ventures. Interestingly, there has even been a reverse flow with African direct investment in China rising to US$14.24 billion in 2012, a 44 per cent increase from 2009 (Xinhua, 2013). The rise of China and the BRICS is leading to significant change in development finance institutions. At the Asian Development Bank, China is increasingly jockeying with Japan for leadership and the BRICS have established the 'New Development Bank', headquartered in Shanghai, to finance infrastructure in Africa and Asia.

A final observation on capital is that in times of crisis capital may flow out of developing countries just when it is perhaps most needed. In 2012, the Argentinian government introduced a range of measures to stem the outward flow of foreign currency that had reached US$21.56 billion in 2011 (*Wall Street Journal*, 17 May 2012) almost approaching the $23.1 billion that had departed in 2008 as a result of the Global Financial Crisis and a farmers' strike. Inflation approaching 25 per cent and a thriving black market in US dollars led to a popular belief that yet another devaluation of the peso was inevitable. But it is not only financial crises that can see capital flee a country. Political crises can have a similar effect especially if they degenerate into civil war. Collier et al. (2003) have estimated that during such wars capital flight increases from 9 per cent of private wealth to 20 per cent and that it continues rising to 26.1 per cent even after the first decade of peace. This is in addition to the destruction of capital stock that occurs during the conflict.

Public finance: revenue mobilization, taxation, foreign aid and debt

Not surprisingly, in low-income countries there are severe constraints on public finance. There are two main reasons for this. First, having small economies and low GNIs per capita mean that there are limited opportunities for personal and corporate taxation. Second, the governments of most developing countries are relatively ineffective in mobilizing domestic revenue. They have a tendency to rely on sales taxes, tariffs from imports and exports and royalties from natural resource extraction while raising very little through taxation. Tax collections is low partly because of tax authority inefficiency; partly because of the often large size of the informal economy, which is usually outside of the tax system; and partly because multi-national companies avoid taxation through offshore registration and transfer pricing. As an example, Bangladesh has a tax-to-GDP ratio of only 13 per cent compared to Denmark's 47 per cent ratio. No wonder public services are much better in Denmark!

Problems of domestic revenue mobilization, shortage of foreign exchange and scarcity of capital led to the development of the foreign aid relationship which binds the low and middle-income economies to the rich nations of the world in a dependent relationship. The flow of foreign aid from the governments of rich nations to those in poor nations has certainly been a leading feature of development in the years following World War II, and the results of such flows have often been disappointing and have contributed to another feature of the economic environment of developing nations – foreign debt.

From small beginnings the amount of debt began to take on enormous proportions: from US$100 billion in 1970 to US$650 billion in 1980, US$1500 billion in 1992 and US$2561 billion in 1999 (UNDP, 1994; 2002). Developing countries struggled to meet repayments that took money away from services and infrastructure investment. This prompted action from the international community. In 1996, the HIPC (highly indebted poor countries) initiative was launched to address the debt problems of poor countries and was later joined by the Multilateral Debt Relief Initiative (MDRI). By the end of 2008, these exercises had not only removed debts of $124 billion from the governments of poor countries but had also improved debt management capacity. This was something that had also occurred in many middle income countries in concert with reformed financial institutions and growing domestic debt markets.

The overall result has been a marked improvement in the debt position of developing countries from the dark days of the 1990s. However, some countries still owe vast sums and struggle to meet repayments or find they must pay significant portions of national income to service their debts.

While action on debts was taking place in the 2000s, the rich countries were pledging to increase the amounts of aid for developing countries so that the latter could achieve their MDG targets. The OECD countries of the EU agreed to increase their aid to 0.56 per cent of GNI within five years. Some have moved in the declared direction while the majority have not. The Global Financial Crisis has resulted in some countries cutting aid budgets and apprehensions that there are more cuts to come. Ironically, there has even been a reverse flow exemplified by Indonesia's US$1 billion to the IMF's European bail-out fund in July 2012 – a far call from the country's humiliation by the IMF in 1998 during the Asian Financial Crisis. Even the arrival of new donors such as wealthy Arab countries and the estimated US$53 billion that now comes annually from non-government sources are unlikely to fill the aid gap. Furthermore, there is ongoing concern over aid effectiveness with a recent OECD survey of 78 countries finding that only one of 13 indices deriving from the Paris Declaration on Aid Effectiveness in 2005 had been met over the five years to 2010 (OECD, 2011). The targeting of aid can also be of concern as it has always tended to be heavily influenced by the geopolitical concerns of donors. This explains why Iraq and Afghanistan have been the largest aid recipients during the 2000s.

Infrastructure

For development a country needs infrastructure. An efficient transport system, reliable and extensive energy provision, adequate sanitation and rapid communication are among key infrastructure needs of developing countries but all too often there are capacity shortfalls. This lack of capacity may be manifest in inadequate port facilities, roads in disrepair or unable to handle the increasing volumes of traffic, obsolescent railway rolling stock, an inability to maintain required electricity output and water supply systems which fail to satisfy personal and organizational demands. While large cities frequently outgrow and hence place insupportable demands on their infrastructure, rural areas are all too often characterized by their lack of infrastructural development. As far back as the 1970s, authors were alleging urban bias in developing countries a state of affairs that has often been sustained (Lipton, 1977; Jones and Corbridge, 2010).

Information is increasingly regarded as the most important commodity in advanced capitalist nations. Gathering, processing and disseminating information using electronic information and communications technologies (ICTs) has become a leading activity in these countries. To service the insatiable demand for information, computers and telecommunications play a major role utilizing ever more sophisticated electronic machines with larger capacities and faster speeds. In the developing world one finds equivalent machines but in much smaller numbers, in fewer places and processing information which is often less plentiful and less reliable. For example, while 77 per cent of under 25s and 71 per cent of over 25s are internet users in rich countries the figures are only 30 per cent and 23 per cent in developing countries. However, mobile phone penetration is much higher with more than half of rural households in developing countries and over 90 per cent in India and China having access to a mobile phone. With broadband and other ICT prices dropping and the greater use of e-government it is inevitable that ICTs will become more available and more familiar to developing country populations. You can monitor the ever-changing statistics on ICT on the website of the UN's International Telecommunications Union.

Technology

In large part, development is about technology. Whether one is promoting indigenous agricultural techniques, modifying machinery for small-scale production, building factories or introducing ICT there are always questions about technology. As technology involves both hardware and techniques all technological activities have a human aspect. In OECD countries the speed of technological transformation during the past century has been unprecedented in human history. Some of what has been achieved is of dubious value for the present and future health of humanity. However, the industrial nations possess a massive store of technology and may be increasing their technological lead over the majority of developing nations although China and India are obvious exceptions. This trend could accelerate as science and technology are increasingly privatized by transnational corporations and made available only to those who can afford to pay. The flow of royalty and license fees is still largely in the direction of rich countries. For example, New Zealand with a population of 4.4 million in 2011 received $669 million in royalty and license fees while middle-income Philippines with a population of almost 95 million received only $445 million. Low-income countries as their name suggests reaped the most meagre benefits from royalties while at the other end of the scale, USA brought in $33 billion in 2011.

Technology in developing countries is often less complex. It may also be inefficient and less effective than more expensive alternatives although one should exercise extreme caution before making value judgements about 'backward' technology in developing nations as compared to superior advanced technology in the OECD. 'Simple' can also be efficient, effective, well-tested and environmentally friendly. But, technological innovation in developing nations is frequently concentrated in 'modern' activities such as large-scale manufacturing, the national airline, agribusiness plantations, and offices in the central business district of the capital city. This technology and much more has traditionally been acquired overseas, in large part from the industrial nations but increasingly it is originating from a few more industrialized developing countries such as China and Brazil. Third World research and development (R&D) capacity has grown considerably over the past two decades but it is heavily concentrated in a few countries. In many developing countries R&D is highly restricted, constrained by capital shortages, foreign exchange shortfalls and other environmental factors. Both in amounts and percentages of GDP, R&D expenditure in developing nations falls far short of that in OECD countries. Administrators and policy-makers face an environment where they must make continual technological choices. Many items on the shopping list derive from the industrial nations but increasingly these are being supplemented by products from the BRICs but whatever a product's origin there are always questions about its appropriateness. What is appropriate in Australia or the UK might well be inappropriate in Nigeria or Pakistan and what works for Brazil or China may not be so effective in Nepal or Paraguay.

Poverty and inequality

In 1990, the World Bank identified the reduction of poverty as the most pressing issue now facing the 'development community' (World Bank, 1990). In 2000, this message was strongly reiterated by the global community in the first of the MDGs – eradicate extreme poverty and hunger. There has been substantial progress in achieving this goal with the UN announcing that in 2010 the global poverty rate measured at US$1.25 per day per person had fallen to half the rate it was in 1990. Although there has been progress in all regions, much of this gain has been achieved by remarkable success in China where persons living on US$1.25 per day constituted only 12 per cent of the population in 2010 as compared to 60 per cent in 1990 (UN, 2013). The figures in Southeast Asia have also declined considerably from 45 per cent in 1990 to 14 per cent in 2010. In stark contrast is Sub-Saharan Africa where 48 per cent were still classified as living in poverty and South Asia, where despite significant advances, 30 per cent of the population were still in poverty. And lest we get carried away by apparent MDG success, it should be remembered that even with the poverty reduction target achieved there will still be over 1 billion people living on less than US$1.25 per day in 2015 (see Table 2.2).

In many developing nations there is also massive inequity in the distribution of resources and in incomes, a matter that is assuming increasing concern to policy-makers (*Economist*, 2012). In China, sustained economic growth has led to improvements in the living standards of the vast majority of the population but there have still been considerable widening of income inequalities – rural compared to urban, north and west compared to south and east, and within urban areas. By contrast, governments in Brazil have been able to reduce the massive economic inequalities although large income differences are still much in evidence. With the growth of middle classes, many people in developing countries, especially in Asia and Latin America, have access to educational resources, health facilities, food, accommodation and consumer goods which are similar to people in Western countries. Some are fabulously wealthy but alongside them exist the millions in urban squatter settlements and those hidden in rural villages and remote locations who daily battle with poverty. They have few assets, live in larger households, have lower incomes, have less access to social services, and live shorter lives than the middle and upper classes. The details vary from country to country and region to region but the bottom line is always the same – an inability to attain an adequate standard of living. The situation is also worrying some political leaders who acknowledge that feelings of 'relative deprivation' can fuel political instability.

Poverty and inequality should not be recorded simply as a matter of economic statistics. Vulnerability and powerlessness are two important characteristics which both define and perpetuate poverty (Sen, 1999). The poor lack buffers against contingencies such as weddings, funerals, natural disasters, sickness and accidents. This makes them highly vulnerable. Attending to these contingencies frequently results in the sale or irreversible loss of their already meagre assets. The poor in rural areas have also witnessed the relative ease with which rural elites intercept benefits intended for the poor who lack the political resources to bargain. Such powerlessness is especially common for women, and the physically weak, disabled and destitute. In an effort to ensure that development does not bypass the poor and vulnerable, the World Bank (2013a), in its World Development Report 2014, has stressed the importance of risk management as a 'powerful instrument' to build resilience and seize opportunities among these groups of people.

Informal sector

A final and particularly distinctive economic feature of developing countries is the prevalence of the informal sector; that is, the multitude of unregistered micro-businesses that operate outside of state regulation. They typically include food preparation and sale, petty trade, transport hire, repair activities, scavenging and manufacture. In 1991, it was estimated that such unofficial economies employed between 35 and 65 per cent of the labour force of most developing countries and provided between 20 and 40 per cent of GDP (Chickering and Salahdine, 1991: 7). Two decades later and the statistics remain remarkably similar. In many developing countries up to 60 per cent of workers are involved in the informal economy (Bachetta et al., 2009) while 41 per cent of GNI has been estimated to derive from it (Schneider, 2002). Typically in Middle Eastern and North African countries 27 per cent of the GDP is produced by the informal sector and 67 per cent of the labour force is employed in it (Angel-Urdinola and Tanabe, 2012). In Kenya, in 2011, 64 per cent of total employment was estimated to be in informal economic activities (IIFLS, 2013). Such burgeoning informal sector activity provides an environmental challenge to public sector managers and policy-makers. They cannot ignore the unofficial economy as it is ubiquitous, vast and frequently growing. But do they regulate it, do they encourage it or do they watch it erode the power and authority of the bureaucratic state?

Cultural factors

Policies and plans may be technically feasible but a group of cultural factors places limits on what policy-makers and administrators can actually achieve and indicates the acceptable directions for policy and management. Culture is manifested in beliefs, values, attitudes and norms of behaviour. It is the meanings we attach to behaviour. These meanings are the products of elements such as history, tradition and social structure. We have made a broad sweep of these elements in the group of cultural variables we discuss below. This complex cluster exercises a major influence on how actors will perceive the rest of the environment and how organizations and managers will operate.

Ethnicity

Ethnic identity may be perceived in various ways – according to race, culture, language, religion or place of origin. A unique combination of such attributes differentiates each ethnic community from others and provides the basis for self-consciousness particularly among members of ethnic minorities. According to both modernization and Marxist theories of development, ethnic identities would weaken as economic development proceeded. History has proved this assumption incorrect. In the late twentieth and early twenty-first centuries this has been most graphically demonstrated in widespread inter-ethnic strife in the form of secessionist movements and civil wars. While ethnic differentiation and political action based on ethnic identity have occurred in the Western nations it is in the developing world that ethnic divisions abound and where the most devastating conflicts have occurred (Cordell and Wolff, 2011a). They are important environmental features for managers and policy-makers which must be taken into account in framing policies, planning and implementation. These state officials may face considerable constraints in devising and implementing development programmes that are acceptable and implementable, especially where there has been a history of violent conflict.

Ethnic configurations vary considerably within the developing world. In Latin America and the Caribbean the indigenous populations were decimated by the colonizers. Thus, ethnic diversity is not such a pronounced feature of these societies although relatively small indigenous ethnic communities survive in marginalized and disadvantaged conditions in some countries. In Africa and Asia there can be considerable ethnic diversity which can translate into sometimes violent competition over resources, the allocation of jobs, control of the state or can even challenge the existence of the state. Civil wars caused by ethnic conflict have had particularly adverse consequences for development in some countries of Sub-Saharan

Africa while ethnic-based secession movements have been highly disruptive in Asia-Pacific countries such as the Philippines, Papua New Guinea and Indonesia. Indeed, Cordell and Wolff (2011b: 1) have described ethnic conflicts as the 'most prevailing challenge to international security in our times' with the capacity to generate large amounts of 'sheer human misery'. For the public sector manager and policy-maker there is always the consideration that their actions can be interpreted by ethnic groups in a framework which focuses on inequity between ethnic groups and that such analysis can have severe repercussions. But rapid economic and social advancement is certainly possible in conditions of ethnic diversity as the examples of Malaysia and Mauritius demonstrate.

Family and kinship

While family and kinship define important human relationships throughout the world, it is not an exaggeration to say that they have greater significance for determining behaviour in developing nations than in the Western world. There is a multitude of kinship systems in the developing world. Imagine Papua New Guinea where there are more than 800 language groups and so an equivalent number of kinship terminologies, each demonstrating some features which distinguishes it from the next. Whatever the operating system, the affective relationships of kinship are important determinants of behaviour. They create obligations and behavioural expectations. In some societies when kinship links do not exist, fictive ones will be sanctioned to cement significant personal relationships. In the Philippines, sponsors or godparents at a christening will be linked to the child, to its parents and perhaps to the wider family and even to the other godparents. One cannot generalize about the degree of intensity of particular kinship relations as differences between societies, individuals and contexts work against uniformity. The vital matter is that kinship forms an important frame of reference for individuals operating in society and the language of kinship has a wide currency in metaphors and analogies.

Values and norms

Among the most important components of culture are values and norms. They serve to determine, explain and legitimate human actions, and they show extraordinary variance between societies and even within them. Their importance to the administrator and policy-maker is quite obviously profound although this has not always been appreciated. In the 1970s, Gert Hofstede (1980) asked the simple question 'do American theories apply abroad?' concerning motivation, leadership and organization. One hundred and sixteen thousand questionnaires later, Hofstede concluded that national cultures provided distinct patterns of mental programming which cast severe doubts on the appropriateness of certain American management practices in different national cultural contexts. In East and Southeast Asia there has been vigorous debate about the need to utilize 'Asian values' in determining developmental visions and policies rather than being overwhelmed by alien Western values (Mauzy, 1997; Mahbubani, 2009).

Managers and policy-makers derive values from the wider society in which they live and from other collectivities to which they belong, such as ethnic groups, religions and social classes. They import such values and norms into their work organizations, and perhaps add a few specific items of organizational culture from that particular office or department. The values and norms guide and give meaning to what they do and what is acceptable or feasible in their dealings with the wider society. The wider society also evaluates the actions of the policy-maker and administrator using values and norms as tools. There is no Third World value system, and even within a nation-state values can vary considerably between groups, or particular groups can operationalize the same values in different ways.

Religion is also concerned with values. From their philosophical foundations, all religions espouse a core group of values on which beliefs and practices are founded. Such values may also influence or determine state policy such as has happened with Islam in Iran, Sudan or Afghanistan under the Taliban. Values deriving from Roman Catholicism may influence policy on matters such as marriage and education in Latin American countries and the Philippines. However, both adherents of a religion and outsiders may interpret the values and their application to daily life and national development in different ways. For example, there is considerable contrast between moderate Indonesia and stricter Middle Eastern countries yet both are Islamic. In India, certain sections of the powerful Bhartiya Janata Party use religion to justify radical policies while others within the party adopt less extreme interpretations.

Values also assume a very important position in the popular concept of 'social capital' which has been increasingly used to explain developmental success or failure. Social capital is 'the ability of individuals in a group to form relationships of trust, cooperation and common purpose' (Lall, 2002: 103). It is about the relations which connect people and is characterized as the metaphorical or social glue which holds a society together. It 'inheres in relationships rather than in individuals and objects' and can be seen in values and networks (Francis, 2001: 77). People do not usually set out to deliberately create social capital. At least until now it has generally emerged during the course of activities established to achieve other objectives in economy and society.

The importance of social capital for development draws on Putnam's (1993) view that it can provide societies with more effective governance and economic dynamism. Thus, countries with strong social capital are allegedly able to function better or, in economic terms, 'reduce transaction costs, facilitate information flows, lower risk, allow joint activities ... and supplement formal contracts and property rights' (Lall, 2002: 103). Part of the contemporary development agenda should therefore be to build social capital in such areas as community development. But problems attend this task. Firstly, there are competing views concerning the scope of what comprises social capital. Secondly, there is often vagueness associated with these definitions unlike the more tangible notions of physical, natural and human capital. These definitional problems contribute to a third difficulty – that of measurement. What indicators of social action best reflect desirable social capital and how are they accurately measured? Fourthly, the operationalization of social capital may establish an analytical and operational separation between the economic and the social when the two are inter-linked (Fine, 1999). There are continuing debates on cause and effect regarding social capital. For example, is poverty necessarily alleviated by building social capital? Finally, there is negative social capital which 'enables conspiracy against the public by cartels, criminals and cronies' (Francis, 2001: 84). Social capital may be utilized by the rich and powerful to maintain privilege rather than to improve the lot of the poor (Olson, 1965).

Gender

Women's issues have become major concerns for administrators and policy-makers only relatively recently. They were certainly part of the environment before the 1970s but their perception was generally undertaken using patriarchal instruments which both understated and misconceived the situation of women in development. The United Nations Decade for Women 1976–85 marked 'the acceptance of women's concerns as legitimate issues for national and international policy' (Tinker, 1990: 4). But this acceptance had been won through the political actions of women not as a result of some natural evolutionary process (Visvanathan et al., 2011).

The overriding theme in the study of gender is inequality and its persistence in relations between men and women (see Table 2.2) (Momsen, 2009). The nature and degree of inequality vary between countries and social classes. The inequity between women in different social classes can in fact be greater than that between men and women. For example, the lives of middle class and elite women in Latin America are vastly different than those of poor rural and urban women in terms of status, power, life chances, education, work, health and conditions of existence. If we are to understand the status of women in development then it is important to see it in the context of both class and gender relations.

Another element of our cultural environment – values – must also be taken into account as they furnish the ideological setting in which inequities are generated and maintained. In developing countries it is sometimes alleged that the Gender and Development (GAD) agenda is determined by interest groups in rich countries or multilateral finance agencies. Policies and projects are criticized as being 'Western' and disrespectful of recipient country norms. But is the call to respect local culture sometimes a device to maintain hierarchies of inequality? Also, local culture is rarely if ever a monolithic entity but is constituted from a variety of values which are subject to reinterpretation and whose individual importance changes over time.

Over the past two decades the situation of women in developing countries has undoubtedly improved. The gender gap in primary education has been closed and that in secondary and tertiary education is closing. In some countries girls now outnumber boys at these levels of education. More women have entered the labour force and now account for 40 per cent of employment (World Bank, 2012a, 2012b, 2012c). Women are living longer than men everywhere and in low-income countries women now live for 20 years more than in 1960. But this does not mean that inequality has been eliminated. Females are more likely to die relative to males in low and middle income countries; there are inequalities of economic opportunities, voice differentials in households and, in some countries of

Sub-Saharan Africa and South Asia, significant educational inequalities between boys and girls still prevail.

History

Public sector managers and policy-makers seldom acknowledge history as a component of their organizational environments, yet it is one of the most significant. John Toye (1987) has argued persuasively that the Third World has acquired a common identity through anti-colonial and anti-imperialist struggles. While the details of individual cases may vary, all developing countries have engaged in these struggles. For most it has been the decolonization process. Even the relatively few developing nations which were not formal colonies of Western powers have been forced to fight against imperialism and to be vigilant in dealing with it. There is a collective psychology wrought in the process of anti-colonial struggles which leaves a deep and lasting imprint on nations. Whatever the specific experience the outcome is a sense of shared experience, a common history. And in the post-colonial era it can be expressed in the ideology and practice of development.

This notion should not be taken to extremes as historical diversity is also evident. The legacies of colonial rule are evident today. For example, national boundaries established by imperial powers often incorporated different ethnic groups. Such ethnic diversity may become a principal consideration in policy-making and even in the survival of the state. Economic structures established under colonialism which focus on export crop production may be difficult to dismantle in post-colonial times. Imported colonial values concerning gender relations may become deeply embedded and survive unscathed long after the colonial power has departed. While at one level there may be a collective identity among developing nations forged out of broadly similar historical relations with the West, on another level one sees diversity between say the details of Hispanic colonialism in Latin America and British imperialism in South Asia. Both have left their mark and are addressed either explicitly or, more likely, implicitly by public sector managers and policy-makers engaged in the process of national development.

Demographic factors

The changing size, composition and location of populations are vital data for policy-makers and administrators. Such information enables them to know what services are needed, how fast they should grow, where they should be located and what to expect in the future. These population dynamics place societal demands on the state and must be monitored by government if informed decisions are to be made. Whether the needs and demands are fulfilled will depend on the interaction of these demographic factors with other clusters of environmental variables and the politics of the policy process. Health is also included in this demographic grouping. Good health for the population is a major objective of development and the MDGs and it is vital to have knowledge of disease patterns and the availability of health services for the attainment of this objective. Furthermore, an unhealthy population produces at far below the optimum level and therefore acts as a constraint on development (see Table 2.3).

Population growth

For most of human history population growth has been slow but during the second half of the twentieth century there was a population explosion as the number of people on the planet doubled to reach 6 billion. In 2012, the figure passed 7 billion. Much of this explosion has taken place in the developing countries and future growth is set to be even more concentrated in these countries: 9 billion people in the world by 2050 with the additional 2 billion being from developing countries. Developed country population growth is projected as minimal with declines only being avoided by the 2.4 million migrants expected annually from developing regions.

In stark contrast to the rich countries are the poorest countries, especially in Sub-Saharan Africa, where there are still relatively high fertility rates. Even allowing for substantial declines in these fertility rates, it is expected that populations in these countries will triple between 2011 and 2100. Indeed, UNFPA (United Nations Population Fund) (Singh and Darroch, 2012) has noted that despite the availability of affordable, safe high quality contraceptive devices, 215 million women still lack access to them.

The implications of continued and considerable population growth for policy professionals and administrators are not hard to discern. There will be a need for more schools, more health professionals, more houses, more roads, more jobs, more food – in short, more of everything. The difficulty is how to accommodate these requirements within tight budgets and limited resources in

Table 2.3 Demographic and health factors

Country	Population 2013 (millions)	Average annual population growth rate (%) 2010 and (1985)	Life expectancy at birth 2013	Under 5 mortality rate per 1,000 live births 2013 and (1985)	Improved water source (% of rural population with access) 2012
Low income					
Madagascar	22.9	2.8 (2.6)	59.9	58 (179)	35
Ethiopia	94.1	2.7 (2.9)	63.6	68 (222)	42
Bangladesh	156.6	1.1 (2.7)	70.7	41 (173)	84
Lower Middle Income					
Ghana	25.9	2.5 (3.3)	61.1	72 (155)	81
Bolivia	10.7	1.6 (2.4)	67.3	41 (147)	72
Indonesia	250.0	1.4 (2.2)	70.8	31 (102)	76
Upper Middle Income					
China	1,385.6	1.5 (0.6)	75.3	14 (53)	85
Gabon	1.67	2.4 (2.6)	63.5	100 (62)	63
Brazil	200.4	1.0 (2.2)	73.9	14 (75)	85
High Income					
United Kingdom	63.1	0.6 (0.1)	80.5	5 (11)	100
Japan	127.1	0.1 (0.7)	83.6	3 (8)	100
Australia	23.3	1.8 (1.6)	82.5	5 (11)	100

Sources: World Bank data: Countries and economies. available from: http://data.worldbank.org/country; UNDP, Human Development Reports, Data, 2014. available from http://hdr.undp.org/en/data

organizational environments where other wicked policy problems such as climate change, water shortage and poverty alleviation are demanding attention. As we have seen, the countries with the most pressing problems associated with population growth will also be the poorest and potentially the least able to cope.

Age structure

While the proportion of young people in developing nations' populations has generally been declining they still make up substantial proportions of those populations, considerably more than in the rich countries. Thus, 29 per cent of the populations of developing countries are under the age of 15 years while another 24 per cent fall into the 15–24 years bracket (UN Population Division/DESA 2009). In absolute terms this entails very large numbers with 1.7 billion persons in developing countries below 15 years of age and 1.1 billion between 15–24 years. For the least developed countries the youthfulness of their population is even more pronounced with 40 per cent of their populations under 15 years. For policy-makers and public sector managers this means devising ways of delivering education to ever-increasing numbers of children at all levels and creating an environment that will provide them with jobs when they graduate from their educational and training institutions.

Somewhat paradoxically, while developing countries have characteristically youthful populations (with some exceptions, notably China) they also face the phenomenon of rapidly ageing populations. One notable example is that life expectancy in Shanghai has surpassed that in the USA, 82 years as against 79 years. The numbers of over-60s in the developing regions are expected to grow from 475 million in 2009 to 1.6 billion in 2050 creating yet another set of policy issues for public officials. Where pensions are inadequate or non-existent and where new patterns of family responsibilities are emerging regarding care of the old, the state will be expected to come up with solutions.

Urbanization and migration

While developing countries generally have larger rural populations than OECD countries one of the remarkable features of the past five decades has been the huge growth of urban population in the developing world. In 1975, only 26 per cent of the population in developing countries lived in urban areas (UNDP, 2002). By 2000, the figure had risen to 40 per cent while by 2010, 45 per cent of the populations of less developed countries and 29 per cent of least developed countries were urban dwellers and it should be remembered that this urbanization has taken place in the context of overall high population growth rates. Furthermore, growth is continuing, perhaps not at the same rate but in absolute numbers the expansion is staggering. For example, in Africa between 2005 and 2010, 13 million persons were added to the urban population each year (Martine, 2011). In the less developed countries between 2010 and 2050, we are expecting urban populations to swell from 2.556 billion to 5.186 billion and in least developed countries from 249 million to 914 million (Credit Suisse, 2012).

In all countries the urban population has been expanding at a more rapid rate than the rural population due to natural increase and migration from the countryside. Some believe that the most able and skilled rural inhabitants are those who comprise the bulk of the rural-urban flow. However, compared to the existing urban population they usually occupy lower socioeconomic levels and have lesser qualifications. These are demographic patterns and processes which must be addressed by public sector managers and planners although all too often they appear to be overwhelmed by them. The poor who make up the vast majority of the developing world's urban population are all too evident in squatter settlements and slums throughout the world, living in cramped, insecure and often unhealthy conditions and displaying low levels of formal employment. The poor have in large part provided for themselves through the informal economy and have built their settlements despite the officeholders of the state rather than with their assistance.

The degree of urbanization varies considerably between developing countries. Some Latin American countries are among the most urbanized in the world. Ninety-two per cent of Argentina's population and 87 per cent of Brazil's lived in urban settlements in 2010, with the overall regional figure being 72.2 per cent (Credit Suisse, 2012). By contrast low-income countries have lesser proportions of their populations in urban areas. For example, in Kenya the figure was 22 per cent in 2010 while for Sub-Saharan Africa as a whole it was 37 per cent.

There has often been a tendency for the largest urban centres to grow most rapidly creating extensive 'megacities' or 'urban agglomerations' which carry huge populations far in excess of their infrastructural capacity and in which environmental problems such as air, water and noise pollution have become acute. Apart from Tokyo, the world's largest cities are now in developing countries and this situation will become even more pronounced with continued urban growth. In 2014, Delhi had 25 million residents, Shanghai, 23 million, and Mexico City, Mumbai and Sao Paulo each had around 21 million, while seven of the world's top 25 fastest growing cities were in China and another six in India (UNDESA, 2014).

In addition to the flow of rural populations to metropolitan centres there is significant migration to other countries. This flow is mostly comprised of skilled and semi-skilled workers and has focused on OECD countries and oil-rich/labour-short Middle Eastern countries although there are major movements within the developing world. Indeed, of the 215 million people that lived outside their country of birth in 2010, more were in other developing countries than in high-income countries. Some of the migration is temporary, for example in the construction industry, while many may be making permanent moves in search of better opportunities. For administrators and policy-makers this 'brain drain' comprises a loss of highly trained human capital but it may be offset by remittances of foreign exchange and by easing pressure on domestic labour markets. Migrant workers' remittances have grown considerably to become one of the major global financial flows to developing countries: from $55.2 billion in 1995 to $77.1 billion in 2000 to $410 billion in 2013, a figure three times that of ODA (Official Development Assistance) from the OECD countries (World Bank, 2013b). And future projections show remittances continuing to grow by 9 per cent per year to reach US$540 billion by 2016. Countries can become dependent on remittances and while economists point to their positive role in reducing the level and severity of poverty other social observers worry about adverse social effects of temporary labour migration on families. For example, Tajikistan was recorded as having half of its working males abroad. Their remittances of US$4.1 billion made up almost half of the nation's GDP (World Bank, 2013a). There are also South–South flows. In upper middle income Malaysia foreign labour rose from 380,000 persons in 1990 to between 2 and 4 million workers in 2010, 9.5 per cent of the country's workforce. The migrants mainly come from poorer countries of the region, especially Indonesia and the Philippines, and undertake low-wage jobs.

Health

One of the success stories of the development process has been improvement in health. However, there is still enormous scope for further improvement as the health status of populations in many developing countries lags far behind than in the OECD countries. Life expectancy at birth in middle income countries has increased dramatically from 46 years in 1960 to 69 years in 2010 and more modestly in low income countries from 43 years to 57 years over the same period (UN, 2013). Mortality rates for children have been drastically reduced, immunization has been made available to most infants, deaths from malaria have declined by 20 per cent between 2000–2009 while safe water has been made increasingly available. Maternal deaths in developing countries have been halved over the past two decades, down from 543,000 in 1990 to 284,000 in 2010.

Despite these overall improvements some countries with low human development still have major health problems. For example, the mortality rate for children under five years was 129 per 1,000 live births compared to 44 in countries with medium human development. The maternal mortality rate in Sub-Saharan Africa was still 500 per 100,000 live births as compared to 150 in Southeast Asia and 80 in Latin America (UN, 2013). There were still 1.1 billion people in 2010 who did not have access to improved water supply and 2.4 billion who did not enjoy improved sanitation facilities, situations contributing to the 2 million deaths per year from diarrhoeal diseases, the majority of which affected children under five years of age (WHO, 2012). Ninety per cent (285 million) of the world's visually impaired and blind people live in developing countries. Eighty per cent of this visual impairment and blindness could be prevented by the right diet, immunization against measles and other diseases, and low-cost surgery. In Ethiopia and Niger in 2009, there were approximately 50,000 persons for each doctor, compared to 57.5 in the Philippines and 60.5 in Algeria, and about 150 or more in many OECD countries (WHO, 2012).

Development itself can change lifestyles leading to new health problems. The spread of diabetes in certain South Pacific island nations following the Westernization of dietary habits is a case in point. Traditional root crops and seafood have often given way to cheap imported foods such as fat-laden lamb flaps and turkey tails which, when accompanied by more sedentary lifestyles, have led to diabetes rates of 44 per cent in tiny Tokelau, 28 per cent in Kiribati and 14 per cent in the Solomon Islands as compared to 3.6 per cent for Australia (Harris-Cheng, 2010). In China, there are three times more persons with diabetes (92.4 million) than there are with HIV in the world. However, AIDS is still a major epidemic with 34 million persons living with the disease in 2010. New cases were down in number to 2.7 million in 2010 as compared to 3.1 million in 2001 with HIV-related deaths reducing from 2 million to 1.8 million over the same period (WHO, 2011). The re-emergence of the deadly Ebola virus in 2014 in West Africa is a grim reminder that the health situation is ever-changing and provides yet another series of considerations and contextual conditions within which and with which administrators and policy-makers must work.

Political factors

A message that we will keep reiterating is that development management is an intensely political affair. Thus, special importance attaches to the cluster of political factors that we discuss in this section. But, it is not an exhaustive list, and there will be considerably more reference to power and politics in the rest of the book. It is also important to note that all of the other factors discussed under different headings have political aspects to them. Political scientists used to search for explanatory models which could encompass the entire developing world. Their demise was an acknowledgement of diversity and 'that peculiar open-endedness of history that is the despair of the paradigm-obsessed social scientist' (Hirschman, 1971: 356). There was no ideal-type Third World state and no ubiquitous Third World political processes. But equally we should not advocate anarchic exceptionalism where dissimilarity makes conceptualization and the comparative method redundant. It is still possible to identify regularity in diversity. For example, states in Sub-Saharan Africa may share some (never all) experiences and features. The histories of East Asian states may also reveal commonalities. Even then, certain historical patterns such as the nature of leadership or the origins of institutions can transcend such classifications. The items discussed in this section reveal these paradoxical themes of similarity and diversity.

Social class

One of the most fundamental divisions in society is that of social class. Although there are competing definitions, classes are 'large-scale groups of people who share common economic resources which strongly influence the types of life-style they are able to lead' (Giddens, 1989: 209). The class structures of developing nations have evolved in different circumstances than those in high-income countries and display far greater diversity and complexity than found in the First World.

Developing countries have large rural populations and a variety of class arrangements which not only distinguish Third World from First World but also differ between countries of the Third World and even within countries. The 'peasant' is ubiquitous in the literature and is found in different relationships with landlords, other peasants and landless labourers. There are often upper, middle and lower peasantries in addition to the landless who have only their labour to sell. Some peasants own their land, others enter a variety of rental agreements with landlords – a direct payment, a share of the crop, a set proportion of the production expenditures. In Latin America there are large landowners known as latifundistas who control vast armies of landless labourers either on 'traditional' farms or modern agribusiness estates. Especially in middle-income economies, rural class structures are often more complex as rural inhabitants may have access to urban employment and to rural non-farm employment in marketing, transport, repair and other services.

The level of development may also affect the size and nature of the middle class. In the rapidly expanding Asian economies there has been substantial growth and rising affluence among the middle class. In many of the poor countries it is the meagre development of anything resembling a middle class which is most noticeable. At the upper ends of the class system other complexities may arise as different fractions of a dominant class compete for policy supremacy: landed interests, industrial exporters, manufacturers for the domestic market and technocrats of the state machinery.

The critical political issue relating to social class is whether people belonging to social classes or fractions of them move beyond a simple awareness of their similar class position to taking action based on their class interests. This class consciousness is expressed in class conflict where particular classes or class fractions pursue political strategies to promote their own interests. Revolution is the most extreme expression of class action, and while it was regularly pursued by armed insurgency in earlier decades, its appeal has waned considerably although in a few countries including the Philippines and Columbia there are well-established Marxist insurgencies. Institutions are sometimes interpreted as being established to articulate class interests in the political arena – labour unions for the urban working class and peasant farmers, business organizations for the bourgeoisie and consumer groups for the middle class. Political parties may have a class character and adopt policies which benefit their membership and class supporters. Leaders can mobilize support from particular classes and use it in opposition to other groups, institutions or classes. Finally, classes may engage in strategic alliances with other classes in the furtherance of mutual interests.

Legitimacy

Concern over regime legitimacy is something which affects developing countries far more than OECD nations. Even military juntas and self-appointed presidents-for-life all share an interest in seeking legitimacy by justifying their holding political power on legal and moral grounds and with the consent of the citizens. They have, nonetheless, been fighting against the tide as since the 1980s, democratization has been the dominant global trend, one which has greatly affected developing nations. But democratic features do not ensure legitimacy, the matter becoming more complex in many developing countries which exhibit elements of both democracy and authoritarianism (Diamond, 2002).

In Sub-Saharan Africa following independence in the 1950s and 1960s, for example, 'regime uncertainty' became the norm, making the search for 'workable political arrangements' a leading issue (Chazan, 1989: 325). Multi-party democracies had short lifespans and were replaced by one-party states, tyrants, military rulers and other authoritarian variants. But they too were often overthrown as their legitimacy was tenuous. In the late 1980s, in line with international trends, many African countries, such as Zambia and Nigeria, began to plan the reintroduction of democratic rule. Other authoritarian regimes followed. Legitimacy was a leading issue and the arrangements for a transition were central policy concerns. This concern has remained until the present with ethnic unrest, civil war, terrorism and other conflicts still being fought to establish the legitimacy of those who would rule.

President Marcos of the Philippines, now somewhat of a distant historical figure, nevertheless provides an excellent demonstration of how, even under authoritarian rule, there can be close attention bordering on preoccupation with claiming legitimacy for a particular type of regime and its incumbents (Turner, 1990). He employed a variety of techniques: establishing the legality and constitutionality of martial law, using performance in socioeconomic development, manipulating history and culture, and securing international support. And all this was done to establish the obedience-worthiness of the institutional order which he had imposed. Hugo Chavez, former President of Venezuela is a more recent example of a national leader seeking to legitimate his radical changes to political institutions and the policies they produced. He reached back in time more than 150 years to utilize the writings and inspiration of Simón Bolívar, the hero of Latin American independence struggles, to justify the new twenty-first century order (McCarthy-Jones and Turner, 2015).

Policy concerns and capacity

The history of the modern Western state has been one of bureaucratization and of the encroachment of the state via the policy process into almost all aspects of everyday life. Rules, regulations, policies and officials determine much of what is done and the manner in which it is done. Even given the recent market orientations of some Western governments the policy coverage of the state is enormous as are the resources gathered by the state for this purpose. Quite obviously, the Third World state cannot hope to have the same scale of policy coverage especially in the area of social welfare. It simply does not have the same resources at its disposal. This is immediately apparent from our discussion of socioeconomic and demographic indicators in this chapter. One should take care, however, to avoid simply reading off policy coverage from indicators such as GNI per capita. Other contingencies such as regime type, political ideology and budgetary tradition can profoundly influence which policies are given priority. For example, low-income Sri Lanka has operated a form of welfare state for more than half a century.

Nevertheless, it is evident that developing countries have less reliable knowledge and technical analytical capacity than are available in OECD countries. In the latter, the state institutions collect and analyse enormous quantities of information on the grounds that policy decisions can only be made with expert knowledge and specialized information, what is often referred to as 'evidence-based policy'. Even the realization that political processes rather than rationality determine decisions has not diminished the passion for data gathering and processing. While greater knowledge and analytical capacity do not guarantee more successful policy decisions and outcomes they have the potential to be of considerable assistance.

Developing country policy-makers and implementers are frequently hamstrung by a lack of knowledge. Their actions are more likely to be guided by guesswork or political preference rather than systematic analysis. Their environments are necessarily and undeniably 'enacted'. The cost of generating information is high; the logistical difficulties are numerous while the immediate political returns are minimal. Furthermore, governments and bureaucrats have frequently had a Western or technocratic orientation and have ignored the contributions that indigenous knowledge can make to the policy process. What farmers know, for instance, has often been treated as inferior knowledge when in reality it can be of great use and can be gathered by cheap innovative methods (Chambers, 1993).

A further difference both between the OECD and Third World and within the Third World is not in the scale but in the nature of policy coverage. There are issues, areas and activities which are of concern to the state in developing countries but which are of little concern in the West. Matters of morality and religious freedom can be 'zones of immunity' into which Western policy-makers rarely wander but which may be of great importance to their developing country counterparts (Ellis and Ter Haar, 2004). Many contrasting policy concerns are simply a product of environmental differences. For example, land reform can be an area of vigorous policy conflict in developing countries but not on the agenda in the West. Reducing population growth has been of major importance especially in large-population countries such as China and Indonesia while in the West the leading issue is how to cope with low rates of natural increase and ageing populations.

Generic labels such as economic policy or agricultural policy apply to all types of countries but conceal major differences and orientations. While the European Union policy personnel may focus on the level of agricultural price subsidy and wonder what to do about butter mountains and milk lakes, in the Third World some policy personnel are analysing how to increase food production and how to reach the poor tenant farmer with low-cost technologies. Others, however, are dealing with multinational agribusinesses and their purchase or lease of vast tracts of land in poor countries. According to Oxfam, up to 227 million hectares, an area equivalent to Germany, have been affected since 2001 with adverse consequences for the world's poorest people (BBC, 2011).

The weak state

The existence of weak states is a critical item for understanding the policy process in much of the developing world, and not surprisingly the topic which has generated the most debate.

In the early days of development planning it was often assumed that states had a far greater degree of control over the environments which they wished to change than was actually the case. The falseness of this assumption was soon realized and academics began exploring the ways in which state–society relations in the developing world were different from the West. Myrdal (1968: 66) identified 'soft states' where 'policies decided on are often not enforced, if they are enacted at all'. Huntington (1968: 1) argued that 'the most important political distinction among countries concerns not their form of government but their degree of government'. The developing countries, said Huntington, often have a shortage of political community and of effective, authoritative, legitimate government – 'in many cases, governments simply do not govern' (Huntington, 1968: 2). Migdal (1988) then wrote about 'weak states and strong societies' where there is an ongoing struggle between the state and societal actors over who has the right and ability to make the rules that guide people's social behaviour; and just because state legislation exists it does not necessarily mean that it is enforced. Migdal (1988) pointed to the power of 'traditional' institutions and practices and to various forms of 'strongmen' organizations which both thwart and penetrate the state. This theme has been carried over into contemporary literature dealing with the prevalence of patronage institutions in government and in their links to society in many developing countries (Khan, 2005; Blunt et al., 2012).

Expressions of the weak state are many and widespread. They can be seen in the inability of the state to collect taxes and in the ability of the society to avoid them. The administration of official statutes can be altered by corruption, by the force of custom or by the demonstrated capacity for violence of local strongmen. Land reform legislation may be passed but minimally implemented. Tenancy arrangements may lay down a particular division of the crop between landlord and tenant but local practice may enforce another arrangement. The state may establish upper limits for interest rates but usurious rates may prevail. Representatives of the state may recast their official roles in rural locations to better fit with the expectations and practices of the local populations. Official mechanisms of accountability may be weak so that the occupants of state office can simply use those offices for personal gain or for the benefit of groups based on kinship and ethnicity.

At the extreme, the weak state can simply disintegrate as in Somalia or Mali. Such 'failed' or 'fictitious' states only claim to existence may be international recognition of something which is not actually there.

But the weak state is not ubiquitous. China, Malaysia, Ethiopia and many other developing countries are inadequately described or totally misrepresented by the uncritical application of the weak state model. Back in the 1950s, Zinkin (1953: 214) wrote that 'There is in Asia less mental resistance to State intervention than in the West, for Asia has a long history of effective and helpful State action'. Recent experience confirms this. The enormous economic success of East Asian countries has not been simply the triumph of the market but also has had much to do with strong state institutions. For example, South Korea's economy grew at an average annual rate of 8.3 per cent between 1962 and 1985, in large part because of government intervention:

> Presidential political leadership and a significant proportion of the bureaucratic elites have given their top priority to economic development.... there has been a host of price controls, distribution controls, and other government interventions through direct and indirect taxes, tariffs, quotas, export subsidies and the protection of import-substituting industries ... Through government intervention the Korean economy was directed more to export promotion than to a neoclassically efficient allocation mechanism. (Kim, 1991: 136)

Care should be taken not to assume that authoritarian regimes and strong states go hand in hand. Authoritarian rule has undoubtedly been associated with economic success stories but it has also been party to economic and social disasters. Military juntas have frequently returned to barracks because they failed to live up to their claims for legitimacy based on performance (for example, more jobs, less corruption, better social services). Dictators have often been primarily concerned with staying in power. Policy can then all too easily focus on survival rather than on the broader needs of the nation. In some cases this can mean that there is minimal state penetration of the routines of everyday life apart from the threat of state violence to maintain consent (but not necessarily legitimacy). In short, authoritarian regimes are often associated with weak states.

But we should not force an all or nothing categorization of weak or strong on Third World states. We should be aware that elements of the weak and the strong can be simultaneously present.

Neo-patrimonialism

According to Weber's ideal type, the modern state is based on principles of rational-legal authority. This involves legally defined structures of authority and power oriented towards the achievement of widely accepted goals. The public officials follow rules, regulations and laws in an impersonal manner and maintain strict distinction between their public and private lives. While this theory may live on in ideological form as a legitimating device we know that the ideal type does not exist anywhere in its pure form.

Greater insight into the nature of the Third World state is provided by invoking the notion of neo-patrimonialism. According to Weber, and historical experience, the traditional ruler frequently lacked the coercive capacity to impose his rule. His power depended on his ability 'to win and retain the loyalty of key sections of the political elite' (Crouch, 1979: 572). Assuming that the masses could be kept in a state of apathy and acquiescence then the successful patrimonial ruler could focus on keeping his potentially troublesome elite loyal through awarding them fiefs and benefices. The contemporary environments enacted by developing country rulers differ from those of their traditional patrimonial forebears. Most importantly, the trappings of rational-legal authority are very apparent in such institutions as formal constitutions, legislative bodies and huge state bureaucracies. However, patrimonialism seems not only to have survived in the Third World but has prospered in the context of development (Khan, 2005; Blunt et al., 2012). The impersonal universalistic systems and rules of the rational-legal have been employed for private, particularistic purposes. The modern ruler whether at national or subnational level fulfils the patrimonial role by rewarding followers and kinsmen by giving them jobs, contracts or licences which should go to those satisfying the rational-legal requirements.

The neo-patrimonial ruler depends on the state being pervasive in the formal economy. Thus, the ruler can protect followers from competition by enacting tariffs and quotas, and by access to subsidized credit, grants and foreign loans. The rent-seeking state is the home of the neo-patrimonial ruler. This is where one finds the dual political systems – of the verandah and of the air-conditioner (Terray, 1986). The latter can be viewed in the form of 'State ... President, Ministers, Parliament, Administration, Party, Constitution, Laws, Rules and airport with VIP lounge, company of paratroopers ... motorcycle outriders with siren' (Terray, 1986 as quoted in O'Brien, 1991: 151). Bureaucracies headed by highly trained technocrats should be added. These are the symbols of the rational-legal which give legitimacy or the appearance of substance to the regime and state, especially for outsiders bearing gifts in the form of loans and grants.

Meanwhile on the verandah the real business of government is conducted according to the informal practices of patron–client ties. It is here that significant decisions are made and loyalties secured. If the patrimonial ruler cannot maintain control over scarce resources then loyalties falter and replacement becomes possible. Political arts are employed to avoid the admonitions of the World Bank and IMF to 'get the prices right' and promote 'good govern-ance'. The patrimonial ruler's success in many instances reflects the ability to communicate the image of the air-conditioner while prac-tising the politics of the verandah. Survival also depends on main-taining mass acquiescence. Signs of disquiet among the masses are frequently met with repression especially if economic development is not happening.

This approach goes a long way to identify apparent irrationality in policy-making. We can understand why certain policy choices are made and why seemingly inefficient government expenditures are sanctioned. It certainly assists in explaining policy failure or the maintenance of the status quo but it often overlooks the ques-tion of how change occurs. How do you explain successes in pat-rimonial contexts? How can reformist policies be introduced? If politics is always seen as negative and elites are always exclusively self-interested then the answers to such questions are difficult. Policy simply cannot be explained in exclusively neo-patrimonial terms. Grindle (1991: 66) suggests an alternative political economy model in which we should not examine the pursuit of self-interest as if it existed in a void but look at the bargains, pacts and compromises of politics in terms of 'problem-solving through negotiation and the use of political resources in the context of great uncertainty'. She acknowledges that the results of these processes can be good, bad or indifferent for the economy, society or for sectors of the society. However, that such a range of possibilities exists means that there is 'space' in which policy elites even under conditions of neo-patrimonialism can manoeuvre to achieve policy choices that are both economically and politically wise (Grindle, 2012).

Democratization

The antidote to neo-patrimonialism and the weak state is supposedly democracy. In the 1960s, Western governments feared that developing countries would tumble like a row of dominoes as they embraced communist rule. Apart from a few Asian countries and Cuba the dominoes failed to fall to communism. Instead, more than a decade later, the dominoes were authoritarian regimes. In the mid-1970s, 68 per cent of the world's states were under authoritarian regimes (Potter, 1997). By the mid-1990s the figure had reduced to only 26 per cent. The Third World had been swept up in the 'third wave' of democratization (Huntington, 1991). The first wave began at the end of the nineteenth century and continued into the early twentieth century while the second wave was associated with developing countries achieving independence. Their hastily constructed post-colonial democracies often collapsed as authoritarian rulers took over and were only re-established in the third wave.

While the majority of developing countries are formally classified as having democratic political regimes, there is wide diversity in institutions and practices. Many regimes are hybrids comprised of elements of both democracy and authoritarianism (Diamond, 2002). Thus, Cambodia has been classified as a hegemonic electoral authoritarian regime where various political and civil rights are absent or poorly enforced and where only one party ever wins national elections. The Philippines is often viewed as an elite democracy in which regular elections are held, a vibrant civil society operates and there is press freedom but where elite families dominate the political offices and process and often for their personal benefit. Neo-patrimonialism can thrive under supposedly democratic rule. In democratic Indonesia many academics have noted the ability of patronage institutions to adapt to the new formal political arrangements with leading government officials at national and subnational levels using their public offices to further personal agendas (Hadiz and Robison, 2005). A country can even be ranked as an exemplar of political democracy but demonstrate many of the traits of bad governance. Papua New Guinea has never been under authoritarian rule since independence in 1975 and has always held democratic elections at the constitutionally defined time but it suffers from a host of governance problems including corruption, electoral violence and candidates who can sometimes win seats with under 5 per cent of the votes cast.

In an attempt to distinguish the 'real' democracies some authors have established check lists of essential characteristics. These include such things as regime legitimacy, the acceptance of democratic practices, the existence of a substantial middle class, the absence or successful alleviation of extreme poverty, and the passage of time which supposedly helps to embed democratic institutions (Polidano, 2002). But some analysts have warned that new democracies may 'drift' as 'frozen' or 'delegative' where power remains with government rather than with the people (Shin, 1994). Furthermore, there is no agreement on which democratization factors are most important, which other factors they need to interact with and how long particular processes take. The relationship between democracy and development is also a murky area, not least because so many causal interconnections are possible. Leftwich (2000) has suggested that democratic governance may not be the most appropriate political arrangement for economic development. It is even debatable whether good governance equates absolutely with democracy. For example, Vietnam has made remarkable progress on a number of measures of good governance but is not a liberal democracy.

The natural environment

Some of the most hotly contested issues in development today concern the natural environment, and what we inhabitants of the earth have done to it. At the beginning of the 1970s, the first major warning shots were fired to raise the alert that the planet was in peril from environmental problems of 'such severity as to require the attention of all nations of the world' (Dasmann, 1972: 14). A report commissioned by the Club of Rome think-tank posed the possibility of future scenarios where the current patterns of production and consumption could be unsustainable (Meadows et al., 1972) while Schumacher (1973) coined the catchy and oft-repeated phrase that 'small is beautiful' when critiquing the economics of development and pointing to its leading role in environmental destruction. Thus, by the mid-1970s the environment was firmly established as a significant consideration for policy-makers, public sector managers and officials of international donor organizations. Subsequent reports and conventions have increased the perceived importance of the environment in any decisions relating to development.

Sustainability

The key term in the global and national debates on the environment is 'sustainability' and the UN's global goals for 2015–2030 are almost certain to be identified as Sustainable Development Goals (see http://sustainabledevelopment.un.org/). All parties appear to feel the need to assure citizens of their commitment to sustainable development but differ in their interpretations of what it means. Many still adhere to the general definition that appeared in the 1987 Brundtland Report which saw sustainable development as 'development that meets the needs of the present without compromising the ability of future generations to meet their own needs' (WCED, 1987: 43). However, the broadness of the definition provides little advice on practical policies while critics see it as giving legitimacy to models of development that focus on economic growth. To provide some clarity in the contestation over the meaning of sustainable development, Hopper (2012) has divided the protagonists into two types – those advocating the weak version and those pushing for the strong manifestation. The weak type follows from the Brundtland Report and places faith in 'technology, economic growth and effective management of resources' (Hopper, 2012: 220). The strong type questions reliance on markets for environmental solutions and argues that 'sustainable development is promoted at grassroots level with local contexts, knowledges and participation all prioritized' (Hopper, 2012: 221). It opposes the principles and application of neoliberal economics in which everything has a price and instead calls for a new order involving a radical change in human behaviour that entails humans living in harmony with the natural environment rather than seeking mastery over it.

Environmental degradation

There is widespread agreement that in order to progress towards environmental sustainability it is necessary to halt and reverse the disturbing trends of environmental degradation. Deforestation commenced in colonial times in developing countries but accelerated in the post-independence era with considerable growth in the demand for wood products or the conversion of forests to agricultural land in contexts where environmental legislation was either lacking or weakly enforced. In the last 50 years about half of the world's natural forest cover has been removed with dire consequences for erosion, watershed management biodiversity and carbon capture. Today, the level of deforestation is still 'alarmingly high' but has at least slowed down from 16 million hectares in the 1990s to 13 million hectares in the 2000s (FAO, 2010; 2012). New tree plantings have lessened the overall loss to 5.2 million hectares per year in 2000–2010 from 8.3 million hectares per year in 1990–2000. However, most new plantings are in temperate and boreal zones while most of the deforestation occurs in the developing countries of the tropics. South America and Africa are the continents which are most affected by this forest destruction.

Despite the dramatic increase in protected ecosystems (150,000 sites in 2010) biodiversity is still in decline. Species of birds, mammals and amphibians are reducing in numbers with more coming under threat each year. Other organisms such as coral reefs and cycads are also under great stress in many parts of the world. Overfishing, pollution and loss of habitat have contributed to declining fish stocks. Our fish consumption is at unsustainable levels – 145 million tonnes as against the sustainable figure of 80–100 million tonnes Thus, the proportion of fish stocks that are underexploited or moderately exploited has plummeted from 40 per cent in the mid-1970s to 15 per cent in 2008 (FAO, 2011). Poor fishermen in developing countries face particular hardship as their numbers increase and their catches decline leading them into more destructive methods such as dynamite fishing which not only kills the fish but also ruins the reefs and ecosystems. Such environmental degradation poses policy and management problems for developing countries that are trying to improve the welfare of their populations. The degradation may be seen as a necessary condition of economic growth and poverty alleviation but can pose sustainability problems while in some instances unscrupulous officials seize opportunities in environmental exploitation as ways to amass personal wealth at the expense of current and future citizens and nature itself. Another severe environmental problem in Third World cities is air pollution. Details are presented in Box 2.1.

Climate change

Of particular concern in recent years has been climate change. While there are some sceptics the overwhelming weight of scientific opinion is that the planet's climate is changing. This state of affairs has now been confirmed by the Fifth Report of the authoritative Intergovernmental Panel on Climate Change (see www.ipcc.ch/report/ar5/wg2). Basically, temperature is rising, human activity is mainly responsible and there are adverse consequences. Furthermore, the latter will be felt more in developing countries of the tropics than in the rich countries of the temperate zones. The main problem

---

Box 2.1   Air pollution in developing countries

Success in economic development can bring about new problems for policy-makers to tackle. One of these is air pollution, now identified by the United Nations Environment Program as the 'world's worst environmental health risk'. It has especially affected the burgeoning cities of developing countries and we have seen graphic evidence of it in television news reports of Beijing swathed in smog for days on end or the thick smoke from agricultural fires in Indonesia crossing the Straits of Malacca and South China Sea to envelop the Malaysian Peninsula. More cars, increased demand for electricity, rising industrial output, land clearing, and greater usage of fossil and biomass fuels for heating and cooking are the principal causes of dramatic rises in air pollution. The costs are high. In China between 2005 and 2010, the death rate from outdoor air pollutants rose by 5 per cent, in India by 11 per cent. The cost of air pollution to China is estimated at US$1.4 trillion, for India US$0.5 trillion. The anticipated growth of Africa's cities is expected to result in massive increases in air pollution so that the continent may be responsible for 50 per cent of global emissions from fossil fuels and biomass by 2030. There are solutions and some are being implemented: phasing out leaded petrol, increasing vehicle engine efficiency, reducing reliance on coal power, making more efficient cooking stoves, using clean energy and enforcing air quality standards. But further economic development could increase the numbers of vehicles on the roads of developing countries and they account for 50 per cent of the health impacts of air pollution – the benefits of more efficient motor vehicles outweighed by the increase in the numbers of them.

---

is development itself or at least the longstanding model that has involved more people consuming ever more goods and services. This has led to massive increases in carbon emissions that in turn have raised global temperatures.

The effects of climate change are felt in three principal areas: rainfall, sea level and 'natural' disasters. It appears that in tropical areas small temperature rises can 'severely disrupt' natural conditions creating problems for water availability and crop productivity (UNDP, 2011). Sea level is rising and if present rates of increase are maintained then the sea level will be 31 cms higher in 2100 than in 1990. This means that large populations in low-lying coastal zones, especially in East Asia, will be inundated and that small island countries such as Kiribati, Tuvalu and the Maldives will sink below the waves. Finally, natural disasters such as tropical cyclones and droughts are on the increase more almost tripling from 132 a year in 1980–1985 to 357 in 2005–2009 (UNDP, 2011). While this increase has been linked to global warming the complex causal relationships are yet to be properly understood. However, what is understood is that climate change can have a potentially devastating effect on the planet and all its species and that development must be oriented both to reducing carbon emissions and to addressing their adverse impacts. However, selling such a message to populations in developing countries is a difficult task especially in a situation where two-thirds of the world's population, mostly in developing countries, are unaware of climate change and its causes. If one is poor, and millions are, the challenges of earning enough to get by are what preoccupies the mind and body not debates about carbon emissions and whether environmental protocols have been ratified.

The public sector and its environment

Having placed various environmental components under the microscope and examined them in isolation it is time to consider them together in order to make some general observations about public organizations and their environments in developing countries.

Distinctiveness

We have presented ample evidence to demonstrate that the environments encountered by public sector managers and policy-makers in the developing world can be distinguished from those facing their OECD counterparts. While there is by no means one typical developing country environment there are clusters of interrelated environmental factors and forces which give some distinctiveness to development management. It is this contextual distinctiveness of management and policy which is one of the most important defining features of development management, what makes it a specific field of enquiry and practice.

Frequently, the differences are a matter of degree. For example, poverty affects OECD nations as well as the developing world although the criteria for distinguishing the poor and the incidence of poverty vary. Particular values found in developing nations may also be present to a greater or lesser extent in rich countries. But the causal texture, that interrelationship between the components of the environment and between them and the public organizations, invariably gives distinctiveness to the developing world.

Diversity

It seems somewhat paradoxical that having made the case for distinctiveness we now argue for diversity in developing country environments. However, within the group of countries collectively identified as the South, the developing world or the Third World there is considerable differentiation which perhaps questions the appropriateness of such labels. What constitutes the environment for public sector managers and policy-makers in Bangladesh varies, perhaps considerably, from that facing similar persons in Botswana, Barbados and Brazil. Whether one uses GNI per capita, female participation in education, level of foreign debt or any other indicator of development the findings are always the same: there is considerable variation between developing countries. There are groups of nations which are quite alike. For example, many small states face similar economic and administrative problems which may be amenable to similar, but never identical, solutions. Many Latin American countries face some of the same environmental issues. Common problems are found among many Sub-Saharan African nations. However, there are also contrasting historical experiences and developmental trajectories and these have become more marked over time and have created increasing differentiation between developing countries.

Turbulence

Focus on the statistics of development can easily lead to static images of the environment. Nothing would be further from the truth. The environments of policy-makers and managers in developing countries are characteristically uncertain and have become increasingly turbulent. For example, there may be new technology, regime change, rapid urban population growth, the rise of pressure groups, global financial crises, new demands from the World Trade Organization (WTO) and severe resource constraints. There may even be a war. Such environmental turbulence is not new. Back in the 1980s, Sagasti (1988: 43) observed that in developing countries 'the very ground on which the actors stand is shifting'. This was supported by Munene (1991: 455) who found that in Africa 'extreme environmental uncertainty is a defining characteristic and ... predictability is almost nil'. This environmental turbulence has remained a constant but this does not make success unattainable. It means that managers and policy-makers need certain management techniques, political skills, organizational structures, implementation capacities, external support and moral commitment to deal with such flux if developmental interventions are to be successful.

Opportunities and constraints

A basic aim of development management is to change the environment. Practitioners are trying to bring about improvements in people's lives and as such are attempting to alter environmental conditions; for example, make clean water more available, increase rural income-earning possibilities, provide more educational opportunities. But, the environment can be seen as presenting both opportunities and constraints in the pursuit of such goals. Certain conditions, such as population pressure and climate change, limit policy options while others, such as labour surplus, suggest avenues of action which could utilize such surplus. Some environments are more restrictive than others and much literature seems to dwell on these constraints rather than on the opportunities. Encouraging creativity which would both identify and make use of the latter while not losing sight of the constraints would seem to be a leading requirement of contemporary development management.

Competing perceptions

We have already noted the diversity and interrelatedness of components in developing country environments. Now we can add a further complexity: different people perceive the environment in different ways. Peasant farmers, top bureaucrats, rural teachers, NGO workers and politicians will have different ideas on what is important in the environment, what happens in the environment and what actions should be taken to alter the environment. Academic rivalries may make the water even muddier. Within the public sector there may be considerable divergence in environmental interpretation, in forecasting what will happen if certain actions are taken and on what are the existing conditions. Environmental perception is not some universal science with a single inviolate set of rules and tools – despite the apparent finality of World Bank statistics and HDI rankings. We bring values and interests into our understanding of the environment. We look at the environment and make judgements. We may express different rationalities. But what this means is that interpreting the environment and taking actions to improve it (the tasks of the policy-maker and manager) have strong political components.

Politics determine what issues are put on the agenda, what actions are planned and how they will be implemented.

Cause and effect

Public organizations are affected by their environments. Much literature in organization theory has been devoted either to the ways in which organizational structure and behaviour are determined by the environment or to how organizations must adapt such features to achieve 'fit' with their environments. Making such conscious adaptations will allegedly make organizations more efficient and effective. But we should be equally aware that public organizations exist interdependently with their environments and that these organizations adopt various strategies to alter their environments. More recently there has been focus on the complexity of environments and the interrelationship between environments and public organizations, where, where boundaries between organizations and environments are at best vague and where organizing rather than organizations should be our principal concern.

Foreign models and Third World realities

Following from all these general points about the environment is the observation that we should be extremely cautious in applying models of management structure and action imported from the West. We should not automatically reject Western ideas as inappropriate. There may be lessons to be learned and advantages to be gained. But we must also accept that many ideas from OECD managerial experience may be unworkable and undesirable in developing country contexts. The institutional, demographic, economic or social environments are different and often require alternative responses. Political behaviour and structures are also different despite superficial similarities. Even imported developing country ideas and models must be modified for use elsewhere to cope with the diversity of environments encountered in the Third World.

Chapter 3

Law and Order: Insecurity, Crime, Conflict and Violence

For classical political theorists the most important role of the state is to provide its citizens with security and ensure law and order. It is surprising therefore that, until recently, development theory and practice have tended to treat law and order (and insecurity and conflict) as a side issue, or assume that the existence of a state means that law and order are somehow automatically in place ... or soon will be. Indeed, the neoliberal paradigm that dominated late twentieth century thinking assumed that minimizing the state was a prescription for economic progress – this is no longer credible. As Francis Fukuyama (2005: 162) argues, in the post 9/11 world '... the withering away of the state is not a prelude to utopia but to disaster ... They [developing countries] do not need extensive states, but they do need strong and effective ones'. In their global analysis of state formation Acemoglu and Robinson (2012: 308) see the Glorious Revolution of 1688 in England as unleashing social forces that helped to gradually promote law and order around the world: '...[o]nce in place, the notion of the rule of law not only kept absolutism at bay but also created a type of virtuous circle'. Increasingly, laws applied to everybody, ruler and ruled, ensuring that all were constrained to act within these laws and if it were perceived that someone had not, then they would be guaranteed a fair trial in return. In turn, according to Acemoglu and Robinson (2012), this shift to inclusive institutional forms fostered increased rates of economic growth and accelerated social progress.

By contrast, insecurity, conflict and violence not only have a huge impact on individual human lives, but have detrimental consequences for entire societies and for their economic prospects. The *World Development Report 2011* stated that no fragile or conflict-affected country had been able to achieve a single MDG by that year (World Bank, 2011). For development, insecurity and disorder present a serious challenge: '[d]evelopment is ultimately impossible without stability and, at the same time, security is not sustainable without development' (Duffield, 2001: 16). While a perusal of the media would suggest that in today's world we are engulfed by violent conflict and things are getting much worse, Stephen Pinker's (2012) thoughtful analysis of the history of violence reveals that contemporary levels of violence are much lower than in earlier periods.

There are two main theoretical frameworks for analysing issues of law and order (and disorder): liberal democratic and political economy. The liberal democratic approach takes the implicit assumption that law and order is always there and is not something that needs to be established prior to development intervention. If there is disorder, it can be attributed to the state encroaching too much on civil society and civil society not organizing itself enough (Bilgin and Morton, 2002). This liberal model does not account for contexts where the pre-requisites of political and economic institutions do not exist (Brett, 2008). In effect, it assumes that democracy plus capitalism will in themselves create law and order.

By contrast, the political economy perspectives adopt a historical lens and see the establishment of law and order in societies as complex and case specific. As the history of Western countries reveals, development is a process fraught with violence and conflict, and it has taken centuries of violence and disagreement for law and order to become established (Bates, 2001). The pages which follow look at how these two analytical perspectives have situated themselves with regards to law and order. First, we consider how law is created and defined within different societies and examine key components which may prove to be obstacles for individuals in societies to achieve justice. Second, the chapter looks in detail at the concept of the fragile state and how it is used within development theory and practice. Finally, theoretical approaches to violent conflict and peace are examined in order to understand how societies emerge from conflict and move towards stability.

The rule of law and development

This section considers how the rule of law is defined and what this means for societies and development actors. It then takes a closer look at: property rights; the judiciary and judicial reform; policing;

and, the shadow economy and its implications for security and development.

The rule of law

The rule of law is viewed as fundamental for establishing internal and external peace and ensuring the freedom of individuals (Peterson, 2010). In development theory it is seen as an essential pre-requisite for economic 'take-off'. For the UN, the rule of law is a 'principle of governance, in which all persons, institutions and entities, public and private, including the State, are accountable to laws that are publicly promulgated, equally enforced and independently adjudicated, and which are consistent with international human rights norms and standards' (UN, 2004: 4).

The World Bank (2012c) identifies three main ways of defining the rule of law, formally substantively and functionally. The formal definition refers to standard criteria which include establishing a judiciary, making and enforcing public laws, and checks on government actions. The substantive definition relates more closely to a moral appreciation of how justice and fairness should be established in a society. Finally, the functional approach focuses on how well law and the legal system function in a society. When functioning well the rule of law secures legitimacy for governance and produces effective state-building, especially for fragile states (Domingo, 2009). Further, it forms an important component of the 'broader effort to reform governance in the interest of growth and poverty alleviation' (Haggard et al., 2008: 206). As a result, it has been strongly associated with the liberal peace project (see later).

Although the meaning of the rule of law is constantly debated, both liberal and radical/Marxian perspectives agree it is a good thing. From a liberal viewpoint the rule of law prevents arbitrary action by the state and protects the rights of individuals (Rose, 2004). From a more radical position, E. P. Thompson (1976: 266) wrote that despite facilitating class domination in some societies, the rule of law was still an 'unqualified human good' which should exist in all complex states. Within the literature on rule of law and development, meanings have ranged from narrow understandings, focusing on property rights, to broader interpretations encompassing legislation to make governments accountable, judiciaries effective, provide security and establish rights-based citizenship (Domingo, 2009).

Property rights

Property rights have been the major focus for theorists and practitioners interested in economic growth and private sector development. In Africa, for example, many works have dealt with the conflicts resulting from the ambiguity of traditional land rights and indigenous institutions (Boone, 2007; Benjaminsen and Lund, 2003; Van Donge and Pherani, 1999). Authoritative figures have argued that the establishment of property rights is essential for economic growth and prosperity (Acemoglu and Johnson, 2005) and for enabling people to be lifted out of poverty in developing countries (De Soto, 2000). Many of these discussions follow the ideas of New Institutional Economics pioneered by Nobel Laureate, Douglass North (2009, 1995). From this perspective, secure property rights (especially those modelled on Western notions of individual property ownership) are seen as essential for encouraging greater domestic and foreign investment in a country. In turn, this has a knock-on effect that is likely to be economically and socially progressive on the evolution of other institutions and on state formation.

Acemoglu and Robinson (2012) compare North and South Korea to demonstrate differences in their economic and political outcomes. They argue that despite having an authoritarian political system after independence, South Koreans now experience longer life expectancy and better living standards compared to their Northern counterparts, due to the private property rights which were established early in the country's state-building process. These were rights denied to North Korean citizens. As a consequence of secure property rights in South Korea, investment and foreign trade followed and political elites were encouraged to invest in the health and education of their citizens. For the North's citizens, poverty and seclusion from a globalizing world was their lot.

Questions have been raised about the difficulty of establishing effective and well-enforced property rights along the lines of the orthodox Western liberal legal model (Jayasuriya, 1996; Evans, 2004). In East Asia, it has been pointed out that the concept of property related to an individual's rights does not sit as comfortably in the institutional norm of *rule through law* (as opposed to *rule of law*). Instead it is the enterprise which is the focus: 'regulations govern institutional entities rather than the individual's property claims' (Jayasuriya, 1996: 374). Further, some have critiqued the idea that property rights can and should precede other legal institutions to provide effective law and order. For property rights to function effectively, a plethora of institutions are required including a 'social contract' between state and society, security and a functioning judicial and legal system (Haggard et al., 2008).

The judiciary

The judiciary is a crucial component for establishing a functioning government. As Dakolias (1995: 167–8) points out, 'promoting private sector development, encouraging development of all other societal institutions, alleviating poverty and consolidating democracy' all require an effective judiciary. Moreover, the rule of law cannot be enforced without a judiciary to resolve conflicts over the law (Dam, 2006). If development agencies seek to establish democratic systems of governance, then an independent judiciary creates 'confidence in the multi-party democratic process and in encouraging people to participate in the democratic process in an unrestrained, and most importantly fearless, way' (Sen, 2006: 45). For example, with democratization in Latin America, ideas of citizenship and civil society have emerged (Chapter 9), which have placed greater pressure on the state to ensure that basic rights are protected through reforms of the judiciary (Domingo, 1999).

There are, however, numerous issues which can affect the reliability, independence and effectiveness of the judiciary (see Box 3.1 for the example of India). First, frequent changes in government can result in constant changes in judicial arrangements and rules; second, and especially when there is insufficient funding, corruption and bribery may develop as a means of supplementing low incomes or from greed; third, the complexity of procedures can cause delays to legal processes, leading to a back-log of cases building up (Domingo, 1999). The approach of bilateral and multilateral development agencies to judicial reform has been described as 'instrumentalist', due to their failure to understand the structures of power which play a fundamental role in determining how judiciaries work (Rodríguez-Garavito, 2011: 157). In Latin America, judicial reform has received a great deal of funding, particularly from the US. However, the projects have usually been centred around a neoliberal agenda which, instead of forging more equal access to the law, permits elites and foreign investors to interpret reforms in ways that benefit themselves. This indicates the importance of having a contextualized understanding of legal institutions in developing countries.

Box 3.1   Criminal justice in India

According to Dabhoiwala (2003), the Indian police force is a 'largely unaccountable body' which lacks any respect for human rights and the rule of law. Between 2001 and 2010, there were 1,504 deaths in police custody and 12,727 deaths in judicial custody, the majority of which were as a direct consequence of torture (ACHR, 2011). In Mumbai, deaths as a consequence of *encounters* have become increasingly common. This term refers to impulsive and unprompted 'shoot-outs' where the alleged criminal is killed by the police (Belur, 2009). In such instances, it is not always made clear whether the deceased was a direct threat to the lives of the public and police officers present. However, it has been seen as a police response to rising levels of crime in the city, ignoring processes of criminal justice. Belur's research points to the complicit role which society has in approving police actions which facilitates an acceptance of such lethal justice.

Despite the recent rise in campaigns for the human rights of the accused to be upheld, there is a significant disparity in the amount of action campaigning for the rights of victims to be considered. In particular, female victims are not provided with support to overcome trauma such as rape (Sarkar, 2010). Furthermore, for all ordinary Indians access to the legal system is beset with problems such as high costs, delays and ineffectual help (Galanter and Krishnan, 2004; Galanter, 2009). In fact, Kumar (2012) estimates there are 30 million cases pending in India's courts, taking on average of 15 years to be resolved. These figures can be attributed to a number of reasons including a severe lack of court officials such as judges compared to the population of the country and the number of crimes. In sum, the criminal justice system in India, and the police force in particular show scant respect for the human rights of both alleged criminals and victims (Gehlot, 2002). Widespread demands for reform are publically acknowledged by political leaders but there is little subsequent action.

Policing and internal security

Policing and internal security in developing countries has only attracted scholarly interest in recent times, and in regions such as Sub-Saharan Africa, with the exception of South Africa, there is little research (Ruteere and Pommerolle, 2003; Baker, 2004). Policing is the component of governance which seeks to ensure order, security of people and property, and peace on an internal scale – through crime prevention and the punishment of law-breakers (Baker, 2004). While it is commonly assumed that policing is a state-run institution this is not necessarily the case. Clegg et al. (2000) point out that there is 'no universal formula of good policing' and identify the various options available. These options are set out for Africa in Box 3.2. Protection at the local level may be provided by a variety of groups, some independent from the state, some community run, some cooperating with the state and others working on behalf of the state. These different strategies have emerged as a consequence of historical and political factors and explain why efforts to implant Western models of policing into developing countries have met with resistance and difficulties, especially due to implicit assumptions about the relative availability of financial, human and technological resources (Baker, 2004; Hills, 2011).

Comparisons of policing approaches and effectiveness are difficult because of how crime and policing are perceived by the citizens of different countries. In some instances, the police are seen as

---

Box 3.2   Types of policing in Africa

Analysts of law and order in Africa identify a variety of approaches to policing, locally and nationally in a country. In some instances, these policing groups may be coordinated by the state and in others, they may be organized locally, with varying degrees of state involvement. The following are some of the different types of internal policing:

Conventional state-run policing – the operation of national or regional police services staffed by public servants and accountable to the legislature

Community-organized security groups – these are formed to provide security on a local basis. Their priorities are crime prevention and punishment. They may work closely with local leaders and, in some cases, local residents may be required to join membership schemes in order to have this protection in their area. Associations may be made with local state police to share duties.

Private informal security groups – in some instances where the state fails to provide adequate security provision, the market takes its place. The state may decide to pay for security groups in areas where it cannot provide adequate policing. In other circumstances, commercial security firms may be employed if businesses or households require higher levels of security.

State-approved civil policing – in cooperation with the state, such groups provide not-for-profit security, working closely with local citizens but still enforcing state legislation and regulations. Police officers in these groups are usually local volunteers who are inducted into the police service.

Source: Adapted from Baker, 2004; Ruteere and Pommerolle, 2003.

'maintaining a certain order and representing the interests of some dominant groups or individuals' in society (Ruteere and Pommerolle, 2003: 592). In Kenya, for example, there is very little data on crime statistics and the constant changing of political interpretations of what constitutes crime results in a great deal of confusion for citizens and police alike. The prevalence of crime in cities such as Nairobi has led to the population losing trust in the effectiveness of the police, to the point where over half of victims do not bother to report crimes to the police (Ruteere and Pommerolle, 2003).

It must also be noted that the police may only have a limited impact on levels of crime. In most societies where law and order prevails this is as much due to social norms and citizen behaviour – obeying the law and reporting lawbreakers to their families and communities – as it is to direct police action.

Shadow economies

Shadow economies and illegal economic activity occur in all countries. However, in developing countries, it has been suggested that they may constitute half or even more of total economic activity (Eilat and Zinnes, 2000). The shadow economy, defined as employment, production and exchange which are not officially reported to government authorities, presents a major challenge for legal institutions (Schneider, 2000; Choi and Thum, 2005). Informal activities, such as household production do not necessarily fall outside of legal parameters, but others such as unrecorded payments for labour activities through to the global trade in drugs, people and arms are clearly illegal (Fleming et al., 2000). In Nigeria, for example, it is estimated that the shadow economy constitutes 50 to 65 per cent of total economic output (Schneider, 2008).

Varying factors affect the extent to which a criminal or illegal shadow economy can persist: elite corruption, weak law enforcement and integration into criminalized global value chains. The extent to which a shadow economy exists within a society can suggest the limitations which political and legal processes have, demonstrating how current economic policies are either ineffective or 'oppressive' (Fleming et al., 2000). Further, due to the inability to tax such transactions, the shadow economy adversely impacts on the state's capacity to collect revenue and subsequently provide economic and social services (Fleming et al., 2000; Eilat and Zinnes, 2000). However, as some scholars have argued, the shadow economy should not always be viewed in a negative light. In some cases, such practices may high-light state-created economic distortions, when government officials use the formal economy for private rents. Choi and Thum (2005: 818) argue that:

> ... the entrepreneur's option to flee to the underground sector con-strains the corrupt official's ability to introduce distortion into the economy for private gains. The unofficial economy thus mitigates government-induced distortions and, as a result, leads to enhanced economic activities in the official sector. In this sense, the pres-ence of the unofficial sector plays as a complement to the official economy instead of as a substitute.

The preceding sections have illustrated the challenges facing the establishment of the rule of law in developing countries but we must remember that the levels of law and order in the advanced economies are the product of generations of reform and political struggle. Until relatively recently major police forces – in New York, Chicago, Los Angeles and London – were bywords for criminality and corruption. However, in some countries and regions today the rule of law is so weak that states are diagnosed as being fragile.

Fragile states: concepts and experiences

Since the end of the Cold War the concept of the fragile state has become a lynchpin of development thinking and policy. The West's forays into Afghanistan, Iraq, Libya and Somalia, and its dither-ing over Syria, have meant that this issue now attracts considerable media attention. This section of the chapter tracks the concepts and taxonomies applied to those states which are perceived to be failing to achieve minimal levels of functioning. It outlines the complexities of labelling states in such a way, which can lead to counterproductive analyses of what states *do not* do as opposed to investigating what *does* actually happen in these situations.

Terms such as soft states, weak states, failed states, collapsed states, crisis states and most recently, fragile states cover a broad set of characteristics. As Zartman (1995: 1) comments, with refer-ence to the collapsed state, '[i]t refers to a situation where the struc-ture, authority (legitimate power), law, and political order have fallen apart and must be reconstituted in some form, old or new'.

In the collapsed states, Zartman sees central authority over the national territory and its citizens as having disappeared and power and order being dispersed to the local level. These characteristics are reflected by others who have been discussing the soft/weak/failed/fragile state (Migdal, 1988; Jackson, 2002; Duffield, 2007). Helman and Ratner (1993) provided an early analysis of failed states and gave examples of Haiti, Somalia and Sudan, countries in which the state failed to prevent violence and anarchy within their borders, leading to regional instability. In other cases, such as Cambodia, Bosnia, Kosovo and East Timor, failed states have been the cause of 'major humanitarian and human rights disasters' (Fukuyama, 2005: xix).

It is the collapse of law and order which is seen as the central characteristic of state failure (Mazrui, 1995; Bates, 2008). If a state cannot ensure law and order operate within its borders, then that leaves little room to provide other services and for the state to retain its legitimacy. The more recent concept of the fragile state develops the concept of state failure by recognizing that a fragile state is not a 'void', but instead, an entity which can be reconstructed and developed (Duffield, 2007). This newer concept takes into account the inability of the state to protect human security and that state's relationships in the wider geopolitical arena, emphasizing the consequences which fragility can bring domestically and internationally (Duffield, 2007; OECD, 2007; O'Gorman, 2011). Thus, the fragile state has become a globalized concept: it not only impacts on its own citizens, but may also impact on the rest of the world. As Fukuyama (2005) points out, it was not until the 9/11 attacks that the US and other countries realized that fragile states were not just localized problems but were challenges to global security.

Terminological changes over the last two decades to describe these types of states, demonstrate the difficulties of forming a robust conceptualization which academics and policy-makers can deploy to deepen the understanding of these states and their prospects. Taxonomies in this field tend to emphasize what a state cannot do. Although this may be useful for providing statistics about what the state provides for its citizens, it leads to analyses which focus exclusively on state deficiency and failure (Bilgin and Morton, 2002). In turn, this leads the international community to perceive these states as being an 'intractable problem' (Collier, 2009: 238).

As an alternative, assessments can be made about what these states and societies *can* achieve. This has been highlighted by the case of Somalia, the classic example of a failed state (Collier, 2009). A more in-depth investigation of Somaliland and Puntland shows that, within local contexts, statehood does exist, and there may be local institutions from which to start rebuilding the state (Box 3.3).

The labelling of states as collapsed or failed means that answers to important questions are neglected: 'why are some poor countries unstable and particularly subject to violence and warfare while others have achieved long periods of peace even in conditions of poverty and low economic growth?' (Putzel, 2010: 1). As Putzel (2010) and others (Beall et al., 2011) explain, while poverty in Tanzania, Zambia and Malawi is a severe problem, these states are resilient. In contrast, Afghanistan, the Democratic Republic of Congo, Somalia and Haiti, also experience profound poverty, but this is compounded by violence and instability. Putzel and di John (2012) have tried to provide a concept of state fragility which is more sensitive to these issues and can ultimately provide a tool which is of greater use for

Box 3.3   Somalia – the 'failed' state?

Since the fall of the Syad Barre regime in 1991, Somalia has been described as the 'stateless' state. In spite of many efforts to establish a central authority in Somalia, some regions have taken a different tack by embarking on their own processes of state formation. For example, Somaliland, an area in North-West Somalia, declared itself a republic, with a defined territory, a government and parliament, a provisional constitution, and has gradually introduced means for revenue collection. More recently, the Somaliland state has taken initiatives to install multi-party democracy and forge economic development. In 1998, another region in Somalia, Puntland, was established as a new state. Its charter followed the similar formula for state-building set out by Somaliland a few years earlier. However, in contrast to Somaliland, Puntland did not declare secession from Somalia; instead its actions aim to be the initial step in establishing a federal system in the country. Despite Somaliland's 20 years of attempts to achieve international recognition of its independent status and Puntland's desire to remain within Somalia, both states have exhibited characteristics of statehood within what is typically described as the 'failed' state of Somalia.

Source: Adapted from Hoehne, 2011.

development policy-makers seeking to strengthen state resilience. Four indicators have been identified, whereby a state is classified as fragile if it:

- fails to protect citizens from violence and to provide internal security;
- fails to function bureaucratically, including the capacity to collect taxes;
- fails to ensure that the state's rules and institutions take precedence over non-state actors;
- and finally, demonstrates an inability to control its borders (Adapted from Putzel (2010: 3) and Putzel and Di John (2012: v)).

These four specific indicators, it is argued, can draw attention to particular problem areas, enabling critical practical steps to be identified that might move states from fragility to resilience (Earle, 2011).

Taxonomies of state failure, weakness, collapse and fragility do raise questions about the fundamental definitions of a state. Indeed, despite a general unease about drawing comparisons with Western, developed states (Mamdani, 1996), there remains an underlying assumption that the Weberian model of a state is the ideal (Hagmann and Hoehne, 2009). Since the end of the Cold War, fragile states have received major intervention from external actors, often spearheaded by military powers, to impose an exogenous idea of sovereignty based upon Western interpretations and ideals. This is usually accompanied by neoliberal development and state-building schemes with international aid agencies and NGOs performing the functions that the state is normally expected to provide (Fukuyama, 2005). But, as Brett (2008) reminds us, the ability of fragile states to overcome their perceived difficulties does not only rely upon international interventions, but also requires actions from the regimes themselves and social and political movements within the country.

Violent conflict and peace

Violent conflict remains horrifyingly prevalent in the contemporary world. Around 1.5 billion people, almost one in four of the world's population, live in societies which are affected by high levels of violence, whether through conflict, criminal behaviour or the breakdown of law and order (World Bank, 2011). In the period between

1945 and 1999, 73 states were involved in 127 civil conflicts, from which it is estimated that 16.2 million people died (Fearon and Laitin, 2003: 75). Intra-state conflicts or civil wars have become increasingly common since the end of the Cold War involving not just regular armies, but armed and unarmed civilians. Civilians have become the main targets of violent conflict: 'at the turn of the twentieth century, the ratio of military to civilian casualties in wars was 8:1. Today this has almost exactly reversed: in wars of the 1990s, the ratio of military to civilian casualties is approximately 1:8' (Kaldor, 2006: 9). In addition, such violence severely disrupts institutions within a country increasing civilian mortality by disrupting health services and access to food.

Many scholars and policy-makers now argue that development needs to be considered alongside the issue of violent conflict as persistent poverty and violent conflict are so closely interrelated (Mac Ginty and Williams, 2009; O'Gorman, 2011). As Mac Ginty and Williams (2009: 1) argue, 'one of the oddities of social science research has been that theories of development and theories of conflict have largely evolved in isolation from one another'. The costs of violence and conflict in developing countries on short and long-term processes of development are significant with Collier (2007) estimating the financial cost of an average civil war as $64 billion and a reduction in economic growth of around 2.3 per cent per year. But, the costs of conflict go well beyond lost growth: conflict increases the spread of diseases, involuntary migration flows and displacement, and reduces levels of educational attainment and health status (Blattman and Miguel, 2009; Chamarbagwala and Morán, 2011). This is notwithstanding the loss of lives with the direct suffering that is caused and subsequent impacts on households and communities, affecting social networks, livelihoods and income generation (Justino, 2012).

Sierra Leone provides an example of the extreme social and economic costs of conflict. In just over ten years of civil war there were over 50,000 civilian deaths and the displacement of more than one million people. The country fell into the bottom ten of the Human Development Index and has remained there since the end of the conflict (in 2014 Sierra Leone was ranked 183 out of 187 countries on the HDI); and, tens of thousands of child soldiers missed out on a significant period of their schooling, which has had long-term consequences for the country's future (UNDP, 2007). Economically, the conflict has stunted business growth as human capital has reduced, as peoples' skills have declined and qualified Sierra Leonean professionals have left the country. This has a long-term negative effect on the country's competitiveness and its prospects for economic reconstruction.

The forms of violence within developing states vary enormously, which makes it difficult for policy-makers and peacekeepers, to distinguish between the lines of war and peace. More than three-quarters of all victims of lethal violence die in non-conflict settings (Krause, 2014). In the case of El Salvador for example, the peace agreement was signed in 1992 after 12 years of conflict. However, since that time, El Salvadorian society has become even more violent, with a homicide rate of 68 per 100,000 in 2008 (Howarth and Irvine, 2011), making it the most violent state in the world according to the Geneva Declaration (2011). It has since been overtaken by Honduras with 90.4 homicides per 100,000 population in 2012 especially due to gang warfare and the penetration of Mexican drug cartels (Rama, 2014). The effect of organized crime has been for Latin America to become the region with most murders – 40 per cent of the global total in 2012 but under 10 per cent of the world's population. This adversely affects social capital with Latin Americans expressing the lowest feelings of security in their communities of all the world's regions (Sonnenschein, 2014).

This demonstrates that high levels of violence can persist outside the realms of intra-state conflict. Since the second half of the twentieth century, there has been a tendency within the literature to describe this blurring of war, organized crime and large-scale human rights violations as 'new wars', forging a strong distinction from the 'old wars' of inter-state conflicts prevalent prior to this era (Kaldor, 2006). Contemporary violence is not just civil wars, but also includes the war on terror, warring amongst criminal gangs, vigilante justice, political violence, foreign invasion, the fallout after recent revolutions such as the Arab Spring and domestic violence against women.

Theoretical approaches to conflict and violence are varied and span across many disciplines (Gurr, 1970; Jacoby, 2008). Within the development literature, three theoretical models appear more frequently than others. First, and in use for over 70 years, is the *grievance* perspective as a theory for explaining conflict. This argues that when particular groups or regions are explicitly or implicitly neglected or marginalized by the state then they may take up arms in an attempt to redress this neglect or exclusion. The state's response – sending in soldiers to eradicate armed opposition or mobilizing local militias – often fuels higher levels of grievance through the extra-judicial murder, rape and corruption that is often associated with such interventions so that levels of violence also increase.

Paul Collier and colleagues have challenged the grievance hypothesis with a *greed* hypothesis. Emerging in the 1990s, 'greed' was the neoclassical economists answer to understanding the causes of conflict. Adopting a rational choice perspective, this approach sought to provide econometric evidence to pinpoint the instigating factor of civil conflicts as the greed of individuals (Berdal, 2005; Cramer, 2006). The most commonly cited works (Collier and Hoeffler, 1998; Collier, 2000; Collier and Hoeffler, 2004) argue that civil wars start and continue because individuals find that they can profit out of the associated breakdown in law and order by gaining control of economically valuable resources – such as diamonds and oilfields. In countries where civil wars take place, the predatory acts of armed groups are influenced by the gains and profits to be made from the high prevalence (at least 25 per cent) of primary commodity exports (Collier and Hoeffler, 2000). Rebels resemble groups of organized criminals in their pursuit of loot and extortion, making conflict a 'lucrative business' (O'Gorman, 2011: 32). The 'scientific' nature of this analytical approach proved appealing to policy-makers and had a direct impact on actions in conflict zones by international agencies such as the UN and the World Bank (Berdal, 2005).

Although it is widely accepted by those working in conflict analysis that natural resources can contribute to conflict, that some combatants make profits from war and that some seek to extend the length of a conflict for personal gain (Cramer, 2006), the 'probabilistic nature' of the greed thesis has been extensively challenged (Ballentine and Sherman, 2003: 5; Jacoby, 2008). Increasingly, researchers are working to overcome the methodological and analytical shortcomings of the greed approach through a more historical and structural analysis that weaves greed and grievance into a common framework (Cramer, 2006). Analytical focus shifts from an exclusive focus on individual and rational choice to a consideration of the role of the state, horizontal inequalities and rents from non-lootable resources. To illustrate, in Sierra Leone, it is argued that both greed and grievances have interacted to perpetuate the civil war. Bellows and Miguel (2006) point out that while the profits from diamond smuggling helped to encourage all armed forces to extend the conflict – greed – the failure of the state to provide economic growth, employment and public services – grievances – also contributed to the violence. In Colombia, it is claimed that although grievances were the underlying factors for the instigation of conflict, greed perpetuated the conflict. '[V]iolence in Colombia seems to have become an end in itself, a development in which greed, as reinforced by the availability of large profits from illegal activities, certainly played a decisive role and is, in turn leading to an increase in grievances' (Röhl, 2004: 13).

The third concept is *structural violence* mooted by Johan Galtung in 1969. This type of violence accounts for the difference between potential and actual life experiences, referring to non-behavioural or indirect violence. An example of indirect violence would be of a child suffering (or even dying) from lack of access to basic medicines in a society in which such medicines are easily available to those with the economic resources to purchase them. Society is structured in such a way as to allow such unnecessary suffering to occur. As Jacoby (2008: 29) explains, an early death from tuberculosis at the beginning of the nineteenth century would not be classed as structural violence as the medicines for treatment did not exist at that time. However, if this happens today, when the medicines exist, then the circumstances are described as structural violence due to the 'inequitable distribution of the world's resources' (Jacoby, 2008: 39). In other words, 'the poor are denied decent and dignified lives because their basic physical and mental capacities are constrained by hunger, poverty, inequality, and exclusion' (Uvin, 1998: 103). Farmer's (2004) analysis of Haiti adopts a structural violence framework viewing both direct acts of physical violence and lack of access to HIV/AIDS medicines as interrelated factors.

While many analysts have examined the causes of conflict, an alternative perspective is to analyse the processes of peacebuilding (Berdal, 2014). This activity is of great relevance for those charged with promoting peace. The UN has launched 34 missions with peacebuilding mandates between 1989 and 2011, many of which have aimed to completely transform the landscape of societies affected by conflict (Berdal and Zaum, 2012). Once a truce or peace agreement has been established and the Security Council has given authorization, UN peacekeepers are allowed to enter a country with the aim of protecting civilians from further violence and helping countries achieve the transition from violence to peace (Brahimi, 2000). The act of establishing peace however is a complex and ambiguous process for international actors mediating in fragile situations. Unfortunately, such attempts sometimes fail to recognize 'underlying power relations' and contextually specific structures which can significantly impact the ability to create peaceful situations (Goodhand and Sedra, 2010). Peacebuilding is not a neutral activity and 'peace processes are disparate and divergent in their economic and social impacts – benefitting some while harming others, or at the very least raising troubling questions about who they might leave behind' (Selby, 2008: 11).

Western efforts at establishing peace in developing countries have been critiqued for their imposition of the 'liberal peace' project (see Box 3.4), using a one-size fits all model which crowds out indigenous approaches to peace-making (Mac Ginty, 2008). Development agencies, such as bilateral aid agencies, the EU, the IMF and the World Bank, are central to the liberal peace project,

---

Box 3.4 Liberal and illiberal peacebuilding processes

Described as the 'currently dominant Western form of peace-making and peace support', liberal peace is the theory and practice, promoted by Western states, international organizations and international financial institutions, of interventions in post-conflict arenas which aim to stabilize financial institutions and the 'international *status quo*' (Mac Ginty, 2008: 143). In turn, liberal market democracy is endorsed as the form of governance which all states should adopt. The process consists of a format of

- Ceasefire monitoring
- Creating formal peace negotiations
- Disarmament, demobilization and reintegration (DDR) of combatants
- Security sector reform
- Building the capacity of civil society
- Elections
- Restructuring of the economic system (adapted from Mac Ginty, 2008).

The liberal peace project allows little, if any, space for indigenous peace-building institutions and practices and can sometimes result in 'troubling and destructive' consequences (Paris, 2010: 362). As Richmond (2010) points out, initiatives such as 'do no harm' become internationalized rather than engaging with the local context and the everyday life of citizens.

By contrast, illiberal peacebuilding is managed by local elites in the post-conflict country. It involves hidden negotiations and dispenses with aspects of the liberal peace agenda and interventions from external organizations. Notable examples of such processes include Angola, Lebanon, Sri Lanka and Rwanda. While illiberal peacebuilding can bring stability, this can lead to elites re-structuring society in order to increase their own economic rents and strengthen their hold on political power (Soares de Oliveira, 2011).

ensuring that post-conflict societies are reconstructed to stabilize their economies, promote economic growth and also service their debts. The World Bank in particular has become a major financier of programmes in fragile and conflict-affected states (Independent Evaluation Group, 2013).

The liberal peace project is challenged by scholars and activists who argue for an alternative approach that emphasizes building peace along contextual lines (Mac Ginty, 2008; Özerdem, 2010). This involves establishing internally driven disarmament, demobilization and reintegration (DDR) processes (collecting and disposing of small arms; disbanding militias and armed groups; and, returning former combatants to their communities and integrating them into economic and political life) and supporting locally designed grassroots institutions to create not only law and order, but also provide a stable and secure society for civilians and former combatants. It demands that international agencies must also pay attention to the unintended consequences of their actions in preventing peace and exacerbating conflict. The directions that external agencies give for the re-integration of conflict affected states back into the global economic system is seen as particularly problematic (Pugh et al., 2008).

NGOs have become a key player in reconstruction processes, attempting to bridge the gap in services between the state and citizens and adding *development* to the peacebuilding process. Whether NGOs have comparative advantages in community level activities (a grassroots orientation, participatory approaches, local accountability and capacities for innovation – see Chapter 9) remains an important question. NGOs are also constrained by their funders and at times, 'NGOs have felt obliged to undertake 'quick impact' projects, which are [...] less concerned with meeting local needs and more to do with donors' geopolitical interests' (Jacoby and James, 2010: 9).

Conclusion

While normative theories, and particularly the concepts of liberal democracy and the liberal peace, inform policies for establishing law and order, conflict resolution and peacebuilding it is political economy theories that provide deepened understanding of the causes of conflict and the prospects for the rule of law and/or peace. Political economy approaches take into account how Western countries have developed, and in contrast to liberal approaches, do not assume that it is possible to transfer Western arrangements into developing countries (Evans, 2004). These theories take into account the case-specific, and often violent and unjust processes, that have established law and order in the advanced industrial countries.

Political economy frameworks accept that lessons can be learned from other contexts, especially ones in the same region, but stress the difficulty of imposing law and order onto a country. Instead, emphasis is placed upon historical precedents and the identification of interventions that build on 'what is available' rather than on 'what we would like to start with'. At the same time, there is a clear need for development researchers and policy-makers to engage more with these debates to ensure that issues of law and order, security and insecurity, and conflict and peace feature significantly in discussions about development. The tendency for international development agencies to adopt normative 'best practice' approaches to problem-solving must be resisted. There are positive indicators that these lessons are starting to be learned:

> Increasingly, development actors are learning the lessons of 'do no harm' by recognizing the inherent need to 'mainstream' con-flict sensitivity in their programs, and to be innovative in their planning, if development resources are to be conscious resources of peacebuilding rather than hostages or fuel to the conflict. (O'Gorman, 2011: 15)

The perception that the rule of law automatically means justice for all must be counterbalanced by understandings of the extent to which the law applies to all within specific societies. The examples of the judiciary and policing in this chapter illustrate the complexi-ties of trying to establish equitable, functioning legal systems when underlying power relations have not been addressed. There is also a need for development thinking and action to move beyond the prior-itizing of property rights: although these may be important for econ-omic development, they themselves require other economic, legal and political institutions to be in place in order for them to take effect.

The concept of the fragile state has received great attention from development agencies and academics since 9/11 and the invasions of Afghanistan and Iraq. Different labels to describe these states have caused confusion about what constitutes a fragile state and what in turn, should be done to make fragile states stronger. It has also raised questions about what defines a state in general; to what extent is the Weberian model a true depiction of an effective state in today's world? Taxonomies of fragility, failure or weakness neglect to account for what states *can* do. The examples of Somaliland and Puntland, in Somalia, demonstrate that forms of statehood do exist even in the worst cases of fragile states.

These discussions on the role of law and order and conflict and peace in development engage more broadly with those dealing with issues of state-building and state formation. They bring to the fore questions about the processes which developing countries have undertaken and should undertake in order to build states which reflect the desires and wishes of their societies. They also emphasize the extent to which the state needs to be considered within development debates but also how these debates can only be informed through analyses which are context specific and which connect to the history of developing countries (Fukuyama, 2005).

Chapter 4

The Policy Process: How and Who

Most of what public sector organizations do is routine or reactive. The routine concerns tasks like admitting children to schools, issuing driving licences and authorizing business permits. But there are unexpected and novel occurrences, 'events, dear boy, events', which former UK prime minister Harold Macmillan told a journalist were the hardest part of his job (a natural disaster like a flood would be an example). Public agencies' priority is not to decide what they should be doing, but how best to do it. Such questions of administrative structure and management are discussed in Chapters 5 and 6. Moreover, politicians and civil servants occupy some of their time pursuing personal objectives, capturing resources and playing the political game: 'court news ... who loses and who wins; who's in, who's out,' as Shakespeare's King Lear puts it, anticipating modern journalistic accounts of government trajectories (for example, Woodward, 2010).

But it is also the job of a government, and possibly its most important job, to set a course in response to the new concerns that are forever crowding in on its attention. They may come from outside: a rise in the price of oil which dictates a new energy policy; or from inside, such as an election manifesto commitment to universal secondary education. In either case, acting on them is what citizens expect governments to do, and policy is how governments do it: policies in areas such as economic development, education, personal safety, job opportunities. The process of making and implementing policy is the subject of this chapter. We look at it in terms of *how* and *who*: the policy process through which policy arises, is analysed and implemented (*how*) and the policy actors who push it along or try to block it (*who*).

Models of the policy process

What is policy?

To commence our exploration of the world of policy in developing countries we must first understand what the word 'policy' means. Unfortunately, it is an imprecise term: 'something bigger than particular decisions, but smaller than general social movements' is the best that one authority could come up with (Heclo, 1972, quoted in Parsons, 1995: 13). The broadness of this definition highlights a recurrent problem in the social sciences, that many terms, such as 'development' and 'policy', have multiple meanings and it depends on who is using the term and in what context as to its meaning. The crucial issue is not which one is right but that students develop an awareness of multiple meanings and identify the versions which have greatest analytical insight. Hogwood and Gunn (1984) have provided a useful classification of the meanings of policy employed by those trying to intervene in the 'real world'. We have recast their various meanings in a developmental context in Box 4.1.

We regard policy as process. This gives policy a historical dimension and alerts us to different foci (for example, policy-making and implementation) during that process. Policy is also about decisions – series of decisions, in fact – and decisions are about power. Sometimes such expressions of power may be revealed in the capacity not to act: the 'non-decision'. Policy is also purposive behaviour, although officially stated goals may mask other intents, and rationalizations about policy initiatives and outcomes may come after decisions have been made and actions taken. Finally, policy is constructed by human agents and we need to understand their behaviour. For this we need to appreciate that these agents have multiple, often conflicting and sometimes changing political goals and that they may enter and exit the policy process at different stages. What must be banished is any lingering idea that policy is some highly rational process in which expert technicians are firmly in control using highly tuned instruments to achieve easily predicted outcomes. Such an image is inappropriate for rich Western countries let alone the developing world where environments are more unpredictable and turbulent. Dror's (1986: 98) notion of policy-making as 'fuzzy betting attempting to influence the probability of future situations' is particularly appropriate for the developing world.

Box 4.1   How does the word 'policy' get used?

As a label for a field of activity
For example, broad statements about a government's economic policy, industrial policy or law and order policy

As an expression of general purpose or a desired state of affairs
For example, to generate as many jobs as possible, to promote democratization through decentralization

As specific proposals
For example, to limit agricultural landholdings to ten hectares, to peg the currency to the US dollar or to provide universal primary education

As decisions of government
For example, decisions on industrial relations or tax reforms announced by a president or in the national assembly

As formal authorization
For example, acts of parliament, ministerial decrees or other statutory instruments

As a programme
For example, as a set of activities in a defined and relatively specific sphere of government responsibility such as a land reform programme or an immunization programme

As output
For example, what is actually delivered such as the amount of land redistributed in a reform programme and the number of tenants affected

As outcome
For example, what is actually achieved such as the effect of a land reform programme on farmer income and living standards

As a theory or model
For example, if you do x then y will happen; if more economic opportunities are provided in rural areas then migration to cities will slow down

As a process
As a long-term matter starting with the issues and moving through objective-setting and decision-making to planning, implementation and evaluation

Source: Adapted from Hogwood and Gunn (1984).

A rational or political model of the policy process?

A deep conflict runs through common attitudes toward policy making. On the one hand ... [people] want policy making to be scientific; on the other hand, they want it to remain in the world of politics. (Lindblom, 1980: 12)

To talk about process implies a 'systems' view in which the entity in question goes through a series of stages. There are a number of such systems models of policy that have been around for a long time (for example, Easton, 1965; Hogwood and Gunn, 1981). The one shown in Figure 4.1 comes from Jenkins (1978).

Such models have an appealing simplicity, coherence and neatness. But the date of Jenkins' model, and others like it, is significant as in the last decade or so, stages models have been called into question. The essential criticism is that while they are rational and orderly, reality is political and chaotic. When a questioner complained that his plots were difficult to follow, the great film director Jean-Luc Godard replied, 'A film should have a beginning, a middle and an end – but not necessarily in that order.' Similarly, policies emerge in the real world of public affairs from a hurly-burly of political contestation which refuses to conform to any logical sequence. Stages

Figure 4.1   *A 'stages' model of the policy process*

Initiation
↓
Information
↓
Consideration
↓
Decision
↓
Implementation
↓
Evaluation
↓
Termination

Source: Jenkins (1978).

© John Wiley & Sons, Inc.

models give us merely 'the shell of policy, presented for political and media consumption,' says John (1998: 27), who goes on to suggest that their parcelling up of reality appeals to bureaucrats and journalists. The bureaucrats use them to restrict outsiders' participation in policies that they prefer to see as their prerogative while journalists have readers who require clarity, however crude, rather than complexity, however faithful to reality that is (see also Thomas and Grindle, 1990).

Bebbington and McCourt (2007) have proposed an alternative model in a development context which responds to the criticism of stages models as apolitical (Figure 4.2). Reflecting on seven cases of long-run policy implementation from across the developing world, they suggest that policy has its 'initiation', as Jenkins would put it, in an upsurge of 'social energy', a notion which they borrow from Hirschman (1984) to express a momentum for change which is precipitated by dramatic events like Bangladesh's independence in 1971 which led to the birth of the Grameen Bank and the microfinance movement in Bangladesh, or the new Brazilian constitution of 1988 that led to Brazil's National Health System. The energy crystallizes in a policy idea around which a coalition assembles, which in turn throws up a leader who acts as a spearhead to get the idea on the policy agenda and overcome opposition from supporters of the old dispensation that the new policy seeks to displace. The coalition is then 'institutionalized' in a formal structure which empowers

Figure 4.2 *A political model of the policy process*

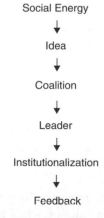

Source: Bebbington and McCourt (2007).

the policy's beneficiaries, and it is consolidated over time through feedback to adapt the policy to changing circumstances. None of this is inevitable: a policy may fall by the wayside at any stage. But Bebbington and McCourt (2007) find that it applies reasonably well to their seven cases, which were deliberately chosen as instances of successful policies.

Bebbington and McCourt's (2007) six-stage model addresses the criticism that stages models ignore politics. However, it neglects the other main criticism of stages models, that they attempt to impose order on a disorderly reality, even though it is more faithful to reality in giving an explicit role to policy feedback (a stage in the policy sequence that we will return to later in the chapter). To take just one example which does not conform to the stages sequence in Figure 4.2, a policy may be initiated by a leader already in power.

In the end, we agree with Hill (2009) that as long as we don't make the mistake of seeing stages models as a faithful description of reality, they remain useful analytical tools which help us to organize our thinking about policy. And so Jenkins' (1978) model provides a partial structure for this chapter: we will highlight the information and consideration stages (under the heading of policy analysis), and also implementation and evaluation. We will also discuss policy feedback, a further stage in the policy process highlighted in Figure 4.2. And we will have the Bebbington and McCourt (2007) model in mind more generally when we discuss the role of policy actors.

Policy initiation: policy windows and political opportunity structures

Where do policies come from? How much weight should we give to ideas, and how much to political factors? In one sense, policies *are* ideas. At any given moment there is a multitude of ideas in circulation, bobbing up and down, as it were, in what Kingdon (1995) has called the 'policy primeval soup'. In trying to understand why some ideas but not others are fished out of the 'soup', it is suggested that policy emerges from the interplay of ideas and interests. Like the proverbial chicken and egg, it is futile to ask which comes first. However, we can fruitfully ask in what circumstances an idea is taken up in the form of a policy.

From a public policy perspective, Kingdon's (1995) research in the US finds that ideas gain traction when a 'policy window' opens.

That in turn occurs when there is 'a change of [government], a shift in the ... distribution of seats in the [legislature], or a shift in the national mood' (Kingdon, 1995: 168). Tarrow's (1998) account of the conditions necessary for social movements to take off is similar. He suggests that the 'political opportunity structure' should facilitate, among other things, a rapid diffusion of collective action from more mobilized to less mobilized sectors of society and a rapid pace of innovation in the forms of political contention. Social movements are mass movements for change in society, such as the civil rights movement in the US in the 1960s or the present anti-globalization movement.

These observations drawn from American experience also fit with some, but not all developing country experiences. For example, some of the elements of policy initiation noted above can be seen in the origins of Brazil's conditional cash transfer (CCT) policy (see Box 4.2).

CCTs only became possible when political liberalization opened up a policy window (in Tarrow's terms, when the 'political opportunity structure' became favourable). Even then, the idea had to be

---

Box 4.2   Conditional cash transfers (CCTs) in Brazil

Brazil's increasingly influential 'conditional cash transfer' policy had its origin in the transition from military to democratic rule which began in the 1970s and which culminated in the new constitution in 1988. The constitution conferred new powers on Brazil's states and municipalities, including control of revenue. The opening up of the political system allowed new parties to emerge, including the Worker's Party (PT). PT senator Eduardo Sulpicy had been promoting the idea of a universal basic income since the late 1980s, influenced by the American economist Milton Friedman's idea of negative income tax and the European Basic Income Network. His idea was seen as eccentric and utopian, and was only taken up by Sulpicy's own party when the economist José Márcio Camargo proposed making it conditional on families guaranteeing to send their children to school.

As politicians of all parties and at every level of government saw the popularity of the scheme, there was a bandwagon effect, with political actors competing to offer the most attractive cash transfer scheme to voters. By 2005, income transfer programmes had reached 8.7 million families, benefiting 34 million family members, and their cost had risen to an annual US$2.2 billion, or 2.5 per cent of GDP.

Source: Melo (2007).

reshaped before it could take off. However, it must be admitted that neither Kingdon's nor Tarrow's account is wholly satisfactory. For example, a review of the social movement literature notes that 'scholars disagree on basic theories of how political opportunities affect [social] movements' (Meyer, 2004: 125). In public policy terms, it is difficult to predict when a policy window will open (or close). Still, these two very different streams of research, taken together, give us a sense of the process though which ideas can become policies when the political conditions are right.

Information and consideration: policy analysis

Even if policy-making is intensely political, policies can still be informed by data. In today's jargon, they should be 'evidence-based', that is where 'rigorous research evidence [goes into] policy debates and internal public sector processes' (Head, 2010: 13). There is longstanding realization of the need for evidence-based policy decisions in developing and transitional countries. Unfortunately, in many of these countries the desired data are sometimes of questionable accuracy, in short supply and not produced in a timely manner. However, in some favourable circumstances, the 'scientific' judgement of an expert can provide the correct policy. For example, Sachs (2005) describes how the Bolivian government adopted his remedy for hyperinflation, stopping it virtually overnight in 1985 in the teeth of those who believed that it would take several years to bring it under control. This 'shock therapy' did, however, incur considerable social costs and has been described as 'a classic example' of neoliberalism being 'shoved down Latin Americans' throats' (Boudin, 2009: 203).

Features of successful policy

One of the most important contributions of policy analysis is that it should lead to successful policies. But can we identify a specific set of characteristics of successful policies that policy analysis should aim to achieve? In the UK, the new government, elected in 1997, spent a lot of time discussing this question and improving the policy machinery (Strategic Policy Making Team, 1999). It suggested that successful policy would have the following features:

- *Forward looking*: outcomes are defined, based on a long-term view informed by statistical trends and political predictions
- *Outward looking*: takes account of the international setting and draws on foreign experience
- *Innovative, flexible and creative*
- *Evidence-based*
- *Inclusive*: involves key stakeholders directly
- *Joined up*: looks beyond institutional boundaries to strategic objectives for the government as a whole
- *Review*: existing policy is constantly reviewed to ensure it remains appropriate
- *Evaluation*: systematic evaluation is built into the policy process
- *Learns lessons*: a learning approach to policy development

In order to produce those features, it was argued that there would need to be:

- *leadership* from ministers and senior officials, via briefing on what policy analysis might provide, so that they would demand better analysis
- *openness* from analysts and policy-makers, since pressure from the public would make government raise its analytical game
- *better planning* to match policy needs and analytical provision
- *spreading of best practice* across departments and professions
- innovative solutions to *recruit and retain the best people*

The government's report (Strategic Policy Making Team, 1999: 13) further noted that policy analysis would only be useful where the government had some room to manoeuvre:

> Detailed manifesto commitments can also constrain a Government's scope for manoeuvre. They are usually seen as binding on the Government. More often – and more helpfully – manifesto commitments do not take the form of specific pledges but are couched in broad strategic terms ... The role of analysts and policy makers in Government is then to translate these broad goals into detailed and workable policy options.

While the features of successful policies and the means of facilitating them set out above were drawn up for a rich country, the advice can still be useful for developing countries. However, the latter should not be trying to emulate rich country experience but they can use the check list to identify shortcomings in the policy process and the areas in which they can make improvements.

Strengthening policy analysis

The development implications of the last quotation become clearer if for 'manifesto commitments' we substitute 'loan conditionalities'. One reason for the detailed conditionalities that were a feature of development, especially World Bank and IMF loans in the 1980s and 1990s, was that donors doubted governments' ability to come up with targets of their own based on sound policy analysis. Thus, strengthening policy analysis while worthwhile in its own right also helps donors resist the temptation to tie borrower governments' hands.

In principle, developing countries have three main sources of analysis:

* the government's own cadre of policy analysts, which can be improved through, for example, employing economists on attractive terms in central agencies such as the Ministries of Finance and Planning
* 'contracting out' to external national resources in universities, think-tanks and NGOs
* drawing on international resources, possibly via a donor agency

In practice, there are problems with all of these. As we discuss elsewhere in this book, relying on international resources such as a donor agency risks creating a problem of policy 'ownership': an inappropriate policy to which national policy actors are not committed. National resources are often weak. As recently as 2009, an international conference convened by the Egyptian government's own think-tank, the Information and Decision Support Center, noted that think-tanks in developing countries lacked sustainable funding, capacity building and independence (IDSC, 2009; see also IDRC, 2009).

Where government's own resources are concerned, even when good quality analysts are available, the structure of government needs to allow their skills to be used. When the new Prime Minister of Zambia, Frederick Chiluba, took office in 1991, he found that only 25 per cent of cabinet decisions were being implemented

(Koenen-Grant and Garnett, 1996). To remedy this, his government introduced five reforms all relating to policy analysis. First, a Policy Analysis and Co-ordination Unit was established in the Cabinet Office with a permanent secretary, nine policy change specialists and administrative staff. Second, workshops were held for senior officials both appointed and elected. Third, inter-ministerial committees of officials were set up to define policy issues and develop responses. Fourth, more systematic policy analysis was introduced in a new standard format for presenting policy proposals. Finally, cabinet liaison officers were identified for each ministry as points of contact between the cabinet office and ministries. The reforms were reported to have improved the policy process although the new unit was still required to spend time in more traditional bureaucratic pursuits such as preparing detailed minutes of committee meetings (Koenen-Grant and Garnett, 1996). The new Zambian policy analysis structure is shown in Figure 4.3.

Reflecting on Zambia's experience and on similar experience in Latin America, Crosby (2000) has identified the following success factors for policy units:

- *Ownership/patronage*: The Unit needs a senior politician or official as an active sponsor
- *Linkage to policy makers*: It should be structurally close to where policies are formed
- *Technical capacity*: Unit staff should be technically excellent
- *Donor role/commitment*: It is helpful for a donor to support this initiative in an unobtrusive way
- *Policy/political congruence*: The Unit needs to work on the policy issues that matter to governments, not the professional priorities of the Unit
- *Collaborative environment*: The Unit needs collaborative links with line ministries

Attaining these desirable characteristics is a challenge for all countries but particularly so for developing countries. Some factors may be more difficult in particular contexts while others may be of varying importance. In many instances the best option may be for a 'good enough governance' approach. But if top-level patronage is removed or agencies can ignore the unit's advice and instructions then all the technical expertise in the world will count for nothing.

108

Figure 4.3 *The policy analysis structure in Zambia*

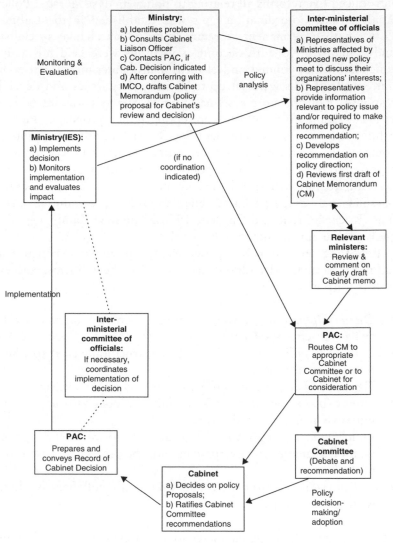

Source: Koenen-Grant and Garnett (1996).

Implementation

Coping with complexity: feedback and policy learning

The myth persists that politicians make policy and public servants implement it mechanically 'as if implementation was something utterly simple and automatic' (Lane, 1993: 93). While both politicians and bureaucrats are frequently active in promulgating and maintaining this myth, the reality is somewhat different. In this section we consider implementation first in terms of feedback and learning, and then in terms of politics.

It is at the implementation stage that policy-makers become forcibly aware that the real world which they are trying to affect is complex. This is a headache for the policy-makers, but a source of relief for the people on whom the policy is being imposed since, as the philosopher Roger Scruton (2010: 113) has observed, 'The worst kind of government is not that which makes mistakes but that, while making mistakes, is unable to correct them.' Correcting a mistake of course entails feedback, and feedback loops decorate many models of the policy process. Like most such processes, policy-making is an *iterative* activity, one that is repeated.

Just as the German field marshal Helmuth von Moltke remarked that no battle plan survives contact with the enemy, probably no policy survives unaltered after contact with reality. In the early 1990s, Uganda set an initial target for staff reduction in the civil service of 34,000 jobs. But when it implemented its job reduction programme it found that it had 42,000 'ghost workers' (employees who existed only as names on the payroll, allowing their salaries to be fraudulently diverted) on the books. Numbers were to decrease eventually by about 150,000, representing almost 50 per cent of civil service employees. Such 'running repairs' are a normal part of policy learning and 'lesson-drawing' in public policy (Sabatier, 1988; Rose, 1993).

Political factors in policy implementation

We know that policy-makers often fail to learn from experience. Sometimes that happens even when it is in their interests to learn. Often, however, it is because implementation is not only complex, but also a highly political process, an arena where those who advocate a policy engage with opponents who believe that the policy harms their interests. This 'politics of implementation' has been a special interest of Merilee Grindle over many years, and it is to her work that we now turn.

Grindle (1980: 15) notes that in the US and Western Europe, policy activity is focused on the input (policy-making) stage but that in developing countries, where interest aggregating structures are often weak, 'a large portion of individual and collective demand-making, the representation of interests, and the emergence and reso-lution of conflict occur at the output stage' (implementation). This is the stage where those interested in particular policies are best able to participate. Also, politics based on factions, patron-client ties and other affective forms is highly suited to 'individualized demand on the bureaucratic apparatus for the allocation of goods and services' (Grindle, 1980: 18). The implementation phase may thus be seen as an arena in which those responsible for allocating resources are engaged in political relationships among themselves and with other actors intent on influencing that allocation.

Emphasis on political factors leads Grindle to reject the classic stages models, or what she calls the 'linear model of implementation', and suggest that policy-makers

> face opposition in attempting to pursue reformist initiatives; in con-sequence, they need to consider feasibility in terms of support and opposition to change, what stakes they and the government they serve have in the pursuit of reform, and the political and bureau-cratic resources needed to sustain such initiatives. (Thomas and Grindle, 1990: 1165–6)

Analysis of implementation feasibility thus becomes an essential part of policy analysis and can be determined using an 'interactive model' of policy implementation (see Figure 4.4). Analysis com-mences with looking at the characteristics of any public policy in terms of the reaction it will generate. Then governments must assess what their resources are and how they can be mobilized to promote successful implementation. Decision-makers must evalu-ate political resources while public managers attend to bureaucratic resources. Such analysis can lead to a more realistic approach to policy where the question of implementation feasibility assumes major importance. Failure can be better anticipated, modifications

Figure 4.4   *The linear model of policy reform*

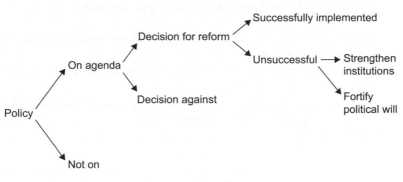

Source: Thomas and Grindle (1990: 1165).

can be better judged and resources can be more efficiently and effectively allocated.

Monitoring and evaluation

Still following the stages of Jenkins' (1978) model, we arrive at evaluation. In this section, we bracket it with monitoring, in line with contemporary development practice. Evaluation involves systematic analysis of what has happened and why, while monitoring is the systematic collection of data and scrutiny of what is happening. Evaluation, when it is not carried out exclusively at the end of a programme – at which point it can sometimes mean no more than shutting the stable door after the horse has bolted – provides perhaps the most obvious policy feedback loop: from evaluation back to the earlier policy stages, and notably what Jenkins (1978) calls the 'consideration' stage. We have already noted the attempt in the UK to make evaluation an integral part of the policy process. The attempt has been even more thoroughgoing in the international development agencies, which have put significant resources into monitoring and evaluation of development programmes over the last quarter-century.

Kusek and Rist (2004), working under the auspices of the World Bank, have proposed a ten-step model of monitoring and evaluation (M&E). They stress the use of evaluation at the end of a programme (*ex post* evaluation) to identify the outcomes or impacts of the programme intervention, but evaluation in the form of monitoring should occur continuously during the programme. The steps are as follows:

1. *Readiness assessment*: what incentives and demands are there for M&E in the political system?
2. *Agreeing on outcomes to monitor and evaluate*: what are the strategic priorities for the programme?
3. *Selecting Key Performance Indicators to monitor outcomes*: for example, a programme outcome 'to improve student learning' might translate into 'change in student scores on school achievement tests' as an outcome indicator
4. *Setting baselines and gathering data on indicators*: a performance baseline takes the form of data establishing the 'state of play' at the beginning of the monitoring period.
5. *Selecting results targets*, defined as baseline indicator levels plus desired degrees of improvement
6. *Monitoring for results*
7. *Evaluation* at suitable intervals during the programme lifetime as well as at the end
8. *Reporting findings* to stakeholders
9. *Using findings* to inform future programme development
10. *Sustaining the M&E system* through embedding M&E, capacity building etc.

Box 4.3 shows how one developing country government, that of Sri Lanka, has attempted to embed monitoring and evaluation in its practice. Note the multiple activities and how they interrelate to other developmental activities and how stakeholders from outside of government can be involved in M&E.

M&E is much more firmly established in international development agencies than in national governments. Paradoxically, accountability for programme performance via M&E is less to developing country governments and citizens than to the development agencies themselves, and to the rich country governments and taxpayers who lie behind the development agencies, demanding evidence that aid spending is having the desired impact (White, 2006). For example, in Sri Lanka, government M&E efforts are reported as being partly geared to donor needs, and are not fully embedded (Sivagnanasothy, undated). Thus, while M&E has made governments and other recipients of development funding more accountable to donors, for the most part, it has not made developing country governments more accountable to their citizens.

Box 4.3   Policy evaluation in Sri Lanka

The government of Sri Lanka's National Evaluation Policy seeks to:

• create an evaluation culture and to use evaluations to manage for results
• promote evaluation through capacity building with respect to staff, institutions, tools and methodologies
• enable learning of lessons from past experiences
• improve the design of development policies and programmes through integration of evaluation findings
• establish accountability, transparency and good governance

As part of the evaluation policy, the government is mandating the use of performance indicators for all policy, programme and project preparation initiatives. For this purpose, the government is encouraging partnerships with civil society organizations (for example, the Sri Lanka Evaluation Association) and NGOs to introduce participatory evaluations in the public sector. The government is also encouraging universities and public sector training institutions to include evaluation modules to share knowledge on evaluation techniques and methodologies.

Source: Kusek and Rist (2004).

Policy actors

Policy 'drivers' and the role of the state

We move from the *how* of the policy process to the *who* of policy actors: the agencies that influence policy and make it happen. In keeping with the view we developed in Chapter 1, national and subnational governments will be at the centre of our attention. Perhaps we are influenced here by a democratic bias; that is, by a belief that governments *should* be in the driving seat, because they are directly accountable to their citizens, unlike the other policy actors that we are going to review.

Over the last decade we have moved a long way from the traditional view that policy is made by politicians who may be accountable to their electorates, but are insulated from them when making policy, and is then implemented by politically disinterested civil servants, acting as a mere transmission belt. The new emphasis on the politics of policy has led to studies sponsored by the World Bank and the

Swedish and UK governments of 'drivers' of policy change in individual countries (Dahl-Østergaard et al., 2005). These studies have pointed to generic factors like technical capacity, insulation from societal interests and building incentives for politicians to embark on reform (Robinson, 2007); but also to the role of policy actors, whose identity and influence vary from country to country. For example, civil society and the media have begun to influence policy in Zambia (Duncan et al., 2003).

But perhaps our thinking has moved just a little too far from the state-centred view, so that state policy-makers have sometimes appeared as not so much the drivers as the passengers of change. Against that, Kingdon's influential study of policy-making in the US concluded that 'to describe the roles of (internal and external) participants in agenda setting, a fairly straightforward top-down model, with elected officials at the top, comes surprisingly close to the truth' (Kingdon, 1995: 199). In a development context, an equally influential study of Lesotho concluded that in that country, 'the development "apparatus" is not a machine for eliminating poverty ... it is a machine for reinforcing and expanding the exercise of bureaucratic state power' (Ferguson, 1990: 255), which is a backhanded way of recognizing that governments do have real power, even if they sometimes exercise it in an undesirable way.

Mozambique and, more recently, Timor-Leste became very different entities once their governments were accountable to their citizens rather than to the distant rulers of Portugal and Indonesia. We regard influences from outside government, whether from national society or from abroad, as a constraint on government's autonomy and an influence on its policy-making rather than as usurping its autonomy outright. Policy-makers do have room to manoeuvre. And so the emphasis in this chapter on the political dimension of policy entails an emphasis on the character and interests of policy actors.

From 'how' to 'who': political commitment

When problems arise in policy implementation, they are often attributed to a lack of political commitment (or will). Academic analysts are united in finding this an unsatisfactory concept. For Thomas and Grindle (1990: 1164), it is 'a catch-all culprit, even though the term has little analytic content and its very vagueness expresses the lack of knowledge of specific detail'. Even writers who use it admit that it is 'conceptually difficult' or '*ad hoc*' (Heaver and Israel, 1986: 1; Killick, 1998: 91). Yet it has been the centrepiece of many explanations of policy outcomes, for example in World Bank project evaluation reports (Nunberg, 1997), and is habitually invoked by policy-makers up to the level of IMF and World Bank presidents and managing directors. It remains a concept that many practitioners find indispensable.

McCourt (2003) has proposed a model of commitment which draws on political economy studies of policy reform and psychological studies of individuals' commitment to achieving personal goals. It suggests that we can estimate whether commitment to a given reform exists by assessing whether what McCourt (2007) calls the 'antecedents' of policy implementation are present (so there is a similarity with 'readiness assessment' in Kusek and Rist's (2004) monitoring and evaluation model), and then whether the policy in question contains 'elements' which will contribute to successful implementation.

Box 4.4 presents the model and applies it to civil service reform in Swaziland leading to the conclusion, in 2001, that commitment

---

Box 4.4   Commitment to civil service reform in Swaziland

Antecedents

Political capacity

Political base:	**positive:** monarchy and cabinet government were well established, and political opposition was weak
Leadership:	**positive:** Prime Minister was personally involved in reform

Administrative capacity

Reform team:	**mixed:** united, but weakened by its low profile and the loss of its director
Overall capacity	**mixed:** structures and funding were adequate, but administrative decisions regarding staff were frequently struck down by the courts

ELEMENTS

Voluntary	**positive:** programme was not imposed by a donor or other external agency
Explicit	**negative:** no firm targets had been set
Challenging	**negative:** commitment was only to carry out reviews, not to take demanding action
Public	**positive:** Prime Minister had advertised his commitment in speeches and interviews
Irrevocable	**negative:** government had an easy line of retreat from the limited action it had taken

Source: Kiragu and Mukandala, 2004.

to civil service reform was weak, and that reform was unlikely to proceed. However, the analysis was not fatalistic, and recommended making the Civil Service Board, the body responsible for civil service recruitment and discipline in Swaziland, fully independent from politicians. This would have constituted an 'irrevocable' step, that crossing of the policy Rubicon which is pre-eminently the proof of commitment. (The new constitution of 2005 in fact restored the Board's independence.)

Stakeholder maps and policy networks

We noted in our discussion of Bebbington and McCourt's (2007) political model of the policy process that an interest in the politics of policy entails an interest in policy actors. We will not discuss individual actors in this chapter, since the most significant of them – politicians, bureaucrats, the private sector and civil society – feature heavily throughout this book. The policy circle is, of course, not confined to those groups, but its membership may be nation- or issue-specific, and members' relative strength can vary over time. In the Middle East, the military has sometimes played a decisive role. Since 1958, the monarchies of Iraq, Egypt and Libya have fallen to officer-led initiatives while Syrian politics, before the civil war, which was still raging at the time of writing, focused on factional shifts within the military. In Myanmar, political changes which followed the release of opposition leader Aung San Suu Kyi in 2010 allowed parliament to flex its muscles at the expense of the executive arm of government.

But there are many countries where participation of citizens outside the elite is weak, sporadic or non-existent. Some members of the elites that have often determined policy may claim to represent the interests of the masses, but it is evident that the majority of the populations in developing countries have not enjoyed access to, or influence over, policy circles. Authoritarian regimes by definition have narrow policy circles. Democratically elected assemblies may have restricted powers or consist of members of privileged classes and dominated by family dynasties. Mass organizations have often been discouraged, made illegal or ignored by decision-makers. Coercion by state agencies or private forces has been common. The result is exclusion from the policy process of the bulk of the population in the developing world: women and subsistence farmers, both female and male, are two such groups. Perceived apathy of these populations may result from the rigours of attending to daily subsistence needs, the demands of patron-client networks, the difficulty of organization in hostile political environments and the systematic closure of policy circles by elites.

Policy actors as stakeholders

We turn from considering individual policy actors to examining clusters of actor groups, using the analytical lenses of the stakeholder and network concepts.

The concept of 'stakeholder' refers to a person, organization or group that has an interest in a particular policy. It gives us a way of mapping constellations of policy actors. Public sector pay reform in Benin in the 1990s is an interesting example of a situation where the political leadership was committed to reform, but reform still failed because important stakeholders opposed it. These included the Constitutional Court which was required to rule on the legality of the leadership's reform after it was challenged, and ultimately the voters in a general election.

Another example of stakeholder mapping is provided in Figure 4.5. It shows numerous organizations that can be considered stakeholders in relation to Bangladesh's National Social Protection Strategy (NSPS). The map plots the location of each stakeholder in terms of their degree of interest in the policy and their relative power to influence the policy.

The use of the stakeholder concept in development discourse has two important limitations. First, in the mainstream management literature where it originated, a stakeholder is defined as any grouping which 'can affect or is affected by the achievement of the organization's objectives' (Freeman, 1984: 46; see also Mitchell et al., 1997). However, the development discourse tends to confine its use to groups which can affect objectives, rather than groups which are affected. This important limitation effectively privileges the groups which have power over an organization rather than groups over which the organization has power. A second limitation of stakeholder analysis has been to treat all stakeholders as if they have equal power although the stakeholder map in Figure 4.5 shows how this can be overcome diagrammatically. Brinkerhoff and Crosby (2002) have developed a useful stakeholder matrix that deals with this.

Figure 4.5   *Institutional and context analysis for the National Social Protection Strategy (NSPS), Bangladesh*

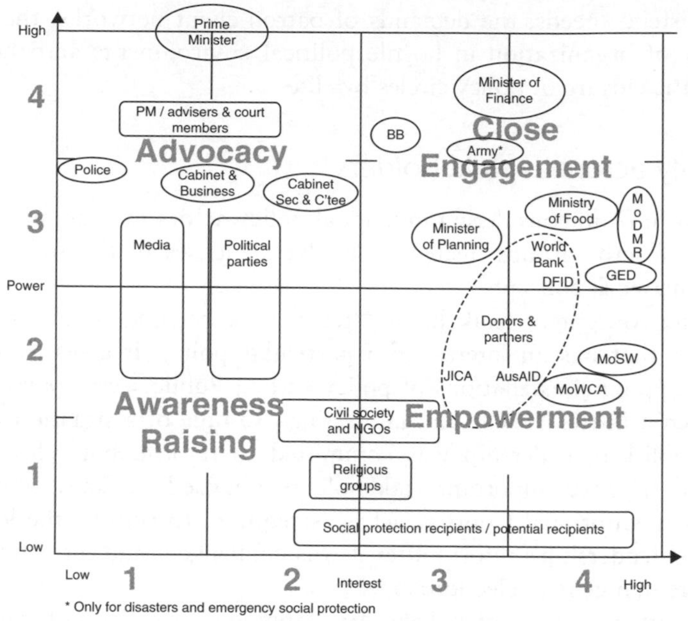

* Only for disasters and emergency social protection

Source: Koenen-Grant and Garnett (1996).

Table 4.1 is an excerpt from their analysis of stakeholders in the case of a Central Bank (they list 13 important stakeholders: we have listed only the first three). The matrix not only identifies the stakeholders but also provides a concise summary of their interests, resources and positions on the issue.

Policy networks

The second way in which we will consider clusters of actor groups is by deploying the network concept, which has been one of the most interesting theoretical developments in public management over the last decade. Our interest in them derives from the attempt in industrialized countries to cut the size of the state in the 1980s and 1990s. It had the unintended consequence of increasing the complexity of public policy through the larger number of actors who now became involved in state action. The first stage was the marketization of

Table 4.1 *Stakeholder analysis: independence for the*
Central Bank of Honduras

Group	Interest in issue	Resources available	Capacity to mobilize resources	Position on issue
Large banks	Maintain influence over central bank decisions	Economic power, high political influence, intelligence, access	Very high	−3
Foreign banks	Level playing field, objective central bank decisions	Linkages with outside banks, donor access	Very low	+2
Other banks	Avoid greater control by central bank, loose compliance	Moderate economic strength, low political influence	Low	+1

Source: Brinkerhoff and Crosby (2002).

public services through contracting them to supposedly more efficient private or voluntary providers, and the introduction of competition within the state itself, as between hospitals. As hierarchical managers found themselves rubbing shoulders with the new contractors, and also with the plethora of special purpose bodies that governments created to bypass public agencies, often seen as sluggish and politically unreliable, networks were born.

But are networks more effective than traditional bureaucratic hierarchies in the policy process? Do they deliver better results? According to Rhodes (2000), there are eight situations in which policy networks can be effective. These occur when

- Actors need reliable, thicker information,
- Quality cannot be specified or is difficult to define and measure,
- Commodities are difficult to price,
- Professional discretion and expertise are core values,
- Flexibility to meet localized, varied service demands is needed,
- Cross-sector, multi-agency cooperation and production is needed,
- Monitoring and evaluation incur high political and administrative costs, and
- Implementation involves haggling.

While Rhodes (2000) was essentially looking at rich countries, his observations can also be applied to developing countries where networks have long been evident in the policy process. However, networks may also adversely affect policy, diverting its implementation from original intentions or favouring a particular powerful interest. This means that we must also consider the potential costs of networks. These include where networks are

- Closed to outsiders and unrepresentative,
- Unaccountable for their actions,
- Serve private interests, not the public interest (at both local and national levels of government),
- Difficult to steer,
- Inefficient because cooperation causes delay,
- Immobilized by conflicts of interest, and
- Difficult to combine with other governing structures (Rhodes, 2000).

The private sector, communities and civil society have long been involved in providing public services in developing countries and have hence often been involved in policy networks. For example, in Papua New Guinea the church has been a longstanding supplier of health services. Religious and private sector organizations have played major roles in tertiary education in the Philippines while in Kenya, community or 'harambee' schools are very well established. In the past three decades, the growing importance of civil society (see Chapter 9) has meant organizations from this sector have increasingly entered policy networks on a variety of issues.

Although networks have sometimes been deliberately created in developing countries, as with the network of water users, suppliers and others in Ceará, Brazil (Lemos and De Oliveira, 2004), their increased prominence there has often been a reflection of government impotence, if not outright state failure, as non-state agencies are sucked into a service vacuum. Hence the extreme cases of NGOs standing in for a state that does not properly exist, as in Palestine, or providing what few services citizens actually receive, as in post-conflict Angola in the mid-1990s (Christoplos, 1997); and also the less dramatic but steady growth of NGOs through the 1980s and 1990s even in a stable democracy like Bangladesh (Edwards and Hulme, 1992).

Such policy networks can operate at international as well as national or local level. The matter of tropical deforestation is illustrative of this. The issue was first raised in the 1970s by epistemic or knowledge-based communities who used their research findings to influence the policy agenda. Activists politicized the issue in the 1980s. For them, 'the issue ... was not ultimately forests or dams ... but leverage over institutions that make a difference' (Perkin and Court, 2005: 23). International networks developed between Northern academics and campaigners and Southern grassroots activists bringing grassroots testimony into the debate. Both key individuals and civil society organizations played major roles. The Brazilian government, one of the targets of the non-state policy network, did not respond to local campaigners but when the latter's testimony was relayed to partner organizations in the USA the situation changed. The US organizations lobbied the US government whose influence inside the World Bank led the latter to exert pressure on the Brazilian government in a 'boomerang effect'.

Assessing policy characteristics

Brinkerhoff and Crosby (2002) have developed a simple heuristic that brings together much of the discussion in this chapter (see Table 4.2). It offers a rough-and-ready yardstick by which to assess the likelihood that a policy will be implemented, but at the expense of inevitable simplification. It is essentially a descriptive tool that provides a basis on which further analysis can build to generate greater understanding of what policies have greater chances of success, why some should be left for now and what steps might be taken to promote more effective implementation.

Conclusion

In this chapter we have examined public policy and its political context. People everywhere expect governments to make and implement policy, and there are increasing pressures for this to be done with consultation and assistance from non-state actors. There are multiple meanings to the word policy. None is wrong but we should be aware of these alternate usages and for analytic purposes adopt a

Table 4.2   *Policy characteristics checklist*

	Simplifying factor	(✓)	Complicating factor	(✓)
Where did the impetus come from?	• Inside the country • Inside government	☐ ☐	• Outside the country • Outside governmentl	☐ ☐
Who decided the policy and how?	• With democratic legislative process • With widespread participation	☐ ☐	• Without democratic legislative process • Without widespread participation	☐ ☐
What is the nature of the benefits and to whom do they accrue?	• Visible • Immediate • Dramatic	☐ ☐ ☐	• Invisible • Long term • Marginal	☐ ☐ ☐
What is the nature of the costs and who bears them?	• Invisible • Long term • Marginal	☐ ☐ ☐	• Visible • Immediate • Dramatic	☐ ☐ ☐
How complex are the changes?	• Few changes • Few decision-makers • Small departure from current practices, roles and behaviours • Limited discretion • Low technical sophistication • Low administrative complexity • Geographically concentrated • Normal pace • Single event • Low level of conflict about nature and value of changes	☐ ☐ ☐ ☐ ☐ ☐ ☐ ☐ ☐ ☐	• Many changes • Many decision-makers • Large departure from current practices, roles and behaviours • Large discretion • High technical sophistication • High administrative complexity • Geographically dispersed • Urgent/emergency pace • Permanent changes • High level of conflict about nature and value of changes	☐ ☐ ☐ ☐ ☐ ☐ ☐ ☐ ☐ ☐
Total number of ticks				

Source: Brinkerhoff and Crosby (2002: 160).

meaning in which process is emphasized. In a few East Asian countries there has been great success with development policy which has made a major contribution to rapid economic and social gains, but the 'Asian Miracle' model has been difficult to transfer to other continents, and even other Asian regions. This diversity may partially explain why various models have been applied to policy processes in developing countries. Some are state-centred and rational, emphasizing the policy stages that policy insiders go through. Others are society-centred and political, and focus on the interplay between societal actors such as classes or interest groups. We believe that both perspectives have explanatory validity, and that elements of both need to be combined to illuminate the nature of the policy process in any specific developing country. Looking at who actually makes or influences policy decisions is useful data for the policy models. There is also the question of implementation. At this stage in the policy process many political battles are fought over the allocation of scarce resources and any policy model must incorporate this reality. Indeed, politics and power permeate the entire policy process rather than rational and technical matters. To understand the policy process in the developing world you must first understand the political context, and to secure improvement in policy-making and policy outcomes it is not enough to simply increase the capacities of state bureaucracies.

There must also be action on the political front. We should move beyond the shrugging of shoulders accompanied by references to lack of political will and attempt to construct a politics of policy improvement as Thomas and Grindle (1990) have done, or canvass ways of facilitating the participation of groups outside the charmed policy circles, especially disadvantaged groups.

There are significant structural constraints on effective policy-making, but even under adverse conditions there is room for manoeuvre. Both public and private actors do have some autonomy in decision-making which means that getting more policies right is possible. Politics is not going to be removed from the policy process. Perhaps the challenge policy actors face most of all is to produce policies and outcomes which are more equitable and effective, which are viable in winning the consent of key stakeholders, and which make efficient use of scarce resources.

Chapter 5

Structuring and Managing Government Organizations for Developmental Success

The growth of bureaucracy or administrative organizations was one of the leading features of twentieth century development. Whether one looks at OECD countries, former and present communist countries or developing countries, bureaucratization was ubiquitous. While some OECD countries have invested great effort into reducing the roles of such organizations, in developing and transitional countries the bureaucracies of the state maintain high visibility and importance in the twenty-first century. Their performance is seen to be one of the major determinants of development success or failure. Our contention, in this chapter, is that the way organizations are structured and oriented to pursue their tasks has considerable influence on what they will achieve.

In the first section of this chapter we outline and review the bureaucratic model of public service organization and its 'executive agency' modification. In the second section of the chapter we present a model of strategic and staff management, and discuss to what extent management offers an alternative to structure as a way of improving service performance. Performance is the thread that unites the first and second parts: the idea that the various organizational structures and management approaches are all, in one way or another, an attempt to order the business of public agencies so that their objectives are achieved.

The bureaucracy model and its consequences

If we characterize the public sector's style of operation as 'bureaucratic', few readers will think that we are paying a compliment. As one classic study put it,

124

[Bureaucracy] evokes the slowness, the ponderousness, the routine, the complication of procedures, and the maladapted responses of 'bureaucratic' organizations to the needs which they should satisfy, and the frustrations which their members, clients, or subjects consequently endure. (Crozier, 1964: 3)

It is the image portrayed in a photograph of Writers' Building, the headquarters of the West Bengal state administration in Kolkata, taken in the 1970s by the great Indian photographer Raghubir Singh (1988). From a vantage point just below the ceiling, we see rows of clerks receding into the distance, each behind a desk, all of them hemmed in by tottering towers of overstuffed files. Nor is the image wholly outmoded in the computer age: as recently as 2004, a senior Sri Lankan civil servant complained to one of the authors that 'When you go to the PSC office, it's like a storeroom' (McCourt, 2007: 437); the PSC, or Public Service Commission, is one of the Sri Lankan government's central agencies, and it was the PSC's backlog of paper files that the officer was complaining about. Many readers will be able to supply similar mental images from their own experience.

Why would any organization, and most of all an organization set up to serve the public, want to manage its business like this? To answer that question, we need to go back to Max Weber, one of the early giants of sociology, and his observations on the professionalization of administration in the modernizing societies of the late nineteenth century. His model is still used widely as a yardstick for the degree and form of bureaucratization in societies and organizations.

For Weber, bureaucracy represented the 'rationalization of collective activities' and was 'capable of attaining the highest degree of efficiency'. It was characterized by a formal division of labour, an impersonal authority structure, a hierarchy of offices and the possibility of a career through progression through those offices, dependence on formal rules, employment based on merit and the distinct separation of members' organizational and personal lives (Gerth and Mills, 1948). There was a stage in history where bureaucracy was a progressive force, an advance on the personalized and arbitrary administration that revolved around kings and absolute rulers, as it did at the court of Emperor Haile Selassie of Ethiopia as recently as the 1970s (Kapuscinski, 1983). Even now, it has been argued that there are inherent reasons why most organizations will continue to arrange themselves into hierarchies for the foreseeable future. According to McCourt and Brunt (2013), most organizations rely on hierarchies, first, in order to minimize the 'transaction costs' (a term from economics) that otherwise arise if every employee had to relate freely to every other employee; and second, because senior managers are needed to act as arbiters between the interests of different stake-holders such as employees, clients and members of the community who are affected by the organization's activities.

State expansion and bureaucratization

The Weberian inheritance is evident in the history and the current operation of the public sector in developing countries.

> Colonial states tended to create an administrative hierarchy through the concentration of political and administrative functions in the hands of the colonial civil service. [The colonizers] went about the task of governance by establishing a bureaucratic network staffed by officers who had charge of specific duties such as revenue collection, public order, medicine, education, infrastructural organization, adjudication, social services, and even in the later colonial period, development projects. (Chazan et al., 1988: 40)

In the colonial bureaucracy, indigenous politicians were largely absent or severely restricted in their powers. The precise arrangements of the bureaucracies varied between colonial powers, but they were all designed to regulate (laws and rules) and extract (taxes and raw materials), and they were backed by coercive force. Control was the theme of colonial bureaucracy but this did not necessarily entail penetration of the routines of everyday life. Much could be left to 'traditional' institutions and indirect rule.

Those tendencies survived independence, intensifying if anything: bureaucracy has been one of the strongest institutional inheritances of post-colonial states. A study in the 1960s declared that 'The subject of bureaucracy has acquired a new lustre, a result of current concerns with the emergence of a host of new nations' (Siffin, 1966: 1). The post-independence period saw the expansion of state bureaucracies as new governments moved beyond the restricted regulatory scope of colonial administration and took on new responsibilities (for example, foreign affairs) and embarked on ambitious schemes of planned development.

New institutions were created and existing ones expanded. Within a decade of Indian independence in 1947, the government had created the Central Secretariat Service, the Central Health Service, the Central Legal Service and the Central Information Service. Then came the Indian Economic Service and the Indian Statistical Service (Maheshwari, 1990). In 1951, there were 1.529 million central government employees. By 1960 there were 2.025 million; by 1980, 3.678 million. The story at state level is similar with the number of state functionaries growing from 1.202 million in 1958 to 4.414 million in the 1980s (Maheshwari, 1990). In Malaysia, the decade of the 1970s was seen as the golden age of the civil service, when the so-called administrocrats enjoyed 'a position of power perhaps unequalled by any other civil service in a democratic country' (Puthucheary, 1987: 107). Malaysia was 'an administrative state' (Esman, 1972) or a 'bureaucratic polity' (Crouch, 1996: 199).

The expansion of the state has been beneficial in important ways. For example, under-five child mortality declined in India from 234 per 1,000 live births in 1960 to 1969 in 2008; and in Malaysia from 90 to 6 over the same period. To be sure, a number of factors outside the state's direct control contributed, including rising incomes, birth spacing and personal sanitation standards. But public services, and in this case child health interventions such as oral rehydration therapy and immunization, played a major part (Claeson et al., 2000).

Bureaucracy as 'anti-poor'

An expanding state delivering services which improve quality of life through an efficient bureaucratic structure: that is the view which is most flattering to public servants. But while he does give the bureaucracy some credit for developmental initiatives, Robert Chambers (1983) argues that in operation state bureaucracies are biased against poor people, and especially poor people living in rural areas, a specific manifestation of 'urban bias'. Chambers (1983) identified six manifestations of bias against the rural poor which derive from the way that what he calls 'rural development tourists' in government ministries, aid agencies and other urban-based groups with a stake in rural development interact with the poor. They include 'project bias' (a tendency to focus on projects which are atypical islands of activity) and 'professional bias' (a tendency to view rural poverty through an inappropriate professional lens).

Chambers (1992) went on to elaborate his criticism of public bureaucracy as 'the self-deceiving state'. He argues that the state misrepresents the reality of rural areas and persistently applies inappropriate models of rural development. The 'false positive feed-back' which fuels the self-deception occurs through misreporting, especially in the exaggeration of government performance; selected perception using unrepresentative sources; methods such as question-naire surveys which systematically mislead; diplomatic evasion by researchers, monitors and evaluators; and willful neglect of incon-venient evidence.

Bureaucracy as 'anti-politics'

Ferguson's (1990) anthropological study of the Thabo-Tseka Development Project (TTDP) in Lesotho adds to Chambers' concern. With funding mainly from the Canadian International Development Agency (CIDA) and the World Bank, TTDP ran from 1975 to 1984 with the aim of developing agriculture, particularly livestock pro-duction, in a mountainous region in the centre of the country. The lion's share of project expenditure went on upgrading infrastructure, notably the construction of a regional centre and a road linking Thabo-Tseka with the capital Maseru. There was also an attempt to decentralize services from the capital to the region.

By 1984, the project was acknowledged to have failed by most observers, and its main funder, CIDA, was pulling out. The infra-structure was in place, but there was little evidence of the planned improvement in agriculture or local incomes, and the decentraliza-tion initiative had abjectly collapsed. However, Ferguson (1990) argues, the project was still a kind of success, though not for its intended beneficiaries. By casting the region's problems in the techni-cal terms of animal husbandry and local governance rather than the political terms of Lesotho's structural dependence on South Africa and its apartheid government, for which Lesotho served as a labour reserve and a granary, it bequeathed the Lesotho state a new local apparatus of control over Thabo-Tseka. The project was, in fact, an 'anti-politics machine' which deflected attention from the politi-cal roots of the region's, and Lesotho's, problems. Its main lasting effect, remarked a development worker, was that 'Now the taxman lives down the valley rather than in Maseru' (the nation's capital). In Lesotho and many other countries including Tanzania and Zimbabwe, Ferguson (1990: 252, 257) suggests, ' "Development", insistently formulated as a benign and universal human project, has been the point of insertion for a bureaucratic power that is neither benign nor universal in its application.'

Sri Lanka's political experience of reform contrasts with Lesotho's in an interesting way as illustrated in Box 5.1. The story in Sri Lanka regarding human resource management (HRM) in the public service is one of a tug-of-war between politicians and bureaucrats to get control of HRM decision-making. As you can see in the case study, control by one or other of the contestants had specific and different

---

Box 5.1   Strengthening bureaucracy in Sri Lanka

Sri Lanka is one of the former colonies which inherited a bureaucratic structure at independence in 1948 in which appointed administrators had a great deal of power relative to elected politicians. After two decades of independence, the government felt that it should act to redress the balance. Its first step, in 1972, was to abolish the Public Service Commission (PSC), the agency responsible for appointments and promotions. The PSC was reinstated in 1978, but required to report directly to the Cabinet.

These steps were a conscious *de jure* politicization of the administration, with the aim of breaking down the elitism of the civil service and harnessing it to national developmental objectives. Their effect, unfortunately, was to turn the civil service into a vehicle for political patronage, which has been viewed as endemic in Sri Lanka (de Silva, 1993). As a civil service trade union leader remarked in an interview to one of the authors, 'From time to time politicians have recruited without considering the need to recruit ... Politicians consider that government exists to provide jobs for their supporters.'

After several ineffectual rounds of reform, the government passed a constitutional amendment in 2001 which restored the independence of the PSC. It was only possible because of the support of the Janatha Vimukthi Peramuna (People's Liberation Front), a revolutionary movement which had turned to electoral politics and was a member of the governing coalition. The reform came at the expense of increasing central bureaucratic power over civil service management. Familiar bureaucratic dysfunctions began to appear. Processing of promotions and other staffing decisions were now centralized, and slowed down accordingly. A police officer who had mugged up for his or her promotion exam, possibly at the expense of their duties, might now get promoted ahead of an officer whose boss's high opinion of their performance was discounted as 'subjective'. But most civil servants and their union representatives saw the dysfunctions as an acceptable price to pay for getting rid of political patronage, which in the police was estimated to have gone down 'from 90–100% to 5–10%' according to one knowledgeable insider.

Source: McCourt (2007).

implications for performance. It was in order to avoid similar problems to Sri Lanka that the government of Nepal drew back from a donor proposal in the late 1990s to devolve staff management responsibility from its PSC to line ministries (McCourt, 2001).

At the start of this section we wondered why any government would embrace the bureaucratic model of service delivery. We now have two opposing answers, one negative and one positive. 'To consolidate the bureaucratic power of the Centre,' say Chambers and Ferguson. 'To break the power of political patronage,' McCourt suggests. Is, then, bureaucracy a good or a bad thing? Ferguson correctly recognizes (it seems to us) that this question hinges on one's view of the state itself, and of its capacity to reform itself when it strays from its espoused objectives. Chambers is optimistic about that. Ferguson is not. For the moment we will leave the question hanging, and turn instead to a different approach to structuring public services.

Managerial devolution and executive agencies

As we saw, Ferguson's (1990) criticism of bureaucracy is that it puts power in the hands of central bureaucrats, at the expense of political struggles by or on behalf of the poor and powerless. Yet as Sri Lanka's government belatedly realized, politicians taking control of administrative decisions creates problems of its own. In a sense, managerial devolution, a central plank of the New Public Management (NPM) model of public management (see Chapter 1), is an attempt to steer between the depredations of political interference and the straitjacket of control by unaccountable central bureaucrats by delegating service delivery to a lower administrative level, turning that level into what is called an 'executive agency' in the UK (Pollitt and Talbot, 2003). Executive agencies are typically discrete activities within a government department which are placed at arm's length from the parent department: a vehicle licensing agency as an offshoot of a Department of Transport would be an example.

Executive agencies are meant to be operationally independent of the government ministry to which they relate, subject only to the objectives which the ministry hands down and the budget it prescribes – unless the agency is in the lucky position of having its own revenue source (as a vehicle licensing agency might be through its license fees). There is an important change in the relationship between the agency and the ministry. As an official who led the agency reform in the UK put it, 'We are moving from a hierarchical system to a system in which the minister and the chief executive are in a quasi-contractual position' (Sir Peter Kemp, quoted in Pollitt et al., 2004: 39). In other words, the ministry supervises its agency offshoot through a quasi-contractual performance agreement rather than through hierarchical control along Weberian lines.

Executive agencies have been created in many developing countries although their creation has often relied on aid funding from the UK. The freestanding revenue authorities which have been set up in at least 14 African and seven Latin American countries over the last quarter-century, including Bolivia, Ghana and Tanzania, have a separate origin, but share the operational autonomy which is the executive agencies' essential feature. They also have a couple of distinctive features of their own, such as discretion to pay salaries above civil service pay scales and, most notably, the objective of increasing government revenue, in a context where a large proportion of potential tax revenue was going uncollected. There has also been the objective of reducing political interference in day-to-day operations (Taliercio, 2004; Fjeldstad and Moore, 2009).

That is the theory. What has the practice been? Ministers and governments have found it hard to resist the temptation to interfere. The autonomy of Tanzania's executive agencies has been compromised by the tight grip kept by the President and his Secretary General, in a country where the centre has historically kept control even after authority has nominally been decentralized or devolved (Kessy and McCourt, 2010). In the UK, autonomy has flown out the window when ministers have felt the need to respond to a public outcry, as in the case of well-publicized escapes from what was notionally a high-security prison. This impelled the relevant minister to browbeat the chief executive of the Prisons Agency into sacking the prison governor (Polidano, 1999). In the case of Africa's revenue authorities, one might have expected that their clarity of purpose would have facilitated effective performance. However, Fjeldstad and Moore (2009) found that after an initial increase in revenue, performance dropped back. Moreover, they suggest that by creating these autonomous agencies, governments have created a new problem of coordinating tax collection with tax policy.

Ideal types and messy contexts

The executive agency model turns out to have problems of its own, just like the bureaucracy model that it seeks to improve on. A further complication is that similar organizational structures have had different outcomes in different places: as we saw, centralizing control in Lesotho and centralizing control in Sri Lanka were two very different things.

Throughout this book we emphasize that public management in any given country will be shaped by the interaction of prescriptive models and contextual factors. It was a distinctive feature of Weber's approach that he sought to identify 'ideal types' in society. But Weber was not a management consultant advocating an early version of 'best practice'. His model of an ideal type bureaucracy was built up from many observations of emerging organizational forms and the consequent identification of a pattern of particular characteristics that could be present to a greater or lesser degree. Thus, the bureaucracy he described did not exist empirically but was his creation. Since then, some have fallen into the trap of treating the analytical model as a description of reality – or, even worse, making reality conform to the model, so that the model becomes a standard that is enforced without regard for individuality. What Weber's model is very useful for is as a comparative tool by which we can assess the degree and form of bureaucratization in a society or organization.

Pollitt et al. (2004) take a similar view in their study of executive agencies in Finland, the Netherlands, Sweden and the UK. While they find common factors across the four countries, such as the widespread use of performance indicators, they find so much variation between the countries that they develop a model of 'task-specific path dependency' to account for it. They find that the new agencies have been strongly influenced by 'task-specific' factors such as the extent to which agencies are self-financing. They also find that the pre-existing pattern of relationships between the agency and its parent ministry constitutes a historical 'path' from which the agency is unlikely to deviate, despite the nominal autonomy which agency status has given it. Thus, in the Netherlands, activities which had substantial effective autonomy before being given agency status were more likely to have substantial autonomy afterwards as well.

So we see that bureaucracy and managerial devolution have had different effects in different places. Moreover, as abstractions from reality rather than faithful descriptions of reality, their practical manifestations can sharply differ. We turn now to an alternative approach to improving public service performance, the objective which every structural model has in common.

Strategic management

Improving public services: restructuring or management?

> The major lesson of the review ... is that two of the five sets of variables emerge as the most consistent influences on performance: resources and management ... The best advice to reformers may be to leave regulatory arrangements, organizational structure, size and market structure as they are ... [There is] some basis for believing that more money and better management are likely to lead to service improvement. (Boyne, 2003: 390)

We saw in the last section that managerial devolution is not a panacea, and neither is centralization, its polar opposite. Relocating decision-making, whether upwards or downwards, solves some problems – the appeal of restructuring is not wholly irrational – but at the expense of creating others, which may become evident only once the restructuring is set in cement.

Seen against that background, Boyne's review of 65 studies of public service performance, mostly from the US with a sprinkling from Western Europe, is very striking. Boyne (2003) acknowledges the data limitations in the studies he reviews, and of course they are all studies of developed rather than developing countries. Moreover, the finding of a relationship between money and service improvement will not come as a surprise to most readers: it seems that as in many walks of life, governments get what they pay for. But keeping in mind the notion of performance which is the thread running through this chapter, Boyne's (2003) conclusion that management is a more promising route to service improvement than restructuring is very significant. For the remainder of this chapter we will explore that route.

The strategic management model

In Chapter 3 we focused on the policy process. We want to emphasize now that the fact that it is a staple of the public management literature should not make us lose sight of the fact that at bottom, it is no more than an approach to setting a direction for a public agency; in other words, to specifying a goal for public management, and a route towards it. Strategic management offers an alternative approach. While it has its origin in military strategy, and therefore in the public sector (despite the use of mercenaries and private security services in some countries), the techniques of strategic management have mostly grown up in the private sector.

Strategic management assumes that the essence of work organizations is the specific purpose which they exist to fulfil, and it offers a way of clarifying and achieving it. At the risk of over-simplification, strategy boils down to a four-stage process: Purpose (or 'mission'), objectives, strategy and implementation (Armstrong, 2008). The strategic approach has three characteristics (Johnson et al., 2009):

- Strategies are achieved by using the *resources* available to the organization: this has been called the 'resource-based view of the firm' (Prahalad and Hamel, 1990)
- Having a single strategy for an organization implies an *integrated* approach to management
- Strategies are *distinctive* with organizations crafting strategies which are appropriate to their needs

We shall explore the first and second characteristics in Chapter 5 on 'managing people', where we will consider the staff of public agencies as a strategic resource, and what it might mean to manage them in an 'integrated' way. An example of the third characteristic is the Swedish home furnishings company IKEA (www.ikea.com), which has an international presence that includes developing countries like China, Malaysia, Thailand, Jordan and the Dominican Republic. It sets out its vision as follows: 'How is IKEA different from other furnishing stores? They offer a wide range, or good design and function, or low prices, while we offer all of these. That's our business idea.'

That is a 'distinctive' vision, and consciously so. It may seem very distant from the concerns of public agencies – we have deliberately chosen a private-sector example to give a flavour of strategy in the private sector where the strategic model originated – but strategic management is now widely applied in the public sector. Malaysia's ambitious 'Vision 2020' is perhaps its earliest application to the public sector in a developing country. It was formulated in 1991 under Prime Minister Mahathir Mohammad as an elaborate blueprint for a transition over a 25-year period to developed country status. It has inspired imitations in several developing countries, including Nigeria and Rwanda. It is true that its ambitious goals were not on track to be realized fully at the time of writing in part due to the adverse effects of the GFC (National Economic Advisory Council, 2009), but they had a galvanizing effect in many areas of government activity. In particular, they carried through to a series of public management initiatives which culminated in an elaborate regime of key performance indicators for government departments (Adam, 2009). Malaysia's score for 'government effectiveness' in the World Bank's Governance Index climbed from the 69th percentile among the world's countries in 1998 to the 84th percentile ten years later.

Let's look at another example in a development context. This time we will focus on a donor's, DFID's, use of strategic management (Box 5.2). As can be seen in Box 5.2, DFID conformed fairly well to our simple model of the strategic process despite its complexity, specificity and global reach: there was a mission (or 'aim'), it was translated into objectives, and then into strategies (or 'plans') which were implemented through project and programme activities.

Readers may have noticed that in large part, DFID's strategic objectives are 'read across' from the MDGs. The MDGs are worth mentioning as an example of strategic management in their own right. Essentially, they are a list of development goals and targets (Goal One, 'eradicate extreme poverty and hunger', breaks down into two targets, the first of which is 'halve, between 1990 and 2015, the proportion of people whose income is less than $1 a day'). They represent the application of strategic management on a global scale. That is no accident. The UN's adoption of the MDG strategic framework reflects the shaping influence of the OECD and its Development Assistance Committee (DAC), one of the principal players in the process that led to the MDGs. The OECD was drawing on the audit culture of the NPM that was very powerful in many OECD countries in the 1990s (Hulme, 2007).

So we see that when a developing country government was setting a policy direction at the beginning of the 1990s, and two major development agencies, DFID and the United Nations, were doing the same thing about ten years later, it was to the private sector techniques and language of strategic management that all of them turned, rather than the established policy analysis and policy process approaches which we reviewed in Chapter 4.

The 'logical framework': a tool for strategy implementation

The examples we have just discussed are at the national and international levels, but strategic management techniques are also used at the

Box 5.2   Strategic management at DFID

At the time of writing, the UK's Department for International Development, DFID, presented its mission as follows:

DFID's overall aim is to reduce poverty in poorer countries, in particular through achieving the Millennium Development Goals (MDGs)

That aim translated into seven 'departmental strategic objectives', of which the first was to 'promote good governance, economic growth, trade and access to basic services'.

As a large and complex agency, DFID had a number of separate substrategies. There was a 'country plan' for every country where DFID operates. The India Country Plan 2008–2015 was typical. It set out three themes:

- Working with *Global India* as it takes its rightful place in the world to help deliver the MDGs globally
- Supporting *Developing India* nationwide to achieve the MDGs across India
- Providing more intensive assistance to *Poorest India*, focused in the highest poverty states, and tackling gender discrimination and social exclusion

The Country Plan went on to say that it would advance those themes through education, inclusive growth, health and nutrition, and governance reform. In governance reform, it further specified that

> DFID will back reforms to help modernise government at the national level and in focus states. People will receive better training and computer systems will be installed to help make government more efficient and responsive to its citizens. And in India's expanding cities, DFID will use its experience in urban development to raise living standards in slums and then use these lessons to help inform national urban management policies.

These themes translated finally into project activities: the 'Support Programme for Urban Reforms in Bihar' is an example of DFID's support to urban development. Its components included improvements to planning and monitoring, financial management and facilitating private investment in housing and commercial activities.

Source: DFID, 2008a, 2008b, 2010, 2014.

level of individual development agencies and projects, where the 'logical framework' method – 'log frame' for short – has become widely used. Parts of a log frame produced by two of the authors for the first 18-month phase of a five-year project in one developing country appear as Table 5.1. It concerns the Public Service Commission, the body which in many former British colonies is responsible for civil service recruitment. There are many more entries in the original log frame columns than appear in Table 5.1, too many for this book. However, our purpose is to show readers the essential elements of

Table 5.1 *'Logical framework' for a project in a developing country: Public Service Commission (PSC)*

Goal	Objectively verifiable indicators	Means of verification	Assumptions
Enhancement of PSC's effectiveness so as to contribute to sustainable economic development, poverty alleviation and reduced regional imbalances.	e.g. Lower ratio of vacant to established positions in civil service.	Records at Ministry of General Administration (MGA).	Political stability.
Purpose:			**Purpose to goal**
PSC using and promoting better recruitment, selection and promotion procedures.	e.g. Time for recruitment falls.	PSC records.	PSC's autonomy is not compromised by petitions.
Outputs:			**Output to purpose**
e.g. Job analysis programme	Programme is published.	Documentation.	New systems are better than existing system.
e.g. Screening system.	System is designed and staff trained.	Documentation and observation.	Stability of senior management at PSC.

a log frame and Table 5.1 fulfils that objective. For those wishing to look at log frames in more detail, we suggest looking at the websites of bilateral donors such as DFID and AusAID.

The log frame has a four-level structure which, like DFID's strategic framework, should be recognizable in terms of the strategy process outlined in Table 5.1:

- *goal*: the overall aim of the project
- *purpose*: what the project is designed to achieve in operational terms
- *outputs*: the tangible results of the project
- *activities*: the activities which will produce those results

The advantages of the log frame are clear. It provides transparency in specifying the results that the activities or project are meant to produce. Transparency, in turn, facilitates accountability: the organization or sponsor to which the activity or project is accountable can assess relatively easily whether the activity is meeting its objectives.

Limitations of strategic management

While the strategic model has been increasingly applied in developing countries, it has its own limitations, just like the policy analysis and policy process approaches with which it is in competition. Some of them have been identified in the model's association with the private sector and the industrialized countries where it originated, and others in its development application. We shall see that they converge on common concerns.

In the private sector, Herbert Simon (1976) noted that in its extreme form, the strategic model assumes that the use of strategic techniques will give businesses complete data from which they can then 'read off' a strategy. He pointed out that in reality, data is usually incomplete, or complex even when it is complete; in the latter case our ability to grasp its full implications is limited. Strategies could only ever be partly rational. Such *bounded rationality* was the basic condition of strategic decisions. More recent research by Kahneman (2011) and others reinforces Simon's insight: we have learnt that we have inherent cognitive biases which militate against a purely mechanical application of strategic management.

Simon retained a faith in rational planning: he suggested, for instance, that strategists could become more rational by using computer-based data processing models to grasp more complex data. Writing again in the US, but this time in a public sector context, Charles Lindblom (1959) shared Simon's belief that strategists have a limited ability to absorb data, but thought that strategists should, and probably would, compensate for it by proceeding step by step: taking a single decision, assessing its effects, taking a second decision and so on. In this rather messy and fragmented way, they would 'muddle through'. Organizations could make radical changes, but they would do so in small, single steps rather than in one grand strategic leap. Lindblom (1959) called this fitful process of decision-making 'disjointed incrementalism' and believed it was an accurate description of what happened most of the time.

Henry Mintzberg (1987) took Simon and Lindblom's criticisms a step further. He argued that far from the mechanical rolling out of a pristine plan, the strategic process resembles the way a potter crafts a pot, and involves feeling, long experience, commitment and a 'fluid process of learning'. Chinese Premier Deng Xiaoping was making much the same point when he memorably described his government's conduct of economic reform as 'crossing the river by feeling the stones', an expression that will be recognized by anyone who has forded a river in bare feet, and which contrasts sharply, as it was no doubt intended to do, with the top-down thinking embodied in China's 'Great Leap Forward' of the 1950s which led to a catastrophic famine.

Similar criticisms have been levelled in a development context, especially by David Korten (1980). In his analysis of development projects in Bangladesh, India, the Philippines, Sri Lanka and Thailand, he found that when projects failed, it was often because they were planned in such unrealistic detail – something he called the 'blueprint approach' to development – that as soon as implementation began, they parted company from reality in ways that the strategists could never have predicted. He proposed a 'learning process approach' as a corrective where, rather than concentrating strategy in the planning stage, strategic thinking would take place throughout the implementation period, with continuous adjustments being made to reflect what project staff were learning as they went along.

Yet log frames and blueprint approaches are, if anything, more widely used now than they were when Korten criticized them. The way they allow observers to monitor the progress of a project almost at a glance – or at least to believe that that is what they are doing – has been attractive as monitoring and evaluation have grown in importance (see Chapter 4). In theory, any deviation is relatively easy to spot, and the project can be steered back on track. This ease of monitoring has an obvious attraction to any funder, whether a national public agency or a foreign aid provider, the latter wanting to keep tabs on how a local development agency is spending its money. A jaundiced observer of the public sector might argue that log frames are another way of bringing citizens within the clutches of the bureaucratic state (see also Kerr, 2008). These benign or devious attractions are probably powerful enough to ensure a future for log frames and blueprint approaches.

What can we conclude about the application of the strategic approach to development agencies? Certainly 'the approach best suited to any particular circumstance is dependent on the objectives of the intervention and the specific context,' as Bond and Hulme (1999: 1354) suggest. More specifically, what both blueprint and process approaches have in common is an emphasis on *strategic thinking*. They both serve to remind us that every so often we should lift our eyes from the mindless routine into which bureaucratic organizations are always prone to slip in order to ask the fundamental questions: What are we trying to do? Where are we going? How will we know when we get there? In the midst of the Allied forces' preparations for the invasion of France in 1944, American President Eisenhower remarked that 'Plans are nothing; planning is everything.' And as we suggested at the beginning of this section, strategic management is in essence a method for asking and acting on fundamental questions about the direction of public agencies.

Human resource management (HRM)

Strategic HRM and the governance effectiveness studies

We saw at the beginning of the last section that the strategic management model posits that strategies are achieved by using the resources available to the organization. Also, since organizations should have a single strategy, the strategic management model entails an integrated approach to managing those resources. Money, information, people and physical resources such as equipment are the major resources in question. In this section we will focus on people – the 'human resource' – and on what it might mean to take an 'integrated' approach to managing them.

We can usefully conceptualize human resource management (HRM) as a series of activities which roughly follow the life cycle of a job, and of the employee who does it:

- human resource planning, the activities that organizations carry out to plan the overall staffing of the organization
- job analysis/competence development, through which the content of individual jobs is identified and the knowledge and skills needed to do them
- pay (or 'reward management')
- employee selection
- performance management
- learning, training and development

We should also include employee relations, which stands outside the life cycle of jobs and employees. It is concerned with the relationship between the employer and its staff, sometimes via a trade union or unions.

All the major HRM activities have been established for at least half a century, but the attempt to conduct them 'strategically' is more recent. The strategic human resource management model (SHRM), the application of strategic management principles to HRM, is by now well documented. It has two relevant features on which most writers agree. The first is the notion of strategic integration, to which we have already referred in our outline of strategic management. Strategic integration means aligning HRM activities like recruitment and selection with organizations' overall strategic objectives ('vertical integration') and with each other ('horizontal integration') (Purcell, 1995). An example of vertical integration in relation to DFID's strategic objectives (see Box 5.2) would be for DFID to help its staff in India to upgrade their knowledge of urban development, one of DFID's priority areas, through training and development. An example of horizontal integration would be ensuring that new appointments are based on an explicit competence framework, and that staff performance is managed in its light.

The second relevant feature is 'line manager ownership'. This is HRM jargon for what we have previously called 'managerial devolution'. It refers to attempts to push HRM decisions down from upper to lower administrative levels.

The empirical evidence for the value of these HRM approaches is strong but patchy. At the level of HRM as a whole, there is good evidence of an association between 'professional' HRM approaches and organizational performance (Huselid, 1995). There is also positive evidence for the value of strategic integration (Becker and Gerhart, 1996), though not line manager ownership. Among the individual activities, the positive evidence for sophisticated selection methods such as assessment centres is exceptionally strong (Schmidt and Hunter, 1998), but at the other extreme we have no evidence at all about the value of different approaches to employee relations. Indeed, since those approaches are rooted in different views of what the balance between employers and employees ought to be, there is basic disagreement about what effective employee relations should look like.

All of this evidence comes from industrialized countries, especially the US and the UK, and especially the private sector. However, some of it is corroborated by a group of studies that have converged in the last ten years on the public bureaucracy as an enabler of economic growth in developing countries. The World Bank commissioned the first of them in the run-up to the 1997 *World Development Report*. Alluding to Weber's bureaucracy model, its authors constructed a 'Weberian' scale of the quality of public bureaucracy, and found a statistical relationship between public bureaucracy and economic growth. Their data suggested that merit-based recruitment was the most important factor, followed by promotion from within and career stability for public servants, with salaries that were competitive with the private sector coming some way behind (Evans and Rauch, 1999).

A little later, Daniel Kaufmann (1999), again under World Bank auspices, constructed a governance index in which bureaucracy was one of three components of 'government effectiveness', which in turn was one of six components of his overall model. His evidence suggested that government effectiveness was actually one of the causes of higher national income. Moreover, the business people in developing and transitional countries whose opinions Kaufmann and his colleagues drew on ranked government effectiveness ahead of economic factors like high inflation and distortions in the exchange rate régime, and behind only control of corruption in its importance to the success of their businesses.

Finally, a UN-sponsored study found that public agencies in Africa do better – they provide better services, and are less corrupt and more responsive to private sector concerns – if the staff they employ are paid well and have access to internal promotion that is not distorted by patronage, and if they have a decent amount of autonomy from the centre of government (Court et al., 1999).

As usual, there are data limitations in all the studies we have discussed above. Different studies of HRM and organizational performance use different models of HRM. The World Bank's governance index leans heavily on surveys produced for overseas investors which mostly rely on self-report data. And the SHRM and bureaucracy studies are not wholly consistent, as is to be expected when they emphasize different aspects of HR. However, taken together these heterogeneous and imperfect findings do provide powerful suggestive evidence that an investment in staff management could have a beneficial effect on service quality.

HRM in developing country governments: the 'human factor' study

What notice have governments taken of that 'powerful' evidence? That is the question posed by McCourt (2006) in a book which studies the way governments manage their employees in seven developing countries (Malaysia, Mauritius, Morocco, Namibia, Sri Lanka, Swaziland and Tanzania).

Strategic management

At the level of strategic management, it was found that the basic strategic framework was widely applied at the time of the study, with all the countries having at least the basic apparatus of mission statements, apart from Morocco, the Francophone exception. In the majority of them, however, strategies existed only on paper in central and line ministries: they were not living realities. Underneath them, hand-to-mouth management continued much as before. Where strategy was real, as in Malaysia and Namibia, it made a positive difference. Namibia's success in creating and training a cadre of enrolled nurses was a direct outcome of its national primary health care strategy. Malaysia's 'Vision 2020' led to the creation of central strategic agencies, and to the introduction of performance indicators.

Strategic integration

The question of strategic integration only arises if an overall strategy already exists. In the countries where strategy was rudimentary at best, namely all but Malaysia and Namibia, it is not surprising that there was little evidence of integration. But even in Malaysia and Namibia, integration was piecemeal. From time to time a policy area would become important – such as Total Quality Management (TQM) in Malaysia and HIV/AIDS in Namibia – and the government would demand a HRM response. This was very different from the systematic and comprehensive HR strategy of the textbooks, with its point-by-point correspondence with organizational strategy. Moreover, those piecemeal responses were not usually initiated by HR specialists in government, and might even bypass them completely; the professional HR function was characterized by unimaginative rigidity. From the insouciance of a HR official in Mauritius whose response to our question about major HR initiatives was 'Well, have there been any?' to Morocco's 'finicky' Civil Service Ministry (as a donor evaluation described it) with its consuming interest in enforcing regulations, the picture was of central agencies dedicated to policing conformity rather than promoting a professional service function to facilitate improved performance.

Line manager ownership

One reason why strategic integration was usually piecemeal at best was the typically centralized but also fragmented structure of HRM. In most countries all significant decisions were made by the centre. Surprisingly, line ministry officials on the receiving end were as often reassured as frustrated by this. Awareness of bureaucratic pathologies was often outweighed by the belief that central management was a bulwark against political influence. A well-known study by Crook and Manor (1998) found that while decentralization might initially increase corruption, in the long run it tended to decrease it as local scrutiny began to operate. But in McCourt's 2006 study, few civil servants or civil service unions saw it that way.

A complicating factor is that given the size and complexity of government, HRM responsibility was parcelled out among several agencies even when it was concentrated at the centre. Table 5.2 is, in Weber's terms, an 'ideal-type' picture of this division of labour, based on the Commonwealth model. This balkanized structure made strategic integration all but impossible, as each agency had its own priorities, and especially the Commonwealth PSCs, whose roles were fixed by national constitutions. At a more basic level, fragmentation often meant duplication of functions.

Table 5.2 *Responsibility for HR in Commonwealth central government agencies*

Agency	Functions
Office of the Prime Minister	Overall government policy
Ministry of Finance	Pay and pensions
Ministry for the Civil Service	Deployment and conditions of service for public servants
Public Service Commission	Appointment, promotion, transfer and discipline
National Administrative Staff College	Training and development

HRM *activities*

At the level of the HRM activities such as employee selection, most governments were much more concerned with integrity than quality. Sri Lanka's experience, discussed earlier in this chapter, highlights this point. In re-establishing the PSC as an independent constitutional body, the government opted to make integrity its exclusive objective. The system was less efficient than before and sophisticated selection methods were ruled out. But the civil service unions and most central officials considered that an acceptable price to pay. Likewise, determination to prevent line managers from making nepotistic or communalist decisions about their employees' pay or promotion meant that performance management was usually reduced to 'an annual ritual of stocktaking', in the words of a Mauritian government report.

Reflecting on the experience of the seven countries which he studied, McCourt (2006) proposed a two-stage normative model of HRM. In it, governments that need to concentrate on the integrity of staffing (such as in Sri Lanka and Swaziland) work through a first stage of strengthening the institutional framework and inculcating a bureaucratic culture of rule-following, while governments in countries where lapses of integrity are exceptional rather than systemic can concentrate on improving staff performance, possibly using a modified SHRM model so to as to improve the quality of public services (such as Malaysia and Namibia).

Conclusion

In this chapter we have reviewed some experiences with two contrasting approaches to service improvement: the structural approach, through the bureaucratic model and managerial devolution; and the management approach, focusing on strategic management and its strategic human resource management sub-set. Neither of the approaches is a panacea although we feel a little more confident about the potential of the management approach, but even it is fraught with problems. Perhaps the fundamental problem is that all of these 'ideal-type models' mutate as soon as they interact with the environments into which they are introduced, and it is impossible to predict what form the interaction will take because it is impossible to specify which features of the environment will be operative. Thus, returning to the question that we posed at the end of our discussion of the bureaucratic model, it is not meaningful to say whether bureaucracy or any of the other models is a good or a bad thing in the abstract.

That is inconvenient, but it should be no surprise in the light of our discussion of the policy process in Chapter 4, where we quoted the German field marshal Helmuth von Moltke's remark that no battle plan survives contact with the enemy in order to make the point that policies rarely survive contact with reality unaltered. Even within this chapter we have seen David Korten, Henry Mintzberg and, for that matter, Deng Xiaoping making essentially the same point about the application of strategies. It turns out that strategies are distinctive not only in their content, as Johnson et al. (2009) indicated, but also in the process by which they are arrived at and implemented.

There is no need to be nihilistic here. Models of organizational structure and management do have a great deal to offer us. But in order to capitalize on them we will need to adapt them to the environments into which we introduce them. Models are made to meet the needs of people, and not the other way round. There will probably always be a need for public managers to exercise analytical skill, judgement and flexibility so that models such as those we have discussed in this chapter do make a positive contribution to public service quality.

Chapter 6

Administrative and Civil Service Reform

In the early days of what we have come to call the New Public Management (NPM), one of the models which we review in this chapter, there was a great deal of discussion about whether managing in the public and private sectors was essentially the same thing. There are similarities, to be sure. For one thing, the permanent revolution of civil service reform in public management has the same restless, unremitting quality as 'continuous improvement' in the private sector. But where continuous improvement was a technique for staying ahead of the competition in the private sector – one of its key handbooks has the sub-title 'the key to Japan's competitive success' (Imai, 1986), civil service reform has been a response to changes in the political and economic environment. In development, it is convenient to date those changes from the independence of countries in Africa and Asia from the 1940s onwards, starting with independence itself in the political sphere, and with other changes in the subsequent decades such as the economic crisis that resulted from the oil price shocks of the 1970s. As we shall see, as a response to those changes, civil service reform has had a very different dynamic from management improvements in the private sector, even though borrowing methods from the private sector (a large part of what constitutes NPM) has been one of the responses to external change. In this chapter we review and analyse the experience of administrative and civil service reform in developing countries.

Civil service reform as administrative problem-solving

As the fields of public sector practice and analysis are cluttered with similar-sounding terminology we need to define the meaning of the term that is the focus of this chapter – civil service reform. It involves 'interventions that affect the organization, performance and working conditions of employees paid from central, provincial or state government budgets' (GSDRC, 2013). We take a problem-solving approach, viewing the different reform interventions as ways of dealing with the problem situation as different national governments have defined it. We have borrowed 'problem situation' from Karl Popper (1989: 129; see also Fritz et al., 2009; Andrews, 2013). Popper (1989: 129) argues that at any given point in the history of science, there is an agenda which arises from problems which current theories have created: 'You pick up, and try to continue, a line of inquiry which has the whole background of the earlier development of science behind it.' Similarly, at any given point in the development of public administration in a particular country, there is an agenda of problems which confronts national policy-makers and other stakeholders.

We emphasize 'national governments'. It is their preoccupations and not development agencies', or domestic civil society's either, which will be at the centre of our analysis. Certainly, much domestic policy-making in our globalized world is informed by international policy models and by the experience of governments elsewhere which are regarded as role models. But our thinking is unapologetically state-centred on democratic principle – because governments are elected by their own people, but other actors are not – and on pragmatic grounds, because as we shall see later, governments only reform when they want to: donors and reform advocates can take the horse to water, but they can't make it drink. It is also because even in low-income countries, it is governments which control the most powerful levers of deliberate social and economic change. We recognize that governments' and other stakeholders' preoccupations often coincide: that, after all, is what 'development assistance' is supposed to mean in the case of the development agencies.

And so we view reform as having its origin in problems which a government poses to itself or which circumstances thrust upon it. Abstracting from the practice of developing country governments over recent decades, we identify six major problems (see Table 6.1); and, at the cost of schematization, we list major reform approaches which we regard as attempted solutions

There is nothing new in the idea that governments will tailor approaches to suit their circumstances. Nunberg (1997: 14) and Turner (2002a), among others, have argued similarly. Still, this simple problem-solving approach provides a convenient structure for this chapter. Readers, however, should not take it too literally. When

Table 6.1 *Civil service reform problems and approaches*

Problem	Approach	Main action period
1. How can we put government on an orderly and efficient footing?	'Weberian' public administration and capacity-building	Post-independence period in Asia and Sub-Saharan Africa
2. How can we get government closer to the grassroots?	(Administrative) decentralization	1970s to present
3. How can we make government more affordable?	Pay and employment reform	1980s and 1990s
4. How can we make government perform better and deliver on our key objectives?	New Public Management	1980s to present
5. How can we make government more honest?	Integrity and anti-corruption reforms	1990s to present
6. How can we make government more responsive to citizens?	'Bottom-up' reforms	Late 1990s to present

faced with a list like ours, some or many policy-makers will say, 'I want it all!' And governments do frequently try to solve more than one of these problems at the same time, and may use a mixture of approaches as they do so. In the late 1990s, the new democratic government in South Africa was trying to make government more responsive and more affordable at the same time, with its flagship 'Batho Pele' (People First) reforms, aimed at creating and improving public services, coinciding with its 'Ghostbusters' and other initiatives aimed at reducing the civil service headcount, especially in the former 'homelands' such as the Transkei whose payrolls had been padded by the former apartheid government. More recently, in Indonesia, the government launched its ambitious Grand Design for Bureaucratic Reform involving a wide range of initiatives that promised to create an efficient and effective First World civil service between 2010 and 2025.

Our warning against a literal reading also applies to what historians call the 'periodization' of the third column in our table. Governments did not suddenly discover honesty in the 1990s, and particular governments (such as Morocco's) were embarking on pay and employment reform for the first time in the 2000s. However, there have been periods when particular questions have preyed on many policy-makers' minds. Public policy issues arise in the order they do partly because external shocks like the oil price rises of the 1970s thrust them onto policy-makers' attention and also because they are what others are doing. But they also arise as reactions to the unintended consequences of the previous generation of reforms (here again we follow Popper, for whom managing unintended consequences was the essence of public policy). The bureaucratization that was the unintended consequence of Weberian public administration created the need for decentralization. The expansion of state capacity had the unintended consequence of creating a fiscal burden which pay and employment reform was framed to relieve. Moreover, just as our grouping of civil service reform approaches in terms of policy questions provides a convenient structure for the chapter, so our periodization gives us a convenient order in which to address the approaches.

In this chapter we will not deal with all six of the problems. Problems Two and Five are dealt with elsewhere in this book. That leaves Problems One, Three, Four and Six, which we shall discuss in turn.

'Weberian' public administration and capacity-building

The public administration ideal in developing countries is essentially the classic Weberian model of bureaucracy harnessed to the needs of the developmental state. Weber located its origins, for both the public and private sectors, in the growth and complexity of the tasks of modern organizations, the rationalization of societal life and democratization, the latter creating an expectation that citizens, and members of an organization, would be treated equally.

Its main features are:

- A separation between politics and elected politicians on the one hand and administration and appointed administrators on the other
- Administration is continuous, predictable and rule-governed

- Administrators are appointed on the basis of qualifications, and are trained professionals
- There is a functional division of labour, and a hierarchy of tasks and people
- Resources belong to the organization, not to the individuals who work in it
- Public servants serve public rather than private interests (Minogue, 2001)

Administration tends to be highly centralized: the model posits an unbroken hierarchical chain from the top (in the capital) to the bottom (in the remotest outpost of government). The tendency is to focus on *inputs*, in the sense of the efficient management of resources rather than *outputs* in the sense of the goods and services that the resources are used to produce, let alone *outcomes* in the sense of the social and economic results that derive from the outputs.

For Weber, the bureaucratic model was the efficient successor to patrimonial regimes which had centred on the personal power of an absolute ruler. He did not anticipate that bureaucracy and patrimonialism would spawn a hybrid which has been called 'neopatrimonialism', where state resources are diverted for patronage purposes such as securing support in an election. This neopatrimonial hybrid is widespread, having been identified in modern times in places as far apart as Greece, Sri Lanka and Chicago in the US (Campbell, 1964; Clapham, 1982). It is especially pervasive in developing countries where it has maintained a tenacious grip and a facility to adapt to changing circumstances such as the developmental state (Kelsall, 2011; Booth and Golooba-Mutebi, 2012) although it is still more often associated with kleptocracy, inefficiency and corruption (Médard, 2002; Turner et al., 2013).

Capacity-building

A distinctive feature of public administration in developing countries is that unlike rich OECD countries, where it generally evolved gradually, developing countries have put in place crash programmes of capacity-building following independence and, more recently, armed conflict and economic crisis. The programmes have centred on staff training and development. The assumption is that public administration is deficient because public administrators lack skills which can be readily imparted through training activities. The training and visit system for agriculture extension workers was a typical example. In the context of a fixed programme of field visits overseen by their supervisors, extension workers received frequent one-day training sessions to impart the three or four most important agricultural recommendations that they should pass on to farmers in the following few weeks.

There is no doubt that capacity affects performance, as even politically oriented studies such as Nelson's (1990) recognize. But we have learned that capacity-building is rarely effective in an organizational vacuum. Interventions to address poor performance must be designed on the basis of an assessment of the context in which performance takes place. Capacity-building at the individual level usually takes place away from the workplace. Learning designs need to make a bridge from training to the 'action environment' of work – its organizational culture, management practices and communication networks – in the form of action plans, supervisor involvement and post-training review arrangements (Grindle and Hilderbrand, 1995; McCourt and Sola, 1999).

Pay and employment reform

In May 2011, the BBC World Service reported that a civil service audit conducted by the consultancy firm Ernst Young in November 2009 had found 13,000 out of Zimbabwe's 180,000 civil servants were absent, and that 75,000 civil servants lacked the qualifications they needed to do their jobs. The sub-text was that this was further evidence of the iniquity of Zimbabwe's government. Thus, the report referred to 'the military and supporters of President Robert Mugabe (being) accused of systematically assaulting those believed to have voted for his rival, Morgan Tsvangirai' (BBC, 2011).

The audit report was leaked, so at the time of writing we had no way of verifying it. But even if the Zimbabwe government's behaviour was as iniquitous as it was portrayed, it was by no means unique. In Zimbabwe's neighbour, South Africa, the ANC liberation movement also faced a problem of corruption in the late 1990s in the form of 'ghost workers', though it was a problem which they inherited from the white apartheid government, which allowed the 'homeland' administrations to pad their payrolls with impunity.

'Pay and employment reform' refers to measures that governments have taken to alter the employment and payment of their staff, typically within some larger programme of macroeconomic reform. It is easy to demonstrate its importance. Firstly, between 1987 and 1996 the World Bank assisted no fewer than 68 developing and transitional countries with civil service reform programmes (Nunberg, 1997), a large figure which excludes those countries that have reformed under their own steam. 'Reform' is often a euphemism, since in practice the most prominent measure has been job reduction or retrenchment, with which reform has frequently been synonymous. Indeed, had we been writing this chapter ten years ago, many readers, especially readers based in developing countries, may have assumed that retrenchment *was* civil service reform.

In the mid-1990s, a World Bank advisor boiled employment reform down into a series of 14 steps (see Box 6.1). It should be self-evident that the list in Box 6.1 is in ascending order of political difficulty. It will be very hard to make civil servants redundant against their will, and governments have almost always tried to avoid it fearing the political backlash such action could generate. But what of the other measures? Specific aspects of them are discussed below.

Box 6.1   Fourteen steps to employment reform

1. Measures to avoid redundancy:
   - human resource planning
   - job flexibility
   - retraining
   - redundancy procedures
2. Remove ghosts
3. Book transfers
4. Delete empty posts
5. Enforce retirement ages
6. Introduce part-time and flexible working
7. Appoint new staff on temporary contracts
8. Natural wastage/ recruitment freezes
9. Suspend automatic advancement
10. Redeployment
11. Voluntary redundancy
12. Privatization/contracting out
13. Freeze salaries
14. Compulsory redundancy

Source: Adapted from Nunberg (1994).

Measures to avoid redundancies

Systematic approaches to avoiding redundancy, a mainstay of personnel practice in rich OECD countries have not been very widely used in developing countries. In the latter, the human resource planning function is often weak, making an orderly reduction in jobs difficult to achieve. Governments have sometimes taken *ad hoc* measures in order to forestall redundancies, especially in Eastern Europe. Five million workers in Russia had their hours cut in 1994 and an additional 7.4 million were placed on involuntary leave. In fact, only 40 per cent of workers there were paid in full and on time in that year (Klugman and Braithwaite, 1998).

Identifying ghost workers

Ghost workers are those personnel whose names are on the payroll and for whom somebody pockets their pay but who don't actually exist. Hunting such ghosts has been a major preoccupation of African governments. One official involved in a 'ghost-hunting' expedition in Malawi even reported finding an entire 'ghost school' with an impressively complete complement of head teacher, teachers and other staff and lacking only a basis in reality. The scale of the problem can be substantial. Ghana eliminated 11,000 ghosts in 1987/1988; by 1997 Uganda had identified no fewer than 40,000 (McCourt, 1998); and, in the Indian capital of Delhi, it was found that US$43 million per year was being paid each year for 22,000 workers who did not exist (BBC, 2009).

Book transfers

This is about removing paid staff from the official books. They have accounted for some ostensible reductions. A significant proportion of the reduction in numbers in Uganda, for instance, was achieved through transfers; for instance, through setting up the Uganda Revenue Authority which took a large number of staff off the books of the traditional public service. 'Book transfers' are, of course, a futile measure, since there is no net saving. But they have still been popular because they allow the ministry from which the employees are moving to look like it's getting tough with its payroll spending.

Deleting empty posts

This has had the effect of removing posts which may have been vacant for some time but which are still listed in the staffing 'establishment'.

Enforcing retirement ages

This has also made a contribution to numbers reduction. In Tanzania, claims by some local government officers that they were still under the official retirement age were so widespread that government felt obliged to ban officers from producing affidavits for that purpose.

Voluntary redundancy

This has been perhaps the most widely used, but also the most unsatisfactory job reduction method. Although in theory voluntary redundancy (VR) should be targeted at staff whose jobs or skills are redundant, in practice the staff who opt to leave are often those one can least afford to lose, as in Sri Lanka (Grindle and Hilderbrand, 1995). Voluntary (and also compulsory) redundancy has been the largest factor in the cost of reform, which is discussed below.

Compulsory redundancy

Although there is reliable evidence for only certain countries, it appears that compulsory redundancy has accounted for only a modest proportion of job reductions in many countries, contrary to the popular image. In Uganda, only 14,000 of the 160,000 job reductions came through compulsory redundancy. Even several years after the fall of the Berlin Wall, in the transitional economies of Eastern Europe public employers were still tending to take a soft line on redundancy, although overall unemployment had definitely increased.

One difficulty in this context was that governments did not always distinguish correctly between compulsory redundancy and disciplinary dismissal. In Ghana, Tanzania and Uganda, many job losses fell into the latter category, as governments removed people identified as incompetents or sometimes, more colourfully, as 'drunkards'. Senior officials in Uganda admitted that the quality of information on which these dismissals were based was weak, leading to unfairness. Staff dismissed in this way are likely to be stigmatized as 'lemons', casting a blight on their re-employment prospects. In rich OECD countries individuals have needed up to five years to eradicate such stains on their reputations.

Privatization and contracting out

In our context, privatization and contracting offer the politician the best of both worlds: a substantial reduction in the number of public jobs is achieved while the service remains intact. Privatization accounted for the lion's share of job reductions in the UK in the 1980s while contracting out was the largest single factor in job reduction in the 1990s (HMSO, 1996). However, there are also political difficulties: privatization and contracting out will almost certainly be opposed by the staff of the public agencies affected, who may mobilize opposition through trade unions. They may also be opposed by the public at large, who fear that they will result in cuts in services, lower quality services or (higher) charges for the same services. Such political unpopularity and the threat to patronage networks also contributes to the lesser use of such measures in developing countries.

There are sometimes legal restrictions affecting the transfer of activities from the public to the private sector. In the member countries of the European Union, there are regulations which often require a private sector contractor who has won the contract to supply a service previously provided by a public agency to employ the agency's staff on their existing terms and conditions of employment. Zimbabwe's contracting out of rubbish collection would almost certainly be covered by those restrictions.

Pay reform

Governments have identified five principal problems with pay (we are applying our problem-solving approach once again here), which they have tackled in different ways. They are listed in Table 6.2.

Across the board pay rises

With evidence of a link between low pay on the one hand and the incidence of corruption and 'moonlighting' (Van Der Gaag et al., 1989;

Table 6.2   *Pay problems and solutions*

Problem	How the problem has been tackled
Inadequate pay at every level	Across-the-board pay rises
Opaque remuneration systems	Consolidation of remuneration
Unclear link between pay and responsibilities	Job evaluation
Unclear link between pay and performance	Performance-related pay
Insufficient pay to retain employees with scarce skills	Pay decompression and pay differentials

World Bank, 1997) on the other, many governments have set the objective of increasing the pay of their public servants. Their success in doing so, however, has been uneven. Pay fell somewhat as a proportion of GDP per capita in developing countries as a whole in the period when reform was at its height, roughly from the early 1990s to early 2000s. Real wages declined over the reform period in nine of the 18 developing countries studied by Abed et al. (1998) on behalf of the IMF, although there were significant rises in a few countries, notably Bolivia and Uganda. Among transitional countries in Eastern Europe, there have been numerous problems with both the value and the payment of wages. Wage freezes have been sometimes been used to avert redundancies, as in the Czech Republic's coalmining industry (Pavlinek, 1998). Budgetary difficulties have also led to wage arrears, which in 1997 were estimated to be running at an average of 122 per cent of the monthly pay bill in four industrial sectors in Russia (Clarke, 1998). Thus the aspirations of governments to improve the pay of their employees have not been realized in any consistent way.

Consolidation of remuneration

Especially in developing countries, housing, transport and other benefits have sometimes been worth as much as the nominal wage. The pay compression ratio between the highest- and the lowest-paid staff of 1:6.8 in Uganda changed to 1:100 after non-monetary allowances and benefits were included (Government of Uganda, 1994). The opaqueness of remuneration in such countries is exacerbated by the difficulty of calculating some of its elements, notably the provision of free housing. There has therefore been a move to consolidate and monetize the remuneration package in some countries, replacing non-monetary benefits such as housing with a single, somewhat increased wage.

Linking pay and responsibilities

Some governments have taken steps to put the grading and relative pay of their staff on a more 'rational' footing. This has often been done through the technique of job evaluation, which we can define as 'the determination of the relative worth of jobs as a basis for the payment of differential wages and salaries'.

In many developing countries pay is based largely on qualifications and seniority, rather than on responsibility. Job evaluation aims to correct this imbalance, giving a more justifiable basis for pay differentials. Job evaluation can also help avoid gender discrimination in pay. Job evaluation has been used in countries like Lesotho, South Africa and Tanzania, normally with donor-funded consultancy support. The technical nature of job evaluation can cause problems: a review of one such scheme in South Africa found that while it was effective in its own terms, the technical nature of the scheme created problems of sustainability once the consultants had withdrawn.

Linking pay and performance

Finding effective ways of linking pay and performance to boost productivity is the holy grail of many public sector organizations across the world. But few if any have located the treasure. The search has been most intense in OECD countries but developing countries have also been swept up in pay and performance fever. For example, in the tiny Pacific islands state of Vanuatu efforts to introduce performance agreements in the 2000s encountered strong political opposition among senior bureaucrats and sank beneath the ocean waves while a predecessor in Samoa was implemented successfully (O'Donnell and Turner, 2005). But relatively few developing countries have made the link between pay and performance, though rather more have floated the idea. This is because of problems of capacity and fairness. PRP decisions are only as good as the judgements of staff performance ratings (normally deriving from some form of performance appraisal system) on which they are based, and such ratings are often inaccurate or biased, especially in countries where nepotism prevails. It is notoriously difficult to quantify the performance of public servants in the way that such a system requires – even the World Bank as an employer seems to find it hard (Reid, 1997). In Malaysia, the civil servants' union is predictably hostile, but privately so too are some senior officials (McCourt and Lee, 2007). The experience of Malaysia, a country that has gone further down the performance-related pay path than most other developing countries is set out in Box 6.2.

Decompressing and differentiating pay

Public sector pay policies in many developing countries shared a common trajectory following independence. Adopting an egalitarian ethos, many took steps to reduce the differential between the highest

---

Box 6.2   Performance-related pay (PRP) in Malaysia

Among developing countries, Malaysia has probably gone furthest in linking pay to performance. Performance-related pay (PRP) in Malaysia was introduced in 1992 as a major feature of the New Remuneration System in an attempt to achieve a 'shift in the work culture' of civil servants. The government had launched a national development policy which aimed to distribute wealth through economic growth, and had identified a number of strategic needs for the civil service in terms of responsiveness, flexibility, innovation and ethical behaviour, and PRP was supposed to support the necessary changes in behaviour.

The new approach had strong political backing: Prime Minister Mahathir chaired the committee which produced the system. PRP awards are made following the annual performance appraisal interview, and are based on a manager's assessment of performance against objectives (called 'work targets' in the Malaysian system) which have previously been set jointly by manager and employee, in the context of overall objectives for their department.

Larger pay increases are given to employees whose performance is rated as high. Each department has a quota for how many employees can enjoy accelerated salary progression: a manager's rating of an employee as outstanding may not be endorsed if the department's quota has been exceeded. The scheme was revised in 2004 to reduce the discretion of managers, who had been accused of favouritism by the civil servants' union, and the scheme is now well established and stable.

Source: McCourt and Lee (2007).

paid (who in the colonial period were almost invariably expatriates) and lowest paid. Zambia is a typical example: the 'decompression ratio' there reduced from 17:1 to 3.7:1 between 1971 and 1986 (Lindauer, 1994). From the early 1980s onwards, some governments acted to reverse that trend. Thus, in Ghana the decompression ratio changed from 2.2:1 in 1984 to 10:1 in 1991 (Burton et al., 1993), and in 1993 the government of Tanzania set the target of raising its compression ratio from 5.74:1 to 12:1 (Stevens, 1994).

Transitional countries in Eastern Europe have experienced one of the biggest and fastest increases in inequality ever recorded, according to Milanovic (1998). However, here it is the external comparison between public and private wages rather than the internal compression ratio between the highest and the lowest paid within the public sector which is significant.

Another form of pay separation is paying more to staff, not necessarily the most senior, who have scarce skills, such as doctors and accountants. It is possible to use job evaluation (see above) to bring this about, or to do it through pay decentralization. Pay decentralization has not been very widely attempted in developing countries, partly because of the heavy load that it places on fragile administrative capacity (Nunberg, 1995). Moreover, and despite all the above, public opinion in at least some countries stubbornly continues to favour narrowing rather than widening the earnings gap between senior and other staff. Public opinion was reflected in decisions by governments in Malaysia and Myanmar to grant across-the-board rises to their public servants in 2012 (see also Robinson, 1990).

There are basic conceptual problems with the compression ratio. In the World Bank and IMF, it is defined as the ratio between the top and bottom earners, whereas the OECD defines it as the ratio between the medians of the bottom and top deciles (i.e. 10 per cent) in the wage distribution, which tends to lower the ratio. In addition, setting the 'right' compression ratio is clearly a subjective judgement. Information about wage movements in the external labour market would make it less arbitrary, but such information is often unavailable in developing countries. The extent of wage compression is in any case hard to determine, since the allowances which tend to be paid disproportionately to senior officials complicate the picture, as we have seen already; and allowances are included or excluded almost at whim in different analyses. Moreover, from a mainstream Human Resources (HR) perspective, the emphasis on the ratio between the top and the bottom earners is idiosyncratic. HR practice focuses instead on the *differentials* between adjacent salary grades, on the assumption that motivation and discretionary effort are keenly affected by those differences, of which individual staff can have an exquisite awareness (the senior teacher who may feel that the small salary increment for a head teacher does not justify the extra work of a head teacher, or the supervisor who resents the fact that a subordinate is actually bringing home more than the supervisor). Staff may be wholly unaware of – and their motivation, in consequence, unaffected by – the compression ratio between their organization's chief executive and its bottom earner: the organization's gardener, say.

New Public Management (NPM)

The concept and practice of NPM was mentioned in Chapter 1 in our review of development management history. Now, we return to it for further scrutiny. In development circles, NPM has sometimes been used as shorthand for 'whatever the World Bank and the IMF did to the public sector in developing countries' (see for example Batley and Larbi, 2004). The version that appears in the OECD's (1995) review of public management developments is a more accurate reflection of the reforms carried out in OECD countries from the early 1990s onwards. It has the advantage of being based on an empirical survey and having an operational form. It has the following elements:

- devolving authority, providing flexibility
- ensuring performance, control and accountability
- developing competition and choice
- providing responsive service
- improving the management of human resources
- optimizing information technology
- improving the quality of regulation
- strengthening steering functions at the centre

The list is heterogeneous. However, we can identify a thread running through it if we contrast it with the public administration doctrine which it implicitly criticizes. As we have just seen, that doctrine was concerned with emphasizing regular, predictable and rule-governed behaviour. It assumed that if a sound framework of rules was put in place and public servants were persuaded to adhere, adequate performance would follow. But the governments that went down the NPM road were setting their sights on better rather than adequate performance. Since continuing pressure to restrain public expenditure meant that better performance could be bought only up to a point, and since there were limits on the extent to which the stimulus of competition could be applied to public services, the application of management techniques, especially those from the private sector, became the formula deployed to square the circle of government that worked better while costing no more, or not much more (Pollitt, 1993).

What has NPM looked like in practice? We have already dealt with 'devolving authority' in the section above on administrative decentralization. In the limited space available, we shall discuss two of the other items on the OECD list: improving performance (rather than 'ensuring' it as the OECD aspires to do: perhaps we lack ambition!) and providing responsive service.

Improving performance

The NPM approach to ensuring performance hinges on the formulation and measurement of performance indicators. In the early days of NPM, such indicators usually addressed the internal operations of individual agencies. In a typical example, Denmark's national library undertook to increase productivity by 10 per cent, increase the number of transactions by 2.5 per cent annually and put purchases prior to 1979 on computer by the end of 1996 (OECD, 1995: 35). Subsequently, the technology of monitoring performance has grown sophisticated, with performance management indicators that are outcome- rather than output- or input-based, and which generate elaborate performance data. Performance management is widely practised by international development agencies; in a sense, the Millennium Development Goals are performance management on a global scale (Goldsmith, 2011).

Public administration as a rule leans lightly on theoretical support. But advocates of performance indicators can point to plentiful evidence for their value from organizational psychology. Locke et al. (1991: 370) surveying numerous relevant studies, characterize goal-setting theory, whose essential claim is that setting goals improves performance, as 'among the most scientifically valid and useful theories in organizational science'. Not just any old goal, though: research shows that goals should be specific and challenging. Those who have to reach them should be committed to doing so, and should receive support and encouragement, and feedback on their performance, as they work towards them (Locke and Latham, 1990).

Malaysia is perhaps the most elaborate example of performance management in the public sector among developing countries. Its National Key Result Areas are the numerical indicators for the Governance Transformation Programme which was the Barisan Nasional government's response to its poor performance in the 2008 election, when the opposition tapped public anxieties on crime, corruption and the economy. Thus, it is an intensely political initiative as can be seen in Table 6.3 that sets out the specific targets in Malaysia's National Key Result Areas and progress towards achieving them.

In January 2011, the Malaysian government assembled an international panel to review its progress. It included an Australian public service commissioner, an IMF Resident Representative and a co-founder of Transparency International. They were fulsome: 'a great success;' 'impressive;' 'extraordinary' (PEMANDU, 2011: 199, 200, 202). However, reservations should be entered. First, there are holes in the data, as Table 6.3 shows. Second, apart from the possibility of a Hawthorne effect, given that Malaysia's initiative was still in its early stages when we wrote, there is the scope for gaming which is inherent in performance management. Agencies have an incentive to perform sub-optimally (a 'threshold effect'), fearful that if they exceed the initial targets, the bar will be set higher next time round (a 'ratchet effect'). They also have an incentive to manipulate the performance data (Bevan and Hood, 2006). There is no evidence that any of this has occurred, but the theoretical concern is reflected in the international panel's report, which recommended that the statistics should be audited 'to preserve authenticity and validity' (PEMANDU, 2011: 206; see also McCourt, 2012).

Providing responsive service

With its emphasis on management techniques as a spur to performance, NPM operates from the top-down, which militates against responsiveness. The oddity of managing service performance over the heads of its beneficiaries has been compensated for through devices

Table 6.3   *Progress on Malaysia's National Key Result Areas*

2010 target	2012 target	Reported progress in 2010
Reducing crime		
20% reduction of street crimes	5% annual reduction in overall reported crime	street crime down 37% overall reported crime down 16%
Corruption		
Malaysia's Corruption Perceptions Index (CPI) score at 4.9 (from 4.5)		CPI 2010 score 4.4
37% approving government efforts on corruption in Transparency International's (TI) global survey (from 28%)		48% approving government efforts in TI global survey
Average audit findings per ministry at 10.6 annually (from 11.2)		
Improving student outcomes		
Pre-school enrolments at 72% (from 67%)	Pre-school enrolments at 87% All children having basic literacy and numeracy skills at end of year three	72.42% enrolment

→

like 'clients' or citizens' charters' which set out minimum standards of service that clients or citizens can expect, based on principles such as:

- *quality* – improving the quality of services
- *choice* – wherever possible
- *standards* – specify what to expect and how to act if standards are not met
- *value* – for the taxpayers' money
- *accountability* – individuals and organizations
- *transparency* – rules/procedures/schemes/grievances

2010 target	2012 target	Reported progress in 2010
Poverty Poverty incidence at 2.8% (from 3.6%) Hardcore poverty at 0% (from 0.72%)		13,471 households removed from poverty hardcore poverty at 0%
Rural infrastructure Peninsula: 91.4% living within 5km of a paved road (from 91%)	close to 100%	
16,000 new/restored houses for rural/ hardcore poor	additional 34,000 houses	
24-hour electricity access: Peninsula: 99.6% (from 99%) Sabah: 81% (from 77%); Sarawak: 73% (from 67%)	ditto	
Access to clean/treated water: Sarawak: 62% (from 57%); Sabah: 59% (from 57%)	90% 90%	
Urban public transport 13% using public transport in Klang valley between 0700–0900 (from 10-12%) 75% living within 400 metres of public transport route (from 63%)	25%	17% usage

Sources:
1. Targets: Government Transformation Programme Roadmap (January 2010).
2. Progress: http://www.pemandu.gov.my/gtp/, accessed 8 February 2011.

They have been introduced in many countries, including India as the case study in Box 6.3 demonstrates.

The reservations about citizens' charters in India presented in Box 6.3 echo findings from the UK. The charter movement was a flagship initiative of Prime Minister John Major, yet only 16 out of 1,000 people polled there in the mid-1990s were both familiar with a charter and satisfied with it (O'Conghaile, 1996). The criticism arose that lip-service was being paid to citizens' views, and that the charters reflected the priorities of managers, not citizens (Clarke and Newman, 1997).

> ## Box 6.3   Citizen's charters in India
>
> Citizen's charters were introduced in India in 1997 in the context of an 'Action Plan for Effective and Responsive Government'. By 2001, 68 citizen's charters had been formulated by central government agencies, and 318 at sub-national level. They were posted on government websites and were open to public scrutiny. A pilot 'exemplary implementation' exercise had been carried out in three national banks.
>   Some reservations about the initiative surfaced in evaluations:
>
> * The initiative was seen as coming from the top, with minimal consultation
> * The employees affected received little training or orientation
> * Staff transfers disrupted implementation in some cases
> * The charter concept was not properly understood by clients
> * Some charter service norms were either too lax or too tight
>
> *Source*: Sharma and Agnihotri (2001).

The involvement of non-state providers is probably of greater significance than 'managerialist' initiatives such as citizen's charters. In this chapter we are not interested in stand-alone service provision, whether by NGOs, for-profit providers or donors, even though in some countries there are areas such as water and sanitation where private provision predominates, but in services that are contracted by or at least aligned with state service provision. Experience here has been mixed yet again, and probably more negative than positive. An early study found that contracting for clinical and ancillary services in the health sector of developing countries found problems created by the limited capacity of slow-moving, rule-ridden bureaucracies to perform even very basic functions such as paying contractors in a timely manner (Bennett and Mills, 1998). A more recent comprehensive survey echoed that finding, and noted that formal policy dialogue between government and non-state providers was often imperfect and unrepresentative, especially in fragile settings, and prone to hijack by large NGO service providers (Batley and Mcloughlin, 2009). However, it also cited a successful example of dialogue in the Ethiopian education sector, albeit on a small scale, where NGOs initiated the engagement by inviting local government staff to training and presentations, and regional education bureaus were set up in some areas to review alternative basic education programmes.

The appropriateness of NPM

NPM has been described as 'truly a global paradigm' (Borins and Warrington, 1996: 65) whose spread is impeded only by bureaucratic isolationism (Thompson, 1997: 13). However, the contributors to a comprehensive review in 2001 found that its incidence in developing countries was limited, and that picture has probably not changed a great deal in the last decade (McCourt and Minogue, 2001). The problem-solving approach that we have taken in this chapter suggests an explanation. If NPM is essentially a response to the problem of improving performance and delivering on a government's objectives, then a prior condition for its application must be that government makes improving performance a priority. Whether that is or even ought to be the case was the subject of a debate over the application of the New Zealand version of NPM (New Zealand was a pioneer of NPM) in developing countries. Bale and Dale (1998), acting as advocates, argued that the New Zealand reforms were relevant to developing countries because they were developed from a broad, system-wide perspective that focused on the causes, not the symptoms, of dysfunctionality, and because having specified the performance standards that the centre expected, the reforms devolved to its line agencies the management authority that they would need to meet the standards. However, they conceded that some stringent conditions were also necessary: a politically neutral, competent civil service; little corruption or nepotism; a functioning legal code and political market; and a competent private sector.

Answering Bale and Dale's case, Schick (1998) argued that Bale and Dale were taking for granted an earlier stage in New Zealand's bureaucratic development, where a framework of rules had been introduced and a culture of following them had been implanted. By contrast, developing country public administration was typically informal, with local managers having virtual impunity to override formal procedures. Deliberately weakening those procedures which were weak in the first place in the interests of giving managers 'the right to manage' would fatally exacerbate the very problems which NPM was proposing to solve.

In terms of the problem-solving framework which we have adopted in this chapter, Schick's (1998) objection is that NPM is a First World solution to the First World problem of improving public sector performance, something that OECD country governments have the luxury of doing because by initially deploying the Weberian model, they have already solved the problem of how to put government on an orderly and efficient footing. Developing countries should follow the same sequence, in Schick's view: walk before they run.

Bottom-up reforms

We are going to discuss the bottom-up model of reform in a bit more detail than the other models, because it is less well known among public management specialists. Indeed some public management specialists may not consider it as a model of civil service reform at all.

All the models we have reviewed so far share an assumption: that when it comes to setting priorities for public management, public managers should be in the driving seat. Reform should come from the top-down – just as it did with India's citizen's charters and Malaysia's National Key Result Areas. Indeed, a great deal of reform effort has gone into ensuring that managers *are* in the driving seat, insulated from clientelistic pressures from society and politicians and public opinion more generally.

That view has changed dramatically. We can see Peter Evans' *Embedded Autonomy* as the first crack in the monolith. Examining the politics of the East Asian developmental state, he accepted that state officials' effectiveness was indeed related to a certain aloofness which they maintained in the face of societal pressures. However, at the same time they participated in a dense network of ties between state agencies and the private sector in the area of economic development and civil society in the area of public service delivery. Evans labelled this distinctive relationship 'embedded autonomy'. Examples of the state playing what he called a 'midwife' role included the Korean government persuading its *chaebol* industrialists to diversify from consumer electronics into informatics products (Evans, 1995: 174).

Evans' (1995) view posited a fruitful tension between autonomy and embeddedness. Implicitly, however, the tension was to be resolved on the public officials' terms. The bureaucrats stayed in the driving seat, even if they now had industrialists and civil society sharing the passenger seat next to them. If anything, Evans' finding of a positive relationship between state bureaucracy and economic growth which fed into the World Bank's annual *World Development Report 1997* which focused on 'the changing role of the state' ensconced the bureaucrats even more firmly (Evans and Rauch, 1999). But arriving just a little later than Evans' seminal work, a new fashion for participation was to displace them in the development discourse, even if not in the actual practice of most state agencies. And just as the World Bank had been in the forefront of the top-down civil service reform efforts, it also played a leadership role with the new bottom-up approach.

By 'bottom-up' we mean, in this context, state programmes where priorities come directly from citizens, placing public officials in a responsive posture. The relevant mechanism is what Hirschman (1970) called 'voice'. Samuel Paul (1992), while still a World Bank official, was perhaps the first to propose it in the recent development literature as an alternative to top-down control.

While voice in the shape of citizen participation in governance goes back at least as far as Athenian direct democracy, its current ascendancy in development dates from James Wolfensohn's restoration of poverty to the centre of the World Bank's mission in the late 1990s. The landmark *Voices of the Poor* report, with a foreword co-written by Wolfensohn, found that public agencies were among the most important but also the least effective institutions in poor people's lives. The Report called for 'organized communities that can participate in devolved authority structures and keep local governments accountable' (see Figures 10.1 and 10.2 in Narayan et al., 2000: 283).

It was this aspect of the Report which went on to make a distinctive – and controversial – contribution to *World Development Report 2000/01*. The Report advocated 'empowerment' of poor communities, including through participation in public services, and making public agencies directly accountable to the public via the media, the courts and advocacy by civil society organizations. It also departed abruptly from the public administration doctrine of accountability with the assertion that 'the quality of public service is reduced when public officials are held accountable more to their hierarchical superiors than to the people they serve' (World Bank, 2001: 101).

The new doctrine was amplified by *World Development Report 2004*, which focused on service delivery. The argument now was that elections are an inadequate way for citizens to control what state agencies do in their name: 'Given the weaknesses in the long route of accountability [i.e. classic vertical accountability], service outcomes can be improved by strengthening the short route – by increasing the client's power over providers' (World Bank, 2003a: 6). In making this argument, World Bank authors were mindful of innovations in developing countries where officials' direct account-ability to their clients has been institutionalized. The Indian exper-ience with citizen report cards and the Brazilian experiment in participatory budgeting, both celebrated in *World Development Report 2004*, are innovations which illustrate both the strength and one or two weaknesses of the new accountability doctrine. These cases are presented in Box 6.4.

There have been problems elsewhere too: an optimistic report of an attempted replication of Porto Alegre in El Salvador admits that participatory budgeting had fallen into disuse in 60 per cent of the locations where it had been attempted; and emerging evidence from Africa is also disappointing (Gaventa and McGee, 2010; Bland, 2011; Booth, 2011). Moreover, 'if one considers the legislature to be an important organ of democratic institutionality, it may seem prob-lematic that the local legislature tends to have its powers diminished by the participatory budget planning' (Teivanien, 2002: 629).

The difficulties with accountability which bottom-up initiatives inadvertently create ('unintended consequences' again!) echo criti-cisms which we have mostly lost sight of in development circles that followed the wave of participation experiments in countries like Libya, Tanzania and Yugoslavia in the 1960s and 1970s, not to men-tion rich countries like the UK and the US (Wolfe, 1970; Richardson, 1983; Pagano and Rowthorn, 1996).

So there are questions of appropriateness with the bottom-up reforms, just as there are with the top-down ones. It is ironic that advocates of bottom-up approaches to reform have been slower than their top-down counterparts to recognize the problems we have just discussed, even though their favoured initiatives have in fact been concentrated in middle-income countries, especially in Latin America, and implemented in idiosyncratic ways. The indifference to context, mixed with the powerful support of international develop-ment agencies, has prompted a concern in an article which is sympa-thetic to the reforms that the voice-based reforms might be 'ground, pasteurized and converted into new appendages of conditionality' (Santos, 1998: 507). Santos (1998) was prescient: 'process condi-tionality' in the form of a requirement for governments to consult civil society has become integral to the design of Poverty Reduction Strategy Papers (PRSPs), the lending vehicle that replaced structural

Box 6.4 'Short-route' accountability in India and Brazil

A 'citizen report card' survey in Bengaluru (Bangalore) in Karnataka state in 1993, initiated by Samuel Paul (admirably putting his money where his mouth was), identified an abysmal satisfaction rating of 9% with municipal services. Following press coverage and action by the state government, satisfaction increased across two subsequent surveys to 48% in 2003. The World Bank evaluated the initiative positively (Ravindra, 2004), and the evidence that 'voice' was improving services, just as the new doctrine had said it would, stimulated replications in countries like Ethiopia, the Philippines and the Ukraine.

However, Paul himself was more cautious than his admirers. He concedes that service quality started to improve in the context of a wider urban reform programme introduced by the Congress Party state government which came to power in 1999. In fact the programme was wound up in 2004 by an incoming state Chief Minister who believed that its urban bias had lost the Congress Party votes. The Report Card initiative was not repeated after the 2004 election in Karnataka. Here is the weakness: just as we reported earlier, Paul's initiative suffered from the perception that it served a sectional (urban) interest.[1] In a democracy, almost every adult can vote, but only some people 'participate': 'a substantial gap will remain between the universalistic conceptions of modern political society and the more restrictive and exacting notion of civil society' (Whitehead, 2002: 76). Bottom-up accountability via civil society is not necessarily more representative than top-down.

The participatory budgeting experiment in Porto Alegre, Brazil is a second example of bottom-up reform. Drawing on a strong history of social movements and neighbourhood associations, participatory budgeting and other participatory procedures were introduced when the Workers' Party took control of the municipality in 1991. By 2000, at least 20,000 residents were taking part in the participatory processes, which covered the full range of municipal budgets from road-building to health care. Review meetings in municipal districts took place at least twice a month, attended by around 50 people on average (Baiocchi, 2003). However, Porto Alegre's budget experiment has accounted for only a modest proportion of the municipal budget: officials still hold most of the purse-strings.

Sources: Paul (undated); Teivanien (2002).

adjustment loans, with initiatives like Porto Alegre and Bengaluru held up as models (World Bank, 2003a). Despite criticisms that what was being promoted was not so much ownership as 'donorship' (Cramer et al., 2006), the model has spread to other development agencies like DFID and UNDP.

Moving beyond failure: evidence and explanations

We turn now to the evidence of failure which we touched on at the start of the chapter. Since we will rely on World Bank project evaluation reports, we should recognize that World Bank projects are a skewed sample in two ways. First, the World Bank operates mostly in low- and middle-income countries where reform is difficult. Second, the Bank is a bank, and its projects reflect its preoccupation with affordability and, consequently, with pay and employment reform among the range of approaches that we listed in Table 6.1.

Having said that, the best evidence of reform outcomes is in reports by the Bank's own Independent Evaluation Group (IEG). The first report found that that only 33 per cent of the civil service reform projects completed between 1980 and 1997 had been rated as satisfactory (IEG, 1999). Reviewing overlapping evidence slightly earlier, Nunberg (1997) found that the success rate was lower than for Bank projects as a whole. When IEG (2008a: xiii) revisited the topic nine years later, it found that public sector performance had usually improved in the wake of projects in public financial management, tax administration and transparency, but not with civil service reform. At the same time, public sector governance as a whole was rated joint eighth among the Bank's 12 project sectors in terms of project success, and its success rate was found to have declined over the previous five years more sharply than all but one of the 12 sectors (IEG, 2008: 83). An important qualification should be made, however: civil service reform has fared roughly on par with the rest of the Bank's project portfolio, after controlling for country. In other words, civil service reform projects are located disproportionately in very poor, and therefore very 'difficult', countries (Blum, 2012).

We are going to cast the net widely as we move from the evaluation evidence to explanations. There are few analytical explanations of the specific outcomes of civil service reform. It makes sense to supplement them with explanations of the progress of reform programmes in general, especially since over the last quarter-century civil service reform programmes have often been implemented in the context of wider structural adjustment programmes and PRSPs.

We will discuss the different explanations in terms of Hyden et al.'s (2005) model of governance as presented in Table 6.4. This model implies that outcomes can be affected by factors at any of the four governance levels – meta, macro, meso and micro. The way in which the levels interact is complicated. The higher levels are logically

Table 6.4   *Civil service reform and levels of governance*

Level	Activity	Concept
Meta	Politics	Governance
Macro	Institutions	Institutional development
Meso	Policy and strategy	Policy-making and strategic management
Micro	Implementation	Operational management

Source: Adapted from Hyden et al. (2004: 17).

prior, of course, since in principle (for example) public policy arises through the political process. In practice, however, a particular reform may start almost anywhere in the governance system. Citizen's (or client's) charters may have been a flagship initiative of John Major's government in the UK, but they were initiated in an almost casual way by a group of civil servants in a central government department.

We shall confine ourselves to the intermediate meta- and macro-levels in Hyden et al.'s (2005) model; politics and institutions in other words. The way in which reforms are affected by factors of policy design and implementation is already well discussed, including in this volume. The influence of politics and institutions is less well understood, and it operates subtly, helping to explain why reforms which look similar at the operational level in two different countries may have completely different trajectories.

The meta-level: politics

Over the last two decades, the most interesting work on civil service reform, and on public sector reform generally, has been done on the interaction between reform models and the underlying political economy. Seeking the reasons for reform success in 12 countries, Nelson (1990) found significant factors to be economic trends, administrative capacity (notably a united economic team) and backing with executive authority. In their survey of 81 World Bank programmes in 38 countries, Johnson and Wasty (1993) found that domestic ownership and the expression of political commitment by the national leadership as most important for successful reform. Williamson (1994), in a study of 11 countries, stressed the need for a coherent economic team, strong political backing and visionary leadership. Finally,

Campos and Esfahani (2000) found that 'reform readiness' (i.e. the ratio of expected gains to costs in reform proposals), trust between government and entrepreneurs, and 'political turnover' as the significant influences on the reforms studied.

When these factors for success are examined together with the frequency of problems in the implementation of World Bank civil service reform projects in the mid-1990s, as identified in World Bank internal evaluation reports in Table 6.5, we begin to build a comprehensive picture of success and failure factors in civil service reform.

Three of the nine problems listed in Table 6.5 have a major political dimension: domestic reform consensus, government commitment and ownership and overall political and economic crisis. Moreover, they are among the most important problems in terms of their frequency of occurrence.

When one considers the pervasiveness of donor intervention in developing countries and the popular equation of reform with donor pressure, it is significant that several studies have found that the key determinants of commitment to reform are internal: 'domestic policies set the basic parameters of government efforts', while external support 'emerges as a sometimes necessary, but far from sufficient, condition for implementation' (Nelson, 1990: 344, 347). The World

Table 6.5   *Problems encountered in World Bank civil service reform operations*

Problem	*Frequency in evaluation reports (%)*
Administrative capacity and financing	21
Domestic reform consensus	17
Project design	17
Government commitment and ownership	15
Overall political and economic crisis	13
Type of lending instrument	5
Supervision or staff continuity	4
Donor coordination	4
Bank and country dialogue	3

Source: Nunberg. 1997. *Rethinking Civil Service Reform.* © World Bank. License: Creative Commons Attribution (CC BY 3.0 IGO).

Bank's (1998) *Assessing Aid* report, despite being devoted to making the case for aid, similarly notes that 'the lending cum conditionality process works well only when local polities have decided, largely on their own, possibly with outside technical help, to address their reform needs'. 'Successful reform,' it concludes, 'depends primarily on a country's institutional and political characteristics' (World Bank, 1998: 52, 53).

Development agencies were quick to grasp the significance of those studies. In 1999, for instance, James Wolfensohn (1999: 9) declared that

> It is clear to all of us that ownership is essential. Countries must be in the driver's seat and set the course. They must determine goals and the phasing, timing and sequencing of programs.

We have been much less quick to agree on the practical implications of that recognition. One view is that only minor adjustments to the existing recipe are needed. Nunberg (1997) argued that the content of pay and employment reforms was broadly correct, and also politically feasible. Only the process was faulty: reform should be deeper (in the sense of the depth of cuts on payroll spending), broader (it should take place in a larger public administration context) and longer (unrolling over a longer period than the typical aid project timetable).

More recently, however, there have been arguments that something more radical is needed. Should reform advocates adjust their reform proposals to the prevailing political economy, so that the issue is reframed as one of political feasibility rather than commitment, even if that means watering down the reform? In this chapter we have anticipated this approach by juxtaposing six reform models and arguing that they can be selected to suit the problem situation – or in this context, the political economy – of a given country. Or – a different approach – should reform advocates concentrate instead on giving policy-makers incentives to implement the 'correct' reform, even if the reform is politically demanding?

On the second approach, the Swedish and UK governments and the World Bank have invested in political economy studies which focus on what drives reform in individual countries (Dahl-Østergaard et al., 2005). These studies have pointed to generic factors like technical capacity, insulation from societal interests and building incentives for politicians to embark on reform; and country-specific factors like the importance of civil society and the media in the case of Zambia (Duncan et al., 2003; Robinson, 2007). The political factors can have a bearing on specific models of reform. Grindle (2006) has shown how capacity-building, for example, can be intimately affected by political preferences and calendars.

Practitioners have sometimes complained that the political economy studies are 'academic', and fail to specify what policy-makers should do differently. However, this seems to be an overstatement as political economy studies can provide good advice about what is acceptable and feasible in civil service reform. For example, in Swaziland, where king and chiefs, held effective power, it was demonstrated to the powerholders that their fundamental interests would be secure if an independent Civil Service Board were introduced. Only their contingent interest in perpetuating the prevailing system would be affected (McCourt, 2003). The leaders agreed to the change in a new constitution that created an impartial and independent Civil Service Commission. A recent DFID (2013) report sums up the practical advantages of political economy analysis in terms of risk identification: identification of agency capacity for reform; identification of situations where government is unable to enforce collective discipline; identification of situations in which political controversy may derail reform; and identification that constitutional preconditions for reform are in place. Being realistic, however, reform achievements drawing on political economy analysis may still be fragile. For example, in Sri Lanka, political economy analysis assisted greatly in re-establishing the independence of the Public Service Commission in 2001.

It functioned well for several years after 2001, but in 2010, the local branch of *Transparency International* and others were expressing fears that the government elected in 2010 was reverting to the old practices of political interference. As with liberty, the price of civil service reform is eternal vigilance.

The macro-level: institutions

Our Swaziland and Sri Lanka examples have enabled us to kill two birds with one stone, because in illustrating the importance of politics for reform trajectories, they also introduce the importance of institutions. A distinctive feature of civil service reform, and of public administration in the context of development activities as a whole, is that it is profoundly shaped by its institutional framework.

Moreover, the institutions which govern and regulate the civil service are even more important in developing countries than they are in rich OECD countries.

This applies very much to the civil and public service commissions in Commonwealth countries, or their equivalents elsewhere. It is a truism among organizational scholars that organizations get the behaviours they reward. If civil servants, and potential civil servants, see that appointments and promotions are decided by a body which is insulated and committed to excellence, they are more likely to strive to be meritorious – study harder for the degree examinations which will equip them for entry, and work harder in the postings that will earn them their promotion.

In this context, when we say 'institutions', we also mean 'laws'. Tanzania's legal framework for public staff management illuminates this. The 1989 Civil Service Act introduced when the country was a one-party state with a politicized civil service concentrated authority in the hands of the president. The constitution and additional legislation also gave the president immense powers with few procedural checks on how he operated. All of this meant that the Tanzanian Civil Service Commission had much less autonomy and authority than the Swaziland and Sri Lankan equivalents discussed above. This led one senior Tanzanian official to remark that 'the President changes the top officers in the service in a similar way as he changes attire'.

One can easily imagine the reluctance of senior Tanzanian officials to embark on a strategic initiative when they hold office at the president's whim, since 'strategic' actions are inherently long-term ones, and officials would be foolish to expect to be around to see them through. Tanzania's staff management dispensation illustrates the way that the institutional, including legal and procedural, framework creates perverse incentives that subtly affect the way that civil servants behave and the service they provide.

Conclusion: from failure to success?

In the years that followed independence, developing countries did dramatically increase the capacity of the state to provide services from the rudimentary level they were at when the colonial rulers handed over. But since roughly 1980, the experience of civil service reform has been disappointing, as even the World Bank, which initiated reform in many countries, has been candid enough to admit. Many development activists have given up on the state, and have put their efforts into projects that bypass the state, ranging from anti-malaria bed nets to microfinance. However, it is governments which control the most powerful levers of deliberate social and economic change, as we noted earlier in this chapter. The difficulties are substantial, but as Leonard (2010) has observed, they are in proportion to the rewards when reform is successful. Just as there are medical doctors who choose to practise in poor countries because of the challenge they offer to their professional judgement and improvisational skills, not to mention their humanitarian commitment, so we hope that among our readers there are a few who will be stimulated rather than daunted by the sheer intricacy and enormity of the challenges we have touched upon here. The experience of countries like Sri Lanka and Malaysia shows that positive change is possible, and can be sustained.

Chapter 7

Planning for Development: From Writing National Plans to Tackling 'Wicked Problems'

In the Prologue to their classic book on planning and budgeting in developing countries, Caiden and Wildavsky (1990: ii) imagine the unlikely situation of a country's leader telling it like it actually is on the deceptive but seductive qualities of planning: 'All right, you want miracles. I can't produce them but I certainly can produce a plan. In that beautiful eighteen-volume document is a rosy future: day by day it curls at the edges, but the charts and the graphs stay resplendent' (Caiden and Wildavsky, 1990: ii). Others have pondered the results of planning such as Scott (1998: 3) who observed that 'the history of Third World development is littered with the debris of huge agricultural schemes and new cities ... that have failed their residents'. These images jar with Waterston's (1965: 2) professional belief in planning during its heyday, that planning is 'an organized, conscious and continual attempt to select the best available alternatives to achieve specific goals'. Decades later, citing Colm and Geiger (1963: 66), Waterston's recent thinking about what planning entails is altogether more modest: '... survey things as they are, observe what needs to be done, study the means you have to do it with, and then work out practical ways of going about it' (Waterston, 2006: 430).

The above views about the process, purpose and results of planning provide a basis for identifying the topics that will be the focus of this chapter, though it must be observed that there are many competing definitions of what 'planning' is. At the heart of debates about what planning is or should be are competing concepts about the nature of the processes of consciously trying to shape social and economic change. On one side are the ideal models of some economists and system analysts envisioning plans as technical products crafted by impartial experts with access to all necessary data and almost infinite analytical capacity. On the other side are the descriptive models of political science and post-colonial studies. Political scientists see planning as a political process involving the interaction of numerous individuals and organizations that bargain and negotiate from varying power bases to achieve objectives that, at least partially, reflect their self-interest (Schaffer, 1984). For the post-colonial scholars, most explicitly presented in the writing of Escobar (1992: 132) planning is a First World structure which '[w]hen deployed in the Third World ... contributed greatly to the production of the socio-economic and cultural configuration that we describe today as underdevelopment'. As we shall see in this chapter, in the twenty-first century planning theorists, such as Innes and Booher (2010) envisage planning as a complex mixture of technical analysis and formal and informal power relations.

But, before we proceed, a third position must be noted. Even in the high modernist heyday of belief in what comprehensive planning could achieve, sceptical voices warned of the false assumptions underpinning such theory. In 1945, Hayek (1945: 530) wrote that '...there is something fundamentally wrong with an approach [national planning] which habitually disregards an essential part of the phenomena with which we deal: the unavoidable imperfection of man's knowledge and the consequent need for a process by which knowledge is constantly communicated and acquired'. For Hayek, and later his followers in the World Bank and IMF, the impossibility of any central authority capturing the knowledge of 'the man on the spot' and the constant and unpredictable changes of economic and social conditions meant that a decentralized approach was needed – markets and prices.

Planning in developing countries: a short history

During the era in which most Asian and African nations came to independence, belief in the efficacy of development planning knew no bounds: 'the national plan appears to have joined the national anthem and the national flag as a symbol of sovereignty and modernity' (Waterston, 1965: 28). Plans would ensure that poor, agricultural countries would become rich, industrialized nations within a few decades. Such faith emanated from a number of sources.

First, there was past experience. Newly independent countries pursuing a socialist path saw the rapid industrialization and resulting strength of the Soviet Union as clear evidence of the fruits of central planning. Those more attuned to the capitalist West heard of the miracles achieved by the Marshall Plan for European reconstruction, the efficiency of war-time planning in Britain and the USA, and of the achievements of the Tennessee Valley Authority. Second, there was theory. Socialist development theory entailed state control of the economy and consequently comprehensive planning of the economy. Contemporary liberal development theory (which was not so closely wedded to the free market at that time) in both its leading sector and big push variants relied on comprehensive planning to kick-start economies into economic take-off (Rondinelli, 1993: 34). The 'high modernism' of both socialist and mixed economy visions promised that rational planning (input-output modelling, cost-benefit analysis, linear programming, critical path analysis and others) harnessing scientific and technological advances, could control the natural environment and deliver economic growth and permanently rising material living conditions. Thirdly, access to international financial resources was usually dependent on having a plan as a basis for negotiation with aid agencies and bankers. Conveniently, those self-same aid agencies and bankers would often write the plans for poor countries. Finally, there were the domestic political pressures on new national leaders to remain popular and bolster their legitimacy. Launching grand plans made it sound as though rapid economic growth and national prosperity would soon be achieved – the new president or prime minister was clearly going to deliver the promises made on attaining independence. As Johnston and Clark (1982: 24) noted:

These arguments and pressures were persuasive and led at times to an almost blind faith in the necessity and efficacy of planning. Characteristic of this was the statement of Prime Minister Nehru of India that '[planning] and development have become a sort of mathematical problem which can be worked out scientifically ... [men] of science, planners, experts who approach our problems from a purely scientific point of view ... agree, broadly, that given certain preconditions of development, industrialization and all that, certain exact conclusions follow almost as a matter of course'.

Unfortunately, national planning in developing countries rarely achieved its ambitious goals and, although it continued in most countries, its significance declined over the 1970s and 1980s. It was during this period that international development agencies shifted their focus and began to emphasize project planning, based on micro-economic analytical principles, and also started to focus on economic policy analysis, particularly 'getting the prices right'. The heyday of project planning was in the 1970s. It came under severe critical scrutiny during the early 1980s as many projects failed to match expectations and methodological flaws became increasingly evident. Nevertheless, project planning has retained a central role in both public and private investment programming through to the present day, although there are heated debates about whether it should be top-down or bottom-up or even 'place-shaping', as we shall see later in this chapter.

The aggressive anti-planning arguments (and especially anti-national planning) of the free-market theorists and practitioners of the 1980s impacted strongly on many aid-dependent countries. National plans were discontinued or sidelined and ministries of national planning and national planning offices were down-sized or merged into ministries of finance as marginal players. The ferocity of these criticisms began to temper in the 1990s. Rather than suggesting that national planning should be abandoned the focus moved on to redefining the nature and quality of development planning (Chowdhury and Kirkpatrick, 1994; Killick, 1989). In less aid-dependent countries, particularly India and China but including Malaysia and Vietnam, economic liberalization became more significant over the 1990s but the commitment to national planning remained.

Planning came back into fashion in development around the Millennium, albeit in a form that met the pressing needs of the most powerful international agencies rather than the national governments of developing countries. As part of debt forgiveness programmes, the World Bank and IMF needed documents showing how highly indebted poor countries (HIPCs) would spend the loan repayments that would be written off on development activities benefiting the poor – rather than on military expenditure or tax cuts for the rich. The Poverty Reduction Strategy Papers (PRSPs) initially required to access HIPC write-offs (and subsequently all concessional loans from the World Bank and IMF) demanded assessments of national and sub-national poverty and analyses of the public policies needed to tackle poverty (Hulme, 2010). Around 2000, the international agencies that had spent the 1980s encouraging the stripping out of planning capacity in the public sector suddenly found they needed planners as their counterparts in developing countries. However, PRSPs, and their successor Poverty Reduction Strategies (PRSs), have often failed to achieve 'national ownership' and senior civil servants in Africa and Asia joke of 'donorship' displacing strategy ownership. Economic growth and welfare improvements over the 2000s have emboldened many developing countries and several (including Bangladesh, Ghana, Uganda and Vietnam) have recently decided to return to a five year planning format and produce National Development Strategies covering all economic and social sectors. These plans are ambitious, in terms of the economic growth rates they pursue, but they are more modest in terms of their faith in state capacity to control the economy. They rely heavily on private sector activity and market-based decisions to take national development forward.

In many aid-dependent countries, donors still drive approaches to planning. Their contemporary 'results' agenda (achieving maximum, measurable short-term impacts), 'cash-on-delivery' approach (aid payments based on ex post target achievement) and 'evidence-based policy' initiatives (randomized control trials to 'scientifically' identify best practice actions) are all premised on the belief that complex technical analysis will identify programmes that yield virtually guaranteed outcomes.

In the following sections we first examine the experience of national development planning and then proceed to a review of project planning.

National development planning

National development planning is

> ...a deliberate governmental attempt to coordinate economic decision making over the long run and to influence, direct, and in some cases even control the level and growth of a nation's principal economic variables (income, consumption, employment, investment, saving, exports, imports etc) to achieve a predetermined set of development objectives. (Todaro, 1994: 566)

In centrally planned economies (this used to be scores of countries but nowadays only North Korea and, to a decreasing extent, Myanmar, Cuba and some Central Asian countries) the emphasis is on state direction, control and ownership whereas in mixed economies national planning involves the programming of state resources to carry out public investment alongside economic policies that seek to stimulate and guide private sector activity. Arguments of market failure (that private sector activity is uncompetitive, non-existent, based on incorrect interpretation of economic signals or cannot deliver public goods), resource allocation priorities (that there is a wide divergence between private and social valuations of what an investment will produce) and attitudinal change (that fac-tionalized and traditionally oriented populations can be united and energized) have supported the case for development planning. A mys-tique grew around the activity which 'was widely believed to offer the essential and perhaps the only institutional and organizational mechanism for overcoming the major obstacles to development and for ensuring a sustained high rate of economic growth' (Todaro, 1994: 566).

Killick (1976) identified six main characteristics of national development plans over the 1950–1970 era:

1. Development plans present the policy objectives of the government, usually with a strong emphasis on economic development.
2. A strategy for achieving these objectives is identified. This varies between cases from the very specific to the very general.
3. The plan seeks to set out a set of internally consistent principles for optimal implementation that can guide day-to-day decision-making.
4. The plan attempts to understand, and influence, the whole of the economy.
5. The plan utilizes a macroeconomic model (ranging from very simple to very sophisticated) to forecast the anticipated performance of the economy.
6. While a development plan is a medium-term document, typically of five years, it commonly involves supplementary annual plans and also presents a longer-term view of national development.

An example of a national development plan in India is presented in Box 7.1. Despite common characteristics different development plans have taken very different forms, varying considerably in the degree of detail and the nature of the analytical tools that have been used. While some plans, especially the early ones, were basically a mixture of descriptions and optimistic projections, others integrate aggregate economic analysis with complex inter-sectoral input-output modelling and subsequently cost-benefit analysis to identify specific

---

Box 7.1   India's five-year plans

In March 1950, the Government of India set up the Planning Commission charged with the formulation of 'a Plan for the most effective and balanced utilization of the country's resources'. The Commission set in motion a large number of discussions with federal departments and state governments and in 1951 produced a draft Five-Year Plan, heavily influenced by the types of plan produced in the Soviet Union. After further negotiations, and decisions to increase planned public expenditure by a third more than the draft plan, the First Five-Year Plan was published in December 1952, to cover 1951–1956.

The First Plan, like later plans, covered virtually all aspects of the economy and social welfare in its 671 pages. It estimated the resources that would be available and set targets for production and service provision through to 1956. These targets covered central government, state governments and the private sector. For example, the private sector was set the target of increasing bicycle production from 99,000 units in 1951 to 530,000 in 1956. Each state government produced a corresponding plan document setting targets within the state.

The early Five-Year Plans were taken very seriously, but by the late 1960s the plans came to be seen as a routine activity, partly because of the arbitrary nature of much of the target formulation and partly because the Second, Third and Fourth Plans' targets were not achieved. Some commentators believe that the plans helped to contribute to the mass of regulations that have discouraged industrialization.

Following the economic reforms of the 1990s, and as Indian policymakers moved away from a command and control regime towards greater reliance on markets, there was a fall in the proportion of state spending deemed to be in the 'planned' categories (mostly capital expenditures). As a consequence, the Five-Year Plans have become less important over time in setting targets and allocating resources to line ministries to meet these targets. The most recent Five-Year Plan (the Twelfth) abandoned target setting in favour of scenario analysis. However, the Indian Planning Commission still remains a powerful government body, staffed by influential members from academia and civil society, and, in the words of its charismatic Deputy Chairman, Montek Singh Ahluwalia, 'has the power to put things on the agenda, to push and persuade'.

---

investment projects such as roads, dams, agricultural schemes, industrial sites, technical training institutes and hospitals.

Promise and performance

The miraculous expectations invested in national development planning were not realized. Waterston (1965: 293) found 'that there have been many more failures than successes in the implementation of development plans ... the great majority of countries have failed to real-ize even modest income and output targets.' In a similar vein, Killick (1976: 161) concluded that 'medium term development planning has in most LDCs almost entirely failed to deliver the advantages expected of it.' Some commentators have taken the argument a stage further, claim-ing it is not simply that planning has failed to deliver, rather national planning is in itself an obstacle to development. For example, Caiden and Wildavsky (1990: 293) lambasted comprehensive multi-sectoral planning as 'a mechanism for decisions to maximize every known disability and minimize any possible advantage for poor countries'. According to this view national development planning has retarded rates of economic growth and discouraged the evolution of institutions and procedures that could lead to more effective decision-making.

What went wrong with development planning? The lists produced by analysts (Killick, 1976; Caiden and Wildavsky, 1990; Rondinelli, 1993) are long but can be summarized in six main points. First, the majority of plans were wildly over-ambitious about the rates at which development could be achieved, assumptions about resource availability and about the degree of control that a government could exert on the private sector in a mixed economy. Second, the data on which such plans were based were poor and at times not available, so that rough guesses and intuition often provided the key parameters (Rondinelli, 1993: 43). Third, there were shortcomings in the analyti-cal methods used in plans. While these were often sophisticated and intellectually demanding they could not model the full complexity and adaptability of an economy. They were often totally inappropriate for low data contexts (Killick, 1976: 181). The fourth major prob-lem was that such plans were incapable of dealing with unanticipated shocks, whether external (e.g. changes in prices) or internal (e.g. civil war requiring a massive reallocation of public expenditure into defence). In particular, the 1974 and 1979 increases in oil prices made the content of virtually all national development plans operating at those times redundant overnight. Fifth, there were institutional weak-nesses. Some related to the positioning of planners in isolated national planning units remote from the sectoral ministries that would have to implement plans. This led to poor communications and friction between planning agencies and other parts of government. More broadly, the low capacity of the public and private sector to imple-ment plans in many countries hampered plan achievement.

Last, but by no means least, comes politics. Much of the theory of national development planning assumed that development was done by technocrats pursuing policies that would optimize some non-contested social good. In practice, policy and implementation were (and are) largely determined by political actors (politicians, political parties and associations, political and bureaucratic elites) and economic actors (leading businessmen and/or wealthy families, bankers and investors). Often the boundaries between political and economic actors overlap considerably. While national leaders were never lacking in rhetoric about development plans, they frequently demonstrated a total lack of commitment to plan implementation and the allocation of budgets for plans. This situation is well illustrated by Sri Lanka, where national plans were prepared largely for show but had minimal influence on actual decision-making (Bruton et al., 1992). However, one should note that not all development planning can be written off. In Japan, South Korea and Taiwan there is evidence of national planning having been a component of effective developmental states, and in Botswana, Indonesia, Thailand and Malaysia national plans have been at least partially successful. It can even be argued, that China and India's recent rise was partly underpinned by capacities created by earlier national planning activities. Nevertheless, the case against development planning is strong, and one can pose the question 'should development planning be abandoned?'

The fall and return of development planning

The criticisms of development planning in the 1970s led to a growing consensus that comprehensive economic planning was infeasible and undesirable. The opening up of former Soviet republics and Eastern European socialist economies in the 1980s and 1990s means that such planning is now only practised by North Korea. However, for some critics reducing the scope and ambition of planning was not sufficient. Throughout the 1980s, neo-liberals at agencies such as the World Bank and IMF argued strongly for the almost complete rolling back of the state and for the abandonment of planning. Planning was seen as an invitation for government to distort markets which, once distorted, could not achieve the allocative efficiency of which they were capable. Planning was not the solution; it was the problem. However, during the 1990s, this position was moderated with the recognition by the Washington institutions that both state and market were essential for national development as highlighted in the *World Development Report 1997: The State in a Changing World* (World Bank, 1997).

In many countries there is now an agreement that planning techniques need to be used on a continuous basis as a part of a process of 'development policy management'. This seeks to provide macroeconomic stability, coordinate public policy, use public expenditure efficiently, anticipate problems and changes in the external and internal environments, ensure competitive markets and stimulate market development. Government intervention is deemed necessary in sectors where markets alone cannot be relied on. According to the World Bank (1991: 9), these include 'education, health, nutrition, family planning, and poverty-alleviation; building social, physical, administrative, regulatory and legal infrastructure of better quality; [and] mobilizing the resources to finance public expenditures'. Such a prescription entails the continuation of public sector planning, often by new approaches and, importantly, with a focus on the development of human capital and institutions as well as the physical infrastructure that was the focus of plans from the 1950s to the 1970s.

Greater attention is also being paid to the most fundamental and routine of national development planning activities: the preparation of the annual budget for public expenditure. More than 20 years ago, Caiden and Wildavsky (1990) pointed out the potential contribution that improved budgeting and management of public finance could make to development. During the 1990s, many countries started to link their annual budgets to modest, medium-term plans (sometimes rolling plans) for capital expenditure and new recurrent expenditures. This helps to ensure that public investment in capital and development works remains a significant budgetary item, and that development projects are carefully screened and analysed. Sri Lanka's rolling, five-year programme for public investment provides an example of such attempts to link annual budgeting to medium-term frameworks and move away from the 'blueprint' approach of earlier times (Hulme and Sanderatne, 1995).

The big change in approaches to national development planning, the return of planning, came in 1999/2000 when the World Bank and IMF decided that countries wishing to access concessional funds would need to prepare Poverty Reduction Strategy Papers (PRSPs, subsequently re-named Poverty Reduction Strategies, PRSs). These are three-year plans that analyse poverty and identify policies to reduce poverty. Usually, a central element of these strategies is promoting economic growth, as virtually all PRSs take it as given that growth is essential for poverty reduction. The PRSP/PRS approach emerged at a particular historic moment that led to it being built on two very different sources of ideas. One was the practical experience of Uganda which independently produced a Poverty Eradication Action Plan (PEAP) in 2007. The other was World Bank President James Wolfensohn's Comprehensive Development Framework (for a detailed account see Hulme, 2010: 131–7). Building on the mood of the Millennium moment, PRSPs were to be based on five principles – national ownership, results focused, comprehensive, partnership oriented and a long-term orientation (Box 7.2). Paradoxically, given the principle of national ownership, the preparation of a PRSP required the use of a 1,260 page manual prepared by the World Bank (Klugman, 2002) and commonly involved large amounts of aid-financed consultancy from expatriates.

While PRSs sensibly rehabilitated the idea that state planning could help promote development this initiative has been heavily criticized. In Ghana, Malawi, Tanzania and other countries, governments were not fully convinced of the utility of PRSs and had separate national development strategies for economic development running alongside PRSs (Peretz, 2009) so that public agencies were implementing two different plans at the same time. An internal IMF evaluation (IMF Independent Evaluation Office, 2004) detailed many shortcomings in the way the IMF managed PRSs and Stewart and Wang (2004) reinforced the finding that IMF culture had not changed. As one Washington DC insider reported, '…the PRSP is a compulsory process wherein the people with the money tell the people who want the money what they need to do to get the money' (Hulme, 2010: 131). While the IMF evaluation saw these shortcomings as technical, Craig and Porter (2006: 88) believed them to be

---

Box 7.2   Five core principles for Poverty Reduction Strategy Papers (PRSPs)

1. *Country-driven:* involving broad-based participation by civil society and the private sector in all operational steps
2. *Results-oriented:* focusing on outcomes that would benefit the poor
3. *Comprehensive:* recognizing the multidimensional nature of poverty
4. *Partnership-oriented:* involving coordinated participation of development partners (bilateral, multilateral and non-governmental)
5. *Long-term:* based on a long-term perspective for poverty reduction

Source: World Bank website, http://go.worldbank.org/ZLBKFM2V90.

deliberate. They argued that the lack of linkage between the PRSP and the Medium Term Expenditure Framework occurred so that the PRSP did not lead to increased pressure to raise public expenditure ceilings to meet poverty reduction targets. Although there is some evidence that over time PRSs have become less generic, more contextualized and more influenced by national governments (Chronic Poverty Research Centre, 2008) it is clear that in most countries the behaviours of international finance institutions (IFIs) contradicted the first principle of the five 'core principles' – that PRSPs should be driven by a broad coalition of interests in the country concerned. All five principles of PRSPs are set out in Box 7.2.

By the late 2000s, several countries that had prepared PRSs decided to move away from this IFI-guided approach to planning and assert their national sovereignty. Bangladesh, Ghana, Uganda and Vietnam have determined to return to preparing five-year national plans in a format that they determine. Uganda provides an interesting example. Led by the forceful President Yoweri Museveni, its parliament has approved a 30-year National Vision Framework that is to see the country move from a peasant economy to 'a modern and prosperous country'. The vision comprises a series of six five-year National Development Plans, each to be reviewed in mid-term. The first five-year plan requires 'state leadership' as it diagnoses that the private sector is not yet sufficiently developed to play a leading role. It seeks to build on the dynamism of private sector activity through a reform path customized to Uganda's specific conditions and tackling the country's 'binding constraints to economic growth'. While poverty eradication remains a goal there is a strong emphasis on 'economic transformation and wealth creation' and a target of achieving annual growth of more than 7 per cent. The National Development Plan is closely linked to the country's Medium Term Expenditure Framework and, through this, shapes the annual budget. The 2009/2014 plan highlights the role of agricultural modernization and many observers see Museveni's thinking as shaping it – despite the plan's claim that it is the product of an 'iterative, consultative and participatory process [involving] bottom up and top down approaches'. Opinions on what will be achieved by this return to national development planning in Uganda vary. Supporters see it as taking the country away from dependence on donor advice and charting a credible route for growth and prosperity. Critics are concerned that 'state leadership' places greater control of the economy (and the new flow of revenues from oil production) in the hands of Museveni, his party and cronies.

This new generation of national plans are vastly different from the comprehensive blueprints of the 1950s and 1960s and, if effective, could improve the programming of publicly financed development projects. It is to such projects that we now turn our attention.

Project planning

'During the 1960s and 1970s projects became the primary means through which governments of developing countries translated their plans and policies into programs of action' (Rondinelli, 1993: 5). Projects were seen as the 'cutting edge of development' (Gittinger, 1982: 1), where resources were converted into improved livelihoods and economic growth. Individual projects had always required some form of planning – at the very least a set of objectives, a rough budget and a schedule of activities – but in the 1960s and 1970s a number of methodological breakthroughs occurred, and these encouraged a belief, particularly among aid donors, that projects could be selected and planned in ways that almost guaranteed the desired results.

At the heart of such methodologies is the project cycle (see Figure 7.1). This conceptualizes projects as a logical sequence of activities in pursuit of known objectives. The planning of projects is seen as rational in that information is gathered and analysed in relation to defined objectives; alternative courses of action are generated; the results and risks of different alternatives are systematically assessed; the optimal course of action (in terms of stated objectives) is selected and subsequently implemented; projects are evaluated, and information from these exercises is fed back into later phases of the project and to policy more generally.

Much project activity, and virtually all new projects in low-income countries, involve assistance from foreign aid agencies. As a consequence, negotiation and supervision need to be fitted into the cycle. Complex project 'spirals' have sometimes been used to describe the process. Donor involvement usually leads to a concentration on the preparation and appraisal stages of the cycle to ensure that investment is justified. Virtually all externally financed projects require very detailed plans before approval, and a cost-benefit analysis to estimate the likely social return on the project. These requirements have meant that most projects involving external finance have been (and still are) designed by specialist planners (often expatriates) using sophisticated techniques.

Figure 7.1   *The conventional project cycle*

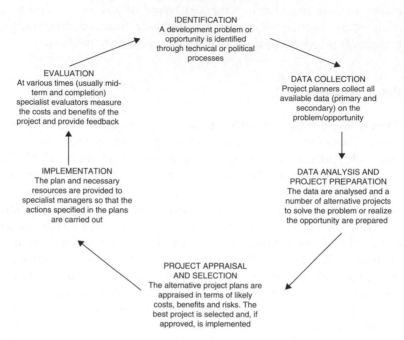

Unfortunately, the rigour that such techniques bring to project analysis has not been reflected in project results. The World Bank (1988: 25) found that some 51 per cent of its rural development area projects over the period 1965 to 1985 failed to achieve the Bank's minimum acceptable rate of return of 10 per cent. While there have been many successful projects in developing countries (for example see World Bank, 1987, on land settlement projects in Malaysia) there are many examples of white elephants such as the well-documented Magarini project in Kenya (Porter et al., 1991) and the Training and Visit agricultural extension projects of the 1990s (Anderson, 2006). A set of problems within the project planning process has been identified as making it likely that projects commonly underperform in terms of their stated objectives. These have been examined in detail by several writers (Johnston and Clark, 1982; Chambers, 1983; Rondinelli, 1993; Hulme, 1994a), and are summarized below.

- *The nature of development problems*: Johnston and Clark's (1982: 23–8) seminal book makes a powerful case that the challenges of development, particularly in rural areas, are not 'well structured' problems, as project planning methodologies assume, but are 'ill structured' or simply 'a mess'. Such problems cannot be 'thought through' by bright technocrats: rather they have to be 'acted out' by processes of social experimentation and interaction. No amount of ex ante expert analysis can identify a solution to such complex problems.

- *Poor data*: Orthodox project planning methodologies demand large amounts of reliable data. In most developing countries such data is not available and so planners have to make assumptions. There is a widespread tendency for such assumptions – about yields, costs and the rates at which people will change their behaviour – to be over-optimistic (see Porter et al., 1991, for numerous examples). Commonly, project planners have compounded the problems of data non-availability by ignoring the indigenous knowledge of intended beneficiaries.

- *Uncertainty*: Central feature of project environments in developing countries are uncertainty and instability. Climate change, rapid economic fluctuations, the systemic financial risks of 'casino capitalism' (Stiglitz, 2010) and the mountains of public debt being run up in the USA and EU mean that in recent times levels of uncertainty have risen. However, conventional methodologies make little allowance for the impact that a sudden or gradual changes in physical factors (e.g. rainfall), economic factors (e.g. prices) or social factors (e.g. the level of lawlessness) will have on a project's effectiveness. The methodologies have pursued analytical sophistication whilst frequently minimizing flexibility and opportunities for experimentation (Chambers, 1993).

- *Separation of planning from management*: Project planning methodologies have distinguished the planners of projects from the managers. The former have been seen as high-powered analysts, technocrats whose 'tools became their power' (Rondinelli, 1993: 8). The latter have been classified as mere implementers who just need to follow the plan. This has led to project management being accorded a relatively low status and at times has contributed to morale problems. More importantly, it has led to an underestimation of the contribution of good management to project performance and of the complexity of creating management capacity.

- *Lack of beneficiary participation*: The failure of conventional project planning approaches to involve beneficiaries in project identification, data gathering, design and selection has fostered beneficiary dependency, discouraged feelings of local ownership of project activities and sometimes alienated the intended beneficiaries of projects.

- *Projects and politics*: Conventional project planning methodologies are based on normative analytical frameworks that ignore
  political factors (Hulme, 1994a). This is a considerable weakness
  given the large body of empirical evidence which indicates that
  project identification, planning, selection and implementation are
  highly political processes in which financiers, political parties,
  local elites, politicians, bureaucrats and others seek to achieve
  outcomes that meet their individual, group, organizational or
  class interests. By avoiding political analysis, conventional methodologies facilitate the concealment of partisan behaviour and
  reduce the opportunity for the powerless (i.e. the intended beneficiaries) to gain influence over the project process.

Alternative approaches to project planning in developing countries

The array of problems identified above has generated a vast critical
literature but as Cernea (1991: 8) argued and correctly predicted that

> despite the recurrent debates on the merits and disadvantages of
> projects as instruments of development intervention, no effective
> alternatives have emerged, and projects are likely to remain a
> basic means for translating policies into action programs.

More than 20 years later, the search continues for approaches that
will make projects more effective. These approaches can be grouped
into three different sets for analytical purposes: refining top-down
approaches, shifting to approaches that are less top-down and/or
participatory, and radical postmodern approaches. However, in practice there is an enormous variety of different proposals combining
different elements of alternative principles and methods.

The first response has been to refine existing top-down methodologies so that as gaps are revealed they are plugged by additional
methods and disciplines. This has been the approach of most international financial agencies and donors. They have upgraded the project
cycle to a complex project spiral, as mentioned earlier; as discussed in
Chapter 5, they have adopted logical framework (log-frame) analysis
for design and monitoring of projects (DFID, 2011); and they have
expanded the content of project planning by the creation of a number
of additional sub-disciplines – social development appraisal, environmental impact assessment, gender analysis and institutional analysis.
This approach sees the problems of project planning as technical – if

the 'gaps' in appraisal that spoil plans can be identified then the addition of new technical analyses (by new sets of experts) will greatly improve project performance.

The second response has been more radical and proposes the replacement of the conventional, top-down approach to project planning. Two different conceptual bases underlie such proposals. One (adaptive administration) highlights the role of project management and implementation vis-a-vis project planning (Rondinelli, 1993). The other (participatory rural appraisal and/or participatory learning and action) emphasizes the role of community participation at all stages of the project cycle (Korten, 1990; Chambers, 1993). These two responses have been combined into 'process approaches' that seek to integrate improved technical analysis and learning with participatory methods. Alternatives that have emerged in the USA and Europe will be discussed later but now we will focus on the two influential and innovative strands of project thinking – adaptive administration and participatory learning and action.

Adaptive administration

Rondinelli (1993) made an impassioned plea for development projects to be conceptualized as 'policy experiments' requiring 'adaptive administration'. Although his book is more than 30 years old it provides a still relevant account of how many of the 'lessons of experience' could be incorporated into an alternative planning model which, while managerialist, permits planners and managers to drop the pretence of having almost perfect knowledge. He argues that an experimental approach which places elements of planning, implementation and monitoring in the hands of project managers, is essential. This is because of the environments in which development projects operate (limited information, high risk, uncertainty and political manipulation) and the capacities that are required to become effective in such environments (learning, experimentation, creativity, organizational flexibility and access to local knowledge).

Development interventions should commence as small-scale 'experimental projects' searching for solutions to local problems that are appropriate to available levels of resources and technological capacity and that can be replicated elsewhere. It may take many years of experiment before such projects begin to produce results. In many cases they may fail and need to be closed down. However, successful experimental projects can be converted into 'pilot projects' that expand the scale of operations or test the applicability of the project in different environments. Significant further innovation and adaptation will be needed at this stage. Successful pilot projects can form the basis for 'demonstration projects … to show that new technologies, methods, or programs are better than traditional ones because they increase productivity, lower production costs, raise income or deliver social services more efficiently' (Rondinelli, 1993: 139). Such projects are still very risky, and selective redesign and adaptation will continue. Finally, for that small proportion of experiments that become fully fledged, comes the process of project 'replication and dissemination'. Simple blueprints are inappropriate as there must be careful consideration of how to develop administrative capacity for service delivery, which institutions should be involved (bureaucratic, civil society or private sector), and how to ensure financial sustainability.

Rondinelli's ideas demand that actors in the project process, particularly donors and financiers, shift their focus from three- or five-year plans into flexible, open-ended experiments that combine planning and management and emphasize administrative capacity-building. This is difficult for politicians, who work on three–five year election time-frames, and aid agencies usually with three-year financial frameworks. In addition, both are under pressure to promise 'magic bullets' that will solve development problems rapidly.

Participatory learning and action (PLA)

For the other radical critics of conventional approaches to project planning, the key themes of adaptive administration – experimentation, flexibility, learning and creativity – are valid, but there remains too great an emphasis on the role of external experts, bureaucrats and aid agencies. Instead, what is required is an approach that permits much greater beneficiary involvement in project identification, selection, design, implementation and evaluation. This ensures that: local knowledge is utilized; activities are consistent with local resource endowments (organizational, material and financial); local preferences and priorities are pursued; and, that the project process contributes to the 'empowerment' of disadvantaged groups. Such approaches evolved in South Asia and have been spearheaded by the work of a large number of local, national and international NGOs as initially described by Robert Chambers (1993; 1994). They were labelled as participatory rural appraisal (PRA). The International Institute for the Environment and Development (IIED) has played a key role in promoting this family of approaches and its Participatory Learning and Action Notes has a vast set of materials about 'what' PLA is and practical examples and discussions of 'how' it can be used (IIED, 2013). The 'how' debates are encyclopaedic, as can be seen from the IIED website, and here we can provide only a simple illustration of the key elements.

A common PLA exercise is the production of a community or village plan. This may be initiated by a trained NGO worker who has been in a locality for some time and is known to local residents. S/he arranges with villagers for a one-, two- or three-day period to be devoted to the exercise. There is an initial briefing in which it is emphasized that PLA is a means by which villagers can systematically analyse their problems, explore possible solutions and draw up a plan of action. Then, villagers (sometimes as a full group sometimes in small sub-groups) produce a map of their village and its resources based on their knowledge. They usually draw it in sand or dirt with symbols (e.g. seeds, old cans and sticks) representing local features. If literacy rates are reasonably high then maps may be drawn on large sheets of paper. During this phase, villagers discuss issues such as which of their resources are over-exploited or under-utilized. On the map, villagers identify individual households (by number, letter or symbol). The next stage is wealth ranking, where the villagers' first task is to agree on a categorization for wealth (e.g. very wealthy, secure, poor, vulnerable). They continue by debating which category is appropriate for which households. During this stage they identify those families that are in greatest need of additional income or welfare services. It must be noted that many PLA practitioners have moved away from wealth ranking exercises as they may encourage social differentiation by labelling household as 'poor' and 'very poor'.

Probably on the second day, they establish (again through village-led discussions) what are the main priorities for the village in terms of problems to be tackled or opportunities seized. A matrix of agreed problems/opportunities is drawn up and then, by a simple technique known as pair-wise ranking (Mascharenhas et al., 1991), villagers compare problems/opportunities and through discussion reach a consensus on their prioritization. In the final stage, villagers agree on a plan of action to tackle priority problems/opportunities. If the process is successful then they will have identified possible local projects, appraised them and agreed on the initial phase of an adaptive implementation plan. If the exercise has gone well the plan of action will be 'owned' by the villagers. The NGO worker will have encouraged

discussion and explained simple techniques but will not have inter-
vened by providing advice or opinions (for a critical discussion of
'who' participates in PRA see Mosse, 1994, and various chapters in
Cooke and Kothari, 2001).

Most NGOs now use PLA in some of their field activities and
major attempts have been made to train public servants in the use
of PRA in countries such as India, Kenya and Sri Lanka. While
participatory approaches have become very popular with NGOs,
some governments and international development agencies, such as
the World Bank with its Community-driven Development projects
(see Mansuri and Rao, 2004 for a review), they have also come in
for criticism. Cooke and Kothari (2001) argue that participatory
approaches have become 'the new tyranny' used by powerful external agencies and national and local elites to mask the ways in which
the practice of participation reinforces pre-existing social relations.
Hickey and Mohan (2004) have similar concerns but they argue
that a critical analysis of participation might allow these practices to
support progressive social change and, in some circumstances, contribute to social transformation. A vast literature has evolved with
proponents of participation arguing for its empowering potential and
critics arguing that it lacks a political analysis and that its progressive
facade can hide oppressive practice.

Process approaches

The nature of the foreign aid relationship means that aid-financed
projects have to be, at least partly, top-down so that aid agencies
can account to their ministers and taxpayers about how aid money
is being spent. Some relatively progressive aid agencies, such as the
UK's DFID and Norway's NORAD, have tried to find ways of combining adaptive management with participatory approaches and they
have used the term 'process approaches' (indicating that they have
moved away from blueprints) to describe these hybrids.

Bond and Hulme (1999) have illustrated the main features of this
approach. It involves:

*   *Flexible and phased implementation* – start small, 10 to 20-year
    time-frames, experimentation and action learning.
*   *Learning from experience* – embracing error, forging links
    between planning and implementation, iterative improvements
    and the selection of appropriate technologies.

- *Beneficiary or client participation* – in problem analysis, planning, resource mobilization, implementation, and monitoring and evaluation seeking to empower clients and communities.
- *Institutional support* – negotiating political support, devolved authority, using only permanent local-level agencies, capacity development and promoting beneficiary organizations.
- *Programme management* – strong leadership, new professionalism (Chambers, 1993), staff retention, short- and long-term technical assistance, creative management and inter-organizational coordination

The case presented by Bond and Hulme (1999) to illustrate a process project, the Moneragala Integrated Rural Development Programme (MONDEP) in Sri Lanka, reveals the ways in which these elements were woven together to produce a programme that was seen as performing strongly during the first ten years, of its 20-year time frame (Moore et al., 1995). However, maintaining such a demanding approach proved difficult in the later years of the programme (Jerve et al., 2005) and generated questions about the effectiveness of project approaches to development that resonated with the criticisms of the 1980s.

Planning in a post-modernist world: place-shaping and collaborative rationality

Over the last ten years, planning theorists have sought to pull together the criticisms of rational planning and create a coherent alternative. As Allmendinger (2002: 168) writes '...planning [is] ... a modernist project in post-modern times'. What would project planning for development look like if it genuinely accepted the complexity of life in the contemporary world? It would need to acknowledge the high levels of uncertainty and unpredictability about actions and their effects and outcomes; that key stakeholders in any initiative have different, and sometimes opposed goals, and that there is not an agreed public goal to pursue; that limited and often poor data mean that understanding about many key processes and their effects is fuzzy at best; and that formal and informal political processes are central to any planning activities. Ostrom's (2010) ideas about 'polycentric governance' have been influential in shaping many of the emerging proposals for 'what' planning in a post-modernist world would look like.

Healey (2004) argues that the 'Euclidian concepts' underpinning orthodox planning have to be replaced by a relational conception that understands planning as a social construct that is: coproduced by multiple actors (i.e. involves actions by the state, private individuals and organizations, and voluntary and community associations); contested, and often fiercely contested; sees development as emergent and with non-linear economic, social and environmental trajectories – there are no starting points and end points; recognizes that governance is multi-scalar; and sees that influence, authority and power are complex network processes not hierarchical structures. From this paradigmatic viewpoint the function of planning is less to programme public investment and more '...to release potentialities and to innovate, and perhaps even to generate new struggles and a different level of politics' (Healey, 2004: 160). The practical output of this theorization is to replace planning with 'place-shaping' and Shucksmith (2010) provides an example of what this might mean in a specific setting. Looking at the planning of rural development in Scotland he argues that the earlier approach of 'integrated rural development' – the technical coordination of state-sponsored programmes across sectors with community consultation – would be replaced by 'disintegrated rural development', with the state promoting mobilization at multiple levels to stimulate action and innovation and the engagement of the people and communities within the physical space being reshaped to not merely engage with processes of governance but to challenge and reform them.

Building on similar ideas, Innes and Booher (2010) provide empirical examples of the ways in which planning and planners might approach 'wicked problems'. They show, for example, how in Sacramento in California planners pursued a 'collaborative policy dialogue' among all of the main players with an interest in the use and management of a river that was being over-exploited and where conflicts between different players (farmers, urban residents, conservationists, public agencies) and different uses (agriculture, household supply, industry, conservation, sport) were widespread (Innes and Booher, 2010: 43–52). Rather than adopting the orthodox approach – conducting technical studies, consulting stakeholders and then producing a technical 'fix', based on a new set of rules and regulations with a 'czar' to oversee implementation – they initiated a series of collaborative processes that brought together the key stakeholders, '...those who are directly affected by the issue, those who could make change happen and those who could block change' (Innes and Booher, 2010: 45). Out of this evolved a Water Forum where different players, sometimes involved in legal procedures against each other, could meet and discuss how to resolve problems. After several years, they produced a 400-page Water Forum Agreement, a memorandum of understanding that included the orthodox elements of a 'plan' – infrastructure investments, agreed monitoring standards for water quality and volumes – but also created new and more collaborative relations between the different parties. Some of this was reflected in new organizations but, equally important, were the different relationships between the key players. While significantly different interests remained between key players it was now easier, and more of a social norm, to try and find a way of negotiating conflicts of interest and to identify common goals, such as drawing down financial resources from the state government, that rewarded collaboration.

The achievements of collaborative policy dialogue are obtained through what Innes and Booher (2010), building on the work of Habermas (1981), theorize as 'collaborative rationality'. This is quite different from the 'rational choice' theory that has dominated much social science in recent decades. They identify three conditions that are essential to achieve the socially valuable outcomes that collaborative rationality can yield. There needs to be a diversity of interests of the participants; participants must have some inter-dependent interests (i.e. their interests cannot be met independently); and, participants must engage in face-to-face authentic dialogue. This is summarized as the DIAD (diversity, interdependence, authentic dialogue) theory (Figure 7.2). While any concrete application of this theory needs to be customized to specific issues and sets of participants such an approach

Figure 7.2   DIAD *(diversity, independence, authentic dialogue) network dynamics for collaborative rationality*

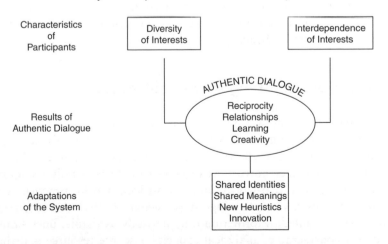

Source: Innes and Booher (2010: 35) © Taylor & Francis.

creates a very different role for the planner than those stipulated in orthodox approaches. While s/he needs technical skills the main focus is on creating a dialogue (e.g. arranging meetings, setting up new forums and organizing site visits) through which the key stakeholders reach agreement. The theory argues that this approach generates new forms of information and understanding across stakeholders and, when successful, does not simply produce a plan or an agreement but changes institutions so that pre-existing agencies become more effective and new organizations and networks evolve that are better able to tackle the 'wicked problems' of our times.

Project planning revisited

While debate remains heated about the relative strengths and weaknesses of orthodox/positivist project planning, adaptive administration, participatory learning and action, and post-modernist approaches, a number of lacunae around which agreement is occurring can be identified. Most planners will now agree that there is no optimal approach to project planning. The approach that is most appropriate in a specific case will depend on the objectives and the context. Increasingly, project planning is recognized as requiring a 'menu' of methodologies in which the very earliest stage of the project cycle involves the selection of the specific approach (or mix of approaches) that is to be utilized. For high specificity objectives in stable environments (e.g. building a road in a politically stable middle-income country), a conventional approach may be best. However, for low specificity objectives in unstable, low information environments (e.g. poverty-alleviation in a semi-arid area of a low-income country), more experimental and participatory approaches are most likely to achieve developmental goals.

Conclusion: planning in the real world

The great faith that was placed in national development planning and project planning in earlier times has eroded. But this does not mean that planning needs to be thrown on the scrap-heap. Rather it calls for new and more effective ways to plan that fully recognize that planning is a real-world, and not an ideal-world, practice. The approaches used for planning must recognize that knowledge is often (very) limited, information only partially available, uncertainty and risk considerable, analytical capacity a scarce resource and that planning is inherently a political process and a component of govern-ance and not some discrete technical realm.

For national planning this means that attempts to control the national economy, as though it was a well-understood machine, must be put aside. Instead, the focus should be on managing a lim-ited number of macroeconomic policies effectively; programming public investment on a medium-term view to ensure that the essential physical and social infrastructure (on which private-sector activity is dependent) is developed; and, strengthening the annual budget-ary process. This is what the governments of Bangladesh, Ghana, Uganda and Vietnam appear to be moving towards now that they have freed themselves from IFI-guided PRSs. For project planning, it entails the recognition that there is a menu of methodologies from which a choice appropriate to specific objectives and contexts must be made. A greater concern with implementation and stakeholder engagement (especially of poor and marginalized groups) is likely to yield dividends well beyond those that will be produced by increas-ingly sophisticated but irrelevant quantitative analysis. In an uncer-tain and rapidly changing world, 'acting out' approaches to societal problem-solving have much to recommend them despite the intellec-tual appeal of pretending that groups of technical experts can 'think through' such problems and come up with 'optimal solutions'.

Finally, many of the problems faced by planning in developing countries are endemic to planning in general – how to balance out public expectations for optimal decisions in a world in which con-flicting goals, limited understanding and data, and high levels of uncertainty and unpredictability are normal. But, some phenomena are specific to development. First, the dependence of developing countries on theories and ideas that tend to come from the North – so that there are long time-lags between the appearance of theoretical changes in the North and their transfer to the South for people there to assess their relevance. For example, while trainee planners in the USA will hear about 'post-modernist' planning, in the South this is rarely the case. Second, the nature of accountability processes around foreign aid means that Northern politicians have to make excessively high claims about how perfect aid investments are, and in order to maintain then the pretence of scientific policy, only positivist assess-ments are allowed.

Chapter 8

Decentralization within the State: Good Theory but Poor Practice?

A major obstacle to the effective performance of public bureaucracies in most developing countries has been the concentration of decision-making authority within central government. Public sector institutions have often been perceived as geographically and socially remote from citizens and acting without knowledge and concerns about actual problems and popular preferences. A common remedy to this malady in developing countries has been decentralization. Identified as 'the latest fashion in development administration' (Conyers, 1983) in the early 1980s, decentralization has subsequently transformed into a seemingly essential component of state reform. It appears to be *de rigueur* for developing countries to have one or more decentralization initiatives. Thus, a World Bank (IEG, 2008) review of its 'decentralization investments' between 1990 and 2006 counted 89 recipient countries. Other donors have been equally enthusiastic in their support of decentralization initiatives with one publication even suggesting that we are in 'the golden era of decentralization' (Siegle and O'Mahony, 2007: 2) in which the question is not whether one decentralizes but what and how one decentralizes (White and Smoke, 2005).

In reality, all national leaders have no choice but to decentralize some decision-making authority. Total centralization (all authority being vested in a single individual who takes all decisions) is infeasible even for the most efficient autocrat in the smallest micro-state. The size of the modern state brought about by its need to provide some services to at least part of its citizenry, to exercise political control over its territory and to bolster its legitimacy require that some authority is delegated and that some decisions are made outside of the national capital. In consequence, all systems of government involve a combination of centralized and decentralized authority.

The persistent dilemma is to find that combination of central control and local autonomy that satisfies popular demands and regime needs.

When central governments decide to engage in explicit decentralization initiatives they are not starting from scratch. There will be governance structures and processes which are already used to manage the affairs of citizens at the subnational level. Patterns of subnational governance vary across and even within countries but efforts to change these patterns should not be considered in isolation from other state-shaping policies. Decentralization is an aspect, albeit an important one, of the whole business of designing the state.

What is decentralization?

Over 50 years ago in the early days of development we were warned by the United Nations (1961) of the 'complexities of decentralization' and that was when only two types of decentralization within the state were acknowledged by officials and academics. Since then, further types of decentralization have been conceptualized, greatly extending the institutional arrangements and fields of activity which are covered by the term. It is therefore essential that when dealing with decentralization the concept is clearly defined. This not only avoids confused debate but also facilitates exploration of some of the leading issues in decentralization.

It is generally agreed that decentralization within the state involves a transfer of authority to perform some service to the public from an individual or an agency in central government to some other individual or agency which is 'closer' to the public to be served. The basis for such transfers is most often *territorial*, that is grounded in the desire to place authority at a lower level in a territorial hierarchy and thus geographically closer to service providers and clients (for example in provincial or district governments). However, transfers can also be made on a *functional* basis, that is, by transferring authority to an agency that is functionally specialized (See Table 8.1).

Such transfers of authority, whether territorial or functional, are of three main types. The first is when delegation is within formal political structures (for example when the central government gives additional authority for health and education services to local governments). The second is transfer within public administration or parastatal structures (for example from the headquarters of the Ministry of Education to its

Table 8.1   *Forms of decentralization*

Nature of delegation	Basis for delegation*	
	Territorial	*Functional*
Within formal Political structures	Devolution (Political decentralization, Local government, Democratic decentralization)	Interest group** Representation
Within public administrative or parastatal structures	Deconcentration (Administrative decentralization, field administration)	Establishment of Parastatals and Quangos***
From state sector to private sector	Privatization of devolved functions (deregulation, contracting out, voucher schemes)	Privatization of national functions (divestiture, deregulation, economic liberalization)

Notes: *In this study, geographical decentralization, such as the establishment of a new capital city or the transfer of parts of headquarters offices to locations outside of the capital city, is not included. This is because such activities merely involve relocation not delegation.

** This form has not received as much attention from writers on decentralization as other forms.

*** Rondinelli and his associates (e.g. Rondinelli and Nellis, 1986) often call this form 'delegation'. However, this is somewhat confusing as all forms of decentralization are, at least in theory, delegations.

provincial and district offices). The third is when the transfer is from an institution of the state to a non-state agency (for example when a government business enterprise, such as an airline or electricity generation organization, is sold off to private shareholders).

If we combine these distinctions then six main forms of decentralization can be identified. However, reality may be less amenable to such neat compartmentalization and the situation can be more complicated, featuring hybrids and 'mixed authorities' (for example when a council is established in which both elected representatives and public servants have voting rights). It is even more commonplace to find several types of decentralization going on at once (for example political decentralization to an elected council accompanied by administrative decentralization to district offices and selling off local government-owned utilities).

The types of decentralization

Having established our six distinctive types of decentralization in Table 8.1 we can now turn our attention to closer examination of them, and to the complexity that characterizes them.

Political decentralization

Political decentralization is the form of decentralization which dominates the popular imagination and has been promoted in the name of 'good governance'. For some it is the true and only valid expression of decentralization (Mawhood, 1983). It focuses on the transfer (rather than delegation) of political power and authority from central government to subnational levels of government. It is manifested in political bodies such as municipal councils, provincial boards and district assemblies and is frequently associated with democratic elections and the push for 'democratic governance' (UNDP, 2004). It is mainly manifested on a territorial basis rather than a functional one. However, there are examples of the latter such as provincial development councils in the Philippines in which a quarter of the members must be from civil society organizations. A leading rationale for democratic political decentralization of the democratic type is that it is a human right for citizens to choose their leaders, influence their decisions and hold them to account. Economics and public administration arguments in favour of political decentralization hold that local politicians will make more informed decisions than distant national-level officials and thus make better use of resources in line with local needs and wishes. Also evident in this optimistic view of political decentralization is that accountability of local officials will be enhanced leading not only to 'good governance' but also to more efficient, effective and responsive management. As we shall see later, the purported benefits of political decentralization are not necessarily reflected in practice (also see Box 8.1 for a case study).

Administrative decentralization

Administrative decentralization refers to the delegation or transfer of authority within government structures and comes in two major forms, one territorial and one functional.

Deconcentration has been the most frequently used type of administrative decentralization and the one that appears in the 'territorial'

Box 8.1   The challenge of deepening democracy and improving services through decentralization in South Africa

Under South Africa's apartheid regime local government was best characterized as deconcentration. It provided services but wielded little power. The African, Indian and Coloured populations were not registered to vote and could only aspire to membership of advisory boards that lacked any semblance of legitimacy. Citizenship was for the white population only.

In post-apartheid South Africa, democracy was given a decentralizing dimension in the constitution of 1996 which stated that there will be 'national, provincial and local spheres of government' and that these will be 'distinctive, interdependent and interrelated'. All South African citizens over the age of 18 were given the vote for national and local elections. All existing political boundaries were abolished and the country was then divided into nine provinces and 800 (later reduced to 283) municipalities of three different categories with legislatures at each level and municipal type. Of the latter, Category A cover the six biggest cities and have over 500,000 voters and Category B account for the rest of the country. They are both divided into wards. Half the councillors are elected by proportional representation and half by residents in each ward. Category C comprises the 47 district municipalities and are made up of local municipalities in a particular area – normally 4–6 municipalities per district. The district municipalities have 40 per cent of councillors elected by proportional representation and 60 per cent are councillors sent by the component local municipalities.

While democracy for all has been extended to the grassroots through the new local government system it has not been a panacea for good governance and improved service delivery by the municipalities. Among the problems have been deteriorating infrastructure; financial stress on local governments; the development of clientelism by politicians; corruption; a lack of capacity to perform routine functions and a neglect of training for them; and disinterested attitudes towards their responsibilities among local bureaucrats. This has resulted in diminishing legitimacy of local governments, regular public 'service delivery protests' and a lack of trust of them among citizens who turn out in low numbers for local elections. Confounding democratization theory is that trust and confidence in government in South Africa increases with its distance from the population. National government (the most trusted level) is aware of the problems of the new local government system and has been taking actions to address them such as the capacity-building Project Consolidate and the Vuna Awards for innovation or improvement in service delivery. However, it will be a long road to achieving participatory democracy, accountable local government and steady improvements in service delivery across the whole local government system.

Sources: Reddy and Maharaj 2008; Tapscott, 2008.

column of Table 8.1. It can be formally defined as 'the transfer of authority over specified decision-making, financial, and management functions by administrative means to different levels under the jurisdictional authority of the central government' (Cohen and Peterson, 1999: 24). No authority is given away by the ministry or other central government organization. It is simply a matter of redistributing some of that authority downwards to ministerial field offices. For example, a Ministry of Education may delegate responsibility for hiring teachers to its provincial field offices; purchasing of drugs may be delegated by the Ministry of Health to provincial hospitals and district health centres. Central governments may favour this mode of decentralization as it gives them 'greater political, administrative and technical control' while aid agencies may like it where it provides a ready-made delivery system and thus should reduce costs (Cohen and Peterson, 1999: 25). While it is perceived as a weaker form of decentralization than the democratic political variety there are benefits that could derive from deconcentration. However, all those listed in Table 8.2 could be gained from political decentralization.

There is, however, no guarantee that these benefits will be realized. For example, field officers may not have the resources or technical skills required to perform their tasks. Inefficient bureaucratic behaviours may still pervade local management. Officials may be more concerned with controlling the behaviour of citizens and establishing the dominance of the state (or even their political party) over society than with responding to the expressed needs of local populations and the delivery of quality services to them. 'Normal professionalism' may prevail whereby the opinions and knowledge of local residents are disregarded (Chambers, 1992). Motivation may be lacking among public servants if field jobs provide poor salaries and conditions. Local-level coordination may suffer where there are disagreements between locally based public servants belonging to different ministries over who has authority over what and the centre may simply not allow decisions or resource control of any significance to be deconcentrated.

Delegation is the functional mode of administrative decentralization that occurs when 'central governments transfer responsibility for decisionmaking and administration of public functions to semi-autonomous organizations not wholly controlled by the central government but ultimately accountable to it' (Rondinelli, 1999: 3). Typically these organizations are state-owned industrial enterprises, public utilities, transport authorities and urban or regional

Table 8.2   *The potential benefits of deconcentration*

- *Accessibility of officials.* Officials are available for consultation, advice and complaint. As local officials can exercise decentralized authority, they make the decisions and do not need to pass them up the line to distant central offices.
- *Mobilization of local resources.* It is easier for locally based officials to identify local resources, both human and physical, and then mobilize them in the pursuit of locally determined developmental purposes. Officials should also be familiar with specific local constraints and the dynamics of local politics.
- *Rapid response to local needs.* Officials are better placed to respond rapidly to local needs as they are located in the territory and fully aware of local conditions.
- *Orientation to the specific local needs.* Because the officials know the local conditions, they are well placed to make decisions and allocate resources which fit with the specific conditions prevailing in a particular territory. Each subnational territory may have some unique features which can be taken into account when planning and allocating resources.
- *Motivation of field personnel.* Appointed government officials are more motivated to perform well when they have greater responsibility for programmes they manage.
- *Inter-office coordination.* Coordination between offices dealing with different functions is more easily achieved at the local level where officials are physically close together and are often familiar with each other.
- *Central agencies.* The decentralization of service functions relieves central agencies of routine tasks. Responsibility for these has been passed down to the local level. Central agencies can thus focus on improving the quality of policy. Monitoring local-level performance and providing assistance to subnational units are key elements of this reformulated government role.

Sources: Turner, 2002b; Blunt and Turner, 2007.

development corporations. Aid agencies have contributed to the delegation mode of administrative decentralization through the promotion of Project Management Units (PMUs). These units were designed to overcome the complexities of inter-agency administration, for example in integrated area development, but have sometimes aroused hostility from staff in line ministries who resent the removal of authority and often superior terms and conditions of PMU staff. Cohen and Peterson (1999) see delegation even extending to some relations between government and private firms and place contracting out, privatization and deregulation under the delegation umbrella. This would seem to make the 'umbrella' unwieldy and reduces the utility of the concept as a particular type of administrative decentralization.

Market decentralization

Economic or market decentralization (from state sector to private sector) has been a relatively recent addition to the decentralization lexicon but one which has been enthusiastically adopted by those who have embraced the idea of a minimalist state (e.g. Rondinelli et al., 1989). It has been described as 'the most complete form of decentralization' as it involves shifting responsibility for functions from public to private sector (Rondinelli, 1999: 4). As such, one may ask whether this is actually decentralization, as responsibilities are being transferred to entities outside of the state. Two major forms of economic decentralization are identified by Rondinelli (1999): privatization and deregulation. Whether these concepts should be subsumed under the ever-expanding umbrella of decentralization is debatable. Rondinelli (1999: 4) admits that privatization itself 'can range in scope from the provision of goods and services based entirely on the free operation of the market to public-private partnerships' (see also Batley and Larbi, 2004). Deregulation, the other type of economic decentralization, involves the removal of legal constraints for private suppliers of goods and services to compete with government or prior monopolies. Whether this should be seen as 'decentralization' is once more debatable and the conceptual waters are further muddied by Rondinelli (1999) placing 'contracting out' in this sub-type.

The different types of decentralization described above provide the framework of reference which can be used by actors in the policy process to conceptualize alternatives, and then analyse, select, implement and evaluate them. But decentralization should not be considered as a process separate from other initiatives which are intended to change the institutional arrangements of the state. Decentralization is an element of state design and these initiatives take place in environments shared by other development policies and involving officials and citizens who are simultaneously affected by and engaging with those environments. It should therefore be seen as a potential contributor to improving the efficiency and effectiveness of the state and economy, but it is part of a larger project and should not be viewed in isolation.

A further complication is that 'the types [of decentralization] are not mutually exclusive and may co-exist in combinations leading to a bewildering range of possible and actual central-local configurations, and even variation within countries' (Turner, 1999: 5). For example, using the classification in Table 8.1: in the Philippines there is territorial based political decentralization which features both popularly elected and functional representatives on subnational councils. There is also deconcentration of some responsibilities which have not been devolved to subnational political authorities and there are parastatal organizations which operate throughout the country. Finally, some local political bodies have experimented with economic decentralization by contracting out and entering into public private partnerships (PPPs). Such complementary mixed modes of decentralization are more the rule than the exception. Whether the right mixture has been put together can vary considerably between countries.

Why do governments choose to decentralize?

There are several rationales for governments to engage in territorial decentralization but liberal democratic theory provides the strongest and most enduring support for it. Smith (1985) categorizes the political benefits which should derive from territorial decentralization of the political variety (see Table 8.3). The first two of these benefits, political education and training, were typically used by colonial powers as they prepared to depart from their overseas territories but are rarely heard now. The third and fourth, relating to political stability and political participation, are the most commonly cited political benefits that contemporary national leaders claim for decentralization. The latter two, accountability and responsiveness, are also often cited, though they overlap with justifications deriving from theories of public administration and management that see decentralization primarily in terms of enhancing the effectiveness and technical efficiency of service delivery (Table 8.3).

Public administration justifications for territorial decentralization focus on the promise of improved management of resources through the delegation of decision-making within organizations and coordination between organizations. The argument is that decentralization should bring better decision-making and this will lead to enhanced organizational efficiency and effectiveness. These gains should be manifested in the following:

Table 8.3   *The political benefits of democratic decentralization*

1. *Political education* teaches the mass of the population about the role of political debate, the selection of representatives and the nature of policies, plans and budgets, in a democracy.

2. *Training in political leadership* enables prospective political leaders to develop skills in policy-making, political party operations and budgeting with the result that the quality of national politicians is enhanced.

3. *Political stability* is secured by participation in formal politics, through voting and perhaps other practices (for example, active support of a party) which strengthen trust in government so that 'social harmony, community spirit and political stability' are achieved. In addition, a mechanism is created to prepare the masses for the profound social and economic changes associated with development.

4. *Political equality* from greater political participation will reduce the likelihood of the concentration of power. Political power will be more broadly distributed thus making decentralization a mechanism that can meet the needs of the poor and disadvantaged.

5. *Accountability* is enhanced because local representatives are more accessible to the populace and can thus be held more closely accountable for their policies and outcomes than distant national political leaders (or public servants). A vote at local elections is a unique mechanism for the populace to register its satisfaction or dissatisfaction with the performance of representatives.

6. *Responsiveness* of government is improved because local representatives are best placed to know the exact nature of local needs and how they can be met in a cost-effective way.

Source: A summary of the writing Smith, 1985.

1. *Locally specific plans* can be tailor-made for local areas using detailed and up-to-date information that is only locally available.

2. *Inter-organizational coordination* can be better achieved because it is managed at the local level.

3. *Experimentation and innovation* are encouraged by the decentralization of decision-making and increase the chances of more effective development strategies being generated and subsequently diffused.

4. *Motivation of field-level personnel* is enhanced through gaining greater responsibility for the programmes and functions they manage.

5. *Workload reduction in central government organizations* is achieved by relieving them from routine functions thus giving them more time to consider strategic issues leading to improved policy.

6. *Accountability* is improved due to the close proximity of citizens to officials, leading to better use of resources and improved service delivery.

Economists support decentralization on the basis of improved efficiency. 'Their rationale is that decisions about public expenditure that are made by a level of government that is closer and more responsive to a local constituency are more likely to reflect the demand for local services than decisions made by a remote central government' (Ford, 1999: 6). This is the principle of 'subsidiarity' which argues in favour of placing decisions about resource allocation down to the lowest level at which appropriate capacities and competencies exist. A further economic support for decentralization derives from the idea that it promotes competitiveness and innovation. This justification for economic decentralization employs arguments about the greater efficiency of markets as distinct from bureaucracies. The basic contention is that 'under conditions of reasonably free choice, the provision of some public goods is more economically efficient when a large number of local institutions are involved than when only the central government is the provider.... a large number of providers offers citizens more options and choices' (Rondinelli et al., 1989: 59). Such competition promotes efficiency with both supply- and demand-side benefits deriving from institutional pluralism (Smith, 1985). But is this line of economic reasoning drawn from wealthy countries equally applicable to developing countries?

While these theoretical arguments can be called upon to justify decentralization they are not necessarily the reasons why governments decide to go down this path. A variety of political factors – not necessarily those in liberal democratic theory – provide the primary impulses for territorial decentralization. These include the pressure generated in national democratization movements which finds further expression in calls for local-level democracy. For example, in the Philippines the 'people power revolution' which contributed so much to the overthrow of President Marcos's authoritarian regime flowed on from the national level to the grassroots with the Local Government Act of 1991. But care should be taken not to assume correlation is cause and effect. For example, the temporal association of democratization and decentralization in Latin America has been judged as 'insufficient to establish causation' (Montero and Samuels, 2004: 17). Thus, in Bolivia the decentralizing Popular Participation Law 1994 was not related to pressure from the subnational territories while in post-authoritarian Chile decentralization was a top-down initiative (O'Neill, 2004; Bland, 2004).

Another form of political pressure comes from the populations of subnational territories making demands for greater decision-making powers over their affairs as in Papua New Guinea following independence. The pressure may derive from a variety of causes including dissatisfaction over resource allocation or ethnic conflict. The central government then sees decentralization as a mechanism for resolving these conflicts while maintaining the overall integrity of the state. Serious ethnic conflict involving armed struggles against the state may also result in the creation of special arrangements in which the territorial entity associated with the ethnic group is given greater authorities than have been given to the other subnational territories of the state. Such 'autonomous regions' include Bougainville (Papua New Guinea), Muslim Mindanao (Philippines), Aceh (Indonesia) and Pakistan's Tribal Areas. All were established after protracted armed struggles some of which are far from resolved.

The creation of autonomous regions can be seen as asymmetrical decentralization where there may be different institutional arrangements for subnational territories. These contingent solutions to the unique problems of individual territories are not confined to ethnic nationalism. The megacities of Asia-Pacific also require special arrangements to cope with the massive populations and particular issues that such huge agglomerations of people present (ADB, 2008a; GlobeScan and MRC McLean Hazel, nd). Governance of a megacity especially requires coordinating mechanisms for services, regulations, infrastructure development and representation which span the many component government units and authorities which will have been swallowed up in urban growth. For example, the Philippines has the Metro Manila Development Authority (12 million population), Thailand the Bangkok Metropolitan Authority (12 million population), and Indonesia the Special Region of Jakarta (9.5 million). Each has a system of governance which differs from those for other subnational territories across the countries because each is geared to the particular demands of the megacity.

In post-conflict states central governments or their advisers may view decentralization as a mode of state-building from below, as in Afghanistan and Iraq. Alternatively, the central government of a post-conflict state may wait until the political regime is stabilized and then extend democratic practices to the local level at least in part to assert greater state control over territory and population, as in Cambodia. Finally, the declining political legitimacy of highly centralized models of governance and fiscal relations has pushed countries towards decentralization (Eckhardt, 2008).

Central governments may also choose decentralization as a mode of improving service delivery. This has been a longstanding rationale (e.g. Rondinelli, 1981; Rondinelli and Nellis, 1986; Smith, 1985, 1993) and has often featured in official statements explaining decentralization. Donors have also shown increasing interest in this rationale possibly because of their commitment to human development especially as expressed in the Millennium Development Goals (MDGs) and also because of disappointments with the results of earlier decentralization initiatives. The advocates of economic decentralization also argue that better services should result from market-friendly measures such as contracting out, public private partnerships and privatization. However, for cash-strapped governments the major impetus to experiment with these market modes of decentralization might be to reduce expenditure.

Rationales for territorial decentralization are numerous, but the extent to which these figure in the calculations of central government leaders who make the decision to decentralize is most often unclear. They invariably face more immediate imperatives, often of a political nature, to which they must respond. The major issue then is not whether to decentralize but rather '*what* and *how* to decentralise' (IEG, 2008: 2).

Accounting for success in decentralization

Despite the great expectations for decentralization, its history is littered with disappointments, yet this does not appear to have dimmed enthusiasm for such reforms. The leading issue is how to derive 'optimal results' from the process (White and Smoke, 2005: 1).

This raises questions of measurability. How do we know when 'optimal results' are achieved? Decentralization initiatives rarely have precise goals against which results can be measured. They may aim to democratize or improve service delivery but the aims are most often broad and unamenable to measurement. Even when minimum service standards are required, as in Indonesia, it may prove a daunting task to reach agreement on the indicators and the desired level of achievement. Insufficiency of data may add further to evaluation difficulties while statistical services in some less developed countries often lack both capability and resources. Perception-based measurement methods, on the other hand, can be problematic as the judgements of different demographic groups may vary. Some perceptions may reflect unrealistic expectations of what decentralization can deliver, and an inability to assess what decentralization has delivered.

Assigning cause and effect to decentralization is a challenging task. Other forces, events and policies in the environment may be responsible for favourable or adverse changes in citizens' welfare. For example, the Global Financial Crisis of 2007–2009 had effects which were most often beyond the power of local governments in the developing world to address. There is also the consideration of time. Thus, we should perhaps distinguish between decentralization transitions and the ensuing stage when the benefits of decentralization are supposedly reaped. In the transition period, action focuses on putting the new systems in place such as inter-governmental financial arrangements, the human resource management system, and the clarification of roles and responsibilities. Once these systems are functioning then local governments can be more attentive to serving the needs of the citizenry. But in some instances, the implementation of new arrangements lasts a long time and the difficulties encountered during this transition period may lead to management problems that adversely affect service delivery and other governmental functions. Finally, diversity in approaches to decentralization means that different combinations of factors will influence success in each instance. Environmental factors may also vary considerably between countries and even within them, for example, the difference between a very poor post-conflict state like Timor Leste and a middle income country with a stable political regime like Malaysia; or the contrast between the weakness of the state and the poverty levels of citizens in conflict-ridden areas of the southern Philippines compared to the relative affluence and order of the provinces around the capital in central Luzon island.

Keeping in mind these provisos and Smith's (1980: 139) still valid warning that the measurement of decentralization 'cannot be a precise exercise, rough judgment will have to be made', we can identify some of the factors which will influence the success of decentralization.

A strong central state: for decentralization to be successful it is highly desirable that the state should be strong. As Hutchcroft (2001: 44) has observed, 'For those countries that begin strategies of decentralization without a strong foundation of *prior* centralization, the tasks at hand may be insurmountable.' It is the central government which assumes responsibility for decentralization. Its leaders make the decision to decentralize, its bureaucrats draw up the plans, and its ministries supervise implementation. It is national legislation which delineates the form of decentralization, the distribution of powers and the nature of fiscal relations. And after the design and implementation of decentralization are accomplished it is the central state which should monitor events to ensure that citizens receive expected levels of service and inequalities do not grow. Central government must ensure that national laws and regulations are obeyed, but it must also assist subnational governments to achieve welfare gains and overcome difficulties. To do all these things, the central state must be effective. It must have the capability, capacity and willingness to support decentralized governance. There is, however, a danger: that is, strong central states may have a tendency to be authoritarian. The central political and administrative organizations may wish to dominate their subnational counterparts. Thus, there is also the need for the strong state to be an enabling state that assists local governments to achieve their potential.

Funds following function: one of the most oft-quoted axioms of decentralization is that 'funds should follow functions'. That is, unless adequate financial resources are made available to those who are responsible for decentralized functions, then the performance of the tasks associated with those functions is likely to suffer. This has been a persistent problem in African decentralization experiments where local governments or organizations may be allocated inadequate funds by central government to cover the costs of their new-found functions or are not granted appropriate revenue-raising powers. It is the central government's responsibility to ensure that funding is adequate and sustainable. Box 8.2 sets out the fiscal options in decentralization.

Planning and politics: it is a self-evident truth that planning is essential for decentralization. In an ideal world, policy-makers would consider all options and consult as widely as possible before making decisions. However, decentralization is never planned and implemented in optimal conditions. These activities are more likely to take place in turbulent environments where political pressures are exerted by a range of interested actors to have their demands incorporated into legislation and implementation plans. Decentralization is a deeply political process, and consequently politics plays a central role in shaping the course of the decentralization process. The centrality of politics requires its management whether in planning or

Box 8.2   The four pillars of fiscal decentralization

Fiscal decentralization is sometimes portrayed as a type of decentralization but it does not occur independently of other forms of decentralization. Whether decentralization is political or administrative there must be fiscal arrangements relating to the management of revenue and expenditure (although most literature deals with it in terms of political decentralization). UNDP identifies four pillars of fiscal decentralization:

PILLAR 1 – Expenditure Responsibilities: the principal of 'subsidiarity' is generally invoked, that is 'government functions should be assigned to the lowest level of government that is capable of efficiently undertaking this function'. This suggests that central government should provide public goods that benefit the entire nation (e.g. defence); deal with income distribution and social policies (e.g. address income differentials between poor and rich regions); and deal with activities that involve spill-overs or 'externalities' between local governments (e.g. immunization against contagious diseases). The assignment of other expenditure responsibilities for the many remaining services depends on the functions decentralized and the capacity of subnational units to perform the associated duties efficiently and effectively.

PILLAR 2 – Revenue Assignments: policy-makers face the question of what sources of revenue should be allocated to subnational government. Easy administration and income stability are preferred qualities for local government taxes as are direct benefits for the local population. Central government may intervene to set the rules, such as tax rates, and thus limit subnational government autonomy and revenue collection.

PILLAR 3 – Inter-governmental Transfer: transfer of grants from central government are frequently the major source of revenue for subnational governments. For example, in Africa the average percentage of revenue from central government transfers is around 60 per cent while in Indonesia and the Philippines, the most decentralized countries in Southeast Asia, transfers account for 70–80 per cent of local governments' income. An important goal of these transfers is to provide fiscal balance, to fund specific national priorities and to counter the effect of inter-regional spill-overs or externalities. However, there can be high dependency of subnational governments on these transfers and where the state has budget difficulties subnational governments can suffer.

PILLAR 4 – Subnational Borrowing: this occurs when a local government's revenue is not balanced with its own source revenue and inter-governmental transfers, Such borrowed funds are generally judged appropriate for capital expenditure but not for recurrent expenditure. In practice, there is limited use of borrowing because of poor creditworthiness and/or central government restrictions.

It should be noted that while the principles of fiscal decentralization may be widely known they are not necessarily manifested in practice.

Source: Adapted from UNDP, 2005.

implementation. Brokers, boundary-spanners, champions and nego-
tiators are needed to forge agreements among stakeholders.

Flexibility: one of the design dilemmas of decentralization is the
degree of flexibility in decision-making that should be awarded to
subnational units of governance. Central government agencies frequently resent ceding their responsibilities to local governments and
have attempted to maintain controls through regulation, oversight,
performance standards or finance. Such techniques can be utilized
to preserve central dominance and in so doing stifle local initiative
and the opportunities which decentralization supposedly provides.
Ideally, decentralization should present local decision-makers with
the flexibility to respond to the preferences of constituents and to
opportunities presented by the specific environment. This is not to
suggest that a *carte blanche* be given to local decision-makers. Such
precipitate action could be a boon to the local purveyors of bad
governance. Rather, there should be policy space in which officials
can manoeuvre when making and implementing policy to encourage
innovation and efficiency. It should be recognized that public servants working at the local level may prefer the security of familiar
centrally imposed rules. For example, in Indonesia despite the radical changes brought about by decentralization in 2001, some things
remained constant. Prime among these was human resource management (HRM) and the dominant role played by central personnel
agencies in defining, monitoring and overseeing the HRM regime
operating at subnational level (Turner et al., 2009).

Doing what is feasible: poorly considered and planned decentralization processes can have dire consequences which are very
difficult to reverse. For example, in 1977 the Papua New Guinea
parliament passed the Organic Law on Provincial Government in
response to a micronationalist secessionist movement and popular
sentiment. Benefits, such as improved income opportunities and better health services, failed to materialize in many provinces leading
interested actors to lobby for change with quite profound differences
of opinion over what form the change would take. Eventually a new
Organic Act was passed in 1995 which has contributed to worsen-
ing levels of government performance in many provinces, with some
institutional arrangements existing only in the law rather than in
reality. In retrospect, the consequences of the original reforms in
Papua New Guinea were not well analysed during policy-making
and planning and the revised decentralized structure has proved to
be infeasible and often dysfunctional given the country's political

dynamics, the territorial distribution of human capability, resource constraints and the nature of inter-governmental relations (see May and Regan, 1997; May, 2005). The lesson is that in order to improve human welfare, decentralization initiatives must take into consideration the constraints imposed by politics, resource availability and organizational capacity. The degree of complexity must also be carefully considered in relation to these factors using the dictum, 'simple as can be, complex as must', as the rule of thumb.

Minimizing risks of elite capture: addressing the possibilities of elite capture is one of the perennial challenges for any decentralization process which aims to improve human development. For example, in a review of Bangladesh's experience with decentralization Hulme and Siddiquee (1999: 25) noted that 'The major focus of local representatives was not to improve service, but rather to seek privileged access for their kin and clients'. Furthermore, local elites were involved in relations of mutual benefit with national-level elites. Political patronage and corruption were features of successive decentralization reforms. There is also strong evidence of elite capture of benefits in the *Panchayats* of India. In a review of the literature, Johnson (2003: 43) concluded that 'the powers and functioning of the *Panchayats* appear to have been undermined by a number of familiar factors: interference from higher level authorities, a resistant bureaucracy, and elite capture'. Even relatively successful examples of decentralization do not appear to be immune from manipulation of the benefits of decentralization by self-interested elites. For example, writing on Indonesia, Priyono (2005: 3) claimed that 'the oligarch-elite has adjusted themselves with democracy, monopolize[d] it and manipulate[d] it for their own interest, including at the local level'. In the Philippines, while pointing to various benefits deriving from decentralization, Cariño (2007: 109) also found that 'bosses and warlords still thrive and enjoy even more powers to manipulate with even less central oversight'.

Decentralization may in fact be used by central governments as a mechanism for retaining power at the centre. In Africa, Crook (2003: 85) has noted the propensity of central government to use funding to create dependent elites or alliances with local elites. Ribot (2003: 56) shows how local committees for forest management in Sub-Saharan Africa are often constituted to reflect the views of 'a few commercially interested parties or are under the control of the local elites'. To address the issue of elite capture requires a central government which is interested and committed to aligning local elites' actions with the goals of decentralization and to effective bottom-up systems of accountability at the local level. (Box 8.3 sets out a range of these devices.) Informed understanding of the local political situation is an essential prerequisite. This may also reveal that not all members of local and national elites are exclusively self-interested. It is not an innate property of 'eliteness'. Some local elites may provide excellent developmental leadership as will be seen in the next item.

Leadership: there is little written about the role of leadership in decentralization yet all anecdotal evidence points to it as being a crucial variable in success. In the Philippines, the annual *Galing Pook* awards for innovation and excellence in local governance have provided many examples of exemplary leadership in pursuit of the

---

Box 8.3   Making local governments accountable to citizens

In 2004, the World Bank noted that 'services fail poor people – in access, in quantity, in quality'. One of the main reasons was that there was a lack of accountability of governments. Traditional vertical upward methods of accountability to political leaders and bureaucrats were not working. Citizens, especially the poor and marginalized, had little or no influence over the services they received and were either dissatisfied or unaware of their entitlements. It was time, said the World Bank, to amplify the voices of the poor to influence governments to provide adequate services.

The way of achieving this was through social accountability defined as a broad range of actions and mechanisms that citizens, communities, independent media and civil society organizations can use to hold public officials accountable. Most actions were at the local level.

Participatory budgeting: involvement of citizens in local budgeting
Public expenditure tracking: following budget allocations to check that there is no leakage en route to their destinations at the local level and that the money is spent on services as planned
Citizen report cards: citizens evaluating local government services in terms of their quality, availability, timeliness and other criteria
Community score cards: communities evaluating services and their delivery
Social audits: citizens mobilize to participate in auditing the performance and expenditures of government organizations at the local level
Citizen charters: citizens participate in defining expected levels of service delivery, monitoring performance and reporting problems for remedial action

public good (Cariño, 2007; Brillantes, 1999). Thus, in writing about the success of poorer municipalities in receiving the awards Cariño (2007: 97) notes that 'visionary leadership by local chief executives and an aroused citizenry' are the common themes in each case. In Indonesia, a series of case studies of innovation in service delivery found leadership to be a major determinant of success (WB-AIDG, 2006). The case studies involved diverse innovations including a community-based water project, participatory planning, the creation of learning communities among children, fee-for-service health services and budget transparency. A common element was local rather than external leadership in a style which exhibited flexibility, personal involvement, trust-building and raising awareness of positive impacts. In Mexico, Grindle (2007: 70) found that the leadership of both elected and appointed officials was the most significant factor in explaining differences in the ways municipalities were 'adjusting' to decentralization. However, she also pointed to other influences and to the fact that the benefits of decentralization should be viewed as 'a palette of possibilities' rather than as inevitable realities.

While it appears that 'transformational leadership' can make a great difference to the success of decentralization at the local level, it is not clear as to the conditions under which such leadership can emerge and how the gains made under such leadership can be maintained. Finally, a word of warning on leadership. As Tendler (1997) has demonstrated we should not assume that all good things in decentralization derive from the 'intentionality' of transformational leadership. 'Inadvertency' can also produce surprising benefits. What we need is to recognize and study such instances 'to enable inadvertency to be turned into intention the next time around' (Tendler, 1997: 165).

Commitment: the reason why governments decide to decentralize may have considerable effect on the effectiveness of decentralization in terms of improved services and welfare gains. Political motives dominate decisions to decentralize. These can include satisfying the demands of local and/or national elites, responding to popular pressure for greater participation in decision-making, or resolving secessionist and autonomy movements. In such circumstances the central government is addressing political issues which threaten the incumbents of national political office and even the maintenance of the political regime. In attending to the resolution of the political issues which lead to decentralization, national governments may be much less concerned about improving service delivery. In such circumstances it is likely that decentralization will bring few positive gains to citizens in terms of their health, education and economic position.

Conclusion: taking stock and looking forward

Decentralization has become a 'must do' policy choice in developing countries. Governments have experimented with a wide and increasing range of initiatives which are placed under the extensive umbrella of decentralization. It has become orthodoxy, one that has been endorsed and funded by donors, although the patterns of central–local relations that have emerged and then evolved show enormous variation.

Political decentralization has been the most common type of decentralization in accordance with the dominant global discourse of democratization. Administrative decentralization has generally played a supporting role. Political decentralization has necessarily been accompanied by fiscal decentralization although the degree of both modes varies considerably according to essentially political causes such as regime type, the power of local elites and the willingness of central bureaucracies to relinquish authority and resources. Market decentralization has received a less enthusiastic reception in developing countries, especially in the least developed where markets are rudimentary at best, but even in middle-income countries bureaucrats and policy-makers have been reluctant to cede control over state resources.

The complexity of decentralization and the difficulty of establishing causal relationships about what leads to improved government performance means that despite the accumulated knowledge about decentralization there is still uncertainty about what works best. Furthermore, there may be differential objectives among decentralization's stakeholders. Central governments may place political stability above performance improvement while some donor staff emphasize accountability. Poor citizens may place the highest value on improved services while local elites can see decentralization as providing opportunities for power and economic gain. Such differentiation demonstrates that decentralization of any type is intensely political, and that politically based actions are evident at all stages in the decentralization policy process. Failure to appreciate the political dynamics of decentralization can lead to serious miscalculations about how to secure developmental benefits from it. Even the desired benefits will be disputed.

While there is no crystal ball to give us precise specifications of the future of decentralization we have lessons available from experience and can make some generalizations which may help to guide future actions:

Decentralization is a component of state design and must be seen in a holistic frame: Decentralization is not a discrete area of policy. It is an aspect of the whole business of state-building and development and can contribute to realizing the rights of citizens, especially those who are poor and marginalized.

Decentralization is context specific: While there are some principles of decentralization which find widespread endorsement, such as in the fiscal field, they must be applied in contrasting environments. Environmental factors mean that each country's decentralization will be different from any other.

Political factors are significant at each stage of decentralization: The importance of politics in determining the design and operation of decentralization has been stressed throughout this chapter. Even where the rhetoric of democratization is trumpeted loudly, elites and leading classes often strive to maintain inequitable status quos by dominating electoral competition and acting to prevent the voice of the poor being articulated or heard. Politics in decentralization is not simply about voting, it is about asserting influence or control over decisions which affect citizens' daily lives.

Decentralization will always build on something that is already there, however weak that something may be: Decentralization takes place within the boundaries of states, and states have structures. Sometimes these structures are weak and in severe cases they collapse, as in the Solomon Islands or Afghanistan. However, even in these extreme cases vestigial and/or informal administration most often continues in subnational territories, the territorial divisions remain, ideas about state responsibilities are still held and shared by citizens, while notions about the appropriate conduct of administration and politics at subnational levels are still evident.

Decentralization and centralization should be seen as ongoing activities in all developing countries – there is no final destination: In all states there are centrifugal and centripetal forces operating at all times. We live in a time when centrifugal (decentralizing) forces appear to be in the ascendancy although it is not difficult to spot centripetal (centralizing) forces as well; and both may be occurring simultaneously. The objective of policy-makers and policy implementers should be to find the balance between these forces which best serves citizens. But environments change, sometimes dramatically, and new policy ideas assume ascendancy. This means that adjustment will be a constant feature of central–local relations as it is in high-income states. It will always be a work in progress.

Chapter 9

Economic Development and the Public Sector: From State Ownership to Enabling Environment

From the start of the first development decade to the present, developing country governments have asked the question 'what should we do about the economy?' They have appreciated that economic development is one of their major concerns. It is a prerequisite for improving the welfare of citizens, addressing poverty and maintaining political legitimacy (with the masses or with the elite). But there have been multiple answers to their longstanding question and these have varied considerably over time as different ideologies have gained ascendancy and led to different degrees of government involvement in the economy. The policy pendulum has swung from governments perceiving that they need to be directly, and sometimes very heavily, involved in economic production through their own businesses to government being urged to leave economic development largely to the invisible hand of the market. In this chapter, we take a historical view of government's role in the economy paying particular attention to public enterprises and their privatization, public-private sector cooperation and to the current concern with creating enabling environments for economic development.

The public enterprise solution

In the early development years, newly independent governments saw their most pressing problem as how to generate the rapid economic growth needed to catch up with the rich countries. But the path from traditional to modern society was strewn with obstacles. The major obstruction was 'market failure' where goods and services are subject to inefficient allocation. In such circumstances, government needed

227

to step in to control the 'commanding heights' of the economy and to intervene where market failure was seen to be inhibiting growth and national progress. One of the policies favoured by developing country governments was to establish public enterprises or state-owned enterprises (SOEs) to fill the gaps that the private sector could not fill. These state-owned production units sold their outputs and were thus directly involved in the market process. Although the organizations assumed various forms, we can provide a checklist, adapted from Praxy and Sicherl (1981: 214), of their typical features:

• owned by public authorities ... to the extent of 50 per cent or more;
• under the top managerial control of the owning public authorities ... including the right to appoint top management and to formulate critical policy decisions;
• established for the achievement of a defined set of public purposes, which may be multi-dimensional in character;
• engaged in activities of a business character;
• involve the basic idea of investment and returns and service

Public enterprises were first established by the colonial powers to facilitate economic development. For example, in Nigeria the British started to set up marketing boards in 1936 and converted selected government departments into public enterprises after 1945, such as the Nigerian Railway Corporation and the Nigerian Ports Authority (Adamolekum, 1983). When India became independent in 1947, the country possessed more public enterprises than Britain, the former colonial power. But the massive expansion of public enterprises in the developing world came after independence in the 1960s and 1970s – and it occurred in all types of economies from communist through to capitalist (see Box 9.1 for the example of Bangladesh).

For socialist and communist countries there was a necessary ideological commitment to the public ownership of the means of production. Private ownership was seen to lead to exploitation and underdevelopment whereas public ownership would ensure that the evils of capitalism were avoided. Nationalism often backed up such views and provided a potent political justification for government intervention in market activities. Such action would ensure that foreigners and multinational corporations would not secure control of the economy. This nationalism was not confined to socialist and communist countries but could be used as justification for the

Box 9.1   The origin of public enterprises in Bangladesh

Bangladesh became independent in December 1971 after nine months of bloody war which took a heavy toll on life and property. The immediate imperatives at independence were to establish a civil administration and to rehabilitate the economy. The political leadership did not design a comprehensive strategy to manage the economy after independence, but it was soon faced with no alternative but to take over the management of industrial units and financial institutions. This included 725 industrial units (47 per cent of the country's fixed assets in the industrial sector) which had been abandoned by their non-local owners who had left the country.

Within three months the government had decided in favour of a much broader nationalization which included the entire jute, sugar and textile industries. This increased the state's ownership of modern industry from 34 per cent to 92 per cent. The government created 10 sector corporations to control, supervise, manage and coordinate different groups of industries. Further, all banks were nationalized and reconstituted into six national commercial banks (NCBs). This expansion of state ownership took place under a political leadership that had traditionally followed a middle-of-the-road economic philosophy. It had neither the ideological conviction nor the cadre nor the organizational capacity to oversee the implementation politically. However, the constitution subsequently strengthened the ideological base for state ownership since it incorporated socialism as one of its basic principles.

The outcome of state ownership and management of industrial enterprises was in general unsuccessful. In the period up to 1975, capacity utilization was low, state-owned industries suffered losses in successive years, and the index of industrial production did not show much improvement.

Source: Adapted from Chowdhury, 1992.

nationalization of foreign enterprises and the creation of new public enterprises in market-oriented economies.

Further justification and encouragement of public enterprise formation came from economic theory and the perceived role of central planning (see Chapter 7). Development was seen as something that did not occur automatically. It had to be engineered by governments through central planning. The examples of the Soviet Union (then seen as a great economic success), the wartime planning of the UK economy and the Marshall Plan for rehabilitating post-Second World War Europe were presented as practical demonstrations of the efficacy of central planning. The need to control the direction of economic development, the absence of domestic capital or the reluctance of the private sector to invest, mistrust of private sector motivations, strategic requirements and inadequate indigenous entrepreneurial skills were utilized as justifications for government participation in market activities. Besides filling the gaps in the economy the new public enterprises would generate profits, which could be used for new investment, and provide jobs for graduates from the expanded educational system.

A commitment to big government complemented this economic outlook. Governments were seen as or claimed to be the only actors with the capacity to engineer the necessary changes for development; and if this meant making steel, marketing crops, running plantations or providing banking services then this was justified. The state was assumed to be a beneficent entity oriented to promoting the welfare of all citizens with central planning as a technical, rather than highly political, affair. Thus, the growing numbers of public enterprises in the 1960s and 1970s indicated a concerted effort to extend the frontiers of the state.

Local political factors have also contributed to public enterprise proliferation and the particular configurations of them in different countries. Some governments have used public enterprises to provide employment or generate political support – or achieve both at the same time by allocating jobs to party members. Conversion of foreign businesses to public enterprises can also distract popular attention from poor government performance. While such motivations can be implicit there are some cases of quite explicit politically driven public enterprise policy. For example, following the racial conflicts in 1969 in Malaysia, the ascendant Malay political elite instituted policies to incorporate and expand the economic role of the Malay upper and middle classes. State intervention in the economy, often through public enterprises, was used as a vehicle to achieve these policy objectives (Woon, 1991). Similarly, in Thailand and Indonesia there are examples of public enterprises being used to take over various economic sectors from local Chinese businesses.

The turning tide on public enterprise performance

The tide began to turn for public enterprises at the start of the 1980s as their poor performance became increasingly obvious. There were success stories but these were outnumbered by enterprises which failed to meet both their economic and welfare objectives. Several reasons for these disappointing results had become increasingly evident as we will now discover.

The leading issue was that public enterprises had often not produced the expected profits and thus had not been the sources of investment capital. In fact, they had frequently been drains on scarce government financial resources and contributed to spiralling levels of national debt. For example, between 1981–87, the Philippine government would have run budget surpluses were it not for the financial haemorrhaging caused by the need to support public enterprises. By mid-1988, the country's state enterprises had incurred US$12 billion in debt, almost 50 per cent of the country's total external debt (Woon, 1991). More recently in India (2003–2004), 156 public enterprises made profits but 116 still made losses and only 42 companies accounted for 80 per cent of the profits (Gupta, 2008). In Africa, a 1985 survey of transport public enterprises in 18 Francophone countries found that only 20 per cent generated sufficient revenue to cover operating cost, depreciation and financial charges (Nellis, 2006). A more vivid depiction of public enterprises in Africa described them as sitting 'like huge white elephants over the African landscape, voraciously consuming what has been produced by others' (Wilson, 1986, as quoted by Haile-Mariam and Mengistu, 1988: 1572).

But profitability is neither a complete nor accurate measure of public enterprise performance. Public enterprises may fulfil non-commercial purposes and even efficient operations can run at a loss because products are priced at below market rates. Even if public enterprises do appear to be making money this may be due to monopoly position and/or pricing policy which makes consumers pay above market rates for inefficiently produced items. Estimating the non-financial contribution of public enterprises to development is a far trickier business. They have been the vanguard of industrialization in some countries. Entrepreneurial and management skills have been developed in some public enterprises and diffused to the wider economy. Substantial employment has been created while regional development has been encouraged through the deliberate decentralization of public enterprises. Some actions by state enterprises, such as the building of a road, may generate external benefits to the economy which are not recorded in the organization's accounts. While all this may be true, such gains may have been made at a high cost. Critics argue that even greater gains could have accrued if resources had been allocated differently or more efficiently.

Management has been another problem area for public enterprises. A fundamental problem has been the vagueness and/or multiplicity of goals. This led to a lack of concern with strategy and the ways in which organizations might adapt to changing environmental conditions. Weak structures of accountability exacerbated the situation and managers have frequently not been held responsible for their operations' poor performance. The absence of appropriate criteria for performance evaluation or the unsuitability of those that exist contributed to disinterest in how performance should be measured and improved. Even today, there are still instances of the once dominant attitude that government is always there to bail out a loss-making enterprise.

The organizational structures of public enterprises have been characteristically bureaucratic in the sociological sense of the term, not surprising since they were the progeny and wards of other bureaucratic agencies of government. These structures emphasize routine, rules, control and hierarchy. This renders them unable to cope with changing environments and makes them risk-averse. Rigidity rather than flexibility has been the norm – following the rules rather than achieving the goals. The managers may be poorly schooled in management techniques and contemporary private sector practices. For example, there may be limited skills in market development, cost control, quality assurance and product diversification especially as such skills have no place in the prevailing model of bureaucratic management.

Managers may have to cope with overstaffing or inappropriate staffing, guided by the relevant 'minister'. They may even encourage it. This is because public enterprises have been ideal vehicles for the disbursement of political patronage. Human resource management may be determined more by political decisions of ministers, local officials and bureaucratic chiefs than sound business principles. Financial malpractice can occur in areas such as procurement, sales or construction as accountability has often been weak. Thus, corrupt practices go undetected or unpunished in situations where decision-making is politicized and the organizational culture is one of 'uncommitment'. Such managerial shortcomings contributed to what Khandwalla (1987) described as 'public enterprise sickness', an ailment not found in all of the species but in enough to lead to increasingly loud calls for reform. These were boosted by an ideologically driven movement to 'rethink' the state (World Bank, 1991).

Rethinking the state

By the early 1980s support for the 'big state' had become muted and the emerging consensus was that the state was overextended, inefficient and needed to be 'rolled back' for effective economic development. The ideological impulse came from the election of conservative governments in the USA, the UK and other parts of Europe and the global ascendancy of neoliberal thinking. They pushed for placing tighter limits on the state's economic activities, and in the case of the UK provided a radical demonstration of how this could be achieved especially through privatization. Multilateral agencies such as the World Bank and IMF added their support to the argument that 'governments need to do less in those areas where markets work, or can be made to work reasonably well. In many countries it would help to privatize many of the state-owned enterprises' (World Bank, 1991: 9).

The floodgates were now opening for privatization in developing countries. Between 1988 and 1993, over 2,700 enterprises in more than 60 developing countries were transferred to private hands bringing governments a revenue of US$ 96 billion (World Bank, 1995; IFC, 1995). Between 1990 and 2003, developing country privatization transactions amounted to US$410 billion from over 8,000 transactions (Kikeri and Kolo, 2005). Privatization peaked in 1997, dropped off at the end of the 1990s but picked up again in the 2000s with 2006 having 248 privatization transactions in 48 developing countries worth US$105 billion. The 2007 Global Financial Crisis (GFC) dramatically reduced privatization receipts in developing countries to $38 billion in 2008, 71 per cent down from the previous year, but did not bring on a wave of nationalizations that had been anticipated (Kikeri and Perault, 2010). In 2009, privatization picked up a little and has remained steady but at much lower rates than in the divestment heyday in large part because of declining opportunities.

There have been regional variations in privatization. Latin America has been the most active region accounting for 55 per cent of total developing country revenue from privatization in the 1990s (Chong and López-de-Silanes, 2004). By contrast, in Sub-Saharan Africa and South Asia privatization was far less significant. Even within regions there can be substantial differences between countries. Overall, the activities of SOEs as a percentage of GDP declined from 11 per cent to 5 per cent in middle income countries and from 15 per cent to 3 per cent in low income countries, with the share of employment falling from 13 per cent to 2 per cent and in the latter from over 20 per cent to about 9 per cent (Sheshinski and López-Calva, 2003).

All of these privatization deals can be grouped under the label of 'denationalization'. This involves selling the businesses on the market either to corporations or through stock flotation. Sometimes, the entire enterprise is sold while in other cases partial privatization occurs whereby government still retains a proportion of the ownership. But simply changing ownership from government to the private sector is no guarantee of success. This is achieved through restructuring, altering culture, human resource management reforms and creating a competitive or regulatory environment that promotes efficiency.

But has the dominant denationalization mode of privatization been successful? There is much data that suggests that from an economic and firm point of view, privatization has been a success. For example, Boubakri and Cosset (1998) studied 79 newly privatized SOEs in 21 diverse developing countries during 1980–1992 and found significant improvement in profitability after divestiture. Efficiency as measured by real sales per employee and net income per employee also showed marked improvement. Capital investment increased as did the owners' dividends. There was even growth in employment in 58 per cent of the firms. Similarly, in their later review of privatization in Latin America, Chong and López-de-Silanes (2004) came to similar conclusions. They found higher efficiency and productivity improvements post-privatization. Beneficial technological overhauls came in some companies and industries such as telecommunications. Government was relieved of paying out subsidies to SOEs. Outputs and profits increased. There were even welfare gains in some instances such as increased access to water and other utilities. These were sometimes offset by price hikes for water and electricity. There was substantial labour retrenchment – down by 24 per cent – and some botched privatization initiatives. Such adverse consequences affected the poorer sections of the community most and sometimes led to civil unrest. The example of water privatization in Manila (Box 9.2) illustrates such a combination of gains and losses that can occur in privatization.

Another problem with privatization is the question of who gains? In some countries, corruption has tainted the privatization process and allowed cronies to make lucrative deals at the state's and people's expense (Stiglitz, 2008). Auctions have allegedly been rigged and certain bidders favoured. Prices have been manipulated and monopolies

Box 9.2   A tale of two water companies

In the mid-1990s, the Metropolitan Waterworks and Sewerage System (MWSS) that provided all of Manila's water and sewerage was in trouble. It was struggling with a massive debt, overstaffed, only connected to two-thirds of households, providing intermittent supply, and subject to water leakages and theft on a grand scale. The government was itself strapped with large international debts and constraints on government spending and had absorbed the pro-privatization attitudes that had accompanied the country's nine Structural Adjustment Programs (SAPs) of the World Bank and IMF. President Fidel Ramos was aware of widespread anti-privatization sentiment in the Philippines and set about building consensus among stakeholders for water privatization. He also ensured that a transparent bidding process occurred. A concession model was adopted whereby Manila was divided into two regions to avoid monopoly, enable comparison of winning companies and to split the debt appropriately. Winners would also need to be at least 60 per cent Philippine owned in line with constitutional requirements. Two bidders were selected and private operations commenced in 1997.

There were improvements in service. Water coverage improved from 67 per cent of households to 82 per cent by 2002. Water availability rose from 17 to 21 hours as did water quality. Responsiveness improved from 74 per cent of leaks attended and repaired in 1996 to 97 per cent and 93 per cent in 2002. Efficiency also grew with the number of employees per 1,000 connections declining from 9.8 in 1996 to 4.1 in 2002. This entailed reducing the labour force by 49 per cent from pre-privatization. There was much less success with dealing with leaks and theft which remained substantial after privatization. Tariffs also increased rapidly, tripling over the 1997–2002 period with one concessionaire and almost tripling in the other. This raised the question of whether the improved services were worth the prices being paid. In terms of company success, one concessionaire attained breakeven in three years while the other was still making a loss after five years. These results derived from different business models, employee management, debt arrangements and failure to do rigorous due diligence analysis on the much greater difficulties in servicing one of the regions. The loss-making concessionaire entered into 'corporate rehabilitation' and succeeded in returning profits in 2005 and 2006.

Source: Adapted from Chia et al., 2007.

privatized before appropriate regulatory systems have been put in place. In short, government officials and their cronies have sometimes personally benefited from privatization and not acted in the best interests of citizens they were supposed to serve.

In other cases there has been political opposition to privatization. Sometimes nationalist sentiments dissuade government from divesting what are perceived to be strategic industries to overseas buyers. Plans to privatize telecommunications in Thailand ran into this obstacle and failed (Chulajata and Turner, 2009). In other cases ethnic minority groups who have been successful in business may have the financial capital to purchase SOEs but lack the political capital. The bureaucracies charged with formulating and implementing public sector reform may demonstrate reactions ranging from reluctant support to downright opposition and recalcitrance (World Bank, 1995b). In the early 1990s in Pakistan, businessmen complained that bureaucrats were loath to surrender their power over SOEs and had deliberately overpriced them for privatization (FEER, 1991). Trade unions often oppose privatization because of potential job losses. The unions can be well organized, numerically strong and have good political connections. Even when privatization has been forced through there can still be labour unrest and disruption as occurred in the Bangladesh textile industry (Lorch, 1991).

But politicians are potentially the major impediments to privatization. As revealed in Box 9.3 the progress of privatization in India has been slow largely because of opposition by politicians at both federal and subnational levels. They fear loss of power, a reduction in patronage opportunities and backlashes from voters if jobs are lost through privatization. In one-party states especially, there can be the persisting view that 'the state must retain a clear responsibility for economic management and an associated competence in management and administration' (Cook and Minogue, 1990: 293). Thus, China, Vietnam and Laos have demonstrated reservations about fully unleashing the market. They value strategic control in the economy and use SOEs to achieve and maintain this state of affairs. In China, despite the massive growth of the private sector and many thousands of privatizations, the big SOEs remain intact or strengthened by amalgamation and infusions of capital. As Box 9.4 shows, China's big SOEs have become more powerful and pervasive and now number among the world's largest companies often with operations of a global scale.

Box 9.3   Why are some countries reluctant to privatize?

Some regions of the world have embraced privatization while others have been far more reluctant. For example, between 1991 and 1999, Latin American governments privatized US$177 billion of assets but South Asian governments only managed to gather $11.9 billion. In part this is due to the commercial unattractiveness of many SOEs in South Asia but it mainly derives from political interests who see privatization as a threat.

Using India as an example, it is evident that SOEs have often been 'extremely inefficient'. This has been due to political interference and rent-seeking by politicians and SOE staff; protection from competition; lack of market-based incentives for workers; reliance on government for bailouts; overcapacity; and public acquiescence to poor performance. As businesses they have performed badly. For example, between 1991 and 1999, the Government of India invested R612 billion but received only R179 billion in dividends. Of 272 SOEs, 116 made losses while 80 per cent of profits were from only 42 organizations.

India's economic development from the 1950s was heavily based on central planning, import substitution industrialization and the liberal use of SOEs to generate the desired economic growth. However, by 1991 this model was proving to be unsustainable due to growing budget deficits, high inflation, low foreign exchange reserves, credit rating downgrade, rising oil prices and the rejection of the Soviet central planning model. Thus, an economic reform package was introduced that did away with the licensing system for private enterprises, liberalized the stock market, allowed entry of new players into previously restricted industries, lowered barriers to foreign investment and liberalized trade law. Furthermore, SOEs were described in the official Industry Policy Resolution 1991 as 'a burden rather than being an asset'. But privatizations remained few between 1991 and 1999. Even the establishment of a Disinvestment Commission in 1996, failed to add any momentum to privatization. The initiatives that did take place between 1991–2000 mostly involved government selling portions of state holdings but not enough to relinquish government control. This avoided political controversy. Some progress was made under a newly elected government in 1999 when the Department of Disinvestment was established. Fourteen SOEs were privatized including the transfer of management control between 2000–2004 but the state still owned 82 per cent of SOE equity. While privatization continues in India, it does so at a very slow pace because an alliance of politicians at national and subnational levels, bureaucrats, labour unions and SOE employees see privatization as a threat to their interests and oppose it.

Source: Adapted from Gupta (2008).

Box 9.4   Grasping the large and letting go of the small

While privatization has been a leading economic development strategy in developing countries for over two decades, in the developing country with the largest economy, China, SOEs are more powerful than ever. Since 1978 when Premier Deng Xiaoping announced that capitalists were not 'class enemies' and that 'to get rich is glorious', the Chinese economy has grown at the unprecedented rate of over 10 per cent each year only slowing down slightly since 2010. The private sector has flourished and the welfare of the population dramatically improved since the days of Maoist central planning and state ownership of all productive assets. Privatization has also proceeded apace with SOEs declining from 1.2 million in 1995 to 468,000 in 2001 and a mere 114,000 in 2010, although the figures do depend on who is telling the story. Whatever the statistical source there have been substantial reductions in SOE numbers and employment but not necessarily in SOE importance to the economy. Privatization has followed a model of 'grasping the large and letting go of the small'. That is, smaller locally based enterprises have been encouraged to privatize or shut down operations while the larger ones have received strong support from the state. Thus, SOEs own 44 per cent of all industrial assets in China (a staggering US$15 trillion) compared to 22 per cent in India and 12 per cent in Indonesia. They also employ 40 million staff and some SOEs are ranked among the world's largest companies. Their survival and growth is in line with the Chinese Communist Party's (CCP's) ideology of economic development as being 'socialism with Chinese characteristics'. Occupying strategic industries such as telecommunications, energy resources and banking, SOEs are vitally important players in promoting national economic and security interests. They are expected to make a profit but also to act on 'backstage' guidance from the CPP – and executives' careers depend on the CCP. Such political control explains why there is such a favourable environment for the SOEs. For example, they enjoy preferred access to capital and receive below-market interest rates. They obtain large capital injections when needed and dominate government procurement. SOEs are quite clearly instruments of government policy both at home and abroad. But despite the trappings of modern corporations and the favourable operating environment, Chinese SOEs remain inefficient compared to the private sector. The latter obtain about 10.4 per cent return on assets compared to the SOEs' 5.9 per cent and produce only 27 per cent of national income from their 44 per cent of national assets. There have been reforms, albeit incremental and cautious. However, in 2014, Sinopec, one of the three oil majors, was reported as floating more radical plans – the privatization of 30 per cent of the company's best-performing assets and perhaps the adoption of a Singapore-style holding company system to control listed entities. Whether these are steps too far for the CCP and the State-owned Assets Supervision and Administration Commission (SASAC) remains to be seen.

Source: Szamosszegi and Kyle, 2011; *Economist*, 2012b; Cai, 2014.

Corporatization

For governments not wishing to go the whole way down the privatization road, corporatization has been an alternative route to performance improvement of SOEs. This has been a feature of the partial privatizations mentioned in Box 9.3 on India and Box 9.4 on China but has been a strategy more widely used in developing countries. It is about transforming SOEs into corporations that are clearly run on private sector lines. The corporations introduce new business processes, improved governance, enhanced performance management and pay close attention to greater efficiency. Corporatization is one of the items on the NPM (New Public Management) menu that we encountered in Chapters 1 and 5 as it seeks to transfer to the public sector the supposedly more efficient and effective management practices of the private sector that are determined by the forces of market competition. Continuing with the NPM logic, corporatization frees SOE management from state control enabling them to pursue efficient and profitable options. But with freedom comes responsibility and greater accountability for results. Corporatization may allow the entry of new minority shareholders but the state retains control.

An Egyptian example illustrates the way in which corporatization is supposed to work (USAID, 2005). In 2004, a presidential decree announced the corporatization of the state-owned Alexandria Water Company (AWCO) and placed it under the public sector's holding company that had responsibility for 13 other utilities. Although seen as a 'better performing' utility, AWCO suffered from poor administrative systems and equipment. AWCO's new status meant that it was no longer bound by civil service regulations on hiring personnel, salaries and retirement. This contributed to AWCO's increased ability to manage its staff on merit rather than seniority. Outsourcing maintenance and other services could now be undertaken thus reducing the need to carry excess staff. Furthermore, AWCO could control revenue and determine investments from surpluses. Corporatization has been linked to AWCO's performance improvement such as coverage increasing from 80 per cent to 92 per cent of households, 15,000 new connections per year and unaccounted water decreasing by 300,000 cubic metres per day (USAID, 2005: 26). Revenues rose and operating costs per unit of water delivered fell.

But there are potential problems with corporatization. First, whose interests are the liberated managers actually working for? Ideally it is for the citizens who theoretically own the corporation but it is possible

Box 9.5   OECD guidelines on corporate governance of SOEs

1. The legal and regulatory framework for SOEs should ensure a level-playing field in markets where SOEs and private sector companies compete in order to avoid market distortion.
2. The state should act as an informed and active owner and establish a clear and consistent ownership policy, ensuring that the governance of SOEs is carried out in a transparent and accountable manner, with the necessary degree of professionalism and effectiveness.
3. The state and SOEs should recognise the rights of all shareholders and in accordance with the OECD Principles of Corporate Governance ensure their equitable treatment and equal access to corporate information.
4. The state ownership policy should fully recognise the SOEs' responsibilities towards stakeholders and request that they report on their relationships with stakeholders.
5. SOEs should observe high standards of transparency in accordance with the OECD Principles of Corporate Governance.
6. The boards of SOEs should have the necessary authority, competencies and objectivity to carry out their functions of strategic guidance and monitoring of management. They should act with integrity and be held accountable for their actions.

Source: OECD, 2005.

that managers are oriented to satisfying specific interests in government or themselves. Second, there could be too much focus on profit and not enough on satisfying social goals. This might even lead to goal displacement whereby the pursuit of profit displaces the goals for which the organization was established. Third, will the corporation be able to retain the profits it earns and reinvest them or will they be grabbed by government for other purposes leaving the corporation bereft of investment capital? Finally, there is a danger that the organization may present a façade of corporate practice but in fact slip back into a business as usual mode.

All of these issues highlight the importance of corporate governance in making corporatization of SOEs work. Corporate governance refers to 'the way power is exercised over corporate entities' (Tricker, 2012: 4). It focuses on the board, which is the governing body of the corporation, and on the board's relationships with shareholders, enterprise managers, the external auditor, regulators and other stakeholders. It does not run the enterprise. That is the job of executive management. The board ensures that the enterprise 'is running in the right direction and being run well' (Tricker, 2012: 4). Corporate governance has become a key concern in the twenty-first century in both OECD and developing countries, especially as its failure contributed in large part to the 2007 GFC. Thus, there is now much written on the subject and guidelines aplenty including the OECD offering on the principles of corporate governance for SOEs. Read it in Box 9.5 and consider the difficulties that might be faced in implementing such guidelines in developing countries.

Public private partnerships

Another offspring of neoliberal rethinking of the state and NPM has been public private partnerships (PPPs) in which government cooperates with the private sector to achieve particular objectives. Although first emerging in rich countries in the late 1980s in infrastructure development, the use of PPPs grew rapidly in developing countries in the 1990s, largely in middle income countries that had legal, financial and governance systems that were able to cope with what are often complex organizational arrangements.

There is no universal agreement on a definition for PPPs, a situation exacerbated by the increasing numbers of arrangements that are placed under the PPP label (MOFAN, 2013). These range from private sector consortiums building and operating roads to contracting out for specific services (see Box 9.6 for the different types of PPP arrangements). Despite the wide range of PPPs, we can identify some common elements in PPPs. First, and as the name indicates, PPPs involve some form of cooperation between public and private sector actors. The latter may include both businesses and non-profit organizations from civil society. Second, the partners share a common goal, normally providing a particular service like a toll road, a hospital or banking. Third, the partners share the risks of the venture. These can be of various sorts including construction (e.g. design problems), financial (e.g. changing exchange rates), performance (e.g. continuity and quality of service), demand (e.g. ongoing need for services) and residual (e.g. the future market price of the asset). As both public and private partners stand to benefit from the PPP, risk sharing can be viewed as an incentive. Fourth, partners in a PPP

Box 9.6   Types of developmental PPPs

Form	Description
Service contract	Government hires a private company or entity for a pre-determined fee to carry out specific tasks or services for a period, typically for 1–3 years.
Management contract	This expands the services to be contracted to include some or all of the management and operation of the public service (e.g. hospital, port authority). Obligation for service provision remains with government while day-to-day management is the contractor's responsibility.
Affermage or lease contracts	The private partner is responsible for the service in its entirety, including quality and service standards, and undertakes the service at its risk usually for ten years in the first instance. Revenues collected are retained by the private contractor which is responsible for maintenance but not new and replacement investment.
Concession	The private sector operator (concessionaire) is responsible, typically for 25–30 years, for full delivery of services in a specified area including operation, maintenance, fee collection, management, and construction and rehabilitation of the system. The government is responsible for performance standards and their enforcement.
Build-operate-transfer (BOT) and similar arrangements	A private sector firm or consortium finances and develops a new infrastructure project according to performance standards set by government, operates it before handing it over to government. There are many variations including: BTO build-transfer-operate; BOO build-own-operate; DBO design-build-operate; and DBFO design-build-finance-operate.
Joint venture	Public and private sector partners can either form a new company or assume joint ownership of an existing one through sale of shares to private sector investors. Both partners share risks and invest in the company.

Source: Adapted from ADB, 2008; MOFAN, 2013.

share resources and activities, and finally, there should be long-term commitment.

There are several attractions of PPPs. Ideally, they enable governments to tap the resources and skills of the private sector (including civil society) in areas where the latter have advantages, experience and records of superior performance. In exchange, the private sector gets access to business opportunities from which they were previously excluded by government, for example, operating toll roads and bridges. Governments see PPPs as politically much safer than full-blown privatization that has often generated vociferous and even violent opposition. However, the IMF regards PPPs as providing similar benefits to privatization and along with the World Bank has been a leading advocate for them (IMF, 2004). PPPs have also relieved financially constrained governments from raising the large amounts of finance required to build major infrastructure items such as roads, ports and bridges. The private sector has stepped in to raise the necessary funds on the open market. A final attraction of PPPs is that partners supposedly feel more secure in their dealings and commitments when risks are shared.

In terms of economic development, PPPs for infrastructure have been the most important and have involved considerable investment. For example, in the late 1980s, the Philippines was adversely affected by infrastructure bottlenecks, particularly in electric power generation and transport. The government, the traditional supplier of infrastructure, was unable to meet the huge costs of building the urgently required power plants and roads. But desperate circumstances meant tradition was abandoned and a BOT (Build Operate Transfer) law was passed in 1990 to allow private corporations to *build* and *operate* public infrastructure before *transferring* the asset back to government, usually after 20–25 years. The BOT law was strengthened and then supplemented by the Electric Power Crisis Act 1993 that gave the president the power to negotiate 'contracts for the construction, repair, rehabilitation, improvement or maintenance of power plants, projects and facilities' (Antonio, 2013: 12). These initiatives were successful in attracting US$6 billion in investments from foreign and domestic corporations and the installation of 4,800MW generation capacity by 1998. However, the era of power sector PPPs appears to have been the precursor for a more thorough process of privatization and entry into a 'retail competition and open access mode' from 2013 onwards. Approximately US$10 billion has been raised from privatization but the Philippines has been left with power prices that are among the most expensive in the world (Antonio, 2013; Molina, 2013).

Even in India, a reluctant privatizer, we can find examples of the more politically palatable PPPs for infrastructure. For example, in the 1990s, economic and population growth led to increased demand for transport infrastructure to maintain economic progress. However, a financing gap between government's financial capacity and road requirements led to experimentation with PPPs (SVBTCPL, 2014). Near the megacity of Kolkata this involved the construction of the second Vivekananda bridge, a six-lane bridge to supplement the original two-lane bridge built in the 1930s. While bidding by interested private sector corporations commenced in the 1990s, considerable time was needed for land acquisition and for government to arrange construction of road links to the new bridge. The winning consortium comprised both foreign and domestic companies. Work on the bridge itself eventually commenced in 2004 and was completed in 2007 with a 30 years concession for its private sector operators. But despite India's love affair with PPPs it has not been plain sailing. Between 2007 and 2012, the private sector invested US$225 billion in infrastructure, much of it in PPPs at both federal and state levels (*Economist,* 2012a). Contract arrangement were often allegedly 'improvised' and there were 'murky' aspects to some of the financial arrangements. Some PPPs have run into serious operating problems and are not making money while delays in construction have been common. And there still are major infrastructure projects being built by the government such as the metros in Delhi and Chennai. Public sector advocates point to these as examples of how the state is able to cope more successfully with finance, construction and red tape than the private sector.

But not all PPPs contributing to economic development are in infrastructure. They have spread into all kinds of activities, even poverty alleviation (Matin and Hulme, 2003). One novel but highly effective and much copied PPP for economic development from Kenya is M-Pesa. 'M' stands for mobile phone and 'pesa' is the word for money in Swahili. M-Pesa is a mobile phone banking system for people without bank accounts who can withdraw funds, make deposits and transfer money using text messages (Graham, 2010; Runde and Zargarian, 2013). Before its launch in 2007, three out of every five Kenyans could not access financial services. This had an adverse economic effect on small businesses especially. With M-Pesa a truck owner can now send money to pay for repairs when a vehicle has broken down 100kms away while thousands of farmers with only a few cattle can receive small payments for their milk and market vendors can purchase their supplies, all using M-Pesa. The system requires registration at a member shop, chemist or petrol station with Safaricom, a mobile phone provider with majority holdings by Vodafone and the Kenyan government. Money can then be loaded onto the phone and sent to the nearest M-Pesa outlet for the recipient to pick up. By 2010, M-Pesa had 13 million customers and was moving US$350 million per month (Graham, 2010). It was reported in 2013 that 70 per cent of Kenya's adult population had made use of the service (Runde and Zargarian, 2013).

While PPPs have been increasingly utilized in developing countries for economic development including poverty alleviation and health services, there have been criticisms. Opponents of privatization may regard them as 'privatization by stealth'. Supporters worry that PPPs can be used to avoid government expenditure controls by moving government spending off budget and balance sheet while government still bears much of the risk (IMF, 2004). A comprehensive survey of the literature on PPPs found that many PPP evaluations pay little attention to risk sharing and revenue distribution while the empirical evidence for evaluation is scarce (MOFAN, 2013). It was also noted that revenue mobilization was the most frequently cited rationale rather than effectiveness; goals have often been very general while 'criteria for specific, measurable, attainable relevant and timely objectives are usually absent' (MOFAN, 2013: 12); and the evidence for the effectiveness of PPPs is mixed.

Creating enabling environments for business

Most developing country governments and international aid agencies now regard the private sector as the engine for economic growth and development. It is the private sector that should be generating the economic growth, new businesses, increased employment and enhanced technology. There have been many initiatives in the past ranging from structural adjustment programs (SAPs) and targeted schemes to improve entrepreneurship, develop appropriate skills and promote particular industries. The SAPs were supposed to provide macroeconomic stimuli to the private sector but largely did not while the targeted schemes mostly produced disappointing results. So does the public sector still have a role in making the private sector the engine of economic growth and development? Experts and institutions in the field say 'yes', the public sector's job is to create an enabling environment in which the private sector can flourish.

There are differing views as to the nature of what the interventions should be: the neoclassical and the neo-structuralist, with the former being divided into two subtypes (UNIDO, 2008). The first of these sub-types focuses on the regulatory business environment and is concerned with those regulations that immediately affect business because of the costs to business of compliance. The second subtype takes a broader view and adds the 'investment climate' to the business regulations. This climate includes such things as infrastructure, health and education. Both neoclassical subtypes assume that the market works fairly well without government intervention. When government does step in things can go 'spectacularly wrong' in what is typically an 'expensive gamble with public funds' according to the World Bank (2004: 160). Government should not be trying to improve enterprises and pick winners although Malaysia, South Korea, China and other economic success stories still appear to dabble in some of this market 'interference' (Turner et al., 2013).

The neoclassical concern with business regulations is expressed most clearly in the World Bank's (2014) Doing Business surveys which chart progress on reducing regulatory impediments to business activity. The 'objective measures' used include the steps and time taken in starting a business; dealing with construction permits; getting electricity; registering property; getting credit; protecting investors; paying taxes; trading across borders; enforcing contracts; and resolving insolvency. Higher scores mean the less the difficulty of addressing these business-related matters. In general, developing countries lag behind the OECD in the business-friendliness of their regulatory environments but the gap has been narrowing due to the removal of much red tape in developing countries (World Bank, 2014). Thus, in 2014, the most improved countries in terms of regulatory reform included six from the Third World and four former communist economies. Furthermore, Sub-Saharan Africa is home to nine of 20 economies that have narrowed the regulatory gap most since 2009. Another aspect of regulatory reform is property titling which according to the work of De Soto (1989; 2000) creates capital leading to better access to finance and infrastructure, and security against expropriation. Simplification of labour regulations is also seen to introduce flexibility into labour markets. While there has been undoubted progress in removing red tape, freeing up labour markets and promoting land titling, the results are mixed. Businesspersons certainly welcome relief from long, annoying and often corruption-ridden bureaucratic processes and land titling gives security but there is no obvious causal connection with private sector performance. The evidence does not show a clear link to improved productivity (UNIDO, 2008).

The second neoclassical subtype supplements the regulatory reforms with the state's responsibility for creating an attractive investment climate. The World Bank website has a page on its website devoted to this mode of desirable climate change. Governance, infrastructure, education and health are among the elements of the investment climate. Bad governance creates investment uncertainty and hampers economic development. Ensuring the rule of law and minimizing corruption are thus important tasks for government. Good infrastructure is also vital for economic development and while government may recruit the private sector to assist in its provision, it is still the government's responsibility to plan and organize that provision. Low levels of education, such as occur in Sub-Saharan Africa, is another cloud in the investment climate. Government may not need to directly provide the education but it must have policies in place that enable a sufficient supply of quality education at all levels. Finally, a problem that particularly affects Sub-Saharan Africa is the combination of underfunded health sectors and devastating diseases such as HIV/AIDS leading to absenteeism, premature deaths and loss of skilled workers. Few would disagree that action on these areas of the investment climate should be government priorities as they comprise central aspects of socioeconomic development, the traditional duty of governments. But once again, while we may approve of such measures, it is difficult to establish a clear causal connection between them and increased private sector productivity, entrepreneurship, growth of SMEs and innovation.

The final perspective is that of the neo-structuralists. While they embrace the neoclassical perspectives, they do point to additional determinants of national business success. The neo-structuralists assume the pervasiveness of market failure and believe governments have an active role to play in correcting it (UNIDO, 2008). The theoretical background is that of comparative advantage which the neo-structuralist see as being increasingly dependent on multiple interactions between the public and private sectors. Private sector development does not simply happen because of a levelling of the playing field, neoclassical style. There needs to be direct intervention and the public sector needs to take a significant role as the market cannot be relied upon to generate the innovation and productivity increases that are needed. UNIDO's study of Sub-Saharan Africa recommends the use of Business Development Services (BDS) and several direct initiatives are identified. These include improved business–state relations, supporting innovative entrepreneurship, strengthening inter-firm linkages, promoting exports and developing financial services for SMEs. But it is stressed that public sector assistance should be given only when markets fail and that government agencies involved in private sector promotion should have improved accountability, and effective and regular monitoring and evaluation. There should also be co-financing by recipients of any BDSs, and involvement of the private sector wherever possible. Markets should be built where possible but government outreach should be used when necessary.

Conclusion

In this chapter we have seen that SOEs have been present in all developing countries. They were established by colonial and post-colonial governments, capitalist and communist regimes, in one-party states and plural democracies. Everybody had at some stage a reason for establishing these state business concerns. The result was a bewildering array of SOEs engaged in activities ranging from coal mining to hotels. However, the theory that justified the state's direct participation in the economy and the disappointing results of that participation led to a critical assault on SOEs.

The neoclassical ascendancy in the 1990s involved the vigorous promotion of privatization. Bureaucrats should not be in business was the message relayed to all parts of the Third World. Sometimes privatization was voluntarily accepted by governments fed up with poor SOE performance but often it was straitened financial circumstances, SAPs and proselytism by international financial institutions and their bilateral partners that precipitated privatization. Thousands of SOEs were sold off or closed down but significant numbers remained. These were often subjected to corporatization in order to get them to operate more like private companies. Meanwhile, the privatized companies often performed better in business terms under their new owners but sometimes social goals were sacrificed. Water privatization was heavily criticized in this regard.

Government has not moved away from the private sector but has become more involved with it through PPPs. Starting in infrastructure but extending to other fields of activity such as health, agriculture and poverty alleviation government has developed a host of different PPP arrangements to cooperate with the private sector to provide public goods. The state has also adopted significant responsibility for creating an enabling environment for private sector development. Governments see the private sector as the engine of economic growth and development and so have increasingly attempted to create environments in which the private sector will thrive. Thus, government is still heavily involved in the private sector, less so directly on its own but more so in cooperation with the private sector and in making life easier for it.

Chapter 10

Beyond the State, Beyond the Market? Civil Society and NGOs

Alongside the state and the market, civil society is the third pillar of governance, constituting the arena in which individuals and groups mobilize around common interests (from political protests to singing in choirs). Encompassing all non-state, non-market and non-family associations, crucially, it is not the organizations themselves that constitute civil society, but the arena or space in which they participate in dialogue and negotiations to advance their interests. Following the state-driven and market-led development ideologies of earlier times, 'strengthening civil society' became an explicit goal in the 'good governance' agenda of the 1990s. Its progress and impact, however, has been limited by the development community's simplistic vision of civil society as a collection of NGOs rather than a space for interaction and negotiation around power.

Since rising to prominence during the 1980s, NGOs have been treated as largely synonymous with civil society by many development agencies. More recently, however, questions about their much lauded comparative advantages have become common, as some have drifted away from people-centred development towards contracting with aid donors and governments. Given the 'non-political' stance many NGOs have adopted, they have limited involvement in tackling the more structurally entrenched causes of poverty and inequality (such as social and political exclusion). Radical critics accuse NGOs of depoliticizing development by treating it as a technical problem that can be 'solved'.

In this chapter we explore the concept of civil society and examine the consequences of international development agencies emphasizing the role of NGOs within civil society. This leads us to look at the recent criticisms of NGOs and to asking whether NGOs can 'return to their roots' and promote genuinely participatory paths to empowerment? Can NGOs move away from their growing role as service providers to that of facilitators and supporters of broader civil society organizations (CSOs), supporting marginalized communities to engage in dialogue, with the state and market, in order to achieve those communities' rights?

Civil society and development

Civil society has become a familiar term in development theory and policy despite the lack of an agreed meaning. The concept is widely seen as having roots in Hegel's philosophy of freedom and community: the creation of a rational state must build on the pre-existing values, reasons and virtues in a society so that citizens, understanding the rational principles on which their community is based, freely choose to serve the state (Singer, 2001). While in this ideal model the interests of the individual and the collective are in harmony, in reality, societies are composed of different individuals and groups with different interests, and states rarely – if ever – can represent and advance the interests of all. Civil society is the arena, separate from state and market, in which ideological hegemony is contested, to both challenge and uphold the existing order (Mohan, 2002; Kamat, 2004; Lewis and Kanji, 2009). To the extent that individuals cannot gain recognition and demand change by themselves, they turn to voluntary associations or CSOs to challenge the existing structures and processes underlying exclusion or disadvantage and to call for social, political and/or economic transformation (Lewis, 2002; Sternberg, 2010). While in mainstream development usage, civil space is often viewed as 'an unqualified "good" ' (White, 1999: 319), it is host to all manner of societal interests and contains many competing ideas and agendas that may not all be good for development such as racist or chauvinist groups (Lewis and Kanji, 2009).

There is huge diversity in the organizations, associations and networks within civil society. The donor community's failure to recognize this has limited the progress of attempts to strengthen civil society, which requires creating greater scope for representation of and interactions between the state and multiple competing CSOs, particularly the inclusion of excluded or underrepresented groups and associations. Context, and particularly historical factors, is key to the analysis and understanding of civil society (Edwards, 2011b).

When the concept of civil society is promoted in non-Western contexts through donor funding, it must allow scope for locally rooted meanings and actors (Lewis, 2002; Encarnacion, 2011; Edwards, 2011a; b).

The actors in civil society are numerous and varied, and include community or grassroots associations, social movements, cooperatives, labour unions, professional groups, advocacy and development NGOs, formal non-profit organizations, social enterprises, foundations, church groups, think tanks and many more. In recent decades, the 'old' social movements of trade unions and labour have been joined by new movements (Bolnick, 2008) – the women's movement, the environmental movement and a nascent anti-globalization movement. Some civil society actors are also becoming much bigger players internationally, with 'mega-philanthropists' and large foundations becoming major funders and shapers of development policies. More recently, we have seen the influence of 'non-organizational' forms of civil society, using blogs and social media, who may not be members of any formal organization but utilize their local and global outreach to mobilize and demand change.

In both authoritarian and democratic settings citizen protests and other forms of engagement are mounted regardless of attempts to weaken or suppress them (Edwards, 2011a). The Arab Spring that commenced in December 2010 illustrates the remarkable power of people-led, 'crowdsourcing' movements to confront and topple authoritarian regimes. Where political parties and governments alienate groups or neglect pressing issues, CSOs can use the space of civil society to confront exclusion and demand change (Rucht and Neidhardt, 2002). Not facing the same pressures as NGOs to be non-political, CSOs can be more assertive in challenging power structures and hegemonic ideas. For this reason some see civil society as oppositional, rather than accommodating, to the state and private sector, bringing together a multiplicity of individuals, groups and organizations around a shared collective identity and common interest (Bebbington et al., 2008; Della Porta and Diani, 2011). The ideal for CSOs is full control and/or ownership of the organization by its constituents through an active membership structure (Joshi and Moore, 2000; Kilby, 2006; Fowler, 2011; Bano, 2012). The CSOs gain legitimacy by working locally through an active membership base that identifies and participates in development activities, and build trust and cooperation with members through regular interaction (Kamat, 2004).

Regardless of CSO diversity, for the past three decades, the inter-national aid community has tended to conceptualize NGOs *as* civil society (Mohan, 2002; Ibrahim and Hulme, 2011). Given this situation, the following sections detail the reasons for and repercussions of NGOs' rising prominence in international development and subsequently look at whether NGOs could be more effective if they returned to seeing themselves as just one actor in civil society. An overreliance by the development community on NGOs with weak roots in society is dangerous, and increasing recognition of such concerns is threatening to dislodge NGOs from their favoured position for new civic actors (Edwards, 2011a; Fowler, 2011).

The rise and rise of NGOs in development

In the 1980s, the perceived failures of state-led development fuelled interest in NGOs which were seen as offering innovative and people-centred approaches to service delivery, advocacy and empowerment. Emerging from historical traditions of philanthropy and self-help (Lewis and Kanji, 2009), NGOs vary widely in origin and levels of formality, rendering taxonomy difficult (Vakil, 1997; Srinivas, 2009). Commonly, NGOs have been defined by what they are not (neither government, nor profit-driven organizations) rather than what they are (White, 1999). Here the focus is on 'development NGOs', but even this masks an extremely diverse set of organizations. NGOs based in one country and seeking development objectives abroad are often referred to as international or Northern NGOs (INGOs or NNGOs). With limited country-level and grassroots knowledge, many INGOs work at the local-level through Southern NGO partners (SNGOs). While often referred to as North–South 'partnerships', these relationships can be highly unequal, favouring Northern partners who control funding and exert compliance requirements on their Southern partners.

The original explanations for the emergence of NGOs centred on their ability to offer a 'development alternative', based on claims about their effectiveness in tackling poverty and challenging unequal relationships (Bebbington et al., 2008; Lewis and Kanji, 2009). Their assumed grassroots linkages were seen as a major strength, enabling them to deliver services using innovative and experimental approaches centred around community participation, and empowering disadvantaged groups. For early proponents of NGOs, the NGO focus on 'empowerment' was seen as their greatest asset. From this perspective, not only do NGOs strive to meet the needs of the poor, they also aim to assist them in articulating those needs themselves through participatory, people-centred and rights-based approaches (Drabek, 1987).

The 'rise' of NGOs over the 1990s and 2000s has continued. Accurate figures on NGO numbers are very limited. There is no international coordinating body and national level data is often inconsistent. For example, in Bangladesh, the Federation of NGOs records 900 members, the government's NGO Affairs Bureau registers 6,500 NGOs, and the Department of Social Services, which includes CSOs in their definition, lists 23,000 registered organizations (Gauri and Galef, 2005). Epstein and Gang (2006) find that for all OECD countries, official development assistance (ODA) to NGOs increased by 34 per cent between 1991–1992 and 2002, and the number of INGOs grew by 19.3 per cent over this decade. In some countries, there has also been a simultaneous trend towards expansion in the size of NGOs, particularly in South Asia (Edwards and Hulme, 1996; Barr et al., 2005) with BRAC in Bangladesh employing more than 100,000 people and operating in more than 12 countries. NGOs are no longer minor actors on the development stage, in some cases receiving as much or more funding than their government counterparts (Brass, 2011). Understanding this expansion must be contextualized within the history in which NGOs are embedded (Box 10.1).

Given the pursuit of state-centric models of development, NGOs were seen as bit-players in development policy until the late 1970s. The ideological ascendency of neoliberalism at this time was accompanied by the rise of structural adjustment, which demanded reductions in public expenditure and the withdrawal of state-provided services. Donor distrust and frustrations with national governments fuelled interest in NGOs as preferred service delivery agencies (Gill, 1997; Barr et al., 2005; Lewis, 2005) and NGOs were incorporated into structural adjustment as private voluntary organizations (PVOs).

Neoliberal policies began to weaken from the mid-1990s and development discourse and policy shifted again. Under the good governance agenda the state became a lead actor again and NGOs were recast as a counterbalance. This pulled in opposite directions for NGOs. On the one hand, re-governmentalization of aid increased state funding and drew attention away from NGOs (Lewis and Kanji, 2009). On the other, the good governance agenda embraced the

Box 10.1   The rising prominence of development NGOs

Until late 1970s: Development policy and practice was dominated by a state-driven vision of change. A limited number of small NGOs receiving little external support constituted the NGO sector. Most were northern-based with a southern presence, often based on religious assistance and/ or in disaster/emergency relief.

Late 1970s to 1980s: 'The NGO decade' took place amidst the Western pursuit of neoliberal policies, putting markets first, with NGOs emerging as a promising alternative service delivery agent as private voluntary organizations (PVOs).

1990s: Alongside the emergence of the good governance agenda, there was a focus restoring the role of the state in development and there were initial concerns surrounding the levels of NGO contribution to development.

2000s: A new international aid regime promised greater consultation and focus on non-growth factors, bringing civil society in as a dominant actor in the development sector's landscape. NGOs with their people-centred, rights-based and grassroots-driven approaches were well-suited to continue riding the NGO wave.

2010s: With persistent concerns about NGOs remaining unaddressed and evidence of their limited success in empowerment, there is increasing recognition that NGOs are only one sector within broader civil society and arguments are being made that they should reorient themselves towards the grassroots.

Source: Adapted from Lewis and Kanji, 2009.

language of democracy, human rights and public participation thus consolidating the centrality of NGOs in the development landscape (Murray and Overton, 2011). Into the 2000s a new aid regime had evolved, promising to promote growth, through an enabling environment, a greater focus on poverty reduction and results, and more consultation between donors and recipients. Amidst this new focus on strengthening civil society, concerns surrounding NGO impacts, activities and organizational structures led to greater recognition that NGOs constitute only one part of civil society.

NGO roles and relationships with the state

Relations between governments and NGOs vary considerably from country to country, region to region and even agency to agency. They range from close cooperation and collaboration to active hostility and overt tensions, depending on multiple influences (Rosenberg et al., 2008; Rose, 2011). To facilitate analysis, we contrast state–NGO relationships between two main roles: NGOs as service providers and NGOs as advocates for the poor.

NGOs as service providers

As service providers, NGOs offer a broad range of services from livelihood interventions and health and education services to emergency response, conflict resolution, human rights, finance and environmental management (Lewis and Kanji, 2009). Interest in the contribution of NGOs to service delivery not only arose because of the enforced rolling back of state services, but also because of their perceived comparative advantages: their ability to innovate and experiment, their flexibility to adopt new programmes quickly, and most importantly, their linkages with communities that offer participatory forms of design and implementation fostering self-reliance and sustainability (Korten, 1987; Bebbington et al., 2008; Lewis and Kanji, 2009). Service provision now constitutes the main activity of most NGOs across the developing world. Ninety per cent of registered NGOs in Kenya, for example, are involved primarily in service delivery (Brass, 2011).

Where governments and NGOs are working towards mutual goals in service delivery and welfare provision there is scope for positive relationships. In Pakistan, for example, Nair (2011) highlights potential for government–NGO collaboration when NGOs focus on service provision, but contrasts this with the generation of conflict when NGOs question government policies. While collaboration with national governments assists programme sustainability it also entails the risk of NGOs pushing out the interests of the poor (White, 1999; Barr et al., 2005; Rosenberg et al., 2008).

NGOs as advocates for the poor

NGOs can be vehicles for social mobilization and advocates for the poor (Bebbington, 2005; Harsh et al., 2010). Exactly how NGOs should participate in the political process, however, is rarely articulated (Edwards and Hulme, 1997). Their efforts lie along a broad spectrum. At one end are NGOs actively intervening in democracy-building and seeking to transform state–society relations. While there were many examples of such NGO activities in the late twentieth century, such as those emerging to mobilize and support radical social movements in the early NGO explosions in Latin America and some parts of Asia (Box 10.2), NGOs are now much more constrained in this sphere, often seeking to convince governments that they are non-political in order to retain 'charity' status.

Many NGOs now claim 'empowerment' is an indirect outcome of service delivery activities. In this orientation, participatory approaches to service delivery are believed to foster a democratic culture which feeds into local and national institutions and processes. It can be argued, however, that NGOs promote democracy *only* when they contribute directly to strengthened citizen participation (Hudock, 1999; Ghosh, 2009). Increases in individual and collective assets are not enough to promote empowerment, which is a process that must be accompanied by wider changes in the structural environment, such as tackling discrimination, that improve the terms of recognition of poor and excluded groups. Others argue that NGOs pursue advocacy by stealth, by working in partnership with the government through which they can demonstrate strategies and methods for more effective service provision (Batley, 2011; Rose, 2011).

NGOs that work in advocacy, human rights and empowerment are often viewed by state officials with suspicion, and sometimes hostility,

---

Box 10.2   NGO trajectories: from radical to mainstream

In both Asia and Latin America, NGOs initially emerged with the goal of transforming state–society relationships. The latter years of the Marcos era in the Philippines was marked by the emergence of numerous protest groups of various political ideologies demonstrating against the authoritarian regime. Some transformed into NGOs with advocacy functions under the new democratic regime while others, past and new, looked to service delivery and cooperation with the state. In India, the explosion of NGOs was fuelled by political parties being increasingly dismissive of excluded castes and groups. In Latin America, emerging from a strong and radicalized body of CSOs opposing authoritarian regimes, NGOs have historically functioned in opposition to the government, playing a crucial role in strengthening civil society. In this form, community development was seen as a secondary goal, justified only on the basis of serving higher goals of social change. Over time, however, these popular movements have experienced fragmentation and weakening, with transitions to democracy preventing NGOs from basing their identity purely on resistance, and with foreign aid fostering a move towards greater collaboration with government in service provision.

especially when explicitly challenging the state. Even when NGOs focus on service delivery and welfare provision this has a political dimension (White, 1999; Townsend et al., 2004; Ghosh, 2009). One account of NGOs in Uganda highlights the delicate balance NGOs play in becoming 'entangled in the politics of being non-political' (Dicklitch and Lwanga, 2003: 3) when trying to convince governments they are non-political while advancing their and their clients' interests in a politically contested arena (Ghosh, 2009). However, pressures for institutional survival favour the gradual erosion of transformative agendas, which over time, become replaced by goals of service provision and organizational survival.

'Big-D' and 'little-d' development and civil society

Given that hostile government–NGO relationships can threaten prospects for NGO sustainability, the role of NGOs as social development agencies has most often taken precedence over their role as political actors (Clark, 1998). This distinction between NGOs as service providers and as advocates for the poor differentiates between the pursuit of 'Big-D' and 'little-d' development agendas (Cowen and Shenton, 1996), and subsequently, NGOs' contribution to civil society as genuine proponents of social, political and economic change.

'Big-D' development sees 'Development' as a project-based activity, the tangible outputs of which have no explicit intention to make foundational changes to society's institutional arrangements. In contrast, 'little-d' 'development' regards development as an ongoing, historical process, emphasizing radical, systemic alternatives that seek different ways of organizing the economy, social relationships and politics (Bebbington et al., 2008). Actors pursuing 'little-d' development are those that can be seen to be socially embedded and attempting to make a significant and direct contribution to the strengthening of civil society. As many NGOs have shifted towards the adoption of technical and managerial solutions to social issues through service delivery and welfare provision, their activities have become professionalized and depoliticized, more 'Big-D'. Arguably, this draws them away from more representative CSOs seeking to address structural issues of power and inequality and expand civil society against unrepresentative states (Kamat, 2004). A classic example is ASA (The Association for Social Advancement) in Bangladesh (Rutherford, 2009). It was originally established to create a revolutionary peasant movement but, over time, shifted to microfinance and is now one of

Bangladesh's most successful market-based microfinance institutions having entirely shed its political and social goals. Other radical NGOs, such as Proshika and GSS, followed a similar path but eventually collapsed when they fell out with donors and/or government.

Mounting concerns about NGOs

The initial hype of NGOs as a development alternative in the 1980s and 1990s was surprisingly uncritical, based more on assumptions than evidence (Bebbington et al., 2008; Lewis and Kanji, 2009; Fowler, 2011). To a degree the high expectations on NGOs meant that some level of disillusion with their activities and impact was inevitable (Bebbington, 2005; Srinivas, 2009; Harsh et al., 2010). By the mid-1990s, empirical studies raised questions about their much-lauded comparative advantages. Edwards and Hulme (1997) expressed concerns about NGOs' close proximity to donors, and asked whether this was compromising their grassroots-orientation, innovativeness, accountability, autonomy and, ultimately, their legitimacy. While these concerns continue today, and research has shed more light on them, this has not led to any systematic re-evaluation of NGOs by NGOs.

Losing a grassroots orientation

It is commonly assumed that NGOs target aid more effectively than state agencies because of closer proximity to the poor and their operations not being subject to commercial considerations (Koch et al., 2009). The centrality of this orientation to the legitimacy of NGOs is strikingly evident, with Drabek (1987: 1) urging NGOs not to 'forget their grassroots origins and links, the basis of their greatest strength'. With their participatory and bottom-up development approach, NGO programmes should reflect local contexts, needs and preferences.

However, the institutional imperatives of organizational survival and growth can lead to strategies that redefine NGO goals and change their relationships with the state, donors and clients (Power et al., 2002; Townsend et al., 2004; Edwards, 2008). Most NGOs have concerns about survival given their reliance on short- and medium-term project-based funding. These concerns can erode an NGO's original values and mission and lead to a focus on financial sustainability, professionalism and survival. Projects with defined time-scales, measurable outputs and an emphasis on physical capital development are not well suited to long-term structural change, particularly when implemented by multiple and competing small-scale NGOs (Murray and Overton, 2011). When donor funds diminish, as happened in the Andean region of South America, NGOs can be forced to become more reliant on national governments drawing them further away from the grassroots (Bebbington, 1997). Many NGOs have become too close to the powerful, and too distant from the powerless (Hulme and Edwards, 1997; Banks et al., 2013).

In a competitive and donor-driven funding environment, NGOs tend to formulate their strategies and policies in line with donor priorities rather than local needs and client preferences. International donors have particular goals to achieve through their spending, creating incentives for NGOs to align their objectives and priorities with donors in pursuit of funds and leading towards the external determination of local agendas (Gill, 1997; Fowler, 2000; Mohan, 2002; Epstein and Gang, 2006; Elbers and Arts, 2011). Donors also heavily influence the choice of location of NGOs (Koch et al., 2009) contributing to uneven patterns of activity (Bebbington, 2004) and drawing NGOs into the 'securitization' of aid in Afghanistan and Iraq (Bebbington et al., 2008; Fowler, 2011). Donor priorities and funding have seen a strong shift to a results-oriented and poverty-targeted agenda in the process taking steps back from goals of empowerment and social change (Clark, 1995; White, 1999; Bebbington et al., 2008).

While donors may claim that NGOs bring in the voices of the poor to design and help hold governments to account, the reality is that at the same time they are funding NGOs to directly supply targeted services, both professionalizing and depoliticizing operations by turning NGOs into contractors (Edwards and Hulme, 1996; Bebbington, 1997; Fyvie and Ager, 1999; Townsend et al., 2004; Bebbington et al., 2008; Elbers and Arts, 2011). Pursuing poverty reduction through projects rather than political change and redistribution depoliticizes the structural condition of poverty by assuming that poverty can be eliminated simply by increased access to resources or services rather than through social, economic and political change (Mohan, 2002; Ebrahim, 2003; Bebbington et al., 2008). The donor-driven rush to achieve measurable 'results' has displaced broader goals of empowerment and structural change (Power et al., 2002). This has depoliticized NGO strategies for promoting 'little-d' development, leading them away from relationships with

social movements towards targeted programs for 'Big-D' development (Power et al., 2002; Bebbington et al., 2008). While theoretically rooted in values of participation, in practice, 'most [NGOs]
appear to do little to advance these goals' (Joshi and Moore, 2000).
Choudry and Kapoor (2013) go so far as to argue that the depoliticization of NGO practice means that NGOs now help to sustain non-
democratic regimes and unregulated globalization.

Other potential negative influences on participation are grounded
in the organizational interests of NGOs (White, 1999; Ghosh, 2009).
Systems of 'resource lodging' – the practice of financial, human and
material resources 'sticking' at various points in the aid chain – mean
that NGOs with headquarters in capital cities have little motivation
to increase the proportion of resources transferred to local communities (Harsh et al., 2010). As Bolnick (2008: 324) argues,

> What needs to be recognized is that it is not possible to talk of real
> people's participation or equal partnership when the decision to
> keep power and resources within the hands of professionals and
> out of the hands of the communities is one of the preconditions of
> the engagement.

Organizational survival also forces NGOs to find a compromise
between their pragmatic and charitable values (Brass, 2012), selecting their programmatic locations not only by relative disadvantage
and need, but in terms of ease of access or the availability of donor
funding (Mohan, 2002; Bebbington, 2004; Koch et al., 2009).

Weak accountability and autonomy

Even NGO enthusiasts highlight that NGO accountability is critical
for the sector to maintain its credibility and legitimacy. A bottom-up
approach to development implies that NGOs are accountable to the
communities they work with, and it is this downwards accountability that should ensure NGO effectiveness (Kilby, 2006). In practice,
however, NGOs must grapple with multiple accountabilities – to
donors, clients, staff and supporters, host governments, and even to
themselves in being true to their values (Fyvie and Ager, 1999; Joshi
and Moore, 2000; Bebbington et al., 2008; Lewis and Kanji, 2009).
With many NGOs 85 to 90 per cent dependent on donor funding
however, prioritizing accountability to donors over beneficiary communities becomes a norm (Fowler, 2000; Tvedt, 2006).

Unequal relationships between donors and NGOs lead to the irreconcilable position in which NGOs appear to represent grass-roots communities but are accountable primarily to external organizations, allowing NGOs to survive and expand so long as they can keep donors satisfied (Mohan, 2002; Power et al., 2002). Accountability to donors is a resource-intensive activity requiring money, time, skills and effort, all of which orient NGOs 'upward' and detract from field operations and client engagement (White, 1999; Harsh et al., 2010; Rose, 2011; Elbert and Arts, 2011). The more time NGOs spend 'professionalizing' and meeting donor requirements for reporting and evaluating (logical frameworks, theories of change, measurable baselines and, recently, random control trials) the less time they spend interacting with clients (Lewis and Kanji, 2009).

There is, of course, good reason for donors to require accountability in fund usage, given the incentives for NGOs to misrepresent or misreport their activities and impact (Alexander, 1998; Barr et al., 2005; Burger and Owens, 2010). Misreporting is not always limited to financial activities. Across 300 NGOs in Uganda, Burger and Owens (2010) found them likely to misrepresent information regarding self-reported finances and community consultation. Good intentions, they conclude, do not provide insurance against 'human fallibility', and they caution against an over-reliance on self-reported data when regulating, monitoring or surveying NGOs (Burger and Owens, 2010: 1274). While it is commonly assumed that NGOs possess an intrinsic value base through which they act on altruistic motives, in reality, as with all organizations, survival is paramount, and sometimes to survive, NGOs put their own interests before those of donors and clients (Hudock, 1999; Power et al., 2002; Burger and Owens, 2010).

There are strategies that NGOs can utilize to reduce this financial dependency on donors and avoid the dangers of co-option – primarily by increasing their financial autonomy. Avoiding reliance on one funding source and achieving some degree of financial autonomy is critical to allow NGOs to make strategic choices and prevent them from becoming passive in the face of structural constraints in the aid chain (Bebbington, 1997; Bebbington et al., 2008; Albert and Arts, 2011; Batley, 2011; Rose, 2011). In many countries, most notably Bangladesh, NGOs have pursued financial autonomy by running profitable microfinance programmes and ploughing the profits back into their organization. This reduces dependency on donors but redefines the role of the majority of field staff as credit officers rather than community mobilizers or catalysts. The recent rise of philanthropists and foundations could be seen as offering another opportunity for financial diversification but it might just allow NGOs to keep operating while avoiding strategic re-thinking (Edwards, 2008; Hulme, 2008).

Do NGOs innovate?

Alongside their people-centred and participatory approach, the ability of NGOs to be innovative and experimental has long been argued to underpin NGO effectiveness (Drabek, 1987). However, this is rarely tested. Donor incentives to scale-up activities and find replicable models for poverty reduction have constrained the innovativeness of NGOs, which can be seen as falling into pursuing a 'predictable range' of activities, varying little by region, country or continent (Fyvie and Ager, 1999). Organizational growth through scaling-up poses a fundamental threat to innovation and experimentation, encouraging NGOs to behave more like businesses than development organizations by shifting focus away from local contexts and client preferences towards the quest for an effective 'model' that can be implemented regardless of context (Korten, 1990; Atack, 1999; Fyvie and Ager, 1999). These pressures leave NGOs unwilling to try risky and unproven pilots for fear of losing their funding (Vivian, 1994; Fyvie and Ager, 1999; Bebbington et al., 2008).

Can NGOs return to the grassroots?

Despite claims to the contrary (Green, 2013) there is growing evidence that many NGOs have become part of the 'Development industry' – dependent on foreign aid, megaphilanthropists or government contracts and focused on programme implementation. This reduces their capacity to pursue participatory and/or innovative initiatives promoting empowerment. Ultimately, this undermines their contributions to civil society in tackling structurally entrenched forms of poverty and 'little-d' development agendas. While NGOs are by definition organizations within civil society, most are not membership organizations and lack the attributes of representative civil society organizations. Some critics go so far as to say NGOs pose a distinct threat to indigenous civil society and grassroots activism by distracting attention and funding from more politicized and socially embedded organizations (Clark, 1998; Bebbington et al., 2008; Chhotray, 2008). For example, in Pakistan, Bano (2012) reveals how donor financing broke down the institutions for collective action (that it claims to promote) by eroding the attributes and character-istics that generate membership and support for CSOs. She argues that in their quest to strengthen civil society organizations, donors failed to understand why people choose to cooperate in groups: col-lective interest, trust and, ultimately, faith in the group leadership's intentions, motivations and commitments to the cause. By bringing in large sums of external financing, donors replaced the psychosocial rewards that incentivize group leadership with material incentives, elite status and professional positions, eroding members' trust in their leaders' motivations and encouraging exit from the group.

While the potential of NGOs to offer development alternatives remains, their leverage over long-run drivers of change will continue to be weak and they will never achieve their mission statements unless they can return to their roots, regain their distinctive val-ues, and remove or re-negotiate the perverse incentives they face (Bebbington, 1997; Bebbington et al., 2008). Banks and Hulme (2012) have identified a model through which greater partnership and support of locally rooted civil society organizations might per-mit NGOs to make a shift away from project-based 'Big-D' develop-ment activities and tackle the processes that perpetuate poverty and structural inequality.

A 'civil society' function for NGOs would entail moving away from a supply-side, service-based orientation and back to a 'demand-side' approach that supports communities to articulate their concerns and participate in the development process (Clark, 1995; Fowler, 2000). It also requires a shift away from conventional approaches to advocacy – in which NGOs generate campaigns on behalf of the poor – to work that directly strengthens the bargaining power of the poor themselves to defend their rights and enhance their capacity for collective action (Ibrahim and Hulme, 2011). One solution may be to develop a paradigm in which NGOs and constituents are both cli-ents simultaneously to each other (Najam, 1996), finding a place for NGOs as the organized face of more deeply seated, networked forms of social action, in which people are already pursuing strategic goals and create NGOs in order to further these strategies (Bebbington, 2004; Banks and Hulme, 2012).

This is a risk-strewn path, away from the existing comfort zone of NGOs, and it entails their repositioning to become secondary actors in the development process, raising questions as to whether NGOs are willing and able to make this transition. Indeed, NGOs have proven unwilling or unable to establish strong connections with social movements that are more embedded in the political processes essential to social change (Edwards, 2008). Paradoxically, civil society may be nurtured most effectively when donors and NGOs do less, stepping back to allow citizens themselves to dictate the agenda and evolve a variety of CSOs to suit their contexts and concerns (Edwards, 2011). Finding ways to support this approach entails a new strategic direction for NGOs, which must evolve to limit their roles to support and facilitation, so as not to take on what individuals and communities can do on their own (Mitlin and Satterthwaite, 2004). In this model, NGOs would work in solidarity and partnership with CSOs, building their capacity as CSOs to mobilize and strengthen their collective assets and capabilities (Kilby, 2006). Locally generated priorities are produced through a long deliberative process and a more egalitarian relationship founded heavily on trust, not only between donors and NGO partners, but within NGO and partner communities too (Racelis, 2008; King, 2014). Shack/Slum Dwellers International (SDI) provides an example of an NGO that has successfully pursued this approach and has learned how to support the evolution of civil society groups at scale (Box 10.3).

Conclusion

The recognition that civil society is an essential element of any attempt to strengthen governance has been a very important lesson for development theorists and practitioners but it has added further complications to the analysis and pursuit of development. To make matters even more complicated, civil society has also widened to include not only local and national CSOs, NGOs and social movements, but also, in today's digital world, the social media that require no physical home or organizational base. Civil society provides a crucial space in which interest groups, social movements and other civil society organizations can contest the existing institutions, structures and processes that underlie their exclusion and/or underrepresentation in the existing social, political and economic order.

The initial focus of development policy on NGOs as the lead agencies in civil society has both confused the understanding of civil society's contribution to development and in many countries created

Box 10.3   Shack/Slum Dwellers International: an NGO supporting civil society

Shack/Slum Dwellers International (SDI) is a movement that has successfully brought together low-income urban communities across 33 countries in Africa, Asia and Latin America. It is first and foremost an organization of and for the urban poor, and illustrates how NGOs can play an important role in supporting community associations that are the primary actors in negotiations and advocacy work with the state. The network has mobilized over 2 million members, all of whom participate in practical activities, daily savings and loans schemes, and in strategic actions that have secured formal land tenure for over 250,000 families (Bolnick, 2008).

In this model, communities take the lead in all strategies and activities. SDI and its national NGO partners work in a supportive role with local community associations to help them build relationships and partnerships with local governments. This approach means that communities have been able to move away from confrontational demands on local government – for land, water, sanitation, electricity and housing finance – to carefully structured negotiation. Strategic successes at the local-level feed up to federated associations at both the national and international level allowing low-income communities to share ideas and lessons learned in promoting their interests and securing resources. While predominantly working at the grassroots, alliances between CSOs and their NGO partners can link local activities with broader national and international efforts to build civic voice and change the underlying systems and structures of power in society (Kunreuther, 2011).

The strength of the SDI model is that within it, NGOs are functional to the needs and demands of the social movement as a whole, supporting it in monitoring public policy, mobilizing members, and creating new information resources, allowing the orientation to maintain its grassroots-driven and participatory approach and encouraging and supporting the urban poor to negotiate with the state and its agencies to obtain entitlements for themselves (Patel et al., 2001; Banks, 2011; Ibrahim and Hulme, 2011). SDI has needed to access aid donor finance to support some of its activities but it has been able to do this in ways that have not compromised its approach.

Another key characteristic of the SDI model is its leverage of information in the processes of social and economic transformation. Organizing around this free resource that they do have, low-income communities have found information to be one of their critical weapons in negotiations with local governments, which have been surprised by the numbers of slum-dwellers as official records under-reported these populations.

an NGO sector that is often closely linked to donor finances (and strategy) or to domestic governments. NGOs rose to prominence on the basis of their strengths as grassroots development organizations offering the potential for innovative bottom-up strategies reflecting the needs and preferences of disadvantaged groups and communities. Early views of NGOs as 'heroic' organizations have been replaced by recognition of their increasingly professionalized and depoliticized nature and their subsequent limitations in promoting long-term structural change.

Despite these limitations, NGOs remain a potentially important part of an emerging civil society that creates a relatively progressive relationship between governments, markets and citizens. An increasing recognition of NGOs as only one component of broader civil society has drawn attention to the need to find a more effective role for NGOs in strengthening civil society. This requires, however, a reorientation of NGOs in line with their original strengths and vision, putting communities back at the centre of their strategies and empowerment back at the centre of their activities. This will not be an easy transition, requiring NGOs to relinquish power over programme design, planning and fund management to the grassroots and requiring deep thinking across the international aid chain.

Chapter 11

Conclusion: What Future for the Public Sector?

Dominant ideas about the role of public sector organizations have changed dramatically. In the early development decades, the 1950s and 1960s, the public sector was awarded undisputed primacy as the creator and implementer of strategies for development. Its technically skilled, and simultaneously altruistic, elites would guide economies and societies along the path to modernization. In the 1970s, critical self-reflection and assault from radical development theory saw the image of an efficacious public sector severely damaged. Could it generate and maintain the impetus for development? By the 1980s, the answer to this question was clearly and widely articulated. The public sector was a pariah that actually hindered economic and social development: it was not the solution, it was the problem. The time had come to roll back the state by privatizing the public enterprises so vigorously promoted in an earlier era and downsizing the ministries which had been encouraged to expand into ever more areas of social and economic life. The invisible hand of the market would unleash the mechanisms to realize the developmental aspirations of the Third World.

Such broad generalizations have frequently dominated debate on development policy and management. But as we have demonstrated in the preceding chapters, they fail to take account of the enormous diversity of management environments, organizational structures, policy processes and public sector performances that the empirical record reveals. Experience is not so neatly characterized when one's object of analysis comprises three-quarters of the world's population and more than 130 independent states.

In the 2000s, blind faith in market mechanisms has waned as neoliberal solutions did not produce the promised results and developing country governments became more assertive in their dealings with rich countries and international financial agencies (IFIs). In an era when China, India and Brazil have economically emerged to reshape the global economy it is clearly foolish to frame think-ing as 'state *or* market'. To achieve developmental goals both 'state *and* market' are needed. The state has been let back in, not to the extent that it had been in the early development decades, and market solutions are now treated more judiciously. One-size fits all solutions that had characterized the agendas of proponents of both state and market approaches to development were more severely criticized. The gloom about developmental prospects that had prevailed in the early 1990s was lifted by the increasing evidence of improved econ-omic and social conditions in East, Southeast and South Asia, and Latin America as the Millennium approached, and subsequently the announcement of the Millennium Development Goals (MDGs) in 2000. This was a global institution of hope which managed to capture the collective imagination of governments and development organizations. There were some dissenters, but that had always been so for all development discourses. For the first time there was a global consensus on what development was to achieve and improved coordination of activity. The MDGs clearly identified the leading problems and measurable targets were set so that progress could be easily monitored. However, prescriptions for how to achieve the goals were left open creating space for countries to take more control of national strategies and forge new alliances – often with the emerg-ing powers of the BRICs.

There was growing agreement that the state had a key role and that governance was of central importance, viewpoints clearly articu-lated in the first edition of this book. Many now agreed that the state needed to be 'sufficiently effective' and governance 'good enough' if growth was to occur and/or human development to advance. Such conditions involve having public sector organizations that can implement basic functions reasonably well and where performance is improving. Government organizations should have competence in macroeconomic management, be able to provide basic services, register citizens, give social protection and guarantee a degree of law and order. Governments should also have priorities for governance improvement with targets that are politically and technically feasible.

There has also been appreciation that ideal type models of Western democracy, especially its Westminster and US versions, have not taken hold in developing countries and in some cases have actu-ally weakened governance. An array of hybrid regimes combining elements of democracy with items of authoritarianism and tradition has been the norm. And the hybrid regimes in developing countries come in many shapes and sizes. Transferring political and governance institutions from Western countries has been fraught with difficulty as they rarely fit the environments of developing countries. The transfer process has drawn criticism from many quarters and decreasing interest from many Third World governments. There are other successful developmental success stories that might be usefully studied – for example, South Korea, China, Brazil, Chile, Mauritius and Botswana. Politicians, public servants and academics in developing countries are interested in these success stories and can often relate to them better than to Western country cases. Thus, uncritical promotion of Western-derived institutions has become increasingly a thing of the past as political economy studies consistently point out the difficulty and folly of trying to fit institutions that have evolved in the West with circumstances that differ markedly in developing countries. Some of these transfers have done more harm than good. This is not to say transfer is wrong, rather that it must be a selective and well thought through process. Countries with similar organizational environments offer the best opportunities for examining transfer possibilities. But even with neighbours, modifications to the transferred item will undoubtedly be necessary and 'policy learning' may be a better guide than 'policy transfer' or 'isomorphic mimicry'.

There has been progress towards achieving the MDGs in most developing countries although the degrees of progress vary considerably. In almost all cases public sector organizations have made significant contributions to MDG progress. Contributions vary: in China it has been through direct involvement in growth processes by state-owned enterprises; in Bangladesh through successful macroeconomic management of the economy; and, in Brazil by enabling growth and directly providing basic services, especially social protection. But this does not mean that developing country governments can rest on their laurels. There are still substantial opportunities to improve public sector performance and it is urgently needed in many of the poorest countries. Throughout this book we have presented a variety of ideas on how this might be done: by maintaining greater awareness of the environment and its ever-changing features (Chapter 2); applying a political economy approach to conflict resolution and peacebuilding and the complexity of establishing legal systems that provide justice for all (Chapter 3); appreciating the crucial role of policy and of politics in the policy process, especially implementation (Chapter 4); using strategic management and its subset of strategic human resource management to secure effective responses to development problems (Chapter 5); taking a problem-solving approach to civil service reform (Chapter 6); abandoning planning for an ideal world in favour of planning for the real world in which knowledge and information are often limited and risk and uncertainty can be considerable (Chapter 7); continuing to experiment with modes of decentralization to improve services especially for the poor and accountability more generally (Chapter 8); engaging with the private sector through PPPs (public-private partnerships) and creating an enabling environment (Chapter 9); recognizing the limitations as well as the potential of civil society organizations for development (Chapter 10) .

These and other ideas that are presented throughout the book are indicative of creativity and diversity. There is no 'one best way'. Rather, experience has provided us with a variety of organizational forms, practices and local applications. What has been successful in one place may be inappropriate in another and the lessons of one country's reforms may be different for the various observers. As time passes, new problems emerge such as adapting to climate change, dealing with ageing populations, widening economic inequality or megacity growth. These require new solutions or updated versions of old ones. Public sector organizations will be expected to take leading roles in addressing the emerging problems and be innovative and resourceful. As has already increasingly happened the public sector will need to engage in partnerships with the private sector, civil society organizations, other governments and aid agencies. We have presented many examples of such cooperation in this book revealing both the advantages to be gained from such cooperation and problems that can occur. But we have not specifically focused on aid agencies. It is to them that we now turn.

IFIs, notably the World Bank and the IMF, and other multilateral and bilateral aid organizations have come up regularly throughout this book. They have been major actors in development. But two phenomena are altering the position of these organizations in development. First, there has been diversification of aid. New players such as China, South Korea, oil-rich Middle Eastern countries, the BRICS' New Development Bank and large philanthropic foundations have entered the scene and are assuming increasingly important roles. Second, there has been growing concern about the effectiveness of aid, especially that delivered by the leading IFIs. Has there been value for money? How big a difference has aid made in the development process? It seems the days of bossing developing countries around and forcing unwanted medicine on them has come to an end. There is also a growing consensus that aid may help in development but that it will not create it. Aid will not generate economic growth or major changes in human welfare. Initiatives to produce such transformations must be indigenous led and supported. Domestic political support and commitment are essential as is capacity in public sector organizations. Making the state work through effective governance and management is, as it always has been, essential for development.

Finally, a consistent theme of this book that has permeated all chapters is the importance of politics. Whether it is the making of policies, the design of civil service reform, the privatization of state-owned enterprises or the implementation of decentralization, there will always be a political dimension. And it is probably the most important dimension as many of the researchers cited in this book have recognized and the authors of this book have witnessed over many years. Different actors struggle to control or influence the development agenda on various levels from the international to the national and down to the local. The actors have different interests and views on such things as what shape development should take, how it should be designed, who should be responsible and what implementation should look like. In all these matters, we find politics – power struggles – that determine the nature of development. Sometimes these struggles are ideological. At other times they are about personal or family or group interests. And, in the messy world of political reality they are often a confusing mixture of several overlapping struggles. We should not, however, think of politics as a malevolent force but rather as a normal state of affairs. It is through political institutions and processes that decisions are made and implemented. The principal task for development management is how to ensure, along with other sympathetic actors, that the poor and marginalized are not only taken into account but that their voices are heard and acknowledged, and that they can take control of important decisions that affect their lives.

Bibliography

Abed, G., Gupta, S., Ebrill, L., Pellechio, A., Schiff, J., Clements, B., McMorran, R. and Verhoeven, M. (1998), 'Fiscal reforms in low income countries: Experience under IMF-supported programs', *Occasional Paper*, 160, International Monetary Fund.

Acemoglu, D. and Johnson, S. (2005), 'Unbundling institutions', *Journal of Political Economy*, 113(5): 949–95.

Acemoglu, D. and Robinson, J. (2012), *Why Nations Fail: The Origins of Power, Prosperity and Poverty* (New York: Crown Business).

ACHR (Asian Centre for Human Rights) (2011), *Torture in India 2011* (New Delhi: ACHR).

Adam, I. (2009), 'Setting targets in the public service: At your service', *The Star*, 31 August.

Adamolekun, L. (1983), *Public Administration: A Nigerian and Comparative Perspective* (London: Longman).

ADB (Asian Development Bank) (1999), *Governance: Sound Development Management* (Manila: Asian Development Bank).

ADB (Asian Development Bank) (2008a), *Managing Asian Megacities* (Manila: Asian Development Bank).

ADB (Asian Development Bank) (2008b), *Public-Private Partnerships Handbook* (Manila: ADB)

Alavi, H. (1982), 'State and class under peripheral capitalism', in H. Alavi and T. Shanin (eds), *Introduction to the Sociology of 'Developing' Societies* (London: Macmillan), pp. 289–307.

Aldrich, H. (2008), *Organizations and Environments* (Stanford: Stanford University Press).

Alexander, V. (1998), 'Environmental constraints and organizational strategies: Complexity, conflict and coping in the non-profit sector', in W. Powell and E. Clemens (eds), *Private Action and the Public Good* (New Haven, CT: Yale University Press), pp. 272–290.

Allmendinger, P. (2002), 'Towards a post-positivist typology of planning theory', *Planning Theory*, 1(1): 77–99.

Anderson, J. (2006), *The Rise and Fall of Training and Visit Extension* (Washington, DC: World Bank).

Andrews, M. (2013), *The Limits of Institutional Reform in Development: Changing Rules for Realistic Solutions* (Cambridge: Cambridge University Press).

Andrews, M., Pritchett, L. and Woolcock, M. (2012), 'Escaping capability traps through problem-driven iterative adaptation (PDIA)', *HKS Faculty Research Working Paper* RWP12–036.

Angel-Urdinola, D. and Tanabe, K. (2012), 'Micro-determinants of informal employment in the Middle East and North Africa region', *SP Discussion Paper*, no 1201, World Bank.

Antonio, H. (2013), 'History of the Philippine power sector', in KPMG Global Energy Institute (ed.), *The Energy Report Philippines: Growth and Opportunities in the Philippine Electric Power Sector 2013–2014 Edition* (Manila: KPMG), pp. 10–14.

Argyris, C. (1957), *Personality and Organization* (New York: Harper and Brothers).

Armstrong, M. (2008), *Strategic Human Resource Management: A Guide to Action* (London: Kogan Page).

Arrighi, G., Hopkins, T. and Wallerstein, I. (2011), *Anti-Systemic Movements* (London and Brooklyn: Verso)

Atack, I. (1999), 'Four criteria of development NGO legitimacy', *World Development*, 27(5): 855–64.

Bachetta, M., Ekkehard, E. and Bustamente, J. (2009), *Informal Jobs in Developing Countries* (Geneva: WTO and ILO).

Baiocchi, G. (2003), 'Emergent public spheres: Talking politics in municipal governance', *American Sociological Review*, 68(1): 52–74.

Baker, K. (1976), 'Public choice theory: Some important assumptions and public policy implications', in R. Golembiewski et al. (eds), *Public Administration: Readings in Institutions, Processes, Behavior, Policy* (New York: Rand McNally), pp. 41–60.

Baker, B. (2004), 'Multi-choice policing in Africa: Is the continent following the South African pattern?' *Society in Transition*, 35(2): 204–23.

Bale, M. and Dale, T. (1998), 'Public sector reform in New Zealand and its relevance to developing countries', *World Bank Research Observer*, 13(1): 103–22.

Ballentine, K. and Sherman, J. (2003), 'Introduction', in K. Ballentine. and J. Sherman (eds), *The Political Economy of Armed Conflict: Beyond Greed and Grievance* (Boulder, CO: Lynne Rienner), pp. 1–15.

Banks, N. (2011), 'Improving donor support for urban poverty reduction: A focus on South Asia', *UNU-WIDER Working Paper* No. 2011/68.

Banks, N. and Hulme, D. (2012), 'The role of NGOs and civil society in development and poverty reduction', *BWPI Working Paper* 171, Brooks World Poverty Institute, University of Manchester.

Banks, S., Butcher, H., Orton, A. and Robertson, J. (eds) (2013), *Managing Community Practice: Principles, Policies and Programmes*, Second Edition (Bristol: The Policy Press).

Bano, M. (2012), *Breakdown in Pakistan: How Aid is Eroding Institutions for Collective Action* (Stanford: Stanford University Press).

Barr, A., Fafchamps, M. and Owens, T. (2005), 'The governance of non-governmental organizations in Uganda', *World Development*, 33(4): 657–79.

Bates, R. (2001), *Prosperity and Violence: The Political Economy of Development* (New York: W. W. Norton & Co.).

Bates, R. (2008), 'State failure', *Annual Review of Political Science*, 11: 1–12.

Batley, R. (2011), 'Structures and strategies in relationships between non-government service providers and governments', *Public Administration and Development*, 31(4): 306–19.

Batley, R. and Larbi, G. (2004), *The Changing Role of Government: The Reform of Public Services in Developing Countries* (Basingstoke: Palgrave Macmillan).

Batley, R. and Mcloughlin, C. (2009), *State Capacity and Non-state Service Provision in Fragile and Conflict-affected States*. Available from http://www.gsdrc.org/docs/open/EIRS3.pdf.

Bauer, P.T. (1984), 'Remembrance of studies past: Retracing first steps', in G. Meier and D. Seers (eds), *Pioneers in Development* (New York: Oxford University Press), pp. 27–43.

BBC (2011a), 'Oxfam warns about effects of land rush', *BBC News*, 22 September. Available from http://www.bbc.co.uk/news/world-africa-15013396.

BBC (British Broadcasting Corporation) (2011b), 'Zimbabwe civil servants exposed by World Bank report'. Available at http://www.bbc.co.uk/news/world-africa-13386762

Beall, J., Goodfellow, T. and Rodgers, D. (2011), 'Cities, conflict and state fragility', *Crisis States Working Papers Series No. 2*, 85. Crisis States Research Centre, LSE.

Bebbington, A. (1997), 'New states, new NGOs? Crises and transitions among rural development NGOs in the Andean region', *World Development*, 25(11): 1755–65.

Bebbington, A. (2004), 'NGOs and uneven development: Geographies of development intervention', *Progress in Human Geography*, 28(6): 725–45.

Bebbington, A. (2005), 'Donor-NGO relations and representations of livelihood in nongovernmental aid chains', *World Development*, 33(6): 937–50.

Bebbington, A.S. Hickey, S. and Mitlin, D. (2008), 'Introduction: Can NGOs make a difference? The challenge of development alternatives', in A. Bebbington, S. Hickey and D. Mitlin (eds), *Can NGOs Make a Difference? The Challenge of Development Alternatives* (London: Zed Books), pp. 3–37.

Bebbington, A. and McCourt, W. (eds) (2007), *Development Success: Statecraft in the South* (London: Palgrave Macmillan).

Becker, B. and Gerhart, B. (1996), 'The impact of human resource management on organizational performance', *Academy of Management Journal*, 39(4): 779–801.

Bellows, J. and Miguel, E. (2006), 'War and institutions: New evidence from sierra leone', *The American Economic Review*, 96(2): 394–99.

Belur, J. (2009), 'Police use of deadly force: Police perceptions of a culture of approval', *Journal of Contemporary Criminal Justice*, 25(2): 237–52.

Benjaminsen, T. and Lund, C. (eds) (2003), *Securing Land Rights in Africa* (London: Frank Cass).

Bennett, A. and Mills, S. (1998), 'Government capacity to contract: Health sector experience and lessons', *Public Administration and Development*, 18 (4): 307–36.

Bennis, W. (1966), *Changing Organizations* (New York: McGraw-Hill).

Berdal, M. (2005), 'Beyond greed and grievance – and not too soon...', *Review of International Studies*, 31(4): 687–98.

Berdal, M. (2014), 'Peacebuilding and development', in B. Currie-Alder, R. Kanbur, D. Malone and R. Medhora (eds), *International Development: Ideas, Experience and Prospects* (Oxford: Oxford University Press), pp. 362–78.

Berdal, M. and Zaum, D. (eds) (2012), *Political Economy of Statebuilding: Power after Peace* (Abingdon: Routledge).

Beswick, D. (2011), 'Aiding state building and sacrificing peace building? The Rwanda-UK relationship 1994–2011', *Third World Quarterly*, 32(10): 1911–30.

Bevan, G. and Hood, C. (2006), 'What's measured is what matters: Targets and gaming in the English public health care system', *Public Administration*, 84(3): 517–38.

Bilgin, P. and Morton, A. (2002), 'Historicising representations of "failed states": Beyond the cold-war annexation of the social sciences', *Third World Quarterly*, 23(1): 55–80.

Birdsall, N. and Fukuyama, F. (2011), 'The Post-Washington Consensus: Development after the crisis', *Foreign Affairs*, 90(2): 45–53.

Bland, G. (2004), 'Enclaves and elections: The decision to decentralize in Chile', in A. Montero and D. Samuels (eds), *Decentralization and Democracy in Latin America* (Notre Dame, Indiana: University of Notre Dame Press), pp. 94–121.

Bland, G. (2011), 'Supporting post-conflict democratic development? External promotion of participatory budgeting in El Salvador', *World Development*, 39(5): 863–73.

Blattman, C. and Miguel, E. (2009), *Civil War* (Cambridge, MA: National Bureau of Economic Research).

Blum, J. (2012), *Towards Better Understanding Risk in Public Sector Management (PSM) Reform: What Predicts the Success or Failure of World Bank-Supported PSM Projects? A Review of the World Bank's PSM Portfolio* (Washington, DC: World Bank).

Blunt, P. and Turner, M. (2007), 'Decentralization, deconcentration, and poverty reduction in the Asia Pacific', in G.S. Cheema and D. Rondinelli (eds), *Decentralizing Governance: Emerging Concepts and Practices* (Washington, DC: Ash Institute and Brookings Institutions), pp. 115–30.

Blunt, P., Turner, M. and Lindroth, H. (2012), 'Patronage's progress in post-Soeharto Indonesia', *Public Administration and Development*, 32(1): 64–81.

Bolnick, J. (2008), 'Development as reform and counter-reform: Paths travelled by Slum/Shack Dwellers International', in A. Bebbington, S. Hickey and D. Mitlin (eds), *Can NGOs Make a Difference? The Challenge of Development Alternatives* (London and New York: Zed Books), pp. 316–33.

Bond, R. and Hulme, D. (1999), 'Process approaches to development: Theory and Sri Lankan practice', *World Development*, 27(8): 1339–58.

Boone, C. (2007), 'Property and constitutional order: Land tenure reform and the future of the African state', *African Affairs*, 106(425): 557–86.

Booth, D. (2011), 'Towards a theory of local governance and public goods provision', *IDS Bulletin*, 42(2): 11–21.

Booth, D. and Golooba-Mutebi, F. (2012), 'Development patrimonialism? The case of Rwanda', *African Affairs*, 111(444): 379–403.

Borins, S. and Warrington, E. (1996), *The New Public Administration: Global Challenges, Local Solutions – A Report on the Second Biennial Conference of CAPAM* (London: Commonwealth Secretariat).

Boubakri, N. and Cosset, J.C. (1998), *Privatization in Developing Countries: An Analysis of the Performance of Newly Privatized Firms* (Washington, DC: World Bank).

Boudin, C. (2009), *Gringo: A Coming-of-Age in Latin America* (New York: Scribner).

Boyne, G. (2003), 'Sources of public service improvement: A critical review and research agenda', *Journal of Public Administration Research and Theory*, 13(3): 367–94.

Brahimi, L. (2000), *Report of the Panel on United Nations Peace Operations* (New York: UN General Assembly and Security Council).

Brass, J.N. (2011), 'Blurring boundaries: The integration of NGOs into governance in Kenya', *Governance: An International Journal of Policy, Administration, and Institutions*, 25(2): 209–35.

Brass, J. (2012), 'Why do NGOs go where they go? Evidence from Kenya', *World Development*, 40(2): 387–401.

Brett, E. (2008), 'State failure and success in Uganda and Zimbabwe: The logic of political decay and reconstruction in Africa', *Journal of Development Studies*, 44(3): 339–64.

Brillantes, A. (1999), 'Decentralization, devolution and development in the Philippines', *UMP-Asia Occasional Paper* 4.

Brinkerhoff, D. and Crosby, B. (2002), *Managing Policy Reform: Concepts and Tools for Decision-makers in Developing and Transitioning Countries* (Bloomfield, CT: Kumarian).

Brown, C. (2012), 'Diplomacy is the only real way forward in the Syrian conflict. Military intervention could make the situation even worse' LSE Comment. Available from http://blogs.lse.ac.uk/europpblog/2012/06/19/syria-diplomacy/

Bruton, H. (1992), *Political Economy of Poverty, Equity and Growth: Sri Lanka and Malaysia* (Oxford and New York: Oxford University Press).

Burger, R. and Owens, T. (2010), 'Promoting transparency in the NGO sector: Examining the availability and reliability of self-reported data', *World Development*, 38(9): 1263–77.

Burton, J., Joubert, C., Harrison, J. and Athayde, C. (1993), *Evaluation of ODA Project in Support of Ghana Civil Service Reform Programme: Volumes I and II* (London: ODA Evaluation Department).

Cai, P. (2014), 'Reforming China's lumbering state giants', *China Spectator*, 27 March. Available from http://www.businessspectator.com.au/article/2014/3/27/china/reforming-chinas-lumbering-state-giants

Caiden, N. and Wildavsky, A. (1990), *Planning and Budgeting in Poor Countries* (New Brunswick: Transaction Publishers, originally published in 1974).

Campbell, J. (1964), *Honour, Family and Patronage: A Study of Institutions and Moral Values in a Greek Mountain Community* (Oxford: Oxford University Press).

Campos, J. and Esfahani, H. (2000), 'Credible commitment and success with public enterprise reform', *World Development*, 28(2): 221–43.

Cardoso, F.H. (1977), 'The consumption of dependency theory in the United States', *Latin American Research Review*, 12(3): 7–24.

Cariño, L. (2007), 'Devolution toward democracy: Lessons for theory and practice from the Philippines', in S. Cheema and D. Rondinelli (eds), *Decentralizing Governance: Emerging Concepts and Practices* (Washington, DC: Ash Institute for Democratic Governance and Innovation and Brookings Institution), pp. 92–114.

Carothers, T. and de Gramont, D. (2013), *Development Aid Confronts Politics: The Almost Revolution* (Washington, DC: Carnegie Endowment for International Peace).

Cernea, M. (1991), *Putting People First: Sociological Variables in Rural Development* (New York: Oxford University Press).

Chamarbagwala, R. and Morán, H. (2011), 'The human capital consequences of civil war: Evidence from Guatemala', *Journal of Development Economics*, 94(1): 41–61.

Chambers, R. (1983), *Rural Development: Putting the Last First* (London: Longman).

Chambers, R. (1992), 'The self-deceiving state', *IDS Bulletin*, 23(4): 31–42.

Chambers, R. (1993), *Challenging the Professions: Frontiers for Rural Development* (London: IT Publishers).

Chambers, R. (1994), 'Participatory Rural Appraisal (PRA): Analysis of experience', *World Development*, 22(9): 1253–68.

Chazan, N. (1989), 'Planning democracy in Africa: A comparative perspective on Nigeria and Ghana', *Policy Sciences*, 22(3–4): 325–57.

Chazan, N., Mortimer, R., Ravenhill, J. and Rothchild, D. (1988), *Politics and Society in Contemporary Africa* (London: Macmillan).

Cheung, A. (2013), 'Can there be an Asian model of public administration', *Public Administration and Development*, 33(4): 249–61.

Chickering, A.L. and Salahdine, M. (1991), 'Introduction', in A.L. Chickering and M. Salahdine (eds), *The Silent Revolution: The Informal Sector in Five Asian and Near Eastern Countries* (San Francisco: ICS Press).

Chhotray, V. (2008), 'Political entrepreneurs or development agents: An NGO's tale of resistance and acquiescence in Madhya Pradesh, India', in A. Bebbington, S. Hickey and D. Mitlin (eds), *Can NGOs Make a Difference? The Challenge of Development Alternatives* (London and New York: Zed Books), pp. 261–78.

Chia, P., Chua Chiaco, K., Kim Fat, C., Toe, S. and Toh, K. (2007), *Water Privatization in Manila, Philippines: Should Water be Privatized?* (INSEAD Economics and Management in Developing Countries).

Child, J. 'Organizational structures, environment and performance: The role of strategic choice', *Sociology*, 6(1): 2–22.

Choi, J. and Thum, M. (2005), 'Corruption and the shadow economy', *International Economic Review*, 46(3): 817–36.

Chong, A. and López-de-Silanes, F. (2004), 'Privatization in Latin America: What does the evidence say?' *Economia*, 37(Spring): 37–111.

Choudry, A. and Kapoor, D. (2013) 'Introduction: NGOization: Complicity, contradictions and prospects', in A. Choudry and D. Kapoor (eds), *NGOization: Complicity, Contradictions and Prospects* (London: Zed), pp. 1–23.

Chowdhury, T. (1992), 'Privatization of state enterprises in Bangladesh, 1975–84', in G. Lamb and R. Weaving (eds), *Managing Policy Reforms in the Real World* (Washington, DC: World Bank, EDI Seminar Series), pp. 57–70.

Chowdhury, A. and Kirkpatrick, C. (1994), *Development Policy and Planning: An Introduction to Models and Techniques* (London: Routledge).

Christoplos, I. (1997), 'Public services, complex emergencies and the humanitarian imperative: Perspectives from Angola', in M. Minogue, C. Polidano and D. Hulme (eds), *Beyond the New Public Management: Changing Ideas and Practices in Governance* (Cheltenham: Edward Elgar), pp. 260–77.

Chronic Poverty Research Centre (2008), *The Chronic Poverty Report 2008–09: Escaping Poverty Traps* (Manchester: University of Manchester).

Chulajata, I. and Turner, M. (2009), 'What happens when policies are transferred? The privatization of the Telephone Organisation of Thailand', *International Journal of Asia-Pacific Studies*, 5(1): 33–53.

Claeson, M., Bos, E., Mawji, T. and Pathmanathan, I (2000), 'Reducing child mortality in India in the new millennium', *Bulletin of the World Health Organization*, 78(10): 1192–99.

Clapham, C. (1982), *Private Patronage and Public Power: Political Clientelism in the Modern State* (London: Pinter).

Clapham, C. (1985), *Third World Politics: An Introduction* (London: Croom Helm).

Clark, G. (1998), 'Nongovernmental organizations and politics in the developing world', *Political Studies*, 46(1): 36–52.

Clark, J. (1995), 'The state, popular participation, and the voluntary sector', *World Development*, 23(4): 593–601.

Clarke, J. and Newman, J. (1997), *The Managerial State: Power, Politics and Ideology in the Remaking of Social Welfare* (London: Sage).

Clarke, S. (1998), 'Trade unions and non-payment of wages in Russia', *International Journal of Manpower*, 1(2): 68–94.

Clegg, I., Hunt, R. and Whetton, J. (2000), 'Policy guidance on support to policing in developing countries' Report prepared on behalf of DFID (Swansea: Centre for Development Studies).

Cohen, J. and Peterson, S. (1999), *Administrative Decentralization: Strategies for Developing Countries* (West Hartford, CT: Kumarian).

Collier, P. (2000), 'Doing well out of war: An economic perspective', in M. Berdal and D. Malone (eds), *Greed and Grievance: Economic Agendas in Civil Wars* (Boulder, CO: Lynne Rienner), pp. 91–112.

Collier, P. (2007), *The Bottom Billion: Why the Poorest Countries are Failing and What Can Be Done About It* (Oxford: Oxford University Press).

Collier, P. (2009), 'The political economy of state failure', *Oxford Review of Economic Policy*, 25(2) 219–40.

Collier, P., Elliott, V., Hegre, H., Hoefflen, A., Reynal-Querol, M. and Sambanis, N. (2003), *Breaking the Conflict Trap: Civil War and Development Policy* (Washington, DC: World Bank).

Collier, P. and Hoeffler, A. (1998), 'On economic causes of civil war', *Oxford Economics Papers*, 50(4): 563–73.

Collier, P. and Hoeffler, A. (2000), 'Greed and grievance in civil war', *Policy Research Working Paper*, 2355, World Bank.

Collier, P. and Hoeffler, A. (2004), 'Greed and grievance in civil war', *Oxford Economic Papers*, 56(4): 563–95.

Colm, G. and Geiger, T. (1963), 'Country programming as a guide to development', in Brookings Institution (ed.), *Development of the Emerging Countries: An Agenda for Research* (Washington, DC: Brookings Institution), pp. 45–70.

Constantino-David, K. (1995), 'Community organizing in the Philippines: The experience of development NGOs', in G. Craig and M. Mayo (eds), *Community Empowerment: A Reader in Participation and Development* (London: Zed Books), pp. 154–67.

Convergences (2013), The 2012 Microfinance Barometer'. Available from http://www.convergences2015.org/en/Article?id=555

Conyers, D. (1983), 'Decentralisation: The latest fashion in development administration', *Public Administration and Development*, 3(2): 97–109.

Cook, P. and Minogue, M. (1990), 'Waiting for privatization in developing countries: Towards the integration of economic and non-economic explanations', *Public Administration and Development*, 10(4): 389–403.

Cooke, B. (2001), 'From colonial administration to development management', *IDPM Discussion Paper Series Working Paper* No. 63, University of Manchester, Institute for Development Policy and Management.

Cooke, B. (2003), 'A new continuity with colonial administration: Participation in development management', *Third World Quarterly*, 24(1): 47–61.

Cooke, B. and Kothari, U. (eds) (2002), *Participation: The New Tyranny?* (London: Zed Books).

Cordell, K. and Wolff, S. (eds) (2011a), *Routledge Handbook of Ethnic Conflict* (Abingdon: Routledge).

Cordell, K. and Wolff, S. (2011b), 'The study of ethnic conflict', in K. Cordell and S. Wolff (eds), *Routledge Handbook of Ethnic Conflict* (Abingdon: Routledge).

Court, J., Kristen, P. and Weder, B. (1999), *Bureaucratic Structure and Performance: First Africa Survey Results* (Tokyo: United Nations University).

Cowen, M. and Shenton, R. (1996), *Doctrines of Development* (London: Routledge).

Craig, D. and Porter, D. (2006), *Development Beyond Neo-Liberalism: Governance, Poverty Reduction and Political Economy* (London: Routledge).

Cramer, C. (2006), 'Greed versus grievance: Conjoined twins or discrete drivers of violent conflict?' in H. Yanacopoulos and J. Hanlon (eds), *Civil War, Civil Peace* (Oxford: James Currey), pp. 164–84.

Cramer, C., Stein, H. and Weeks, J. (2006), 'Ownership and donorship: Analytical issues and a Tanzanian case study', *Journal of Contemporary African Studies*, 24(3): 415–43.

Credit Suisse (2012), *Opportunities in an Urbanizing World* (Zurich: Credit Suisse Research Institute).

Crook, R. (2003), 'Decentralisation and poverty reduction in Africa: The politics of central-local relations', *Public Administration and Development*, 23(1): 77–88.

Crook, R. and Manor, J. (1998), *Democracy and Decentralization in South Asia and West Africa* (Cambridge: Cambridge University Press).

Crosby, B. (2000), *Policy Analysis Units: Useful Mechanisms for Implementing Policy Reform*. Available from http://www.usaid.gov/our_work/democracy_and_governance/publications/ipc/wp-10.pdf.

Crouch, C. (2013), *Making Capitalism Fit for Society* (Cambridge: Polity Press).

Crouch, H. (1979), 'Patrimonialism and military rule in Indonesia', *World Politics*, 31(4): 571–87.

Crouch, H. (1996), *Government and Society in Malaysia* (Ithaca, NY: Cornell University Press).

Crozier, M. (1964), *The Bureaucratic Phenomenon* (Chicago: University of Chicago Press).

Curle, A. (1971), *Making Peace* (London: Tavistock).

Dabhoiwala, M. (2003), 'Policing India in the new millenium, or old? *Article 2*, 2(5): 49–52.

Dahl-Østergaard, T., Unsworth, S. Robinson, M. and Jensen, R. (2005), *Lessons Learned on the Use of Power and Drivers of Change Analyses in Development Cooperation*. Available from http://www.gsdrc.org/docs/open/DOC82.pdf

Dakolias, M. (1995), 'A strategy for judicial refrom: The experience in Latin America', *Virginia Journal of International Law*, 36(Fall): 167–232.

Dam, K. (2006), 'The Judiciary and economic development. *John M. Olin Program in Law and Economics Working Paper*, 287.

Dasmann, R. (1972), *Planet in Peril: Man and the Biosphere Today* (Harmondsworth: Penguin).

Deen, T. (2006), 'Development: Is brain drain robbing poor to pay for the rich?' *Inter Press Service*, 6 September. Available at www.ipsnews.net/2006/09/development-is-brain-robbing-poor-to-pay-for-the-rich/

Della Porta, A. and Diani, A. (2011), 'Social movements', in M. Edwards (ed.), *The Oxford Handbook of Civil Society* (Oxford and New York: Oxford University Press), pp. 68–79.

De Silva, K. (1993), 'The bureaucracy', in K. de Silva (ed.), *Sri Lanka: Problems of Governance* (New Delhi: Konark), pp. 83–98.

De Soto, H. (1989), *The Other Path: The Economic Answer to Terrorism* (New York: Harper and Row).

De Soto, H. (2000), *The Mystery of Capital: Why Capitalism Triumphs in the West and Fails Everywhere Else* (New York: Basic Books).

DFID (2008a), *Department for International Development 2008 Autumn Performance Report* (London: DFID). Available from https://www.gov.uk/government/publications/department-for-international-development-autumn-performance-report-2008

DFID (2008b), *Three Faces of India: DFID India Country Plan, 2008–2015* (London: DFID). Available from http://webarchive.nationalarchives.gov.uk/+/http:/www.dfid.gov.uk/pubs/files/india-cap.pdf

DFID (2010), *DFID in 2009–10* (London: DFID). Available from https://www.gov.uk/government/uploads/system/uploads/attachment_data/file/67675/dfid-in-2009-10-revised-6-sept-2010.pdf

DFID (2011), *How to Note: Guidance on Using the Revised Logical Framework* (London: DFID).

DFID (2013), *Summary Report of the Public Sector Governance Reform Evaluation* (London: DFID-Irish Aid-Sida).

DFID (2014), Support Program for Urban Reforms in Bihar (London: DFID). Available from http://devtracker.dfid.gov.uk/projects/GB-1-114040/

Diamond, L. (2002), 'Thinking about hybrid regimes', *Journal of Democracy*, 13(2): 21–35.

Dicklitch, S. and Lwanga, D. (2003), 'The politics of being non-political: Human rights organizations and the creation of a positive human rights culture in Uganda', *Human Rights Quarterly*, 25(2): 482–509.

Domingo, P. (1999), 'Judicial independence and judicial reform in Latin America', in A. Schedler, L. Diamond and M. Plattner (eds), *The Self-Restraining State: Power and Accountability in New Democracies* (Boulder, CO: Lynne Rienner Publishers).

Domingo, P. (2009), 'Why rule of law matters for development' *Opinion 131* (London: Overseas Development Institute).

Doornbos, M. (2002), 'Somalia: Alternative scenarios for political reconstruction', *African Affairs*, 101(402): 93–107.

Drabek, A. (1987), 'Development alternatives: The challenge for NGOs – an overview of the issues', *World Development*, 15(Supplement 1): ix–xv.

Dror, Y. (1986), *Policymaking Under Adversity* (New Brunswick: Transaction Books).

Duffield, M. (2001), *Global Governance and the New Wars: The Merging of Development and Security* (London: Zed Books).

Duffield, M. (2007), *Development, Security and the Unending War: Governing the World of Peoples* (Cambridge: Polity Press).

Duncan, A., Macmillan, H. and Simutanyi, N. (2003), *Zambia: Drivers of Pro-Poor Change – an Overview* (Oxford: Oxford Policy Management).

Dwivedi, O. and Nef, J. (1982), 'Crises and continuities in development theory and administration: First and Third World perspectives', *Public Administration and Development*, 2(1): 59–77.

Earle, L. (2011), 'Citizenship, the "right to the city" and state fragility', *Crisis States Research Centre Working Paper*, 87.

Easton, D. (1965), *A Systems Analysis of Political Life* (New York: Wiley).

Ebrahim, A. (2003), 'Accountability in practice: Mechanisms for NGOs', *World Development*, 31(5): 813–29.

Eckardt, S. (2008), 'Political accountability, fiscal conditions and local government performance–cross-sectional evidence from Indonesia', *Public Administration and Development*, 28(1): 1–17.

Economist (2012a), 'Special report world economy: For richer, for poorer', *The Economist*, 13 October.

Economist (2012b), 'RIPP: India's love affair with public-private partnerships faces a stern test', *The Economist*, 15 December.

Economist (2012c), 'The state advances', *The Economist*, 6 October.

Edwards, M. (2008), 'Have NGOs "made a difference?" from Manchester to Birmingham with an elephant in the room', in A. Bebbington, S. Hickey and D. Mitlin (eds), *Can NGOs Make a Difference? The Challenge of Development Alternatives* (London and New York: Zed Books), pp. 38–52.

Edwards, M. (2011a), 'Introduction: Civil society and the geometry of human relations', in M. Edwards (ed.), *The Oxford Handbook of Civil Society* (Oxford and New York: Oxford University Press), pp. 3–14.

Edwards, M. (2011b), 'Conclusion: Civil society as a necessary and necessarily contested idea', in M. Edwards (ed.), *The Oxford Handbook of Civil Society* (Oxford and New York: Oxford University Press), pp. 480–91.

Edwards, M. and Hulme, D. (1992), *Making a Difference: NGOs and Development in a Changing World* (London: Earthscan).

Edwards, M. and Hulme, D. (1996), 'Too close for comfort? The impact of official aid on nongovernmental organizations', *World Development*, 24(6): 961–73.

Eilat, Y. and Zinnes, C. (2000), 'The evolution of the shadow economy in transition countries: Consequences for economic growth and donor assistance', *CAER II Discussion Paper*, 65 (Harvard Institute for International Development).

Ekins, P. (1992), *A New World Order: Grassroots Movements for Global Change* (London: Routledge).

Elbers, W. and Arts, B. (2011), 'Keeping body and soul together: Southern NGOs' strategic responses to donor constraints', *International Review of Administrative Sciences*, 77(4): 713–32.

Ellis, S. and ter Haar, G. (2004), *Worlds of Power: Religious Thought and Political Practice in Africa* (Oxford: Oxford University Press).

Emery, F. and Trist, E. (1965), 'The causal texture of organizational environments', *Human Relations*, 18(1): 21–32.

Encarnacion, O. (2011), 'Assisting civil society and promoting democracy', in M. Edwards (ed.), *The Oxford Handbook of Civil Society* (Oxford and New York: Oxford University Press), pp. 468–79.

Epstein, G. and Gang, I. (2006), 'Contests, NGOs, and decentralizing aid', *Review of Development Economics*, 10(2): 285–96.

Escobar, A. (1992), 'Planning', in W Sachs (ed.), *The Development Dictionary* (London: Zed Books).

Escobar, A. (1995), *Encountering Development: The Making and Unmaking of the Third World* (London: Routledge and Kegan Paul).

Esman, M. (1972), *Administration and Development in Malaysia: Institution Building and Reform in a Plural Society* (Ithaca, NY: Cornell University Press).

Esman, M. (1988), 'The maturing of development administration', *Public Administration and Development* (2) 125–34.

Evans, P. (1995), *Embedded Autonomy: States and Industrial Transformation* (Princeton: Princeton University Press).

Evans, P. (2004), 'Development as institutional change: The pitfalls of monocropping and the potentials of deliberation', *Studies in Comparative International Development*, 38(4): 30–52.

Evans, P. and Rauch, J. (1999), 'Bureaucracy and growth: A cross-national analysis of the effects of "Weberian" state structures on economic growth', *American Sociological Review*, 64(5): 748–65.

FAO (2010), 'Deforestation and net forest area change'. Available from http://www.fao.org/forestry/30515/en/

FAO (2011), *The State of the World's Fisheries and Aquaculture* 2011 (Rome: FAO).

FAO (2012), *State of the World's Forests* (Rome: FAO).

Fahmi, W. (2009), 'Bloggers' street movement and the right to the city. (Re) claiming Cairo's real and virtual "spaces of freedom"', *Environment and Urbanization*, 21(1): 89–108.

Far Eastern Economic Review, 29 August 1991.

Farmer, P. (2004), 'An anthropology of structural violence', *Current Anthropology*, 45(3): 305–25.

Fayol, H. (1949), *General and Industrial Management* (London: Pitman).

Fearon, J. and Laitin, D. (2003), 'Ethinicity, insurgency, and civil war', *American Political Science Review*, 97(1): 75–90.

Feeley R., Rosen S., Fox M., Macwan'gi M. and Mazimba A. (2004), *The Cost of HIV/AIDS among Professional Staff in the Zambian Public Health Sector* (Lusaka: Central Board of Health).

Ferguson, J. (1990), *The Anti-politics Machine: 'Development', Depoliticization, and Bureaucratic Power in Lesotho* (Cambridge: Cambridge University Press).

Fine, B. (1999), 'The developmental state is dead – long live social capital?', *Development and Change*, 30(1): 1–19.

Fine, B. (2001), *Social Capital Versus Social Theory: Political Economy and Social Sciences at the Turn of the Millennium* (London: Routledge).

Fjeldstad, O. and Moore, M. (2009), 'Revenue authorities and public authority in sub-Saharan Africa', *Journal of Modern African Studies*, 47(1): 1–18.

Fleming, M., Roman, J. and Farrell, G. (2000), 'The shadow economy', *Journal of International Affairs*, 53(2): 387–409.

Ford, J. (1999), 'Rationale for decentralization', in J. Litvack and J. Seddon (eds), *Decentralization Briefing Notes* (Washington, DC: World Bank), pp. 6–8.

Fowler, A. (2000), 'NGO futures: Beyond aid: NGDO values and the fourth position', *Third World Quarterly*, 21(4): 589–603.

Fowler, A. (2011), 'Development NGOs', in M. Edwards (ed.), *The Oxford Handbook of Civil Society* (Oxford and New York: Oxford University Press), pp. 42–54.

Francis, P. (2001), 'Social capital, civil society and social exclusion', in U. Kothari and M. Minogue (eds), *Development Theory and Practice: Critical Perspectives* (Basingstoke: Palgrave Macmillan), pp. 71–91.

Frank, A. (1971), *Capitalism and Underdevelopment in Latin America* (Harmondsworth: Penguin).

Freeman, R. (1984), *Strategic Management: A Stakeholder Approach* (Boston: Pitman).

Fritz, V., Kaiser, K. and Levy, B. (2009), *Problem-driven Governance and Political Economy Analysis* (Washington, DC: World Bank).

FSM (2013), World Social Forum Website. Available from http://www.forumsocialmundial.org.br/main.php?id_menu=19&cd_language=2

Fukuyama, F. (2005), *State Building: Governance and World Order in the 21st Century* (London: Profile Books).

Fyvie, C. and Ager, A. (1999), 'NGOs and innovation: Organizational characteristics and constraints in development assistance work in the Gambia', *World Development*, 27(8): 1383–95.

Galanter, M. (2009), 'Part I courts, institutions, and access to justice: "to the listed field...": The myth of litigious India', *Jindal Global Law Review*, 1(1): 65–73.

Galanter, M. and Krishnan, J. (2004), ' "Bread for the poor": Access to justice and the rights of the needy in India', *Hastings Law Journal*, 55: 789–834.

Gauri, V. and Galef, J. (2005), 'NGOs in Bangladesh: Activities, resources, and governance', *World Development*, 33(12): 2045–65.

Gaventa, J. and McGee, R. (2010), *Citizen Action and National Policy Reform: Making Change Happen* (London: Zed).

Gehlot, N. (2002), 'Indian police system: Crisis of management', in P. Alexander (ed.), *Policing India in the New Millennium* (New Delhi: Allied Publishers Pvt. Limited), pp. 16–28.

Geneva Declaration (2011), *Global Burden of Armed Violence 2011: Lethal Encounters* (Cambridge: Cambridge University Press).

Gerth, H. and Mills, C. (eds) (1948), *From Max Weber: Essays in Sociology* (London: Routledge and Kegan Paul).

Ghosh, S. (2009), 'NGOs as political institutions', *Journal of Asian and African Studies*, 44(5): 475–95.

Giddens, A. (1989), *Sociology* (Cambridge: Polity Press).

Gill, L. (1997), 'Power lines: The political context of nongovernmental organisation (NGO) activity in El Alto, Bolivia', *Journal of Latin American Anthropology*, 2(2): 144–69.

Gittinger, J.P. (1982), *Economic Appraisal of Agricultural Projects* (Baltimore: Johns Hopkins University Press).

Giustozzi, A. (2008), 'Afghanistan: Transition without end. an analytical narrative on state-making', *Crisis States Research Centre Working Paper*, 2.

Glaeser, B. and Vyasulu, V. (1984), 'The obsolescence of ecodevelopment?', in B. Glaeser (ed.), *Ecodevelopment: Concepts, Projects, Strategies* (Oxford: Pergamon), pp. 23–36.

GlobeScan and MRC MacLean Hazel (ed.), *Megacity Challenges: A Stakeholder Perspective* (Munich: Siemens AG).

Goldsmith, A. (2011), 'No country left behind? Performance standards and accountability in US foreign assistance', *Development Policy Review*, 29(1): 157–76.

Golooba-Mutebi, F. (2008), 'Collapse, war and reconstruction in Rwanda: An analytical narrative on state-kaking', *Crisis States Research Centre Working Paper*, 28.

Goodhand, J. and Mansfield, D. (2010), 'Drugs and (dis)order: A study of the opium trade, political settlements and state-making in Afghanistan', *Crisis States Research Centre Working Paper*, 2.

Goodhand, J. and Sedra, M. (2010), 'Who owns the peace? Aid, reconstruction, and peacebuilding in Afghanistan', *Disasters*, 34(issue supplement s3): 78–102.

Goulet, D. (1992), 'Development: Creator and destroyer of values', *World Development*, 20(3): 467–75.

Government of Rwanda (2008), *Strategy and Budgeting Framework (January 2009–June 2012) for the Republic of Rwanda: Justice, Reconciliation, Law and Order Sector* (Kigale: Government of Rwanda).

Government of Uganda (1994), *Management of Change: Context, Vision, Objectives, Strategy and Plan* (Kampala: Ministry of Public Service).

Government of Uganda, National Planning Authority (2010), *National Development Plan 2010/11- 2014/15* (Kampala: National Planning Authority).

Graetz, F., Rimmer, M. Smith, A. and Lawrence, A. (2011), *Managing Organisational Change*, 3rd Australasian edition (Milton: John Wiley & Sons Australia).

Graham, F. (2010), 'M-Pesa: Kenya's mobile wallet revolution', *BBC News Business*, 22 November. Available from http://www.bbc.com/news/business-11793290.

Green, M. (2013), 'Philanthropists and aid donors must join forces in these straitened times', *The Guardian: Global Development, Poverty Matters Blog*, 30 August. Available at www.theguardian.com/global-development/poverty-matters/2013/aug/30/philanthropists-official-donors-aid-effectiveness

Greig, A., Hulme, D. and Turner, M. (2007), *Challenging Global Inequality: Development Theory and Practice in the 21st Century* (Basingstoke: Palgrave Macmillan).

Grey, C. (2004), *A Very short, Fairly Interesting and Reasonably Cheap Book About Studying Organizations* (London: Sage).

Grey, C. (2009), *A Very Short, Fairly Interesting and Reasonably Cheap Book About Studying Organizations* 2nd edn (London: Sage).

Grindle, M. (ed.) (1980), *Politics and Policy Implementation in the Third World*. (Princeton, NJ: Princeton University Press).

Grindle, M. (2004), 'Good enough governance: Poverty reduction and reform in developing countries', *Governance*, 17(4): 525–48.

Grindle, M. (2006), 'Modernizing town hall: Capacity building with a political twist, *Public Administration and Development*, 26(1): 55–69.

Grindle, M. (2007), 'Local government that performs well: Four explanations', in S. Cheema and D. Rondinelli (eds), *Decentralizing Governance: Emerging Concepts and Practices* (Washington, DC: Ash Institute for Democratic Governance and Innovation and Brookings Institution), pp. 56–74.

Grindle, M. (2012), *Jobs for the Boys: Patronage and the State in Comparative Perspective* (Cambridge, MA: Harvard University Press).

Grindle, M. (2013), 'Public sector reform as problem-solving? comment on the world bank's public sector management approach for 2011–2020', *International Review of Administrative Sciences*, 79(3): 398–405.

Grindle, M.S. (1991), 'The new political economy: Positive economics and negative politics', in G.M. Meier (ed.), *Politics and Policy Making in Developing Countries: Perspectives on the New Political Economy* (San Francisco: ICS Press), pp. 41–67.

Grindle, M. and Hilderbrand, M. (1995), 'Building sustainable capacity in the public sector: What can be done?' *Public Administration and Development*, 15(5): 441–63.

Gros, J. (1996), 'Towards a taxonomy of failed states in the new world order: Decaying Somalia, Liberia, Rwanda and Haiti', *Third World Quarterly*, 17(3): 455–72.

GSDRC (Governance and Social Development Resource Centre) (2013), Civil service reform. Available at http://gsdrc.org/go/topic-guides/civil-service-reform/introduction

Gulrajani, N. (2010), 'New vistas for development management: Examining radical-reformist possibilities and potential', *Public Administration and Development*, 30(2): 136–48.

Gupta, N. (2008), 'Privatization in South Asia', in G. Roland (ed.), *Privatization: Successes and Failures* (New York: Columbia University Press), pp. 170–97.

Gurr, T. (1970), *Why Men Rebel* (Princeton: Princeton University Press).

Haas, P. (1992), 'Introduction: Epistemic communities and international policy coordination', *International Organization*, 46(1): 1–35.

Habermas, J. (1981), *The Theory of Communicative Action: Reason and the Rationalization of Society* (Boston, MA: Beacon Press).

Hadiz, V. and Robison, R. (2005), 'Neo-liberal reforms and illiberal consolidations: The Indonesian paradox', *Journal of Development Studies*, 41(2): 220–41.

Haggard, S., Macintyre, A. and Tiede, L. (2008), 'The rule of law and economic development', *The Annual Review of Political Science,* 11: 205–34.

Hagmann, T. and Hoehne, M. (2009), 'Failures of the state failure debate: Evidence from the Somali territories', *Journal of International Development*, 21(1): 42–57.

Haile-Mariam, Y. and Mengistu, B. (1988), 'Public enterprises and the privatisation thesis in the third world', *Third World Quarterly*, 10(4): 1565–87.

Harris-Cheng, M. (2010), 'Asia-Pacific faces diabetes challenges', *The Lancet*, 375(9733): 2207–10.

Harrison, D. (1988), *The Sociology of Modernization and Development* (London: Unwin Hyman).

Harsh, M., Mbatia, P. and Shrum, W. (2010), 'Accountability and inaction: NGOs and resource lodging in development', *Development and Change*, 41(2): 253–78.

Hatch, M. (2013), *Organization Theory: Modern, Symbolic and Postmodern Perspectives* (Oxford: Oxford University Press).

Hayek, F. (1945), 'The use of knowledge in society', *American Economic Review*, 35(4): 519–30.

Head, B. (2010), 'Evidence-based policy: Principles and requirements', in Productivity Commission (ed.), *Strengthening Evidence-based Policy in the Australian Federation* (Melbourne: Productivity Commission), pp. 13–26.

Healey, P. (2004), 'The treatment of space and place in the new strategic spatial planning in Europe', *International Journal of Urban and Regional Research*, 28(1): 45–67.

Hearn, J. (2007), 'Roundtable: African NGOs: The new compradors?' *Development and Change*, 38(6): 1095–110.

Heaver, R. and A. Israel (1986), 'Country commitment to development projects', *World Bank Discussion Paper*, 4.

Helman, G. and Ratner, S. (1993), 'Saving failed states', *Foreign Policy*, 89(winter): 3–20.

Hickey, S. (2010), 'The Politics of social protection in Africa: What do we get from a "social contract" approach?, Paper prepared for the conference Experiences and Lessons from Social Protection Programmes Across the Developing World: What Role for the EU? Paris, European Report of Development.

Hickey, S. and Mohan, G. (2004), *Participation: From Tyranny to Transformation?* (London: Zed Books).

Hill, M. (2009), *The Public Policy Process* (Harlow: Pearson Longman).

Hills, A. (2011), 'Policing Africa: Internal security and the limits of liberalisation', *International Review of Law, Computers and Technology*, 25 (1–2): 69–77.

Hirschman, A. (1970), *Exit, Voice, and Loyalty: Responses to Decline in Firms, Organizations, and States* (Cambridge, MA: Harvard University Press).

Hirschman, A. (1971), *A Bias for Hope: Essays on Development and Latin America* (New Haven and London: Yale University Press).

Hirschman, A. (1984), *Getting Ahead Collectively* (New York: Pergamon).

Hirschmann, D. (1981), 'Development administration? A further deadlock', *Development and Change*, 12(3): 459–79.

HMSO (Her Majesty's Stationery Office) (1996), *Civil Service Statistics: 1996* (Norwich: HMSO).

Hoehne, M. (2011), 'Not born as a de facto state: Somaliland's complicated state formation', in R. Sharamo and B. Mesfin (eds), *Regional Security in the Post-Cold War Horn of Africa* (Pretoria: Institute for Security Studies), pp. 309–46.

Hofstede, G. (1980), "Motivation, leadership and organization: Do American theories apply abroad?' *Organizational Dynamics*, 4(1): 42–63.

Hogwood, B. and Gunn, L. (1981), *The Policy Orientation* (Glasgow: University of Strathclyde).

Hogwood, B. and Gunn, L. (1984), *Policy Analysis for the Real World* (Oxford: Oxford University Press).

Hopper, P. (2012), *Understanding Development* (Cambridge: Polity).

Howarth, K. and Irvine, C. (2011), 'Mediation's failings in El Salvador and the limits of crusading universalism', *International Studies Review*, 13(2): 354–85.

Hudock, A. (1999), *NGOs and Civil Society: Democracy by Proxy?* (Malden: Blackwell Publishers Inc).

Hulme, D. (1994a), 'Projects, politics and professionals: Alternative approaches for project identification and project planning', *Agricultural Systems*, 47(2): 211–33.

Hulme, D. (2007), 'The making of the millennium development goals: Human development meets results-based management in an imperfect world', *Brooks World Poverty Institute Working Paper* No. 16, University of Manchester.

Hulme, D. (2008), 'Reflections on NGOs and development: The elephant, the dinosaur, several tigers, but no owl', in A. Bebbington, S. Hickey and D. Mitlin (eds), *Can NGOs Make a Difference? The Challenge of Development Alternatives* (London and New York: Zed Books), pp. 337–45.

Hulme, D. (2010), *Global Poverty: How Global Governance is Failing the Poor* (London: Routledge).

Hulme, D. (2015), *Global Poverty: From Poverty Eradication to Sustainable Development* (London: Routledge).

Hulme, D. and Edwards, M. (eds) (1997), *Too Close for Comfort: NGOs, The State and Donors* (London: Palgrave Macmillan).

Hulme, D. and Sanderatne, N. (1995), 'Sri Lanka: Democracy and accountability in Decline', in J. Healey and W. Tordoff (eds), *Votes and Budgets* (London: HMSO), pp. 109–52.

Hulme, D., Savoia, A. and Sen, K. (2014), 'Governance as a global development goal? Setting, measuring and monitoring the post-2015 development agenda', *Global Policy*.

Hulme, D. and Siddiquee, N. (1999), 'Decentralization in Bangladesh: Promises, performances and politics', in M. Turner (ed.), *Central-Local Relations in Asia-Pacific: Convergence or Divergence?* (Basingstoke: Macmillan), pp. 19–47.

Hulme, D. and Turner, M. (1990), *Sociology and Development: Theories Policies and Practices* (London: Harvester Wheatsheaf).

Huntington, S. (1968), *Political Order in Changing Societies* (New Haven: Yale University Press).

Huntington, S. (1991), *The Third Wave: Democratization in the Late Twentieth Century* (Norman: University of Oklahoma Press).

Huselid, M. (1995), 'The impact of human resource management practices on turnover, productivity and corporate financial performance', *Academy of Management Journal*, 38(3): 635–72

Hutchcroft, P. (2001), 'Centralization and decentralization in administration and politics: Assessing territorial dimensions of authority and power', *Governance*, 14(1): 25–53.

Hyden, G., J. Court and K. Mease (2004), *Making Sense of Governance: Empirical Evidence From 16 Developing Countries* (Boulder, CO: Lynne Rienner).

IATT (Inter-Agency Task Team) on Education (2008), 'Teachers living with HIV', *Advocacy Briefing Note*. Available from http://unesdoc.unesco.org/images/0015/001586/158673e.pdf.

Ibrahim, S. and Hulme, D. (2011), 'Civil society and poverty' in M. Edwards (ed.), *The Oxford Handbook of Civil Society* (Oxford and New York: Oxford University Press), pp. 391–403.

IDRC (International Development Research Centre) (2009), *The Think Tank Initiative: Strengthening Policy Research for Development*. Available from http://www.idrc.ca/uploads/user-S/12615187971 Executive_Summary_Dec09.docx.pdf.

IDSC (Information and Decision Support Center) (2009), *The International Conference on the Role of Think Tanks in Developing Countries: Cairo Declaration*. Available from http://www.n2t4dc.net.eg/images/CairoDec.pdf.

IEG (Independent Evaluation Group) (1999), *Civil Service Reform: A Review of World Bank Assistance*, Report No. 19599, World Bank.

IEG (Independent Evaluation Group) (2008a), *Public Sector Reform: What Works and Why? An IEG evaluation of World Bank Support*. Available from http://siteresources.worldbank.org/EXTPUBSECREF/Resources/psr_eval.pdf.

IEG (Independent Evaluation Group) (2008b), *Decentralization in Client Countries: An Evaluation of World Bank Support 1990–2007* (Washington, DC: World Bank).

IFC (International Finance Corporation) (1995), *Privatization: Principles and Practice* (Washington, DC: World Bank).

IIED (2013), International Institute for Environment and Development website. Available from http://www.iied.org.

IIFLS (2013), *Kenya: Making Quality Employment the Driver of Development* (Geneva: International Institute for Labour Studies).

Imai, M. (1986), *Kaizen: The Key to Japan's Competitive Success* (New York: Random House).

IMF (International Monetary Fund) (2004), *Public-Private Partnerships* (Washington, DC: IMF).

IMF Independent Evaluation Office (2004), *Report on the Evaluation of Poverty Reduction Strategy Papers* (Washington, DC: IMF).

Independent Evaluation Group (2013), *World Bank Group Assistance to Low-income Fragile and Conflict-Affected States* (Washington, DC: World Bank).

Ingelaere, B. (2009), 'Does the truth pass across the fire without burning?' Locating the short circuit in Rwanda's Gacaca Courts', *The Journal of Modern African Studies*, 47(4): 507–28.

Innes, J. and Booher, D. (2010), *Planning with Complexity: An Introduction to Collaborative Rationality for Public Policy* (London: Routledge).

IPCC (Intergovernmental Panel on Climate Change) (2014), *Climate Change 2014: Impacts, Adaptation and Vulnerability* (Geneva: IPCC).

Jackson, R. (2002), 'Violent internal conflict and the African Ssate: Towards a framework of analysis', *Journal of Contemporary African Studies*, 20(1): 29–52.

Jacoby, T. (2008), *Understanding Conflict and Violence: Theoretical and Interdisciplinary Approaches* (London: Routledge).

Jacoby, T. and James, E. (2010), 'Emerging patterns in the reconstruction of conflict-affected countries', *Disasters*, 34(1): 1–14.

Jayasuriya, K. (1996), 'The rule of law and capitalism in East Asia', *The Pacific Review*, 9(3): 367–88.

Jenkins, W. (1978), *Policy Analysis* (London: Martin Robertson).

Jerve, A., Lakshman, W. and Ratnayake, P. (2005), *Exploring Ownership of Aid-Funded Projects: A Comparative Study of Japanese, Norwegian and Swedish project aid to Sri Lanka Mimeo* (Bergen: Chr. Michelson Institute).

John, P. (1998), *Analysing Public Policy* (London: Pinter).

Johnson, C. (2003), 'Decentralisation in India: poverty, politics and Panchayati Raj', *Working Paper* 199 (London: Overseas Development Institute).

Johnson, G., Scholes, K. and Whittington, R. (2009), *Exploring Corporate Strategy* (London: Prentice Hall).

Johnson, J. and Wasty, S. (1993), 'Borrower ownership of adjustment programs and the political economy of reform', *Discussion Paper* No. 199, World Bank.

Johnston, B. and Clark, W. (1982), *Redesigning Rural Development: A Strategic Perspective* (Baltimore, MD: Johns Hopkins University Press).

Jones, G. and Corbridge, S. (2010), 'The continuing debate about urban bias: The thesis, its critics, its influence and implications for poverty reduction', *Progress in Development Studies*, 10(1): 1–18.

Joshi, A. and M. Moore, M. (2000), 'Enabling environments: Do anti-poverty programmes mobilise the poor?' *Journal of Development Studies*, 37(1): 25–56.

Justino, P. (2012), 'War and poverty' *IDS Working Paper*, 391.

Kahneman, D. (2011), *Thinking Fast and Slow* (New York: Farrar, Straus & Giroux).

Kaldor, M. (2003), *Global Civil Society: An Answer to War* (Cambridge: Polity Press).

Kaldor, M. (2006), *New and Old Wars: Organized Violence in a Global Era*, second edition (Cambridge: Polity Press).

Kamat, S. (2004), 'The privatization of public interest: Theorizing NGO discourse in a neoliberal era', *Review of International Political Economy*, 11(1): 155–76.

Kapuscinski, R. (1983), *The Emperor: Downfall of an Autocrat* (London: Quartet).

Kaufmann, D. (1999), *Governance Redux: The Empirical Challenge* (Washington, DC: World Bank). Available from http://www.worldbank.org/wbi/governance/pubs/govredux.html.

Keck, M. and Sikkink, K. (1998), *Activists Beyond Borders: Advocacy Networks in International Politics* (Ithaca: Cornell University Press).

Kelsall, T. (2011), 'Rethinking the relationship between neo-patrimonialism and economic development in Africa', *IDS Bulletin*, 42(2): 76–87.

Kenny, C. (2011), *Getting Better: Why Global Development is Succeeding – And How We Can Improve the World Even More* (New York: Basic Books).

Kerr, R. (2008), 'International development and the new public management: Projects and logframes as discursive technologies of governance', in S. Dar and B. Cooke (eds), *The New Development Management: Critiquing the Dual Modernization* (London: Zed), pp. 91–110.

Kessy, A. and McCourt, W. (2010), 'Is decentralization still recentralization? the local government reform programme in Tanzania', *International Journal of Public Administration*, 33(12): 689–97.

Khan, M.H. (2005), 'Markets, states and democracy: Patron-client networks and the case for democracy in developing countries', *Democratization*, 12(5): 704–24.

Khandwalla, P.N. (1987), *Effective Management of Public Enterprises* (Washington, DC: World Bank).

Kikeri, S. and Kolo, A. (2005), 'Privatization trends and recent developments', *World Bank Policy Research Working Paper*, No. 3765.

Kikeri, S. and Perault, M. (2010), 'Privatization trends: A sharp decline but no widespread reversal in 2008', *Viewpoint*, May, World Bank.

Kilby, P. (2006), 'Accountability for empowerment: Dilemmas facing non-governmental organizations', *World Development*, 34(6): 951–63.

Killick, T. (1976), 'The possibilities of development planning', *Oxford Economic Papers*, 28(2): 161–84.

Killick, T. (1989), *A Reaction Too Far: Economic Theory and the Role of the State in Developing Countries* (London: Overseas Development Institute).

Killick, T. (1998), *Aid and the Political Economy of Policy Change* (London: Routledge).

Kim, B.W. (1991), 'An assessment of government intervention in Korean economic development', in G.F. Caiden and B.W. Kim (eds), *A Dragon's Progress: Development Administration in Korea* (West Hartford: Kumarian), pp. 135–43.

King, S. (2014). 'NGOs and political capabilities I: Good governance or popular organisation building', *Brooks World Poverty Institute Working Paper*, No. 193, University of Manchester, Brooks World Poverty Institute.

Kingdon, J. (1995), *Agendas, Alternatives and Public Policies* (New York: HarperCollins).

Kiragu, K. and Mukandala, R. (2004), *Pay Reform and Policies Report* (Paris: OECD Development Assistance Committee).

Kitching, G. (1982), *Development and Underdevelopment in Historical Perspective* (London: Methuen).

Klugman, J. (2002), *A Sourcebook for Poverty Reduction Strategies* (Washington, DC: World Bank).

Klugman, J. and Braithwaite, J. (1998), 'Poverty in Russia during the transition: An overview', *World Bank Research Observer*, 13(1): 37–58.

Knight, M. and Özerdem, A. (2004), 'Guns, camps and cash: Disarmament, demobilization and reinsertion of former combatants in transitions from war to peace', *Journal of Peace Research*, 41(4): 499–516.

Koch, D. (2007), 'Blind spots on the map of aid allocations: Concentration and complementarity of international NGO aid', *UNU-WIDER Working Paper*, No. 2007/45.

Koch, D., Dreher, A., Nunnenkamp, P. and Thiele, R. (2009), 'Keeping a low profile: What determines the allocation of aid by non-governmental organizations?' *World Development*, 37(5): 902–18.

Koenen-Grant, J. and Garnett, H. (1996), *Improving Policy Formulation and Implementation in Zambia*, USAID Implementing Policy Change Project, Case Study No. 2, INSERT.

Korten, D. (1980), 'Community organization and rural development: A learning process approach', *Public Administration Review*, 40(5): 480–511.

Korten, D. (1987), 'Third generation NGO strategies: A key to people-centred development', *World Development*, 15(supplement): 145–59.

Korten, D. (1990), *Getting to the 21st Century: Voluntary Action and the Global Agenda* (West Hartford: Kumarian).

Krause, K. (2014), 'Violence, insecurity, and crime in development thought', in B. Currie-Alder, R. Kanbur, D. Malone and R. Medhora (eds), *International Development: Ideas, Experience and Prospects* (Oxford: Oxford University Press), pp. 379–94.

Kumar, V. (2012), 'Judicial delays in India: Causes and remedies', *Journal of Law, Policy and Globalization*, 4(1): 16–22.

Kunreuther, F. (2011), 'Grassroots associations', in M. Edwards (ed.), *The Oxford Handbook of Civil Society* (Oxford and New York: Oxford University Press), pp. 55–67.

Kusek, J. and Rist, R. (2004), *Ten Steps to a Results-based Monitoring and Evaluation System: A Handbook for Development Practitioners* (New York: World Bank). Available from http://www.oecd.org/dataoecd/23/27/35281194.pdf.

Lall, S. (2002), 'Social Capital and Industrial Transformation', in S. Fukuda-Parr, C. Lopes and K. Malik (eds), *Capacity for Development: New Solutions to Old Problems* (London and New York: Earthscan and UNDP), pp. 101–20.

Lane, J. (1993), *The Public Sector: Concepts, Models and Approaches* (London: Sage).

Larson, A. and Ribot, J. (2004), 'Democratic decentralisation through a natural resource lens: An introduction', *European Journal of Development Research*, 16(1): 1–25.

Lawrence, P. and Lorsch, J. (1967), *Organization and Environment* (Cambridge, MA: Harvard University Press).

Leftwich, A. (2000), *States of Development: On the Primacy of Politics in Development* (Cambridge: Polity Press).

Lemos, M. and De Oliveira, J. (2004), 'Can water reform survive politics? Institutional change and river basin management in Ceará', *World Development*, 32(12): 2121–37.

Leonard, D. (2010), 'Pockets' of effective agencies in weak governance states: Where are they likely and why does it matter?' *Public Administration and Development*, 30 (1): 91–101.

Lewis, D. (2002), 'Civil society in African contexts: Reflections on the usefulness of a concept', *Development and Change*, 33(4): 569–86.

Lewis, D. (2005), 'Actors, ideas and networks: Trajectories of the non-governmental in development studies', in U. Kothari (ed.), *A Radical History of Development Studies* (London: Zed Books), pp. 220–22.

Lewis, D. and Kanji, N. (2009), *Non-Governmental Organizations and Development* (Abingdon: Routledge).

Lindauer, M. (1994), 'Government pay and employment policies and economic performance', in D. Lindauer and B. Nunberg (eds), *Rehabilitating Government: Pay and Employment Reform in Africa* (Washington, DC: World Bank), pp. 17–32.

Lindblom, C. (1959), 'The science of "muddling through"', *Public Administration Review*, 19(2): 79–88.

Lindblom, C. (1980), *The Policy-making Process* (Englewood Cliffs, NJ: Prentice-Hall).

Lipton, M. (1977), *Why Poor People Stay Poor: A Study of Urban Bias in World Development* (London: Temple Smith).

Lizi, E., Lwanda, J. and Matiti, H. (2013), 'Modern medical myth: More doctors in Manchester than Malawi: A preliminary communication', *Malawi Medical Journal*, 25(1): 20–21.

Locke, E. and Latham, G. (1990), *A Theory of Goal-Setting and Task Performance* (New York: Prentice Hall).

Locke, E., Latham, G. and Erez, M. (1991), 'The determinants of goal commitment', in R. Steers and L. Porter (eds), *Motivation and Work Behavior* (New York: McGraw-Hill), pp. 370–89.

Lorch, K. (1991), 'Privatization through sale: The Bangladeshi textile industry', in R. Ramamurti and R. Vernon (eds), *Privatization and Control of State-Owned Enterprises* (Washington, DC: Economic Development Institute of the World Bank), pp. 126–52.

Mac Ginty, R. (2008), 'Indigenous peace-making versus the liberal peace,' *Cooperation and Conflict*, 43(2): 139–63.

Mac Ginty, R. and Williams, A. (2009), *Conflict and Development* (Abingdon: Routledge).

Mahbubani, K. (2009), *Can Asians Think?* 4th edition (Singapore: Marshall Cavendish Editions).

Maheshwari, S. (1990), 'Pruning big government: The Indian experience', in M. Campbell and A. Hoyle (eds), *Government and People: Issues in Development* (Canberra: University of Canberra), pp. 58–74.

Mamdani, M. (1996), *Citizen and Subject: Decentralized Despotism and the Legacy of Late Colonialism* (Princeton, NJ: Princeton University Press).

Manning, N. (2001), 'The legacy of the new public management in developing countries', *International Review of Administrative Sciences*, 67(2): 297–312.

Manning, N. and Parison, N. (2004), *International Public Administration Reform: Implications for the Russian Federation* (Washington, DC: World Bank).

Manor, J. (2004), 'User committees: A potentially damaging second wave of decentralisation', *European Journal of Development Research*, 16(1): 192–213.

Mansuri, G. and Rao, V. (2004), 'Community-based and driven development: A critical review', *World Bank Research Observer*, 19(1): 1–39.

Martine, G. (2011), 'Preparing for sustainable urban growth in developing areas', in UN Department of Economic and Social Affairs, Population Division (ed.), *Population Distribution, Urbanization, Internal Migration and Development: An International Perspective* (New York: UN Department of Economic and Social Affairs, Population Division), pp. 6–30.

Mascharenhas, J. et al. (1991), 'Participatory rural appraisal: Proceedings of the February 1991 Bangalore PRA trainers' Workshop', *RRA Notes* 13 (London: International Institute for Environment and Development).

Matin, I. and Hulme, D. (2003), 'Programs for the poorest: Learning from the IGvgd programme in Bangladesh', *World Development*, 31(3): 647–65.

Mauzy, D. (1997), 'The human rights and "Asian values" ' debate in Southeast Asia: Trying to clarify the key issues', *The Pacific Review*, 10(2): 210–36.

Mawhood, P. (1983), 'Decentralisation: The concept and the practice,' in P. Mawhood (ed.), *Local Government in the Third World* (Chichester: Wiley), pp. 1–24.

May, R. (2005), 'District-level governance in Papua New Guinea: Preliminary report of a pilot survey', *SSGM Report*, Society, State and Governance in Melanesia Project, Australian National University.

May, R. and Regan, A. (eds) (1997), *Political Decentralisation in a New State; The Experience of Provincial Government in Papua New Guinea* (Bathurst: Crawford House).

Mazrui, A. (1995), 'The blood of experience: The failed state and political collapse in Africa', *World Policy Journal*, 12(1): 28–34.

McCarthy-Jones, A. and Turner, M. (2015), 'Policy transfer through time and the search for legitimacy in developing nations', *Politics and Policy*, 43(2).

McCourt, W. (1998), 'Civil service reform equals retrenchment? the experience of staff retrenchment in Ghana, Uganda and the United Kingdom', in M. Minogue, C. Polidano and D. Hulme (eds), *Governance in the 21st Century* (Cheltenham: Edward Elgar), pp. 172–87.

McCourt, W. (2001), 'The new public selection? Anti-corruption, psychometric selection and the new public management in Nepal', *Public Management Review*, 3(3): 325–44.

McCourt, W. (2003), 'Political commitment to reform: Civil service reform in Swaziland', *World Development*, 31(6): 1015–31.

McCourt, W. (2006), *The Human Factor in Governance: Managing Public Employees in Africa and Asia* (Basingstoke: Palgrave Macmillan).

McCourt, W. (2007), 'Impartiality through bureaucracy? A Sri Lankan approach to managing values', *Journal of International Development*, 19(3): 429–42.

McCourt, W. (2008), 'Public management in developing countries: From downsizing to governance', *Public Management Review*, 10(4): 467–79.

McCourt, W. (2012), 'Reconciling top-down and bottom-up: Electoral competition and service delivery in Malaysia', *World Development*, 40(11): 2329–41.

McCourt, W. and Brunt, C. (2013), 'Inherent constraints and creative possibilities: Employee participation in Kenya', *International Journal of Human Resource Management*, 24(10): 1997–2018.

McCourt, W. and Gulrajani, N. (2010), 'The future of development management: Introduction to the special issue', *Public Administration and Development*, 30(2): 81–90.

McCourt, W. and Lee M. (2007), 'Malaysia as model: Policy transferability in an Asian country', *Public Management Review*, 9(2): 211–30.

McCourt, W. and N. Sola (1999), 'Using training to promote civil service reform: A Tanzanian local government case study', *Public Administration and Development*, 19(1): 63–75.

McDonald, C. (2012), 'Malawian doctors – are there more in Manchester than Malawi', *BBC*, January 14. Available from http://www.bbc.co.uk/news/magazine-16545526.

McKenna, R. (1999), *New Management* (Roseville: Irwin/McGraw-Hill).

Meadows, D.L., Meadows, D.I., Randers, J. and Behrens, W.W. (1972), *The Limits to Growth: A Report for the Club of Rome's Project on the Predicament of Mankind* (London: Potomac Associates).

Médard, J-F. (2002) 'Corruption and the neo-patrimonial states of Sub-Saharan Africa,' in A. Heidenheimer and M. Johnston (eds), *Political Corruption: Concepts and Contexts,* Third Edition (New Brunswick, NJ: Transaction Publishers), pp. 379–402.

Melo, M. (2007), 'Political competition can be positive: Embedding cash transfer programmes in Brazil'. in A. Bebbington and W. McCourt (eds), *Development Success: Statecraft in the South* (Basingstoke: Palgrave Macmillan), pp. 31–51.

Meyer, D. (2004), 'Protest and political opportunities'. *Annual Review of Sociology*, 30: 125–45.

Mitchell, R., Agle, B. and Wood, D. (1997), 'Toward a theory of stakeholder identification and salience: Defining the principle of who and what really counts', *Academy of Management Review*, 22(4): 853–86.

Menendez, F. (2013), 'The trend of Chinese investments in Latin America and the Caribbean', *China US Focus*, 19 December. Available from http://www.chinausfocus.com/finance-economy/the-trend-of-chinese-investments-in-latin-america-and-the-caribbean/.

Migdal, J.S. (1988), *Strong Societies and Weak States: State-Society Relations and State Capabilities in the Third World* (Princeton: Princeton University Press).

Milanovic, B. (1998), 'Explaining the increase in inequality during the transition' *World Bank Working Paper* 1935.

Miles, R. (1980), *Macro Organizational Behavior* (Santa Monica: Goodyear Publishing).

Minogue, M. (2001), 'The legacy of the new public management in developing countries', in W. McCourt and M. Minogue (eds), *The Internationalization of Public Management: Reinventing the Third World State* (Cheltenham: Edward Elgar), pp. 1–19.

Minogue, M. (2001), 'Should flawed models of public management be exported? Issues and practice', in W. McCourt and M. Minogue (eds), *The Internationalization of Public Management: Reinventing the Third World State* (Cheltenham: Edward Elgar), pp. 20–43.

Minogue, M. (2002), 'Power to the people? Good governance and the reshaping of the state, in U. Kothari and M. Minogue (eds), *Development*

Theory and Practice: Critical Perspectives (Basingstoke: Palgrave), pp. 117–35.

Mintzberg, H. (1987), 'Crafting strategy', *Harvard Business Review*, July/August: 66–75.

Miraftab, F. (1997), 'Flirting with the enemy: Challenges faced by NGOs in development and empowerment', *Habitat International* 21(4): 361–75.

Mitlin, D. and Satterthwaite, D. (2004), 'The role of local and extra-local organizations', in D. Mitlin and D. Satterthwaite (eds), *Empowering Squatter Citizen: Local Government, Civil Society and Urban Poverty Reduction* (London: Earthscan), pp. 278–305.

MOFAN (Ministry of Foreign Affairs Netherlands) (2013), *Public-Private Partnerships in Developing Countries: A Systematic Literature Review* (The Hague: Ministry of Foreign Affairs).

Mohan, G. (2002), 'The disappointments of civil society: The politics of NGO intervention in northern Ghana', *Political Geography*, 21(1): 125–54.

Molina, J. (2013), 'Power pricing in the Philippines', in KPMG Global Energy Institute (ed.), *The Energy Report Philippines: Growth and Opportunities in the Philippine Electric Power Sector 2013–2014 Edition* (Manila: KPMG), pp. 20–21.

Momsen, J. (2009), *Gender and Development* (Abingdon: Routledge).

Montero, A. and Samuels, D. (2004), 'The political determinants of decentralization in Latin America: Causes and consequences', in A. Montero and D. Samuels (eds), *Decentralization and Democracy in Latin America* (Notre Dame, IN: University of Notre Dame Press), pp. 3–32.

Moore, M. (1995), 'Democracy and development in cross-national perspective: A new look at the statistics', *Democratization*, 2(2): 1–19.

Moore, M. (2001), 'Political underdevelopment: What causes bad governance?' *Public Management Review*, 3(2): 385–418.

Moore, M. and Putzel, J. (1995), 'Thinking strategically about politics and poverty', *IDS Working Paper* 101, University of Sussex, Institute of Development Studies.

Moore, M., Rasanayagam, Y. and Tilakaratne, K. (1995), *Monergala Integrated Development Programme Mid-Term Review* (Colombo: Ministry of Finance and NORAD).

Moore, W. (1963), *Social Change* (Englewood Cliffs, NJ: Prentice Hall).

Morgan, G. (2006), *Images of Organization* (Thousand Oaks: Sage Publications).

Mosse, D. (1994), 'Authority, gender and knowledge: Theoretical reflections on the practice of Participatory Rural Appraisal', *CDS Working Paper* No. 2, University of Swansea, Centre for Development Studies.

Mowles, C. (2010), 'Post-foundational development management – power, politics and complexity', *Public Administration and Development*, 30(2): 149–58.

Munene, J. (1991), 'Organizational environment in Africa: A factor analysis of critical incidents', *Human Relations*, 44(5): 439–58.

Murray, W. and Overton, J. (2011), 'Neoliberalism is dead, long live neoliberalism? Neostructuralism and the international aid regime of the 2000s', *Progress in Development Studies*, 11(4): 307–19.

Myrdal, G. (1968), *Asian Drama: An Inquiry into the Poverty of Nations* (New York: Pantheon).

Nair, P. (2011), 'Evolution of the relationship between state and non-government organisations: A South Asian perspective', *Public Administration and Development*, 31(4): 252–61.

Najam, A. (1996), 'NGO accountability: A conceptual framework', *Development Policy Review*, 14(4): 39–53.

Narayan, D., Patel, R., Schafft, K., Rademacher, A. and Koch-Schult, S. (2000), *Can Anyone Hear Us? Voices of the Poor, Volume 1* (Paris: Editions ESKA).

Narokobi, B. (1983), *Life and Leadership in Melanesia* (Suva and Port Moresby: Institute of Pacific Studies and University of Papua New Guinea).

National Economic Advisory Council (2009), *New Economic Model for Malaysia*. Available from http://www.neac.gov.my/sites/default/files/NEM%20for%20Malaysia%20-%20Part%20I.pdf.

Nellis, J. (2006), 'Privatization-a summary assessment', *Center for Global Development Working Paper*, No. 87.

Nelson, J. (1990), 'Conclusions', in J. Nelson (ed.), *Economic Crisis and Policy Choice: The Politics of Adjustment in Developing Countries* (Princeton, NJ: Princeton University Press), pp. 321–61.

North, D. (1995), 'The new institutional economics and third world development', in J. Harriss, J. Hunter and C. Lewis (eds), *The New Institutional Economics and Third World Development* (London: Routledge), pp. 17–26.

North, D., Wallis, J. and Weingast, B. (2009), *Violence and Social Orders: A Conceptual Framework for Interpreting Recorded Human History* (Cambridge: Cambridge University Press).

Nunberg, B. (1994), 'Experience with civil service pay and employment reform: An overview', in D. Lindauer and B. Nunberg (eds), *Rehabilitating Government: Pay and Employment Reform in Africa* (Washington, DC: World Bank), pp. 119–59.

Nunberg, B. (1995), *Managing the Civil Service: Reform Lessons from Advanced Industrialized Countries* (Washington, DC: World Bank).

Nunberg, B. (1997), *Rethinking Civil Service Reform: An Agenda for Smart Government* (Washington, DC: World Bank).

Nyerere, J.K. (1966), *Freedom and Unity: A Selection from Writings and Speeches, 1952–1965* (Dar es Salaam: Oxford University Press).

Oakeshott, M. (1962), *Rationalism in Politics and Other Essays* (London: Methuen).

O'Brien, D.B.C. (1991), 'The show of state in a neo-colonial twilight: Francophone Africa', in J. Manor (ed.), *Rethinking Third World Politics* (London: Longman), pp. 145–65.

O'Conghaile, W. (1996), 'Current and future developments in service quality initiatives in Portugal, France and the United Kingdom', in OECD (ed.), *Responsive Government: Service Quality Initiatives* (Paris: OECD), pp. 65–70.

O'Conner, V. (2006), 'Rule of law and human rights protections through criminal law reform: Model codes for post-conflict criminal ustice', *International Peacekeeping*, 13(4): 517–30.

ODA (Overseas Development Administration) (1993), 'Good government', *Technical Note* No. 10 (London: ODA).

O'Donnell, G. (1970), *Modernization and Bureaucratic-Authoritarianism* (Berkeley: University of California Press).

O'Donnell, M. and Turner, M. (2005), 'Exporting new public management: Performance agreements in a Pacific microstate', *International Journal of Public Sector Management*, 18(7): 615–28.

OECD (Organisation for Economic Co-operation and Development) (1995), *Governance in Transition: Public Management Reforms in OECD Countries* (Paris: OECD).

OECD (Organisation for Economic Co-operation and Development) (2004), *Issues and Developments in Public Management – Country Reports*. Available from http://www.oecd.org/document/17/0,2340,en_2649_37421_2732241_1_1_1_37421,00.html.

OECD (Organisation for Economic Co-operation and Development) (2005), *OECD Guidelines on Corporate Governance of State-owned Enterprises* (Paris: OECD).

OECD (Organisation for Economic Co-operation and Development) (2007), *Principles for Good International Engagement in Fragile States and Situations* (Paris: OECD).

OECD (Organisation for Economic Co-operation and Development) (2011), *Aid Effectiveness 2005–10: Progress in Implementing the Paris Declaration* (Paris: OECD).

O'Gorman, E. (2011), *Conflict and Development: Development Matters* (London: Zed Books).

Olson, M. (1965), *The Logic of Collective Action: Public Goods and the Theory of Groups* (New Haven, CT: Yale University Press).

O'Neill, K. (2004), 'Decentralization in Bolivia: Electoral incentives', in A. Montero and D. Samuels (eds), *Decentralization and Democracy in Latin America* (Notre Dame, IN: University of Notre Dame Press), pp. 94–121.

Orogun, P. (2002), 'Crisis of government, ethnic schisms, civil war, and regional destabilization of the Democractic Republic of Congo', *World Affairs*, 165(1): 25–41.

Ostrom, E. (2010), 'Beyond markets and states: Polycentric governance of complex economic systems', *American Economic Review*, 100(3): 641–72.

Ostrom, V. and Ostrom, E. (1971), 'Public choice: A different approach to the study of public administration', *Public Administration Review*, 31(2): 203–16.

Ottaway, M. and Lieven, A. (2002), 'Rebuilding Afghanistan: Fantasy versus reality', *Carnegie Endowment for International Peace Policy Brief*.

Özerdem, A. (2010), 'Insurgency, militias and DDR as part of security sector reconstruction in Iraq: How not to do it', *Disasters*, 34(1): 40–59.

Pagano, U. and Rowthorn, R. (eds) (1996), *Efficiency and Enterprise Democracy* (London: Routledge).

Pape, R. (2012), 'Why duty calls: A pragmatic standard of humanitarian intervention', *International Security*, 37(1): 41–80.

Paris, R. (2010), 'Saving liberal peacebuilding', *Review of International Studies*, 36(2): 337–65.

Parsons, W. (1995), *Public Policy: An Introduction to the Theory and Practice of Policy Analysis* (Cheltenham: Edward Elgar).

Patel, S., Burra, S. and D'Cruz, C. (2001), 'Slum/Shack Dwellers International (SDI): Foundations to treetops', *Environment and Urbanization*, 13(2): 45–59.

Paul, S. (undated), 'Holding the state to account: Lessons of Bangalore's Citizen Report Cards'. Available from http://www.pafglobal.org/about-us/publications/Lessons_BRCs_7Oct05.pdf.

Paul, S. (1992), 'Accountability in public services: Exit, voice and control', *World Development*, 20(7): 1047–60.

Pavlinek, P. (1998), 'Privatization of coal mining in the Czech Republic', in J. Pickles and A. Smith (eds), *Theorizing the Transition: The Political Economy of p]Post-Communist Transformations* (London: Routledge), pp. 218–39.

PEMANDU (Performance Management Delivery Unit) (2011), *Government Transformation Programme: Annual Report, 2010*, Putrajaya, Malaysia. Available from http://www.pemandu.gov.my/gtp/wp-content/uploads/reports/GTP_AR2010_ENG_FINAL.pdf

Peretz, D. (2009), *Learning from Experience: Perspectives on Poverty Reduction Strategies from Four Developing Countries* (London: Commonwealth Secretariat).

Perkin, E. and Court, J. (2005), 'Networks and policy processes in international development: A literature review', *ODI Working Paper 252*, London. Available from http://www.odi.org.uk/resources/download/133.pdf.

Peterson, J. (2010), '"Rule of law" initiatives and the liberal peace: The impact of politicised reform in post-conflict states', *Disasters*, 34(1): 15–39.

Pfeffer, J. and Salancik, G. (2003), *The External Control of Organizations: A Resource Dependence Perspective* (Stanford: Stanford University Press).

Pinker, S. (2012), *The Better Angels of Our Nature: A History of Violence and Humanity*. (London: Penguin).

Plato (1969), 'The Apology of Socrates', in Plato (ed.), *The Last Days of Socrates* (Harmondsworth: Penguin), pp. 43–76.

Polidano, C. (1999), 'The bureaucrat who fell under a bus: Ministerial responsibility, executive agencies and the Derek Lewis affair in Britain', *Governance*, 12(2): 201–29.

Polidano, C. (2001), 'Administrative reform in core civil services: Application and applicability of the New Public Management', in W. McCourt and M. Minogue (eds), *The Internationalization of Public Management: Reinventing the Third World State* (Cheltenham: Edward Elgar), pp. 44–69.

Polidano, C. (2002), 'Democratization', in C. Kirkpatrick, R. Clarke and C. Polidano (eds), *Handbook on Development Policy and Management* (Cheltenham: Edward Elgar), pp. 260–68.

Polidano, C. (2013), 'Towards better results for the World Bank', *International Review of Administrative Sciences*, 79(3): 420–25.

Pollitt, C. (1993), *Managerialism and the Public Services* (Oxford: Blackwell).

Pollitt, C. and Talbot, C. (2003), *Unbundled Government: A Critical Analysis of the Global Trend to Agencies, Quangos and Contractualisation* (London: Routledge).

Pollitt, C., Talbot, C., Caulfield, J. and Smullen, A. (2004), *Agencies: How Governments Do Things Through Semi-Autonomous Organizations* (Basingstoke: Palgrave Macmillan).

Popper, K. (1989), 'Towards a rational theory of tradition', in K. Popper (ed.), *Conjectures and Refutations: The Growth of Scientific Knowledge* (London: Routledge), pp. 120–35.

Popper, K. (1999), *All Life is Problem-Solving* (London: Routledge).

Porter, D., Allen, B. and Thompson, G. (1991), *Development in Practice: Paved With Good Intentions* (London: Routledge).

Potter, D. (1997), 'Introduction', in D. Potter, D. Goldblatt, M. Kiloh and P. Lewis (eds), *Democratization* (Buckingham: Open University Press), pp. 1–40.

Power, G., Maury, M. and Maury, S. (2002), 'Operationalising bottom-up learning in international NGOs: Barriers and alternatives', *Development in Practice*, 12(3–4): 272–84.

Prahalad, C. and Hamel, G. (1990), 'The core competence of the corporation', *Harvard Business Review*, 68(3): 79–91.

Praxy, F. and Sicherl, P. (eds) (1981), *Seeking the Personality of Public Enterprise* (Ljubljana: International Centre for Public Enterprises in Developing Countries).

Pritchett, L. and Woolcock, M. (2004), 'Solutions when the solution is the problem: Arraying the disarray in development', *World Development*, 32(2): 191–212.

Priyono (2005), 'Local politics in post-New Order Indonesia', Paper presented at Workshop on 'Democratizing Decentralization and Deconcentration: Implications for Civil Society', Phnom Penh, 25–27 April.

Pugh, M., Cooper, N. and Turner, M. (2008), 'Conclusion: The political economy of peacebuilding – whose peace? Where next?' in M. Pugh, N. Cooper and M. Turner (eds), *Whose Peace? Critical Perspectives on the Political Economy of Peacebuilding* (Basingstoke: Palgrave Macmillan), pp. 390–97.

Purcell, J. (1995), 'Corporate strategy and its link with human resource management strategy', in J. Storey (ed.), *Human Resource Management: A Critical Text* (London: Thomson), pp. 63–86.

Puthucheary, M. (1987), 'The administrative elite', in Z. Ahmad (ed.), *Government and Politics of Malaysia* (Singapore: Oxford University Press), pp. 94–110.

Putnam, R.D. (1993), *Making Democracy Work: Civic Traditions in Modern Italy* (Princeton, NJ: Princeton University Press).

Putzel, J. (2010), 'Why development actors need a better definition of "state fragility" ', *Policy Directions*, Crisis States Research Centre.

Putzel, J. and Di John, J. (2012), *Meeting the Challenges of Crisis States* (London: Crisis States Research Centre, LSE).

Quie, M. (2012), 'Peace-building and democracy promotion in Afghanistan: The Afghanistan Peace and Reintegration Programme and reconciliation with the Taliban', *Democratization*, 19(3): 553–74.

Racelis, M. (2008), 'Anxieties and affirmations: NGO-donor partnerships for social transformation', in, A. Bebbington, S. Hickey and D. Mitlin (eds), *Can NGOs Make a Difference? The Challenge of Development Alternatives* (London and New York: Zed Books), pp. 196-218.

Rama, A. (2014), 'Honduras, Venezuela have world's highest murder rates: UN', 10 April. *Reuters website.* Available from http://www.reuters.com/article/2014/04/10/us-latam-crime-idUSBREA390IY20140410.

Ravindra, A. (2004), 'An assessment of the impact of Bangalore Citizen Report Cards on the performance of public agencies', World Bank, *ECD Working Paper Series*, No. 12.

Reddy, P. and Maharaj, B. (2008), 'Democratic decentralization in post-apartheid South Africa', in F. Saito (ed.), *Foundations for Local Governance: Decentralization in Comparative Perspective* (Heidelberg: Physica-Verlag), pp. 185–211.

Reid, G. (1997), *Making Evaluations Useful* (Washington, DC: World Bank).

Renard, M-F. (2011), 'China trade and FDI in Africa', *African Development Bank Group Working Paper Series*, No 126.

Rhodes, R. (1997), *Understanding Governance: Policy Networks, Governance, Reflexivity, and Accountability* (Buckingham: Open University Press).

Rhodes, R. (2000), 'The governance narrative: Key findings and lessons from the ESRC's Whitehall programme', *Public Administration*, 78(2): 345–63.

Ribot, J. (2003), 'Democratic decentralization of natural resources: Institutional choice and discretionary power transfers in Sub-Saharan Africa', *Public Administration and Development*, 23(1): 53–65.

Richardson, A. (1983), *Participation* (London: Routledge and Kegan Paul).

Richmond, O. (2010), 'Resistance and the post-liberal peace', *Millennium: Journal of International Studies*, 38(3): 665–92.

Robbins, S., Bergman, R., Stagg, I. and Coulter, M. (2011), *Management*, 6th edition (Frenchs Forest: Pearson Australia).

Robinson, D. (1990), 'Public-sector pay: The case of Sudan', in J. Pickett and H. Singer (eds), *Towards Economic Recovery in Sub-Saharan Africa* (London: Routledge), pp. 92–105.

Robinson, M. (2007), 'The politics of successful governance reforms: Lessons of design and implementation', *Journal of Commonwealth and Comparative Politics*, 45(4): 521–48.

Rodríguez-Garavito, C. (2011), 'Toward a sociology of the global rule of law field: Neoliberalism, neoconstitutionalism, and the contest over judicial reform in Latin America', in B. Garth and Y. Dezalay (eds), *Lawyers and the Rule of Law in an Era of Globalization* (New York: Routledge), pp. 156–82.

Rodrik, D. (2008), 'Second-best institutions', *Working Paper* 14050, National Bureau of Economic Research, Cambridge, MA.

Röhl, K. (2004), 'Greed or grievance – why does the FARC keep fighting?' *Peace and Conflict Monitor* (Costa Rica: University for Peace and Conflict).

Rondinelli, D. (1981), 'Government decentralisation in comparative perspective', *International Review of Administrative Sciences*, 47(2): 133–45.

Rondinelli, D. (1983), *Development Projects as Policy Experiments: An Adaptive Approach to Development Administration*, 1st edition (London: Routledge).

Rondinelli, D. (1993), *Development Projects as Policy Experiments: An Adaptive Approach to Development Administration*, 2nd edition (London: Routledge).

Rondinelli, D. (1999), 'What is decentralization', in J. Litvack and J. Seddon (eds), *Decentralization Briefing Notes* (Washington, DC: World Bank), pp. 2–5.

Rondinelli, D., McCullough, J. and Johnson, R. (1989), 'Analysing decentralisation policies in developing countries: A political-economy framework', *Development and Change*, 20(1): 57–87.

Rondinelli, D. and Nellis, J. (1986), 'Assessing decentralisation policies in developing countries: A case for cautious optimism', *Development Policy Review*, 4(1): 3–23.

Rose, J. (2004), 'The rule of law in the Western world: An overview', *Journal of Social Philosophy*, 35(4): 457–70.

Rose, P. (2011), 'Strategies for engagement: Government and national non-government education providers in South Asia', *Public Administration and Development*, 31(4): 294–305.

Rose, R. (1993), *Lesson-drawing in Public Policy: A Guide to Learning Across Time and Space* (Chatham, NJ: Chatham House).

Rosenberg, A., Hartwig, K. and Merson, M. (2008), 'Government-NGO collaboration and sustainability of orphans and vulnerable children projects in southern Africa', *Evaluation and Program Planning*, 31(1): 51–60.

Routley, L. and Hulme, D. (2013), 'Donors, development agencies and the use of political economic analysis: Getting to grips with the politics of development'? *ESID Working Paper 19* (Manchester, Effective States and Inclusive Development Research Centre, www.effective-states.org).

Rubin, B. (2006), 'Peace building and state-building in Afghanistan: Constructing sovereignty for whose security?' *Third World Quarterly*, 27(1): 175–85.

Rucht, D. and Neidhardt, F. (2002), 'Towards a movement society? On the possibilities of institutionalizing social movements', *Social Movement Studies*, 1(1): 7–30.

Runde, D. and Zargarian, A. (2013), 'The future of public-private partnership: Strengthening a powerful instrument for global development', Center for Strategic and International Studies, 25 October. Available from http://csis.org/publication/future-public-private-partnerships-strengthening-powerful-instrument-global-development.

Ruteere, M. and Pommerolle, M-E. (2003), 'Democratizing security or decentralizing repression? The ambiguities of community policing in Kenya', *African Affairs*, 102(409): 587–604.

Rutherford, S. (2009), *The Pledge: ASA, Peasant Politics, and Microfinance in the Development of Bangladesh* (New York: Oxford University Press).

Sabatier, P. (1988), 'An advocacy coalition framework of policy change and the role of policy-oriented learning therein', *Policy Sciences*, 21(2): 129–68.

Sachs, J. (2005), *The End of Poverty: Economic Possibilities for Our Time* (New York: Penguin).

Sachs, W. (1992), 'Development: A guide to the ruins', *New Internationalist*, June, pp. 4–6.

Sagasti, F. (1988), 'National development planning in turbulent times: New approaches and criteria for institutional design', *World Development*, 16(4): 431–48.

Samset, I. (2002), 'Conflict of interests or interests in conflict? Diamonds and war in the DRC', *Review of African Political Economy*, 29(93/94): 463–80.

Samson, D. and Daft, R. (2014), *Fundamentals of Management*, 5th Asia-Pacific edition (South Melbourne: Cengage Learning Australia).

Santos, B. (1998), 'Participatory budgeting in Porto Alegre: Toward a redistributive democracy', *Politics and Society*, 26(4): 461–510.

Sarkar, S. (2010), 'The quest for victim's justice in India', *Human Rights Brief*, 17(2): 16–20.

Schaffer, B. (1984), 'Towards responsibility: Public policy in concept and practice', in E. Clay and B. Schaffer (eds), *Room for Manoeuvre: An Exploration of Public Policy in Agricultural and Rural Development* (London: Methuen), pp. 142–90.

Schaffer, B.B. (1969), 'The deadlock in development administration', in C. Leys (ed.), *Politics and Change in Developing Countries* (Cambridge: Cambridge University Press), pp. 177–211.

Schick, A. (1998), 'Why most developing countries should not try New Zealand's reforms', *World Bank Research Observer*, 13(1): 123–31.

Schmidt, F. and Hunter, J. (1998), 'The validity and utility of selection methods in personnel psychology: Practical and theoretical implications of 85 years of research findings', *Psychological Bulletin*, 124(2): 262–74.

Schneider, F. (2000), 'Dimensions of the shadow economy', *The Independent Review*, 5(1): 81–91.

Schneider, F. (2002), Size and measurement of the informal economy in 110 countries around the world', Paper presented at a Workshop of the Australian National Tax Centre, Canberra, Australian National University, 17 July.

Schneider, F. (2008), 'Shadow economy', in C. Rowley and F. Schneider (eds), *Readings in Public Choice and Constitutional Political Economy* (New York: Springer), pp. 511–29.

Schumacher, E.F. (1973), *Small is Beautiful: Economics as if People Mattered* (New York: Harper and Row).

Scott, J. (1998), *Seeing like a State: How Certain Schemes to Improve the Human Condition Have Failed* (New Haven: Yale University Press).

Scruton, R. (2010), *The Uses of Pessimism and the Dangers of False Hope* (London: Atlantic).

Selby, J. (2008), 'The political economy of peace processes', in M. Pugh, N. Cooper and M. Turner (eds), *Whose Peace? Critical Perspectives on the Political Economy of Peacebuilding* (Basingstoke: Palgrave Macmillan), pp. 11–29.

Sen, A. (1999), *Development as Freedom* (Oxford: Oxford University Press).

Sen, A. (2006), 'What is the role of legal and judicial reform in the development process?' in A. Palacio (ed.), *The World Bank Legal Review: Law Equity, and Development* (Washington, DC: World Bank), pp. 33–50.

Sharma, A. and Agnihotri, V. (2001), 'The citizen's charter: The Indian experience', *International Review of Administrative Sciences*, 67: 733–39.

Sheshinski, E. and López-Calva, F. (2003), 'Privatization and its benefits', *CESifo Economic Studies*, 49(3): 429–59.

Shin, D.C. (1994), 'On the Third Wave of democratization: A synthesis and evaluation of recent theory and research', *World Politics*, 47(1): 135–70.

Shixue, J. (2012), 'Chinese investment in Latin America: A win-win situation', *Hemisphere*, 21(Spring): 12–13.

Shucksmith, M. (2010), 'Disintegrated rural development? Neo-endogenous rural development, planning and place-shaping in diffused power contexts', *Sociologia Ruralis*, 50(1): 1–14.

Siegle, J. and O'Mahony, P. (2007), 'Assessing the merits of decentralization as a conflict mitigation strategy'. Paper Prepared for USAID's Office of Democracy and Governance.

Siffin, W. (1966), *Thai Bureaucracy: Institutional Change and Development* (Honolulu: East–West Center).

Siffin, W. (1976), 'Two decades of public administration in developing countries', *Public Administration Review*, 36(1): 61–71.

Simon, H. (1976), *Administrative Behavior* (New York: Macmillan).

Singer, P. (2001), *Hegel: A Very Short Introduction* (Oxford: Oxford University Press).

Singh, R. (1988), *Calcutta: The Home and the Street* (London: Thames and Hudson).

Singh, S. and Darroch, J. (2012), *Adding it up: Costs and Benefits of Contraceptive Services – Estimates for 2012* (New York: Guttmacher Institute and United Nations Population Fund).

Sivagnanasothy, V. (undated), *National Monitoring and Evaluation System in Sri Lanka: Experiences, Challenges and the Way Forward*. Available from http://stone.undp.org/undpweb/eo/evalnet/workshop/nec/documents/papers/SriLanka.pdf.

Smith B. (1980), 'Measuring decentralisation', in G. Jones (ed.), *New Approaches to the Study of Central-Local Government Relationships* (Westmead: Gower Publishing), pp. 137–51.

Smith, B. (1985), *Decentralization: The Territorial Dimension of the State* (London: George Allen and Unwin).

Smith, B. (1993), *Choices in the Design of Decentralisation* (London: Commonwealth Secretariat).

Smith, W.E., Lethem, F.J. and Thoolen, B.A. (1981), 'The design of organizations for rural development projects', *World Bank Staff Working Paper*, No. 375.

Soares de Oliveira, R. (2011), 'Illiberal peacebuilding in Angola', *Journal of Modern African Studies*, 49(2): 287–314.

Sonnenschein, J. (2014), 'Laton America scores lowest on security', 19 August. Gallup World. Available from http://www.gallup.com/poll/175082/latin-america-scores-lowest-security.aspx.

Srinivas, N. (2009), 'Against NGOs? A critical perspective on nongovern-mental action', *Nonprofit and Voluntary Sector Quarterly*, 38(4): 614–26.

Sternberg, E. (2010), 'NGOs vs civil society: Reflections on the illiberal, the illegitimate, and the unaccountable', *Journal of Economic Affairs*, 30(3): 22–8.

Stevens, M. (1994), 'Public expenditure and civil service reform in Tanzania', in D. Lindauer. and B. Nunberg (eds), *Rehabilitating Government: Pay and Employment Reform in Africa* (Washington, DC: World Bank), pp. 62–81.

Stewart, F. and Wang, M. (2004), 'Do PSRPs empower poor countries and disempower the World Bank or is it the other way round?' *QEH Working Paper* No. 108.

Stiglitz, J. (2004), 'Towards a new global governance', paper delivered at the conference From the Washington Consensus towards a New Global Governance', Barcelona, 24–25 September.

Stiglitz, J. (2008), 'Foreword', in G. Roland (ed.), *Privatization: Successes and Failures* (New York: Columbia University Press), pp. ix–xx.

Stiglitz, J. (2010), *Freefall: Free Markets and the Sinking of the Global Economy* (London: Allen Lane).

Stone, D. (1965), 'Government machinery necessary for development', in M. Kriesberg (ed.), *Public Administration in Developing Countries* (Washington, DC: The Brookings Institution), pp. 49–67.

Strategic Policy Making Team (1999), *Professional Policy Making for the Twenty First Century* (London: Cabinet Office). Available from http://www.nationalschool.gov.uk/policyhub/docs/profpolicymaking.pdf.

SVBTCPL (2014), Second Vivekananda Bridge Tollway Company Private Limited website. Available from http://www.svbtc.in.

Szamosszegi, A. and Kyle, C. (2011), *An Analysis of State-owned Enterprise and State Capitalism in China* (Washington, DC: US-China Economy and Society Review Commission).

Taliercio, R. (2004), 'Designing Performance: The Semi-autonomous Revenue Authority Model in Africa and Latin America', *World Bank Policy Research Working Paper* 3423. Available from http://www.fiscalre-form.net/library/pdfs/taliercio_aras_2004.pdf

Tapscott, C. (2008), 'The challenges of deepening democracy in post-apartheid South Africa', in F. Saito (ed.), *Foundations for Local Governance: Decentralization in Comparative Perspective* (Heidelberg: Physica-Verlag), pp. 213–31.

Tarrow, S. (1998), *Power in Movement: Collective Action, Social Movements and Politics* (Cambridge: Cambridge University Press).

Taylor, F.W. (1911), *The Principles of Scientific Management* (New York: Harper and Row).

Teivanien, T. (2002), 'The World Social Forum and global democratisation: Learning from Porto Alegre', *Third World Quarterly*, 23(4): 621–32.

Tendler, J. (1997), *Good Government in the Tropics* (Baltimore, MD: Johns Hopkins University Press).

Ter Haar, G. and Ellis, S. (2006), 'The role of religion in development: Towards a new relationship between the European Union and Africa', *The European Journal of Development Research*, 18(3): 351–67.

Terray, E. (1986), 'Le climatiseur et la veranda', in *Afrique Plurielle, Afrique actuelle: Hommage a George Balandier* (Paris: Karthala), pp. 37–44.

The Independent (2011), 'Benydin against PMS system'. Available from http://theindependent.mu/2011/02/19/benydin-against-pms-system/.

Thomas, J. and Grindle, M. (1990), 'After the decision: Implementing policy reforms in developing countries', *World Development*, 18(8): 1163–81.

Thompson, E. (1976), *Whigs and Hunters: The Origin of the Black Act* (New York: Pantheon Books).

Thompson, F. (1997), 'Defining the new public management', in L. Jones, K. Schedler and S. Wade (eds), *Advances in International Comparative Management: International Perspectives on the New Public Management* (Greenwich, CT: JAI Press), pp. 1–14.

Thompson, J. (1967), *Organizations in Action* (New York: McGraw-Hill).

Thomson, S. and Nagy, R. (2011), 'Law, power and justice: What legalism fails to address in the functioning of Rwanda's Gacaca Courts', *The International Journal of Transitional Justice*, 5(1): 11–30.

Tinker, I. (1990), 'A context for the field and for the book', in I. Tinker (ed.), *Persistent Inequalities: Women and World Development* (New York: Oxford University Press) pp. 3–13.

TISL (Transparency International Sri Lanka) (2011), 'Presidential report card'. Available from http://www.tisrilanka.org/pub/reports/PRC.pdf.

Tran, M. (2012), 'UK still gathering evidence ahead of aid to Rwanda decision', Guardian, 14 November. Available from http://www.guardian.co.uk/global-development/2012/nov/13/uk-evidence-aid-rwanda-decision?INTCMP=SRCH.

Tod, C. (1991), 'The national silver', *Far Eastern Economic Review*, 29 August.

Todaro, M.P. (1994), *Economic Development*, 5th edition (London: Longman).

Townsend, J, Porter, G. and Mawdsley, E. (2004), 'Creating spaces of resistance: Development NGOs and their clients in Ghana, India, and Mexico', *Antipode*, 36(5):871–89.

Toye, J. (1987), *Dilemmas of Development* (Oxford: Basil Blackwell).

Tricker, B. (2012), *Corporate Governance: Principles, Policies, and Practices* (Oxford: Oxford University Press).

Tuchman, B. (1984), *The March of Folly: From Troy to Vietnam* (London: Michael Joseph).

Turnbull, P. and Wass, V. (1997), 'Job insecurity and labour market lemons: The (mis)management of redundancy in steel making, coal mining and port transport', *Journal of Management Studies*, 34(1): 27–51.

Turner, M. (1990), 'Authoritarian rule and the dilemma of legitimacy: The case of President Marcos of the Philippines', *The Pacific Review*, 3(4) 349–62.

Turner, M. (1999), 'Central-local relations: Themes and issues', in M. Turner (ed.) *Central-Local Relations in Asia-Pacific: Convergence or Divergence?* (Basingstoke and New York: Macmillan and St Martin's), pp. 1–18.

Turner, M. (2002a), 'Choosing items from the menu: New public management in Southeast Asia', *International Journal of Public Administration*, 25(12): 1497–516.

Turner, M. (2002b) 'Whatever happened to deconcentration? Recent initiatives in Cambodia', *Public Administration and Development*, 22(3): 353–64.

Turner, M., Imbaruddin, A. and Sutiyono, W. (2009), 'Human resource management: The forgotten dimension of decentralisation in Indonesia', *Bulletin of Indonesian Economic Studies*, 45(2): 231–49.

Turner, M., O'Donnell, M., Suh, C-S. and Kwon, S-H (2013), 'Public sector management and the changing nature of the developmental state in Korea and Malaysia', *The Economic and Labour Relations Review*, 24(4): 481–94

Tvedt, T. (2006), 'The international aid system and the non-governmental organizations: A new research agenda', *Journal of International Development*, 18(5): 677–90.

UN (United Nations) (1961), *A Handbook of Public Administration* (New York: United Nations).

UN (United Nations) (2004), *The Rule of Law and Transitional Justice in Conflict and Post Conflict Societies, Report of the Secretary-General* (New York: United Nations).

UN (United Nations) (2009), 'Press release: World population to exceed 9 billion by 2050', 11 March. Available from http://www.un.org/esa/population/publications/wpp2008/pressrelease.pdf.

UN (United Nations) (2013), *The Millennium Development Goals Report 2013* (New York: United Nations).

UNDESA (United Nations Department of Economic and Social Affairs) (2014), *World Urbanization Prospects: 2014 Revision, Highlights* (New York: United Nations).

UNDP (United Nations Development Programme) (1994), *Human Development Report 1994* (New York: Oxford University Press).

UNDP (United Nations Development Programme) (1995), *Public Sector Management, Governance and Sustainable Human Development* (New York: UNDP).

UNDP (United Nations Development Programme) (1998), *Governance for Sustainable Human Development* (New York: UNDP).

UNDP (United Nations Development Programme) (2002), *Human Development Report 2002* (New York: Oxford University Press).

UNDP (United Nations Development Programme) (2004), 'Decentralised governance for development: A combined practice note on decentralisation, local governance and urban/rural development', *UNDP Practice Note*.

UNDP (United Nations Development Programme) (2005), *Primer: Fiscal Decentralisation and Poverty Reduction* (New York: UNDP).

UNDP (United Nations Development Programme) (2007), *Sierra Leone Human Development Report 2007* (New York: UNDP).

UNDP (2011), *Human Development Report 2011 Sustainability and Equity: A Better Future for All* (New York: Palgrave Macmillan).

UNDP (2013), *Human Development Report 2013: The Rise of the South: Human Progress in a Diverse World* (New York: UNDP).

UNDP (2014), *Human Development Report 2014* (New York: UNDP).

UNFPA (2011), *State of World Population 2011* (New York: UNFPA).

UN High Level Panel (2013), *A New Global Partnership* (New York: United Nations).

The UN Millennium Project, www.unmillenniumproject.org

UNIDO (United Nations Industrial Development Organization) (2008), *Creating an Enabling Environment for Private Sector Development in sub-Saharan Africa* (Geneva: UNIDO).

United Republic of Tanzania (2002), *Civil Service Circular No.1,* Ref. No. MUF.C/AC/46/205/01 (Dar es Salaam: Civil Service Department, President's Office).

USAID (United States Agency for International Development) (2005), *Case Studies on Bankable Water and Sewerage Utilities* (Washington, DC: USAID).

Uvin, P. (1998), *Aiding Violence: The Development Enterprise in Rwanda* (West Hartford, CT: Kumarian Press).

Uvin, P. (2010), 'Structural causes, development co-operation and conflict prevention in Burundi and Rwanda', *Conflict, Security and Development,* 10(1): 161–79.

Vakil, A. (1997), 'Confronting the classification problem: Toward a taxonomy of NGOs', *World Development,* 25(12): 2057–70.

Van der Gaag, J., Stelcner, M. and Vijverberg W. (1989), 'Wage differentials and moonlighting by civil servants: Evidence from Cote d'Ivoire and Peru', *World Bank Economic Review,* 3(1): 67–95.

Van Donge, J. and Pherani, L. (1999), 'Law and order as a development issue: Land conflicts and the creation of social order in southern Malawi', *The Journal of Development Studies,* 36(1): 48–70.

Visvanathan, N., Duggan, L., Wiegersma, N. and Nisonoff, L. (eds) (2011), *The Women, Gender and Development Reader* (London: Zed Books).

Vivian, J. (1994), 'NGOs and sustainable development in Zimbabwe: No magic bullets', *Development and Change,* 25(1): 167–93.

Wallerstein, I. (1979), *The Capitalist World-Economy* (Cambridge: Cambridge University Press).

Waterston, A. (1965), *Development Planning: Lessons of Experience* (Baltimore, MD: Johns Hopkins University Press).

Waterston, A. (2006), Development planning: Lessons of experience', *Research in Public Policy Analysis and Management,* 15: 427–31.

WB-AIDG (World Bank-Ash Institute for Democratic Governance) (2006), Case studies on innovation in service delivery in Indonesia. Available from http://www.innovations.harvard.edu/showdoc.html?id=6295.

WCED (1987), *Our Common Future: Report of the World Commission on Environment and Development* (New York: United Nations).

Weick, K. (1977), 'Enactment processes in organizations', in B. Staw and G. Salancik (eds), *New Directions in Organizational Behavior* (Chicago: St. Clair Press), pp. 267–300.

White, H. (2006), *Impact Evaluation: The Experience of the Independent Evaluation Group of the World Bank.* Available from http://mpra.ub.uni-mucnchen.de/1111.

White, R. and Smoke, P. (2005), 'East Asia decentralizes', in World Bank (ed.), *East Asia Decentralizes: Making Local Government Work* (Washington, DC: World Bank), pp. 1–23.

White, S. (1999), 'NGOs, civil society, and the state in Bangladesh: The politics of representing the poor', *Development and Change,* 30(2): 307–26.

Whitehead, L. (1990), 'Political explanations of macroeconomic management: A survey', *World Development,* 18(8): 1133–46.

Whitehead, L. (2002), *Democratization – Theory and Experience* (Oxford: Oxford University Press).

WHO (2011), Global Health Observatory: HIV/AIDS. Retrieved at www.who.int/gho/hiv/en/.

WHO (2012), Water Sanitation Health. Available from http://www.who.int/water_sanitation_health/en/.

Williams, G. (2004), 'Evaluating participatory development: Tyranny, power, and (re)politicisation', *Third World Quarterly,* 25(3): 557–78.

Williamson, J. (1990), 'What Washington means by policy reform', in J. Williamson (ed.), *Latin American Adjustment: How Much Has Happened?* (Washington, DC: Institute for International Economics), pp. 7–20.

Williamson, J. (1994), *The Political Economy of Policy Reform* (Washington DC: Institute for International Economics).

Williamson, J. (2004), 'A short history of the Washington Consensus', paper delivered at the conference From the Washington Consensus towards a New Global Governance', Barcelona, 24–25 September.

Wilson, E. (1986), 'The public-private debate', *Africa Report,* July–August.

Wilson, G. (2007), 'Knowledge, innovation and reinventing technical assistance for development', *Progress in Development Studies,* 7(3): 183–99.

Wolfe, T. (1970), *Radical Chic and Mau-Mauing the Flak Catchers* (New York: Farrar, Straus and Giroux).

Wolfensohn, J. (1999), 'A proposal for a comprehensive development framework', Memorandum to the Board, Management and Staff of the World Bank Group, 21 January.

Woodward, B. (2010), *Obama's Wars* (New York: Simon and Schuster).

Woodward, S. (2012), 'The IFIs and post-conflict Statebuilding', in M. Berdal and Zaum, D. (eds), *Political Economy of Post-Conflict Statebuilding: Power after Peace* (Abingdon: Routledge), pp. 140–57.

Woon, T. (1991), 'The role of the state in Southeast Asia', in N. Yuen and N. Wagner (eds), *Marketization in ASEAN* (Singapore: Institute of Southeast Asian Studies), pp. 11–24.

World Bank (1987), Malaysia – Sixth FELDA Land Settlement Project: Project Completion Report. Available at www-wds.worldbank.org/external/default/WDSCContentServer/WDSP/18/1987/10/30/00009265_3960925022839/Rendered/PDF/multi_page.pdf

World Bank (1988), *Rural Development: World Bank Experience 1965–86* (Washington, DC: World Bank).

World Bank (1990), *World Development Report 1990* (Washington, DC and New York: World Bank and Oxford University Press).

World Bank (1991), *World Development Report* (New York: Oxford University Press).

World Bank (1992), *Governance and Development* (Washington, DC: World Bank).

World Bank (1995), *Bureaucrats in Business: The Economics and Politics of Government Ownership* (New York: Oxford University Press).

World Bank (1997), *World Development Report 1997: The Changing Role of the State* (Washington, DC and New York: World Bank and Oxford University Press).

World Bank (1998), *Assessing Aid: What Works, What Doesn't, and Why* (Washington, DC: World Bank).

World Bank (2001), *World Development Report 2000/2001: Attacking Poverty* (New York: Oxford University Press).

World Bank (2003a), *World Development Report: Making Services Work for Poor People* (Washington, DC and New York: World Bank and Oxford University Press).

World Bank (2003b), *Breaking the Conflict Trap* (Washington, DC: World Bank).

World Bank (2004), *World Development Report 2005: A Better Investment Climate for Everyone* (Washington, DC: World Bank).

World Bank (2010), *Malaysia Economic Monitor: Growth Through Innovation* (Washington, DC: World Bank).

World Bank (2011), *World Development Report 2011: Conflict, Security, and Development* (Washington, DC: The World Bank).

World Bank (2012a), *Approach to Public Sector Management 2011–2020* (Washington, DC: World Bank). Available from http://siteresources.worldbank.org/PUBLICSECTORANDGOVERNANCE/Resources/285741-1287520109339/PSM-Approach.pdf.

World Bank (2012b), *World Development Report 2012* (Washington, DC: World Bank).

World Bank (2012c), 'Rule of law as a goal of development policy', World Bank. Available from http://go.worldbank.org/DZETJ85MD0:

World Bank (2013a), *World Development Report 2014* (Washington, DC: World Bank).

World Bank (2013b), 'Migration remittance flows: Recent trends and outlook, 2013–2016', *Migration and Development Brief*, 21, 2 October. Available from http://siteresources.worldbank.org/INTPROSPECTS/Resources/334934-1288990760745/MigrationandDevelopmentBrief21.pdf.

World Bank (2014), Doing Business: Measuring Business Regulation website. Available from http://www.doingbusiness.org.

Xinhua (2013), 'China's investment in Africa increases 20.5 pct annually', *Xinhuanet*. Available from http://news.xinhuanet.com/english/china/2013-08/29/c_132673248.htm

Zartman, I. (1995), *Collapsed States: The Disintegration and Restoration of Legitimate Authority* (London: Lynne Rienner Publishers).

Zifcak, S. (1994), *New Managerialism: Administrative Reform in Whitehall and Canberra* (Buckingham: Open University Press).

Zinkin, M. (1953), *Asia and the West* (London: Chatto and Windus).

Index

Malaysia
  civil servants' union in, 159
  government effectiveness
    score, 135
  National Key Result Areas, 163,
    164*t*, 165*t*, 168
  performance management in, 163
  performance-related pay (PRP)
    in, 159*b*
  racial conflicts in, 230
  strategic integration of HRM
    activities, 143–4
  strategic management in,
    134–5, 143
  TQM in, 144
  Vision 2020, 134–5, 143
managerial devolution, 130–2, 141
  see also executive agencies
Manila, water privatization in, 235*b*
Mao, 28
Marcos, Ferdinand, 61–2, 214, 257*b*
market decentralization, 211–12
  defined, 211
  deregulation, 211
  justification for, 214
  privatization, 211
market failure, 227–8
Marshall Plan, 181
maternal deaths, 58
Mauritius
  Civil Service Ministry, 144
  HR initiatives, 144
McCourt, W., 101–2, 115, 116,
    125–6, 130, 143, 144, 145
MDRI, *see* Multilateral Debt Relief
    Initiative (MDRI)
M&E, *see* monitoring and
    evaluation (M&E)
Medium Term Expenditure
    Framework, 190
megacities, 56
  governance of, 215
Mexican drug cartels, 90
microfinance institutions, 39
middle class, 60
middle powers, 1

midwife role, 168
Migdal, J. S., 64
migrant workers' remittances, 57
migration, 57
  see also urbanization and
    migration
military juntas, 65
Millennium Declaration, 10
Millennium Development
    Goals (MDG), 2, 11–12,
    11*b*, 162
Minogue, M., 27
Mintzberg, Henry, 139
mobile phones
  access to, 43
Mohamad, Mahathir, 134
Mohan, G., 198
MONDEP, *see* Moneragala
    Integrated Rural Development
    Programme (MONDEP)
Moneragala Integrated Rural
    Development Programme
    (MONDEP), 199
monitoring and evaluation (M&E),
    111–12
  governments and, 112
  in international development
    agencies, 112
  ten-step model of, 111–12
Moore, M., 28
mortality rates, 58
Mowles, C., 23
Mugabe, Robert, 152
Multilateral Debt Relief Initiative
    (MDRI), 41
multi-party democracies, 61
multi-sectoral planning, 186
Munene, J., 74
Museveni, Yoweri, 190
Myrdal, G., 64

Namibia
  HIV/AIDS in, 144
  strategic integration of HRM
    activities, 143–4
  strategic management, 143